"Andrew Abernethy and Gregory Goswell have written an important and timely volume that is sure to contribute to the ongoing discussion of the Messiah in the Old Testament. Grounded in careful exegesis and shaped by theological and canonical concerns, this book makes a compelling case for a patient and hermeneutically sensitive reading of the Hebrew canon that appreciates the themes of both divine and human kingship. This, in turn, accentuates the redemptive-historical threads of the Bible, culminating with Christ as the resplendent and glorious Divine King and Messiah. This is a thought-provoking book what will enrich students, professors, and pastors—anyone who is interested in studying the Scriptures."

—**Seulgi L. Byun**, Grove City College

"Jesus is the Messiah, the Christ, the King. So what happens when you look back into the Old Testament for passages that might foreshadow him? If you wonder about the kind of passages that could have fed into an understanding of Jesus as King, then this book will examine them for you and with you."

—**John Goldingay**, Fuller Theological Seminary

"In a world of would-be potentates and disappointing presidents, we have a worthy fascination with the dominant personality of Scripture. He is God's Messiah. In these pages, Abernethy and Goswell open new vistas for a fresh consideration of the only King to ever satisfy. Read this book and rejoice."

—**Charlie Dates**, senior pastor, Progressive Baptist Church, Chicago, Illinois; affiliate professor, Trinity Evangelical Divinity School

"I heartily recommend this canonical reading of Scripture by Abernethy and Goswell. They read the Old Testament as part of a Two-Testament Bible and as a canonical witness to the providential purposes of God in Jesus Christ. They follow the canonical order of the Hebrew text (Torah, Prophets, Writings) and display the pieces of the puzzle with humility. They offer a potential interpretation of the parts in light of Scripture's theological and eschatological design. While the patterns are clear, the figurations are open to a potentiality of connections. In the meantime, God's people wait for the placement of the last pieces of the puzzle—God's final act in Jesus Christ."

—**Willem A. VanGemeren**, Trinity Evangelical Divinity School (emeritus)

God's Messiah in the Old Testament

EXPECTATIONS OF A COMING KING

Andrew T. Abernethy
and Gregory Goswell

Baker Academic

a division of Baker Publishing Group
Grand Rapids, Michigan

Published by Baker Academic
a division of Baker Publishing Group
PO Box 6287, Grand Rapids, MI 49516-6287
www.bakeracademic.com

Printed in the United States of America

Library of Congress Cataloging-in-Publication Data
Library of Congress Cataloging-in-Publication Data
Names: Abernethy, Andrew T., author. | Goswell, Gregory, author.
Title: God's Messiah in the Old Testament : expectations of a coming king / Andrew T. Abernethy and Gregory Goswell.
Description: Grand Rapids, Michigan : Baker Academic, a division of Baker Publishing Group, 2020.
Identifiers: LCCN 2020011975 | ISBN 9780801099755 (paperback) | ISBN 9781540963567 (casebound)
Subjects: LCSH: Messiah—Biblical teaching. | Bible. Old Testament—Criticism, interpretation, etc. | Messiah—Prophecies.
Classification: LCC BS1199.M44 A24 2020 | DDC 221.6—dc23
LC record available at https://lccn.loc.gov/2020011975

20   21   22   23   24   25   26   7   6   5   4   3   2   1

In keeping with biblical principles of creation stewardship, Baker Publishing Group advocates the responsible use of our natural resources. As a member of the Green Press Initiative, our company uses recycled paper when possible. The text paper of this book is composed in part of post-consumer waste.

Contents

Preface

Eight years ago, Andrew and Greg met at a theological library in Melbourne. As our friendship grew, so did our appreciation for one another's work. On one occasion, Andrew joked, "It feels like every journal I open has an article by Gregory Goswell on kingship. Is there a book in the works?" Little did Andrew know that a few years later he and Gregory would begin writing a coauthored book on the subject. We both agree that this book is better because we have written it together. We have interacted with, challenged, and refined one another's work, as we wrote, rewrote, and rewrote some more to try to offer a unified voice across the volume. We strove to keep our primary audience in mind: pastors and students, although we hope scholars will appreciate our work too. Although we may not agree on every minor detail, what unites us is our conviction that Davidic kingship must be seen in light of God's kingship; the royal messiah in the Old Testament is God's agent for fulfilling God's kingdom purposes. Our introductory chapter will offer you a window into the approach of this book, but let us offer a few explanatory remarks here in the preface.

In this volume, we follow the order of the Hebrew Bible as opposed to the order in most English Bibles, which depends upon the ordering in the LXX. This is not to say that there would be anything wrong with adopting the LXX's order, but writers must make choices, and we have opted for the order reflected in the masoretic tradition. Admittedly, choosing an ordering that concludes with Chronicles is advantageous in a project like ours that focuses on messianic expectations. Recent work by scholars such as Christopher Seitz, Stephen Dempster, and Miles Van Pelt has shown the value of adopting the Hebrew order too. We deviate from the Hebrew Bible order in one instance by moving Ruth from the Writings to its location between Judges and 1–2 Samuel. Christopher Seitz argues that the Writings relate extrinsically to the Torah-Prophets core.[1] It is the extrinsic association between Ruth—with its temporal setting during the time of judges (Ruth 1:1) and its genealogy culminating in David (4:18–22)—and Judges and the book of Samuel that led Ruth to find its locale in the LXX's historically oriented order. Given our topic, we believe our audience benefits more by considering Ruth between our chapters on Judges and Samuel. There is nothing sacrosanct about canonical orders, yet even in our choice we affirm the value of reading the books in either the Hebrew or Greek order.

Another choice—admittedly difficult—relates to which books of the Old Testament we would examine. We have not included chapters on Joshua, Haggai, or Ezra-Nehemiah, since we argue that there is nothing "messianic" in those books. On Joshua, we do not see the figure of Joshua as depicted in a royal guise, as a precursor to King Josiah. It is better to see Joshua in the cloth of Moses. On Haggai, we would argue that God's statement to Zerubbabel about God taking him as a signet ring (2:23) is not messianic in nature; instead, it is best understood as a statement about God's care for Zerubbabel. On Ezra-Nehemiah, we believe the book focuses on the community rather than on promoting expectations about the renewal of Davidic rule. For interpretation of those books in relation to the theme of kingship, we recommend other resources.[2] Also, the Wisdom corpus—especially Proverbs, Ecclesiastes, and Song of Songs—does not receive a chapter. Although the association between wisdom and kingship in those books is apparent, we devote space to the intersection between wisdom and Davidic kingship in our chapters on 1–2 Kings, Isaiah, and Jeremiah. Sometimes, less is more, and, by narrowing our chapters to what appear in your hand (or on your screen), we hope the book is both more affordable and streamlined. This is what our editor, Jim Kinney, calls "authorial hospitality." You're welcome.

We would like to express our thanks to Baker Academic for believing in this project and to our copy editor, Melisa Blok, for polishing this volume to make it shine. Andrew would like to thank two Wheaton College Graduate School students for their help: Mason Lancaster and Benjamin Ridgeway. Resources from the G. W. Aldeen Memorial Fund at Wheaton College supported parts of Andrew's work. He dedicates this volume to his wife, Katie, and their children, Anna, Bethany, and Oliver. Gregory dedicates this volume to his friend and mentor, the Rev. C. R. (Bob) Thomas.

---

1. Christopher R. Seitz, *The Goodly Fellowship of the Prophets: The Achievement of Association in Canon Formation* (Grand Rapids: Baker Academic, 2009).

2. Gregory Goswell, "Joshua and Kingship," *BBR* 23 (2013): 29–42; Gregory Goswell, "The Fate and Future of Zerubbabel in the Prophecy of Haggai," *Bib* 91 (2010): 77–90; Gregory Goswell, "The Absence of a Davidic Hope in Ezra-Nehemiah," *TJ* 33 (2012): 19–31.

Abbreviations

General Abbreviations

//	parallel passage	esp.	especially
alt.	altered	etc.	*et cetera* / and so on
ANE	ancient Near East(ern)	i.e.	*id est* / that is
BCE	before Common Era	n.b.	*nota bene* / note well
ca.	circa/about	*pace*	contrary to
CE	Common Era	p(p).	page(s)
cf.	confer/compare	pl.	plural
chap.	chapter	2x	twice
e.g.	*exempli gratia* / for example	3x	three times

Scripture Versions

ESV	English Standard Version	NEB	New English Bible
HCSB	Holman Christian Standard Bible	NIV	New International Version
KJV	King James Version	NKJV	New King James Version
LXX	Septuagint	NRSV	New Revised Standard Version
MT	Masoretic Text	RSV	Revised Standard Version
NASB	New American Standard Bible		

Secondary Sources

AB	Anchor Bible
ABD	*Anchor Bible Dictionary*
ABR	*Australian Biblical Review*
AcBib	Academia Biblica
AGJU	Arbeiten zur Geschichte des antiken Judentums und des Urchristentums
AIL	Ancient Israel and Its Literature
AOTC	Abingdon Old Testament Commentary
ApOTC	Apollos Old Testament Commentary

ArBib	The Aramaic Bible
AYBRL	Anchor Yale Bible Reference Library
AzTh	Arbeiten zur Theologie
BBB	Bonner biblische Beiträge
BBR	*Bulletin for Biblical Research*
BBRSup	Bulletin for Biblical Research Supplement
BDB	Brown, Francis, S. R. Driver, and Charles A. Briggs. *A Hebrew and English Lexicon of the Old Testament*
BECNT	Baker Exegetical Commentary on the New Testament
BETL	Bibliotheca Ephemeridum Theologicarum Lovaniensium
BHQ	*Biblia Hebraica Quinta*. Edited by Adrian Schenker et al. Stuttgart: Deutsche Bibelgesellschaft, 2004–
Bib	*Biblica*
BibInt	*Biblical Interpretation*
BIntS	Biblical Interpretation Series
BLS	Bible and Literature Series
BN	*Biblische Notizen*
BSac	*Bibliotheca Sacra*
BZAW	Beihefte zur Zeitschrift für die alttestamentliche Wissenschaft
BZNW	Beihefte zur Zeitschrift für die neutestamentliche Wissenschaft
CBET	Contributions to Biblical Exegesis and Theology
CBQ	*Catholic Biblical Quarterly*
CBQMS	Catholic Biblical Quarterly Monograph Series
CC	Continental Commentaries
CNTUOT	*Commentary on the New Testament's Use of the Old Testament*. Edited by G. K. Beale and D. A. Carson. Grand Rapids: Baker Academic, 2007
DCH	*Dictionary of Classical Hebrew*. Edited by David J. A. Clines. 9 vols. Sheffield: Sheffield Phoenix, 1993–2016
EQ	*The Evangelical Quarterly*
ETL	*Ephemerides theologicae lovanienses*
ExpTim	*Expository Times*
FAT	Forschungen zum Alten Testament
FBBS	Facet Books, Biblical Series
FC	Fathers of the Church
FOTL	Forms of the Old Testament Literature
FRLANT	Forschungen zur Religion und Literatur des Alten und Neuen Testaments
GKC	*Gesenius' Hebrew Grammar*. Edited by Emil Kautzsch. Translated by Arthur E. Cowley. 2nd ed. Oxford: Clarendon, 1910
HAR	*Hebrew Annual Review*
HBT	*Horizons in Biblical Theology*
HCOT	Historical Commentary on the Old Testament
HSM	Harvard Semitic Monographs
HTR	*Harvard Theological Review*
HUCA	*Hebrew Union College Annual*
IBC	Interpretation: A Bible Commentary for Teaching and Preaching
IBHS	*An Introduction to Biblical Hebrew Syntax*. Bruce K. Waltke and Michael O'Connor. Winona Lake, IN: Eisenbrauns, 1990

ICC	International Critical Commentary
Int	*Interpretation*
JBL	*Journal of Biblical Literature*
JESOT	*Journal for the Evangelical Study of the Old Testament*
JETS	*Journal of the Evangelical Theological Society*
JJS	*Journal of Jewish Studies*
JNSL	*Journal of Northwest Semitic Languages*
JPS	Jewish Publication Society
JSJSup	Journal for the Study of Judaism in the Persian, Hellenistic, and Roman Periods, Supplement Series
JSNTSup	Journal for the Study of the New Testament, Supplement Series
JSOT	*Journal for the Study of the Old Testament*
JSOTSup	Journal for the Study of the Old Testament Supplement Series
JSPSup	Journal for the Study of the Pseudepigrapha Supplement Series
JTISup	Journal for Theological Interpretation, Supplements
JTS	*Journal of Theological Studies*
LHBOTS	The Library of Hebrew Bible/Old Testament Studies
LNTS	The Library of New Testament Studies
NAC	New American Commentary
NCB	New Century Bible Commentary
NIBC	New International Biblical Commentary
NICNT	New International Commentary on the New Testament
NICOT	New International Commentary on the Old Testament
NIGTC	New International Greek Testament Commentary
NIVAC	NIV Application Commentary
NovTSup	Supplements to Novum Testamentum
NSBT	New Studies in Biblical Theology
NTS	*New Testament Studies*
OBT	Overtures to Biblical Theology
OTL	Old Testament Library
OTS	Old Testament Studies
PRSt	*Perspectives in Religious Studies*
ResQ	*Restoration Quarterly*
RHPR	*Revue d'histoire et de philosophie religieuses*
SBLDS	Society of Biblical Literature Dissertation Series
SBLEJL	Society of Biblical Literature Early Judaism and Its Literature Series
SBLMS	Society of Biblical Literature Monograph Series
SBS	Stuttgarter Bibelstudien
SBT	Studies in Biblical Theology
SHBC	Smyth & Helwys Bible Commentary
SJOT	*Scandinavian Journal of the Old Testament*
SNTSMS	Society for New Testament Studies Monograph Series
SOTSMS	Society for Old Testament Studies Monograph Series
SubBi	Subsidia Biblica
TDOT	*Theological Dictionary of the Old Testament*. Edited by G. Johannes Botterweck and Helmer Ringgren. Translated by John T. Willis et al. 15 vols. Grand Rapids: Eerdmans, 1974–2006

THOTC	Two Horizons Old Testament Commentary
TJ	*Trinity Journal*
TOTC	Tyndale Old Testament Commentaries
TynBul	*Tyndale Bulletin*
VT	*Vetus Testamentum*
VTSup	Supplements to Vetus Testamentum
WBC	Word Biblical Commentary
WMANT	Wissenschaftliche Monographien zum Alten und Neuen Testament
WTJ	*Westminster Theological Journal*
WUNT	Wissenschaftliche Untersuchungen zum Neuen Testament
ZAW	*Zeitschrift für die alttestamentliche Wissenschaft*
ZECNT	Zondervan Exegetical Commentary on the New Testament
ZNW	*Zeitschrift für die neutestamentliche Wissenschaft und die Kunde der älteren Kirche*

Introduction

The subject of this book is fundamental to a proper understanding of the faith we profess, for the name of our faith (Christianity) and the name given to its followers (Christians) derive from a core belief that Jesus of Nazareth is the "Christ" (= Messiah). In terms of a definition of "messiah" and "messianism," in this book these terms are understood to refer to the hope of the coming of a royal agent who will serve God's kingdom purposes, an expectation that Christians believe finds fulfillment in Jesus Christ.[1] Put simply, a messianic passage or book in the Old Testament is one in which this royal figure is prefigured, anticipated, predicted, or described. There are many Old Testament portions that Christians see as pointing to Jesus that do not fall under this definition—for example, the Servant Songs of Isaiah, which depict "the servant of the LORD," whom we would classify as a prophetic rather than a royal figure (see, e.g., Isa. 42:1–4);[2] however, such texts are not our concern in this book. In other words, our definition of things messianic is narrower than just any Old Testament passage that can be understood to point to Jesus. In fact, messianism is only one of several strands of Old Testament expectation that lead to Jesus. Other strands include Jesus as the ultimate prophet, the true priest, or God himself. This is an important caveat, for it means that in classifying any particular biblical text or book as "non-messianic," we do not mean to imply or assert that it is unconnected to Jesus.

---

1. On the vexed problem of definition, see, e.g., Gerbern S. Oegema, *The Anointed and His People: Messianic Expectations from the Maccabees to Bar Kochba*, JSPSup 27 (Sheffield: Sheffield Academic, 1998), 21–34.
2. See chap. 6 in the present volume.

Beyond Word Studies

The study of messianism in the Old Testament is not to be tied too closely to occurrences of the term *māšîaḥ* ("anointed one"), the Hebrew word from which we get the term "Messiah," as demonstrated, for example, by the fact that the Davidic ruler of Jer. 23:5–6 is clearly a future ideal figure, but the term "anointed" is not used in this passage.[3] In determining what biblical passages are to be examined, we will not limit their range to those that specifically refer to an anointed one, for the messianic concept is not limited to specific terminology. Though kings are not the only figures said to be anointed in the Old Testament,[4] the main application of the terminology is to kings, and, therefore, kingship will be our exclusive focus in this book. The Hebrew root *mšḥ* occurs as a verb (*māšaḥ*), meaning "to anoint," and as a nominal form (*māšîaḥ*), which in terms of its form is really an adjective with a passive meaning ("anointed"),[5] as shown by its use, for example, to refer to "the *anointed priest*" (Lev. 4:3, 5, 16, etc.), though in the Old Testament most of the time it is used as a substantivized noun ("anointed one").

In terms of the biblical use of the Hebrew root *mšḥ*, both as a noun and as a verb, the place to start is the book of Samuel, where it is found many times and where for the first time in the Old Testament it is applied to royal figures. What is obvious from a survey of nominal uses of the root is that the noun (*māšîaḥ*) is always determined. It can be determined in a number of ways:

> by a pronominal suffix—either "his anointed" (1 Sam. 2:10; 12:3, 5; 16:6; 2 Sam. 22:51) or "my anointed" (1 Sam. 2:35)—where the suffix refers to Yhwh;
>
> by being part of a Hebrew construct chain—usually "the Lord's anointed" (1 Sam. 24:6 [24:7 MT; 2x], 10 [11 MT]; 26:9, 11, 16, 23; 2 Sam. 1:14, 16; 19:21 [19:22 MT]);
>
> once in a poetic passage, "the anointed of the God of Jacob" (2 Sam. 23:1).

This is by no means an unusual occurrence in the Old Testament, since, for example, in the Psalter the expressions that come closest to "the Messiah" are "his anointed" (Pss. 2:2; 18:50), "your anointed" (132:10), and "my anointed"

---

3. A point made by John J. Collins, *The Scepter and the Star: Messianism in Light of the Dead Sea Scrolls*, 2nd ed. (Grand Rapids: Eerdmans, 2010), 17.

4. E.g., the high priest (Exod. 29:7; Num. 35:25), other priests (Exod. 28:41; 30:30; 40:15; Num. 3:3), and prophets (1 Kings 19:16; Isa. 61:1; maybe Ps. 105:15 [= 1 Chron. 16:22]).

5. Paul Joüon and T. Muraoka, *A Grammar of Biblical Hebrew*, rev. English ed., SubBi 27 (Rome: Pontifical Biblical Institute, 2006), §88Eb.

(v. 17), with the personal pronoun referring in each case to YHWH. This pattern of usage suggests that there is a close bond between YHWH and his anointed royal agent (indicating authorization, dependence, or submission).

The verb "to anoint" (*māšaḥ*) is used fourteen times in the book of Samuel. These verbal occurrences make the point that the person in question (usually Saul or David) was anointed by YHWH (1 Sam. 10:1; 15:17; 2 Sam. 12:7), by the prophet under divine instruction (1 Sam. 9:16; 15:1; 16:3, 12, 13), or by the people through their own representatives (2 Sam. 2:4, 7; 3:39 [probably]; 5:3, 17; 19:10 [19:11 MT]). Regarding the last category, except in the case of Absalom (19:10 [19:11 MT]), the action of the people is not out of step with God's purposes and reflects popular knowledge that David was the one whom God wished to be their ruler; we note the statement the northern tribes made about their motivation when speaking to David in 2 Sam. 5:2 ("And the LORD said to you, 'You shall be shepherd of my people Israel, and you shall be prince over Israel'").

The title "the Messiah" is not found in Samuel or the Psalter, or, indeed, in the Old Testament as a whole, and the two obscure references to "an anointed one" (*māšîaḥ* without a definite article) in Dan. 9:25 and 9:26 are hardly exceptions, for there is ongoing scholarly disagreement over to what these refer (king or priest?).[6] Though this surprising fact is often pointed out by scholars, it may not be as significant as it at first sounds. It certainly does not mean that messianism is a postbiblical concept and only *read into* the Old Testament by those wearing Christian spectacles.

Messianism: Defined out of Existence?

Whatever view is taken of the concept of the Messiah in the Old Testament, an essential starting-point for thinking on this subject is the book of Samuel, for it is at this point in the Old Testament that we are first introduced to royal anointed figures, though this way of approaching the subject is not obvious to all.[7] The reason usually given is that those referred to under the title "the LORD's anointed" (and variants on this title) and the persons who are anointed in Samuel are historical figures (notably Saul and David), who are reigning kings rather than eschatological figures. On that basis, Joseph Fitzmyer quickly surveys and dismisses the passages in Samuel that refer to an anointed figure

6. See chap. 14 in the present volume.
7. The material in Samuel is often overlooked in treatments of the theme—e.g., Walter C. Kaiser Jr., *The Messiah in the Old Testament* (Grand Rapids: Zondervan, 1995); Stanley E. Porter, ed., *The Messiah in the Old and New Testaments* (Grand Rapids: Eerdmans, 2007).

(listed above), in each case declaring that they are devoid of messianic connotations, and he sums up his brief study by saying that they do not even *hint* at messianic expectation.[8] Susan E. Gillingham gives the references to an anointed one in eight psalms the same kind of treatment (2:2; 18:50 [18:51 MT]; 20:6 [20:7 MT]; 28:8; 45:7 [45:8 MT]; 84:9 [84:10 MT]; 89:38, 51 [89:39, 52 MT]; 132:10, 17).[9] As a result of this way of proceeding, Joseph Fitzmyer finds what he considers a genuine messianic passage only in the book of Daniel (9:25–26), and the result is that messianism is relegated to the fringe of the Old Testament,[10] such that for scholars like Fitzmyer, messianism becomes predominantly an intertestamental development, and consequently their focus is on the Apocrypha, the Pseudepigrapha, and the Dead Sea Scrolls to provide the background for New Testament thinking about Jesus as the Christ.[11]

To anticipate our findings, our argument to the contrary is that Saul and David are depicted as messianic figures in Samuel, such that their position and roles presage a royal personage promised by God. Though the book of Samuel is not explicit concerning the prospect of a future ideal ruler in the Davidic line, the experiences of Saul and David present a messianic paradigm that helps to shape what God's people are to expect to see in the coming messianic figure. In other words, the portrait of these *historical* messianic figures carries implications for the realization of a messianic ideal in the end time. Likewise, in the case of the Psalter, we find in the psalms of book 5 a nuanced messianism in the form of a future "David" who depends upon and serves YHWH, the Divine King.[12] As a result, in this book we will present a more extended history of messianism in the Old Testament period than is common among scholars in this field of study.

The Messiah and the Kingdom of God

Another distinctive of our approach is that we believe that by coordinating a theology of divine and human kingship, one achieves a more nuanced

8. Joseph A. Fitzmyer, *The One Who Is to Come* (Grand Rapids: Eerdmans, 2007), 13–16.

9. Susan E. Gillingham, "The Messiah in the Psalms: A Question of Reception History and the Psalter," in *King and Messiah in Israel and the Ancient Near East: Proceedings of the Oxford Old Testament Seminar*, ed. John Day, JSOTSup 270 (Sheffield: Sheffield Academic, 1998), 212–20.

10. Fitzmyer, *One Who Is to Come*, 56–64.

11. E.g., Adela Yarbro Collins and John J. Collins, *King and Messiah as Son of God: Divine, Human, and Angelic Messianic Figures in Biblical and Related Literature* (Grand Rapids: Eerdmans, 2008); Jacob Neusner, William Scott Green, and Ernest S. Frerichs, eds., *Judaisms and Their Messiahs at the Turn of the Christian Era* (Cambridge: Cambridge University Press, 1987).

12. See chap. 13 in the present volume.

interpretation of what kind of Messiah is in view in different books. Without claiming that the theme of God's kingship is *the* center of Old Testament theology, but only asserting that it is central, the following outline focuses on God's kingship, to balance and to provide a context for the theme of human kingship. It is no exaggeration to claim that the metaphor of God as king is pervasive within the Old Testament.[13] The kingship of YHWH is intimately connected to his act of creation (cf. Pss. 29:10; 74:12–17; 93:2–4), for in creating the cosmos, God was making a realm to rule, and the earth is thought of as his temple/palace in accordance with the ideology of the ANE, and Adam is his vice-regent.[14] The divine victory over Pharaoh and his hosts at the Red Sea (Exod. 15:1–18), in which the Creator God wielded wind and water as his weapons, leads to the acclamation of God's kingship (v. 18: "The LORD will reign forever and ever").[15] Just as the great kings of the ANE made treaties, God made a "covenant" with his people at Sinai. The cultic regulations of Exodus and Leviticus are controlled by the ideal of oriental royal protocol—that is to say, the proper way in which to approach the king[16]—and James W. Watts argues that the commandments of Exodus through Deuteronomy implicitly characterize their (divine) speaker as king.[17]

It is anticipated in Moses's speeches that Israel will have the institution of kingship (Deut. 17:14–20); however, the king acts alongside other officeholders—judges, priests, and prophets—so that power sharing is the ideal (16:18–18:22), with the king depicted as the "model Israelite" and the "first citizen" in the community of God's covenant people.[18] In this way, human kingship is not allowed to get out of control and threaten God's supreme rule. Compatible with this, Moses, for all his God-given authority,

13. See Marc Zvi Brettler, *God Is King: Understanding an Israelite Metaphor*, JSOTSup 76 (Sheffield: Sheffield Academic, 1989).

14. Gary V. Smith, "The Concept of God/the Gods as King in the Ancient Near East and the Bible," *TJ* 3 (1982): 20–38; John H. Walton, *Genesis 1 as Ancient Cosmology* (Winona Lake, IN: Eisenbrauns, 2011), 178–92.

15. Bruce C. Birch, *Let Justice Roll Down: The Old Testament, Ethics, and Christian Life* (Louisville: Westminster John Knox, 1991), 199.

16. E.g., God's kingship is presupposed in the idiom of people being required to "appear [MT: *rā 'â*, a *niphal* verb form] in the presence of" YHWH, such as found in Exod. 23:15, 17; 34:20, 23; Deut. 16:16 and 31:11; see Abraham Geiger, *Urschrift und Übersetzungen der Bibel in ihrer Abhängigkeit von der innern Entwickelung des Judenthums* (Breslau: Julius Hainauer, 1857), 337–39.

17. James W. Watts, "The Legal Characterization of God in the Pentateuch," *HUCA* 67 (1996): 8.

18. J. G. McConville, "King and Messiah in Deuteronomy and the Deuteronomistic History," in Day, *King and Messiah*, 271–95.

is not depicted in the Pentateuch as a *king*,[19] perhaps because such a move might be thought to detract attention from God's kingship. As a second Moses, Joshua, likewise, is not depicted as a king figure in the book named after him.[20] This raises the implicit question, How does human kingship fit within the theocratic structure of Israel as the covenant nation? Unless this question can be satisfactorily answered, any form of messianism is incomprehensible.

In Judg. 8:22–23 Gideon refuses the offer of kingship by referring to God's own status as king ("the LORD will rule over you"), showing that in the judges' thinking, human kingship appeared to be incompatible with divine kingship. In the speeches of Samuel, the people's request for a king is viewed as a rejection of YHWH as king (1 Sam. 8:7; 12:12). The reactions of Gideon and Samuel suggest that the relationship between divine and human kingship is vital to clarify (this "theological work" is done in 1 Sam. 8–12[21]), and the role of the prophet is to keep this dangerous new institution in check (12:23). The transfer of the "ark" (viewed as the throne or footstool of YHWH; see 2 Sam. 6:2) to the new capital of Jerusalem is to be understood as King David's sincere acknowledgment of God's superior kingship (2 Sam. 6), and this is also the godly motivation behind David's desire to build YHWH a temple/palace (2 Sam. 7). These key passages set the theological parameters for the era of kingship (depicted in Kings and Chronicles).

The sacking (and later destruction) of the temple calls in question the reign of YHWH (Dan. 1:1–2), and the book of Daniel explores the relation of God's kingship and the fate of human kingdoms. Kingship, human and divine, is the main theme of the Psalter, with the climactic confession by David of God as his king (Ps. 145:1: "I will extol you, my God and King"). The links of Old Testament wisdom with kingship are strong (e.g., Prov. 1:1; Eccles. 1:1; 2:1–11), with the implicit understanding that wisdom is something handed down by God as the Wise King. Among the writing prophets, Hosea is the first to articulate a clearly expressed criticism of the (northern) kings (e.g., 8:4, 10; 13:9–11), but he also says that there is a place for a future Davidic king in God's purposes (3:5). Isaiah emphasizes the kingship of YHWH (2:1–4; 6:5b: "For my eyes have seen the King, the LORD of hosts"; cf. 41:21; 43:15; 44:6; 52:7; 66:1). Similarly, in Ezekiel, throne scenes (the appearance and movement of the theophanic glory cloud) form the structural backbone of the prophecy

19. *Pace* Danny Mathews, *Royal Motifs in the Pentateuchal Portrayal of Moses*, LHBOTS 571 (New York: T&T Clark International, 2012).

20. Gregory Goswell, "Joshua and Kingship," *BBR* 23 (2013): 29–42.

21. Lyle M. Eslinger, "Viewpoints and Point of View in 1 Samuel 8–12," *JSOT* 26 (1983): 61–76.

(1; 10; 43:1–5). The prophets depict God as the one who saves his people (e.g., Isa. 12:2; Jer. 23:1–3; Ezek. 34:11–19), so what role is left for a messianic figure to play? The same prophets consistently present a truncated form of human kingship as the model for the future, focused on social justice and domestic rule (e.g., Isa. 9:6–7 [9:5–6 MT]; 11:3–4; Jer. 23:5–6; Ezek. 34:23–24).[22] In the postexilic period, there is a noticeable loss of interest in messianism, perhaps due to the decidedly negative experience with the kings of Israel and Judah, with the later books having a distinctly theocratic emphasis. For example, neither Haggai nor Ezra-Nehemiah describes Zerubbabel, the temple builder, as having Davidic credentials.[23]

Moving to the New Testament, the proclamation of Jesus can be summed up as the preaching of "the kingdom of God" (Mark 1:14–15), with Jesus understanding himself to be the bringer of the kingdom that fulfills Old Testament expectation. So, too, Luke pictures Paul as "proclaiming the kingdom of God and teaching about the Lord Jesus Christ" (Acts 28:31; cf. 20:25), and Rom. 1:1–6 at once confirms that Luke has given an accurate summary of Paul's message (cf. 9:5). The preaching of the kingdom by Jesus and his apostles serves to confirm that Yhwh's kingship is a key theme in the theology of the Old Testament. If in the Old Testament a certain tension between divine kingship and human kingship surfaces at times, any such tension is finally and fully resolved in the person of the God-man, Jesus Christ, who is both the Divine King who saves his people and the hoped-for Messiah who rules in God's consummated kingdom. Some think that the designation of Jesus as the Christ is no more than a second *proper name* (e.g., Rom. 1:1: "Paul, a servant of Jesus Christ . . ." RSV), but that evaluation is not consistent with Paul's reference to Jesus's descent from David (v. 3)[24] or with the fact that Ps. 2 "resonates" in Rom. 1:3–5 (esp. the key themes of the Christ, Son of God, and all the nations).[25] On the other hand, we would not go as far as N. T. Wright, who says that whenever Paul uses the word "Christ,"

22. See chaps. 6, 7, and 8 in the present volume.

23. See Gregory Goswell, "The Fate and Future of Zerubbabel in the Prophecy of Haggai," *Bib* 91 (2010): 77–90; Gregory Goswell, "The Absence of a Davidic Hope in Ezra-Nehemiah," *TJ* 33 (2012): 19–31.

24. This approach is roundly rejected by Giorgio Agamben, *The Time That Remains: A Commentary on the Letter to the Romans*, trans. Patricia Dailey (Stanford, CA: Stanford University Press, 2005), 15–18.

25. N. T. Wright, *Paul and the Faithfulness of God*, Christian Origins and the Question of God 4 (Minneapolis: Fortress, 2013), 2:815–908, esp. 818; cf. Lidija Novakovic, *Raised from the Dead according to Scripture: The Role of Israel's Scripture in the Early Christian Interpretations of Jesus' Resurrection*, Jewish and Christian Texts in Contexts and Related Studies 12 (London: Bloomsbury T&T Clark, 2012), 133–46. More will be said on this issue in chap. 16 in the present volume.

he is underlining the messiahship of Jesus such that it should be routinely glossed as "Messiah."[26]

Postlude: Canonical Reflections

The prevalence of the use of "Christ" in the New Testament means that its application to Jesus must be carefully studied and read in the context of what is said in the Old Testament concerning messianism. In terms of New Testament fulfillment, the Lord Jesus, as God in human flesh, fulfills what the prophets say God will do—namely, regather God's people and effect eschatological renewal (e.g., Isa. 11:6–16), and Jesus is also the promised Davidic ruler who will maintain justice in the end-time kingdom (vv. 1–5).[27] The divine kingship of Jesus is the presupposition for his ability to save his people. The New Testament writers regularly apply what is said about God in the Old Testament—his character and actions—not just to the Father but to Jesus.[28] This realization helps to take the heat out of certain debates and disagreements over "messianic passages," for many such passages find their fulfillment in Jesus on *two* levels—namely, his advent brings together two aspects of Old Testament hope, the coming of God and the coming of the Messiah. We will have more to say about this after we have surveyed the books of the Old Testament for what they teach about messianism.

In this volume, we are not attempting to make every messianic passage across the Old Testament sound the same but will allow the different biblical books to provide their own variations on this vital Old Testament theme. For example, does the "seed" motif from Genesis figure as strongly in the book of Judges? Probably not. Does the view of Chronicles differ in some respects from the view of the book of Kings on things messianic? Perhaps it does. Our aim in writing is not to force these different canonical perspectives into one mold; instead, we will proceed book by book, allowing each biblical book to sound its unique tune as part of a symphonic whole. As well, we will not be moving backward (NT to OT) but forward (OT to NT). This way of proceeding allows the voice of the Old Testament to be heard before we move to consider the New Testament fulfillment of messianic hopes in the person and work of Jesus Christ.[29]

26. N. T. Wright, *The Climax of the Covenant: Christ and the Law in Pauline Theology* (Edinburgh: T&T Clark, 1991), 41.

27. Gregory Goswell, "Messianic Expectation in Isaiah 11," *WTJ* 79 (2017): 123–35.

28. E.g., the use made of the description of God as the unchanging Creator in Ps. 102:25–27 by the author of Hebrews (1:10–12).

29. See chap. 16 in the present volume.

Here is what we believe makes our volume most significant: in providing this survey of the Old Testament, we are mindful of *God's* supreme kingship, with the Messiah seen as God's agent; our focus in this book is on *royal* messianic expectation (other strands such as the priestly and prophetic are beyond our brief); and we work our way through the Old Testament book by book, allowing each book to have its unique witness, confident that the Bible as a whole provides a unified testimony to the coming of Jesus Christ, who is both the Divine King and the hoped-for Messiah.

1

The Seed, the Star, and the Template in the Pentateuch

When my wife and I (Andrew) moved to Melbourne from the US, we expected that encounters with poisonous spiders and venomous snakes would be a daily, or at least weekly, occurrence. After all, every tourism book that we read before our move featured Australia as home to the deadliest spiders and snakes on the planet. As it turns out, after three years in Australia, we had not seen a single snake, and the only scary spiders we had seen were huntsmen (we dare you to do a Google search), which are harmless.

Many Christians have a similar mismatch in expectations when they read the Old Testament. During Jesus's walk to Emmaus, he helps some struggling disciples see how Moses, the Prophets, and the Psalms—all of the Old Testament—bear witness to him (Luke 24:27, 44). With this sort of New Testament passage in mind, some Christians find themselves perplexed by how few explicit references there are to a royal Messiah in the Pentateuch. In this chapter, we will consider how messianic expectations figure into the portion of Scripture Jesus began with in his exposition to the disciples on the road to Emmaus, the Pentateuch, "the law of Moses." As is indicated in our introduction, we will limit our attention to passages containing royal messianic expectations while at the same time factoring in how such passages fit into the bigger picture of the Pentateuch.

Messianic Expectations in Genesis

The book of Genesis launches the story line of Scripture, so how do messianic expectations figure into the Bible's opening book?

Creation

There is no need for a messianic agent in the opening two chapters of Genesis. After all, on both the cosmic scale (Gen. 1) and on a narrower scale in the garden (Gen. 2) there is harmony; there is no rupture in God's ideal for his world.[1] A triangulated ideal for God's world emerges from these opening chapters where *God the King* creates *humanity* (his vice-regents) to govern *creation* as both humanity and the rest of creation experience God's blessing.[2] It is the rupture of this harmonious ideal through the fall that sets in motion a plot that will eventually include messianic expectations whereby God's ideal in creation will be regained.

Genesis 3 and the Seed of Woman

Yes, when Adam and Eve ate from the forbidden fruit, they committed sin. There is, however, more wrong in Gen. 3 than Adam and Eve disobeying God. Through a clever play on a word from the final verse of chapter 2, chapter 3 opens by introducing a snake that is more crafty (*'ārûm*) than all other animals (3:1) and threatens to undo the shameless, naked (*'ărûmmîm*; 2:25) existence of Adam and Eve.[3] This snake is "the mouthpiece for a Dark Power,"[4] an evil force at work to rupture the God, human, and creation interrelationship.[5] As evil's wiles unfold, as humans partake in sinful actions, and as shame sets in, the harmonious ideal of Gen. 1–2 quickly unravels. Any solution to Gen.

1. Alan Jon Hauser, "Genesis 2–3: The Theme of Intimacy and Alienation," in *I Studied Inscriptions from before the Flood: Ancient Near Eastern, Literary, and Linguistic Approaches to Genesis 1–11*, ed. Richard S. Hess and David Toshio Tsumura (Winona Lake, IN: Eisenbrauns, 1994), 383–98.

2. For more on the triangle of God's presence, people, and place, see Christopher J. H. Wright, *The Mission of God: Unlocking the Bible's Grand Narrative* (Downers Grove, IL: IVP Academic, 2006).

3. E.g., Kenneth A. Mathews, *Genesis 1–11:26*, NAC 1A (Nashville: Broadman & Holman, 1996), 225.

4. C. John Collins, *Genesis 1–4: A Linguistic, Literary, and Theological Commentary* (Phillipsburg, NJ: P&R, 2006), 171.

5. Later in Israel's history, particularly in the New Testament, biblical writers refer to Satan as a central figure in bringing about evil influence and relate Satan with the serpent (e.g., Rev. 12:9). For a discussion on snakes and how ancient Israel conceptualized evil, see John H. Walton, *Genesis*, NIVAC (Grand Rapids: Zondervan, 2001), 203, 209–10.

3, then, must seek to remedy all facets of the problem presented there—the power of evil, sinful human action, and the consequences of sin, including alienation of humans from one another, from God, and from creation. Although the rest of Gen. 3 primarily details the negative outcomes of this event for the snake, the woman, and the man, in God's words to the snake a glimmer of hope arises that has implications for understanding messianic expectations in Genesis and beyond.

Genesis 3:15, often referred to as the *protoevangelium* (first gospel), is a difficult passage to interpret. Debate swirls around two major questions: (1) Is the "offspring" of woman singular or collective? (2) Does the passage envisage the ultimate victory of the "offspring" of woman over the snake's "offspring" or a perpetual struggle between them? A comparison of the NIV and ESV translations, along with their footnotes, exposes these issues. In Hebrew, *zera'* can be either singular or collective. Also, the final two clauses use the same Hebrew verb (*šûp*), which the ESV translates with the same English word ("bruise") and the NIV translates with different English words ("crush"; "strike").

NIV	ESV
And I will put enmity	I will put enmity
between you and the woman,	between you and the woman,
and between your offspring [*zera'*][a]	and between your offspring [*zera'*][a]
and hers [*zera'*];	and her offspring [*zera'*];
he will crush [*šûp*][b] your head,	he shall bruise [*šûp*] your head,
and you will strike [*šûp*] his heel.	and you shall bruise [*šûp*] his heel.
a. Or *seed*.	a. Hebrew *seed*; so throughout Genesis.
b. Or *strike*.	

Instead of reviewing all the debates, we will present our understanding of this verse in four points and engage with differing views as needed.

First, Gen. 3:15 occurs within God's curse of the snake. The curse opens with God decreeing that the snake will go about on its belly and eat dust (v. 14). As Walter Kaiser suggests, it is likely that this is a "figure of speech, vividly picturing those who had been vanquished."[6] The curse is directed against an evil agent itself, not snakes (contra the etiology view).[7] Although verse 15 does include some negative implications for humanity (i.e., enmity), the fact that it is part of God's curse spoken to the serpent should lead one

6. Walter C. Kaiser Jr., *The Messiah in the Old Testament* (Grand Rapids: Zondervan, 1995), 39.

7. For an example of the etiological interpretation, see Sigmund Mowinckel, *He That Cometh: The Messiah Concept in the Old Testament and Later Judaism*, trans. G. W. Anderson (Grand Rapids: Eerdmans, 2005), 11.

to interpret verse 15 as a curse primarily for the agent of evil embodied in the serpent. The implications of this will become evident below.

Second, Gen. 3:15 decrees perpetual enmity between the snake's *zeraʿ* (offspring) and woman's *zeraʿ*. Whether *zeraʿ* is singular or collective is the crux of interpreting this verse. On one side, C. John Collins argues for interpreting *zeraʿ* as an individual on grammatical grounds due to the use of singular pronouns for *zeraʿ*.[8] This leads to an interpretation where woman's singular *zeraʿ* is understood as the Messiah who would reign in the future. The other side, however, which is the view we prefer, is to understand *zeraʿ* as collective, referring to humanity generally. Grammatically, this view is defensible, as singular pronouns can also occur with a collective understanding of *zeraʿ*.[9] Also, since all the other curses and consequences in verses 14–19 are perpetual and long term, it seems odd to think of verse 15 as pronouncing an isolated occasion of enmity between an individual seed of woman and an individual seed of the snake at a later date. As one reads on into Gen. 4, the struggle between Cain and "sin" that is crouching at his door (v. 7) seems to illustrate what 3:15 has in mind: a battle for humans to obey God in spite of temptation. It seems most natural, then, to interpret Gen. 3:15 as referring more generally to the continual enmity between evil and the sons and daughters of Eve in general.

Third, Gen. 3:15 may be understood as conveying the expectation of victory over evil. The same verb, *šûp*, describes the actions by the offspring of woman and the offspring of the snake toward one another. This leads some to conclude that 3:15 speaks of a perpetual battle, without any sense of victory by either side. While that is a grammatically defensible interpretation, the body parts referred to in the conflict could have some bearing on this text. "Striking" a *heel* is a logical way for a snake to attack a human, but "striking" the *head* of a snake would be a mortal blow. Since this is part of a curse toward the snake, a negative outcome of death for the snake is not unexpected. So, what would victory over the snake entail? The snake is a symbol of an evil force that aims to lead humanity into sin, resulting in shame, death, and a fracture in relationship among humanity, God, and creation. Victory in Gen. 3:15, then, anticipates the victory of humanity over evil through obedience to God resulting in restored relationships with one another, God, and creation.[10]

Fourth, Gen. 3:15 should be understood in light of its role in introducing the Pentateuch. The expectation is that there will be perpetual enmity between humanity and evil with the hope that Eve's offspring will ultimately

8. C. John Collins, "A Syntactical Note (Genesis 3:15): Is the Woman's Seed Singular or Plural?," *TynBul* 48 (1997): 139–48.

9. See Lev. 11:37–38; 26:16; Deut. 31:21.

10. See Gordon J. Wenham, *Genesis 1–15*, WBC 1A (Nashville: Nelson, 1987), 80.

be victorious over evil. As we will see in the rest of Genesis, what begins as a hope for Eve's offspring in general becomes centered on Abraham's offspring, Israel. Israel carries the hope of humanity to overcome evil. Whereas Adam and Eve face exile from the garden due to sin, Israel will be offspring who enter a new land, with God in their midst, in hope of overcoming evil through obedience to Torah and experiencing God's blessing in the land, which will lead to blessing for all nations.[11]

So far, we have not addressed any specific messianic expectations; we have just been observing the hope that the sons and daughters of Eve will overcome evil. Across the rest of Genesis, we will see how kingship figures into God's plans for Eve's offspring.

The Collective Seed of Abraham and Kingship

If Gen. 1–3 sets the drama of Scripture into motion, the rest of Genesis depicts how one lineage within Eve's offspring fits into God's plans to bless his fractured world. In fact, as many observe, Genesis itself is a collation of genealogies, some of which incorporate extended narratives about God's workings with particular individuals.[12]

Particularization—God's election of a particular lineage among Eve's offspring—becomes apparent from the very first "genealogy" (Gen. 2:4–4:26). While Cain's lineage plunges deeper into sin, Gen. 4 introduces an alternative line among Eve's offspring, that of Seth. By explaining the reasoning behind the name Seth (*šēt*)—God had given (*šāt*) offspring (*zeraʿ*) to Eve (4:25)—and by associating Seth's lineage with calling upon the name of the LORD (v. 26), the narrative particularizes in the line of Seth the hope from 3:15 that the offspring (*zeraʿ*) of Eve will overcome evil. The hope of a righteous "offspring" continues with Noah, who is described as righteous and blameless (6:9). From Noah, primeval history particularizes upon Shem, one who is portrayed as upright in contrast to his brother Ham (9:18–27). As sin, death, and ruptures in God's ideal develop, the particularization within the genealogies of the primeval history elicit hope that somehow, some way, a righteous line among Eve's offspring will triumph over evil.

Just as God spoke the world into existence out of a formless and void reality (Gen. 1:2), so God speaks to an aged, childless man, Abram, promising to

---

11. See Joseph A. Fitzmyer, *The One Who Is to Come* (Grand Rapids: Eerdmans, 2007), 152, who notes how Targum Pseudo-Jonathan, Targum Yerušalmi II, and Targum Neofiti view faithfulness to Torah as what will lead to the death of the serpent.

12. E.g., Walton, *Genesis*, 39–41; T. Desmond Alexander, "Genealogies, Seed and the Compositional Unity of Genesis," *TynBul* 44 (1993): 258–69.

make out of nothing a great nation through which God will bless every clan across the earth (12:1–3). The term *zeraʿ* figures prominently in the promises to Abram and is nearly always collective in Gen. 12–25.[13] In Abraham's line through Isaac (17:19), the *zeraʿ* will be as numerous as the stars of the sky (15:5) and dust of the earth (13:16). They will receive God's gift of the promised land (cf. 12:7; 13:15; 15:13, 18; 17:7–8). This same *zeraʿ* is to live according to God's covenant expectations (17:9, 10, 12). The promise of a collective *zeraʿ* through Abraham is passed on to Isaac (26:3–4, 24) and Jacob (28:4, 13, 14; 32:13; 48:4; cf. 46:6–7). Thus, from the beginning to the end of Gen. 12–50, God's plans revolve around a collective *zeraʿ* that will come from the line of Abraham: the nation of Israel. Since barrenness is overcome by God's help throughout, "it is God himself . . . who is responsible for the birth of the promised 'seed.'"[14]

Up to this point, our argument has been that through its use of *zeraʿ*, Gen. 3:15 and the rest of Genesis primarily anticipate a collective offspring, not a particular Messiah. Some argue, however, that not only in 3:15 but elsewhere in Genesis there are occasions when *zeraʿ* refers to an individual royal descendant. Rejecting the standard collective interpretation of Gen. 22:17b and 24:60b, T. D. Alexander argues for an individual, as is reflected in the following translations:

> Your *zeraʿ* will possess (*yārāš*) the gate of *his* enemies. (22:17b, authors' trans.)

> Your *zeraʿ* will possess (*yārāš*) the gate of those hating *him*. (24:60b, authors' trans.)

Drawing on the use of singular pronouns, the progressive specification in Genesis toward the line of Judah, and a parallel between Gen. 22:18 and Ps. 72:17, Alexander concludes that these verses "anticipate that a future member of this line will conquer his enemies and mediate God's blessings to the nations of the earth."[15] There are several reasons why we are unconvinced. First, a singular pronoun refers to a singular understanding of *zeraʿ* only once in Genesis (21:13 [non-messianic]), and it is possible for a singular pronoun to refer to a collective understanding of *zeraʿ* (cf. Lev. 11:37–38; 26:16; perhaps Deut. 31:21). Second, when *zeraʿ* occurs with the verb *yārāš*, the noun is often

---

13. The exceptions are 15:3; 21:13 (Ishmael); and 19:32, 34 (Lot's daughters' children).

14. Gregory Goswell, "The Shape of Kingship in Deut. 17: A Messianic Pentateuch?," *TJ* 38 (2017): 170.

15. T. Desmond Alexander, "Further Observations on the Term 'Seed' in Genesis," *TynBul* 48 (1997): 363–67, esp. 367.

collective and can occur with a singular (Num. 14:24; Ps. 25:13; Isa. 54:3). In the case of Isa. 54:3, *zeraʿ* occurs with a singular verb form ("Your offspring shall possess [*yāraš*] the nations"), and then *zeraʿ* is the assumed subject of a plural verb form in the following line ("And they [your offspring] shall inhabit the desolate cities"). Third, within the immediately preceding lines in Gen. 22:17a and 24:60a, a collective *zeraʿ* is in view:

> I will surely bless you, and I will surely multiply your offspring [*zeraʿ*] as the stars of heaven and as the sand that is on the seashore. And your offspring [*zeraʿ*] shall possess . . . (22:17)

> Our sister, may you become
> thousands of ten thousands,
> and may your offspring [*zeraʿ*] possess . . . (24:60)

In our opinion these passages most likely anticipate a time when Israel, the collective *zeraʿ* of Abraham, will overtake their enemies—as is apparent in the book of Joshua, wherein kings are not required for military victory.

It is more accurate to say that kingship is one aspect of God's collective *zeraʿ* in Genesis. This is apparent when Gen. 17 expresses the expectation that kings will come from the line of Abraham. God says of Sarah, "I will bless her, and moreover, I will give you a son by her. I will bless her, and she shall become nations; kings of peoples shall come from her" (17:16).

Several points are important: (1) God is the one whose blessing enables Sarah's fertility and her far-reaching impact; (2) the mention of "nations" and "peoples" suggests that multiple nations are in view, such as Edom along with Israel and Judah (cf. Gen. 17:6); (3) the plurality of kings in conjunction with "peoples" suggests that the focus is neither on a singular king in Israel nor on kingship only in Israel. The most one can claim then, in terms of messianic expectations, is that multiple lines of Abraham's offspring will become nations with kings (cf. 35:11).

Thus, instead of a dominant expectation for an individual messianic ruler, the priority in Genesis is on the collective, with kings playing a role within the collective offspring of Abraham as God carries out his mission.

Joseph and a Ruler from the Line of Judah

In the final part of Genesis (chaps. 37–50), "the generations of Jacob," the focus is on the survival of collective Israel through God's providential actions in and through Joseph. The Joseph story within Genesis offers a foretaste of the kingship anticipated in Israel's future. Two observations make this apparent.

First, although the presentation of Abraham's genealogy through Isaac and Jacob unfolds very slowly, the genealogy of Esau in chapter 36 fast-forwards across many generations to highlight the kings who came to rule within Edom (36:31–32; cf. 25:16). Given how this resonates with the expectation of kings emerging in nations stemming from Abraham (17:16; 35:11), it is reasonable for a reader of Genesis to wonder about the place of kingship within the line of Jacob.

Second, the motif of Joseph as "ruler" is prominent in the Joseph narrative.[16] After his first dream about his sheaf rising above his brothers' and theirs bowing down to him, his brothers say: "Will you indeed rule [*mālak*] over us, will you indeed have dominion [*māšal*] over us?" (Gen. 37:8).[17] Of course, the fulfillment of Joseph's dream seems unlikely after he becomes a slave and then a prisoner in Egypt. Joseph's fortunes change dramatically when he takes a prominent role in Egypt after he interprets Pharaoh's dream. He eventually reveals his identity to his brothers as they turn to him for food, and he states: "Now, you yourselves did not send me here, for it was God. He made me a father to Pharaoh and lord toward his house and the ruler [*māšal*] over the entire land of Egypt" (45:8). His brothers continue to highlight Joseph's role as ruler in their first words back to their father Jacob: "Joseph is still alive and indeed he is ruler [*māšal*] over the entire land of Egypt" (v. 26). By opening the Joseph story with the motif of rulership (37:8) and then reintroducing it at these climactic moments (45:8, 26), the narrative directs us to conceptualize Joseph's journey in light of an unexpected ascent to rulership under God's sovereign guidance. Joseph is certainly not a monarchical king in this narrative; nevertheless, in a book that lists kings from Esau's line and expects kings from Jacob's line, Joseph's depiction as a ruler within Egypt—one appointed by God, endowed with wisdom (41:33, 39), and meant as a blessing to many nations—could possibly foreshadow a time when the nation of Israel would have their own wise king in their own land (e.g., 1 Kings 3; 10; Ps. 72; Isa. 11).

Interspersed throughout Gen. 37–50 is an interest in Judah.[18] In what appears to be an oddly placed narrative, the story of Tamar taking initiative to procure offspring and preserve a lineage through Judah (chap. 38) parallels

16. On this motif in the Joseph narrative, see also T. Desmond Alexander, "Royal Expectations in Genesis to Kings: Their Importance for Biblical Theology," *TynBul* 49 (1998): 206; T. Desmond Alexander, "The Regal Dimension of the תולדות־יעקב," in *Reading the Law: Studies in Honour of Gordon J. Wenham*, ed. J. G. McConville and Karl Möller, LHBOTS 461 (New York: Continuum, 2007), 196–212.

17. Our own Scripture translations are used in this paragraph.

18. On the supposed insertion of the Judah materials, along with Gen. 49, into the Jacob story to preserve the legacy of children other than Joseph, see Claus Westermann, *Genesis 37–50*, trans. John J. Scullion, CC (Minneapolis: Fortress, 2002), 21–22, 49.

the Joseph narrative, wherein God uses Joseph's acts of initiative to preserve the entire family of Israel.[19] Additionally, the mention of Judah's somewhat noble actions (37:26; 43:3, 8) and his depiction as a leader and spokesperson for the family (44:18–34) indicate that the final form of Genesis is interested in highlighting the leadership of Judah within Israel. The pinnacle of Judah's prominence emerges in Jacob's blessing of his children in Gen. 49. Although Joseph's rulership in Egypt foreshadows future kingship within Israel, 49:8–10 specifies that Judah's line will be a source of kingship within Israel. Genesis 49:8–10 reads:

> [8]Judah, your brothers shall praise you;
>> your hand shall be on the neck of your enemies;
>> your father's sons shall bow down before you.
> [9]Judah is a lion's cub;
>> from the prey, my son, you have gone up.
> He stooped down; he crouched as a lion
>> and as a lioness; who dares rouse him?
> [10]The scepter shall not depart from Judah,
>> nor the ruler's staff from between his feet,
> until tribute comes to him;
>> and to him shall be the obedience of the peoples.

Although there are several ambiguities in 49:10, three ideas are clearly expressed in this poetic blessing: (1) Judah will have prominence over his brothers and enemies, like a fearsome lion that no one dares to stir (vv. 8–9); (2) Judah will have a perpetual lineage of kingship (v. 10a);[20] (3) although the phrase translated as "until tribute [*šîlōh*] comes to him" yields many emendations and translations,[21] it is apparent that kingship in Judah—whether

19. Lindsay Wilson, *Joseph, Wise and Otherwise: The Intersection of Wisdom and Covenant in Genesis 37–50*, Paternoster Biblical Monographs (Carlisle, UK: Paternoster, 2004), 78–94.

20. The word *šēbeṭ* ("scepter") can refer to the power of a king (Judg. 5:14; Pss. 2:9; 45:6 [45:7 MT]; Isa. 14:5; Ezek. 19:11), and *məḥōqēq* can refer to a "ruler's staff" (Num. 21:18; cf. Isa. 33:22). The context within Gen. 49:8–12, along with the use of *šēbeṭ* in Num. 24:17, strengthens the case that kingship, not simply military prominence or nobility, is in view in Gen. 49:10a.

21. Victor P. Hamilton, *The Book of Genesis: Chapters 18–50*, NICOT (Grand Rapids: Eerdmans, 1995), 659–61, offers a helpful list of options for understanding *šîlōh* in verse 10b: (1) "until Shiloh comes" (i.e., the name of a future ruler); (2) "until he [i.e., Judah] comes to Shiloh"; (3) "until he comes to whom it belongs" (*š* = relative pronoun "whom"; *lô* = possessive preposition + 3ms suffix [pleonastic with the relative pronoun] "to whom it belongs"); (4) "until its rulers come" (*šîlōh* as containing a Semitic term for ruler); (5) "until tribute is brought to him" (*šy* = "tribute"; *lô* = directive preposition + 3ms suffix "to him"). With Walton, *Genesis*,

an individual ruler or a dynasty—will invoke the "obedience" (yᵊqāhâ) of other nations (v. 10b). Within the larger book context, verses 8–10 narrow the anticipation of kings from the line of Jacob to the tribe of Judah, while expanding the reach of the kings' impact to the nations.

Assessing Other Views

Up to this point, we have set forth our own approach to messianic expectations in Genesis in as straightforward a fashion as possible. Now, it may prove beneficial to clarify the approach set forth above by evaluating two alternative evangelical views.

Alexander is a leading voice on messianic kingship in Genesis. For him, when *zeraʿ* is interpreted within the context of Genesis's structure and the story line of Genesis to 2 Kings, Gen. 3:15 should be interpreted as referring to a royal Messiah who would fulfill the promise to Abraham of a future king from the line of Judah.[22] His argument revolves around how the seed in verse 15 comes to be specified across Genesis from Seth → Noah → Shem → Terah → Abraham → Isaac → Jacob → Judah's king. Additionally, 2 Sam. 7 and Ps. 72 particularize Abrahamic promises in Davidic kingship, so when Genesis introduces the larger story line of Genesis to 2 Kings, the promise of a victorious seed is understood to be a king from the line of David who had not yet appeared by the time of Babylonian exile.

Although we appreciate many of Alexander's observations, he takes particularization within Genesis one step too far by making a king from Judah the center of all the Abrahamic promises. Particularization in Genesis ends with Jacob (not Esau) before expanding to the twelve sons of Jacob. Genesis 37–50 emphasizes God's ability to preserve all of Jacob's family, and Jacob's children (including and especially Ephraim and Manasseh) are all recipients of the blessing at the end of the book (chaps. 48–49). Although Judah is identified as the seat of kingship (49:8–10), this is just one among numerous promises made to the tribes as a whole. It is safer to say that God's plans remain for a corporate Israel within which kingship will play a part. It seems, then, to be a stretch to say that "the entire book [of Genesis] highlights the existence of a unique line of 'seed' which will eventually

---

716, it seems that the final option has the advantage of making sense of the parallel noun in the next line: "obedience." Tribute and obedience could refer to a holistic response of submission to kingship in Judah.

22. See especially T. Desmond Alexander, "Messianic Ideology in the Book of Genesis," in *The Lord's Anointed: Interpretation of Old Testament Messianic Texts*, ed. P. E. Satterthwaite, Richard S. Hess, and Gordon J. Wenham (Carlisle, UK: Paternoster, 1995), 19–39; Alexander, "Genealogies, Seed."

become a royal dynasty."[23] Genesis's primary focus is on God's remarkable creation of and preservation of the corporate *zera'*—Israel, who will bring blessing to the entire world.

John Sailhamer's approach is the second we will assess.[24] He argues that poems with a focus on "a future king from the house of Judah" were strategically inserted at the final stages of the Pentateuch's composition (Gen. 49:8–12; Num. 24; Deut. 33:7).[25] These poems cross-reference one another (e.g., Gen. 49:9; Num. 24:9; Deut. 33:7) "along the final boundaries of the Pentateuch,"[26] creating a messianic framework and lens through which the rest of the Pentateuch is to be read. According to Sailhamer, these poems appropriate language from the Abrahamic promises and apply it to the anticipated king (cf. Gen. 27:29 in Gen. 49:8 and Num. 24:9); thereby, "the author of the Pentateuch moves decisively away from a collective reading of the promise narratives and toward an individual understanding of Abraham's 'seed' (Gen. 12:3–7)."[27] Since Gen. 3:15 is poetic too, Sailhamer claims that ambiguity regarding the identity of the "seed" there is clarified through these later poems; the victorious seed anticipated in 3:15 is a ruler from the line of Judah.[28] He concludes, "Within the structure of the Pentateuch, the poems are the author's last and most important word regarding the message of the Pentateuch. . . . The texts and connections that we have examined clearly envision an individual king as the recipient of the patriarchal promise. The 'seed of Abraham' is an individual king."[29]

Sailhamer's schema is problematic for several reasons. First, although Deut. 33:7 mentions Judah, as Gordon McConville states, "The prayer has no messianic hint."[30] If 33:7 is removed from the equation, this greatly weakens Sailhamer's argument regarding the strategic placement of these poems along the boundaries of the Pentateuch. With or without a messianic poem near the Pentateuch's conclusion, how much weight does its final author expect a reader to give to messianic kingship within its overarching message? Can a few scattered poems really play such a dominant role in reframing the Pentateuch's message around a coming ruler from the line of

23. Alexander, "Genealogies, Seed," 269.

24. John H. Sailhamer, *The Meaning of the Pentateuch: Revelation, Composition and Interpretation* (Downers Grove, IL: IVP Academic, 2009).

25. Sailhamer, *Meaning of the Pentateuch*, 335.

26. Sailhamer, *Meaning of the Pentateuch*, 467.

27. Sailhamer, *Meaning of the Pentateuch*, 478.

28. Sailhamer, *Meaning of the Pentateuch*, 321, 587–88.

29. Sailhamer, *Meaning of the Pentateuch*, 479–80.

30. J. G. McConville, *Deuteronomy*, ApOTC (Downers Grove, IL: InterVarsity, 2002), 470.

Judah? Second, the cross-references between poems and their application of language from Gen. 27:29 is not driven by "messianic" concerns as Sailhamer claims. In Num. 24:9, there is a consensus that its subject is Israel, not a singular king:[31]

> He [Israel] crouched, he lay down like a lion
>   and like a lioness; who will rouse him up?
> Blessed are those who bless you,
>   and cursed are those who curse you.

Through a verbatim quotation from Gen. 49:9b, Num. 24:9a applies a prior description of Judah's prowess to Israel as a whole. Through a possible association with Gen. 27:29, Num. 24:9b reverses the order of blessing and cursing to reiterate a prior claim about God's commitment to Israel. In our estimation, there is no basis in these linguistic parallels for a claim that the author of these poems guides the reader to narrow the transmission of the Abrahamic promises exclusively to a singular king. If these poems do not play an overarching role in structuring the entire Pentateuch and if they do not in fact transfer promises from corporate Israel to an individual king, Sailhamer's argument becomes untenable.

Summary

What, then, can we say about royal messianic expectations in Genesis? Instead of there being a dominant expectation for an individual messianic ruler, the priority in Genesis is on a collective offspring from the beginning, when victory over evil is anticipated through Eve's offspring (3:15). As the book progresses, the corporate remains in view, while centering on the collective offspring of Jacob, among whom kings from the line of Judah will play a role as God carries out his mission through the offspring of Israel to overcome evil and restore a world ruptured by sin.

Messianic Expectations in the Rest of the Pentateuch

After Genesis, the focus on corporate Israel continues throughout the rest of the Pentateuch. In fact, Exodus and Leviticus pay no obvious attention to a

---

31. For representative treatments of Num. 24:9, see R. Dennis Cole, *Numbers*, NAC 3B (Nashville: Broadman & Holman, 2000), 422; Baruch A. Levine, *Numbers 21–36*, AB 4B (New York: Doubleday, 2000), 197–98; Jacob Milgrom, *Numbers*, JPS Torah Commentary (Philadelphia: Jewish Publication Society, 1989), 205.

future royal king. Instead, their interest is on God saving Israel from bondage in Egypt so that they can become a *kingdom* of priests (Exod. 19:5–6) who live as a righteous and obedient nation in Canaan with God, their saving and holy king (15:18), in their midst. These books are preparing Israel to be a nation through which victory over evil comes. Generally, Numbers and Deuteronomy retain this same corporate focus, as they recount Israel's wilderness experiences and present a vision for Israel's life as God's people as they are on the brink of the promised land. Two passages, however, in Numbers and Deuteronomy express expectations for future rulers: Num. 24 and Deut. 17.

Numbers 24 and a King of Military Might

As the first generation of those saved from Egypt dies off in the wilderness, Israel heads toward the land of promise and camps on the plains of Moab across from the Jordan River. The king of Moab, Balak, requests that the prophet Balaam curse Israel, for Balak fears their power (Num. 22:6). From the time Balaam receives this request to his final oracle, it is clear that Balaam is unable to curse Israel because God is committed to blessing Israel (cf. 22:6, 12; 23:7–8, 20, 25; 24:9, 10). As King Balak's anger increases because Balaam's oracles favor Israel, chapter 24 offers King Balak a rhetorical punch in the gut through two of its oracles that speak of kingship in Israel (24:3–9, 15–19). A brief comment regarding kingship in verse 7b is expanded on in verses 17–19, which depicts the king as a victorious military figure who will destroy Moab and Edom.

As Balaam looks down from a mountain upon Israel spread across the wilderness, he extols how far Israel's tents will stretch (Num. 24:5–7a) and declares that this people whom God brought out of Egypt will destroy their enemies (vv. 8–9). Amid this depiction of Israel's future greatness, Balaam says, "His king shall be higher than Agag" (v. 7b).

The mention of a future king here is just one of numerous components of hope in Num. 24:5–9. Israel's future greatness will include an expansive population, beautiful and bountiful environs, military prowess due to divine favor, and also a well-known king. As was argued above, there is no reason to believe that promises to corporate Israel are being transferred to a future king; instead, just as having a powerful king like Agag can signify the power of a nation, so the greatness of Israel's king will correspond with the greatness of the nation.

What is mentioned in Num. 24:7b develops into a more expansive portrayal in the next oracle:

> [17]I see him, but not now;
>   I behold him, but not near:
> a star shall come out of Jacob,
>   and a scepter shall rise out of Israel;
> it shall crush the forehead of Moab
>   and break down all the sons of Sheth.
> [18]Edom shall be dispossessed;
>   Seir also, his enemies, shall be dispossessed.
>   Israel is doing valiantly.
> [19]And one from Jacob shall exercise dominion
>   and destroy the survivors of cities! (24:17–19)

Although "star" (*kôkāb*) and "scepter" (*šēbeṭ*) can have nonroyal meanings, astral imagery (e.g., Isa. 14:12–13; Ezek. 32:7) and the "scepter" (e.g., Gen. 49:10; Isa. 14:5) can convey the idea of kingship in the Old Testament.[32] In Num. 24:17, the ESV's translation of the verb associated with the "star" obscures its meaning. The root *drk*, translated as "shall come out," often calls to mind the militaristic notion of treading down enemies—a sense not readily apparent in the English translation.[33] This militaristic depiction of the king extends through the rest of the verses as Moab and Edom are the representative victims of Israel's military valor through the leadership of a king within Jacob. Given the context of these oracles, Balak, king of Moab, would not have missed their message: the very nation he wishes to curse will become a great and powerful nation, whose king will crush Moab. Although this is indeed an oracle about the future, it is not clear whether this oracle refers to a singular king who ushers in a new era or envisions an ideal for greatness among kings within Israel in general. As one reads forward in the story of Scripture, David aligns with the mold presented here, as a king who brings victory to Israel over Moab and Edom (cf. 2 Sam. 8). Due to the cosmic language here and the way Edom can symbolize judgment of nations in general (cf. Isa. 34; Obadiah), it is possible that this oracle would create expectations for a greater display of military might by a king than was seen in David.

Deuteronomy 17 and the King as a Model of Obedience

Deuteronomy offers its own portrayal of kingship. The canonical presentation of Deuteronomy situates Israel at the edge of the promised land, with Moses imparting a final vision of covenant life under Yʜᴡʜ when they enter

---

32. Milgrom, *Numbers*, 207–8.
33. E.g., Levine, *Numbers 21–36*, 200–201.

the land. Peter Vogt has convincingly argued that, according to Deuteronomy, Yʜᴡʜ is the king whose will is expressed *through Torah* to his people.[34] The primary task of leaders across Israel, then, is to promote Torah obedience. Figure 1.1 illustrates this schema.

Figure 1.1
Leadership in Deuteronomy

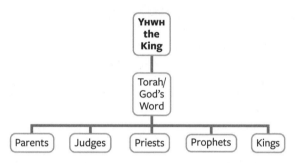

Set among the general (Deut. 5–11) and specific (chaps. 12–26) instructions by which Israel would display their love for God through obedience, many facets of leadership within Israel receive direction for the role they will play within the community of the Divine Suzerain. Parents (6:7), judges (16:18–20), priests (17:8–13; 18:1–8), prophets (18:18–19), and kings (17:14–20) were all to play their role in fostering faithfulness to Yʜᴡʜ through obedience to Torah.

Deuteronomy 17:14–20 does not offer an extensive description of duties for the king; instead, the passage is most concerned with the heart of the king. First, verse 15 gives two qualifications: the king must be chosen by God and not be a foreigner. Second, God specifies what the king *should not do*—all of which pertain to multiplication (vv. 16–17). The king is not to multiply horses, wives, or silver and gold. These prohibitions revolve around protecting the king from trusting in the accumulation of resources available to him. He would not attain security by stockpiling military machinery (horses), strengthening foreign alliances through countless marriages, and hoarding reserves through taxation; instead, he was to trust God as the King of Israel. Third, God describes what the king *was* supposed to do: write out the Torah on a scroll and read it all the days of his life (vv. 18–19a). The reasons for this were to cultivate reverent obedience (v. 19b), to protect the king against any pretension of superiority (v. 20a) and apostasy (v. 20b), and to result in

---

34. Peter T. Vogt, *Deuteronomic Theology and the Significance of Torah: A Reappraisal* (Winona Lake, IN: Eisenbrauns, 2006), esp. 204–26. The following paragraphs summarize his argument.

longevity for the king and his dynasty (v. 20c). Thus, Deuteronomy does not spell out what the king should actually do in his duty as king; presumably, Israel shared with its neighbors a common understanding of what the office of a king would involve. What Deuteronomy aims to impart, instead, is an inspiring vision for the king to be "the model Israelite,"[35] whose love for YHWH through Torah obedience would revolutionize the way an Israelite would fulfill the office of the king. In being such a model, the king was a member of corporate Israel offering leadership that would remind Israel of what the heart of every Israelite should look like.

To what extent is Deut. 17:14–20 messianic? It is not necessarily a promise regarding a future messianic king so much as an ideal through which future kings would be assessed. As will become evident in our chapter on 1–2 Kings, this ideal of Torah obedience looms large as kings such as Solomon and Josiah receive either a thumbs-up or a thumbs-down based on this ideal standard. Since Davidic kingship will ultimately fail to live according to Deut. 17:14–20, this ideal, while not messianic in its first instance, comes to inform hopes for a Messiah who will align with this paradigm.[36]

Conclusion

Let's return to how this chapter opened. My wife and I (Andrew) expected to see poisonous spiders and snakes everywhere in Australia, but we did not encounter any during our three years there. What can one expect to find pertaining to royal messianic expectations in the Pentateuch? The Pentateuch establishes the framework and seedbed by which messianic expectations elsewhere in the Old Testament can be understood. Genesis 3:15 anticipates a time when the offspring of Eve, particularized throughout Genesis to be corporate Israel, will attain victory over evil through obedience amid God's mission to restore what sin had fractured: harmony among God, humanity, and creation. As God's commitment to victory through corporate Israel unfolds, kings (Gen. 17:6, 17; 35:11) through the line of Judah (49:8–10) will play an important part, with Joseph's rule in Egypt possibly foreshadowing this anticipated rule. In Numbers and Deuteronomy, two dimensions of kingship receive elaboration—Israel's king will be a great military victor (Num. 24:17–19) and is to be an exemplar of obedience to Torah as the first among equals within corporate Israel (Deut. 17:14–20).

35. Vogt, *Deuteronomic Theology*, 218.
36. For a more thorough discussion of Deut. 17:14–20 as a paradigm for subsequent messianic expectations, see Goswell, "Shape of Kingship in Deut. 17," 169–81.

Postlude: Canonical Reflections

Without circumventing what subsequent chapters will examine, several reflections on how messianic expectations in the Pentateuch correspond with a theological witness to Christ across both testaments will draw this chapter to a close.

The Church as the Corporate Offspring of Eve

Romans 16:20 alludes to Gen. 3:15, with a number of elements reconfigured. It reads: "The God of peace will soon crush Satan under your feet." Whereas Eve's offspring is the subject that strikes the serpent, Rom. 16:20 makes explicit what is implicit in Gen. 3:15: God will be the one crushing evil, albeit through the feet of the church. Since the verse just prior to this exhorts the Roman Christians to be wise about what is good and innocent about evil, Paul is casting a vision whereby the church is enabled by God to be the obedient offspring of Eve that overcomes evil.

In Rev. 12:9, Michael and his angels throw "that ancient serpent, who is called the devil and Satan," down to the earth, resulting in increased fury by the evil one toward God's people. Heaven, however, breaks out in song because the faithful martyrs "have conquered him by the blood of the Lamb and by the word of their testimony, for they loved not their lives even unto death" (v. 11). The blood of the Lamb enables the redeemed to reign on the earth (5:9–10), living obedient lives that are victorious over Satan under the reign of Christ as King. This corporate outlook, however, looks ahead to a time when the devil meets his definitive demise through being cast into the lake of fire (20:10).

Paul's "Seed" and "Seed" in Genesis

Paul's reference to the "seed" of Abraham as "referring to one . . . who is the Christ" (Gal. 3:16) hovers over any Christian who interprets "seed" in Genesis. Would the apostle Paul disagree with a "corporate Israel" interpretation of seed in Genesis? Several thoughts are in order. First, in Gal. 3:29 Paul uses the Greek word *sperma* in the singular form with a collective referent ("you [pl.] are the seed of Abraham," authors' trans.), so Paul clearly knows that there is latitude for how the word *sperma* could be interpreted in (the LXX of) Genesis.[37] One may infer, then, that Paul knows that an argument purely based on the grammatical singularity of the noun would not be convincing.

37. Douglas J. Moo, *Galatians*, BECNT (Grand Rapids: Baker Academic, 2013), 229.

Second, Paul is utilizing a common Jewish interpretive practice of utilizing ambiguity in terms of singularity or collectivity to make a point.[38] Third, such ambiguity leads Paul to interpret the "seed" promise in Genesis typologically in light of God's culminating work in Christ to bring blessing to the gentiles. It is this salvation-historical framework that enables the grammatical part of his argument to have credence. Fourth, and related to our third point, the corporate is not entirely discarded if Christ is the corporate representative.[39]

Christ as the Obedient King

In Ps. 40:7–8, the psalmist says:

> Behold, I have come;
>   in the scroll of the book it is written of me:
> I delight to do your will, O my God;
>   your law is within my heart.

If this is an allusion to the scroll of Deuteronomy, where it expresses that a king would be devoted to Torah obedience (17:14–20), then the application of Ps. 40 to Christ in Heb. 10:5–10 presents Christ as one who exemplifies the royal paradigm of Deut. 17.[40]

38. E.g., F. F. Bruce, *The Epistle to the Galatians: A Commentary on the Greek Text*, NIGTC (Grand Rapids: Eerdmans, 1982), 172–73.
39. Thomas R. Schreiner, *Galatians*, ZECNT (Grand Rapids: Zondervan, 2010), 229–30.
40. See George H. Guthrie, "Hebrews," in *CNTUOT*, 976.

2

The Need for a King in Judges

In *Lord of the Flies*, a group of British boys become stranded on an uninhabited island, without grown-ups. Playfulness, unity, innocence, and order mark their initial quest to do life without adults. Over time, a hunger for power and a thirst for blood create rival groups among the boys, eventuating in stealing, torture, and even murder as a tribe led by Jack usurps and then attempts to snuff out the initially elected chief, Ralph, and his followers. Throughout *Lord of the Flies*, depravity never resides only in one person; instead, all the boys are capable of great evil. It is not just Jack; it is the tribe. Ralph and his crew, however, are not exempt from the book's depiction of human depravity. This is why, after their first murder, Ralph says to Piggy: "I'm frightened. Of us. I want to go home. Oh God, I want to go home."[1] Although Ralph believes a return to life with grown-ups will remedy their ills, the irony is that adults on a warship eventually save the boys. The warfare between the boys mirrors the depravity evident in the adults, who, too, are waging war. William Golding offers no solution in *Lord of the Flies*; instead, the book's brilliance is in its ability to capture how depravity within human nature wreaks havoc. The book of Judges is similar in its ability to capture depravity within Israel, yet it makes overtures toward a possible solution. This chapter will explore whether the book of Judges presents the institution of human kingship as a solution to Israel's moral and religious unraveling and, if so, in what way.

1. William Golding, *Lord of the Flies* (New York: Riverhead, 1954), 181.

The Unraveling of Israel within Judges

There are high hopes that upon entry into Canaan Israel will overcome evil, as the triangulated ideal of people, place, and God's presence is restored through Israel. As it turns out, Israel is anything but the holy offspring God intended them to be. Judges captures Israel's spiral into disobedience and disarray in three major ways. First, the recurrence of apostasy (3:7, 12; 4:1; 6:1; 10:6; 13:1) in the judge's cycle impresses upon its reader a sense of inevitability; judges were unable to prevent Israel from again and again drifting into sin.

Second, the sequence of the major judges portrays a disintegration of the moral fabric of the judges themselves. Othneil, Ehud, and Deborah are depicted in either a morally neutral or a morally positive fashion. But then we read of Gideon acting out of fear (Judg. 6:27), struggling to trust God (vv. 33–40), and eventually creating an idol that led Israel astray (8:27). Things get worse with Jephthah. Not only does he sacrifice his daughter (11:29–40), but he handles a dispute with Ephraim—a dispute similar to one Gideon peacefully quelled (8:1–4)—through violence that leads to the deaths of forty-two thousand Ephraimites. In Samson, one finds a judge constantly breaking Nazirite laws, forming liaisons with pagan women, and acting only out of personal vengeance. Although God's mercy is on display in his willingness to act through these judges to deliver Israel,[2] the descent of the judges into moral and spiritual decay contributes to the book's aim of capturing the depravity of Israel at the time.

Third, the book's introduction and conclusion display the author's concern to portray Israel's demise while also pointing toward a solution. The book has a dual introduction and a dual conclusion that align to capture Israel's regression from bad to worse.

Figure 2.1
The Introduction and Conclusion to Judges

A   Introduction 1: Israelite Difficulties with Fighting Foreign Nations (Judg. 1)
   B   Introduction 2: Israelite Difficulties with Foreign Gods (2:1–3:6)
   B'   Conclusion 1: Israelite Difficulties with Domestic Gods (17–18)
A'   Conclusion 2: Israelite Difficulties with Domestic (Civil) War (19–21)[3]

2. Barry G. Webb, *The Book of the Judges: An Integrated Reading*, JSOTSup 46 (Sheffield: JSOT Press, 1987).
3. This is an adaptation from K. Lawson Younger, *Judges and Ruth*, NIVAC (Grand Rapids: Zondervan, 2002), 30–33.

Judges begins on a difficult note: Israel has challenges in battles when settling the land of promise and adopts foreign gods. By the end of the book, however, Israel's issues are internal and spread across the tribes: idol making, idol worship, thievery, sexual abuse, and civil war. The narrator helps us assess these devious and heinous actions within Israel by interspersing a refrain across the conclusion of the book:

> In those days there was no king in Israel; all the people did what was right in their own eyes. (17:6)

> In those days there was no king in Israel. (18:1)

> In those days, when there was no king in Israel . . . (19:1)

> In those days there was no king in Israel; all the people did what was right in their own eyes. (21:25 NRSV)

In light of the strategic design of the judge's cycle and the introduction and conclusion, the second half of the refrain comes as no surprise—Judges is recounting how the era of the judges was a time of spiritual and moral collapse within Israel. Everyone was indeed doing what was right in their own eyes. The first part of the refrain, however, introduces something new—it frames this era as a time when Israel lacked a king. Is this suggesting that having a king would somehow remedy Israel's moral and spiritual anarchy? The rest of this chapter will consider a few options for interpreting this reference to kingship. As a recurring refrain in the conclusion to the book of Judges—indeed, even appearing as the book's final verse—this reference to kingship significantly figures into how the author wants us to interpret the book.

The Book of Judges as against Human Kingship

At first glance, the refrain "In those days there was no king in Israel; all the people did what was right in their own eyes" (Judg. 17:6; cf. 18:1; 19:1; 21:25) seems to assert that monarchy is the solution to Israel's problems. But, as William Dumbrell states, "If [the refrain] endorses kingship with enthusiasm, then it contradicts earlier accounts [in Judges] which damn the institution."[4] Earlier in the book, Gideon rejects Israel's request for him to rule over them

---

4. William J. Dumbrell, "'In Those Days There Was No King in Israel; Every Man Did What Was Right in His Own Eyes': The Purpose of the Book of Judges Reconsidered," *JSOT* 25 (1983): 23–33, esp. 28.

because, as he says, "the LORD will rule over you" (8:23). Since Gideon goes on to fail religiously by creating an ephod that becomes a snare to Israel (vv. 24–27), a decision for Gideon not to be king seems to be a good move.[5] The anti-kingship rhetoric continues in Judges 9, where Abimelech's rule is seen in a very negative light. Abimelech garners supporters, hires a posse, kills all seventy of his brothers except Jotham, and then is named king in Shechem. All we learn about Abimelech's reign is that it was filled with turmoil and battles between Abimelech and the people of Shechem, with Abimelech eventually dying after a woman drops a millstone on his head (9:53). From the narrator's perspective, this tumultuous reign of Abimelech stems from the hand of God: "God sent an evil spirit between Abimelech and the leaders of Shechem" (v. 23). The reign of the only Israelite king in Judges is a debacle.

Not only do the negative perspectives on human kingship in the Gideon and Abimelech narratives support Dumbrell's case, but Dumbrell also appeals to the point in time when Judges took its final form—*after* the monarchy had failed. For instance, the narrator in Judg. 18:30 notes that a line of priests from Dan served "until the day of the captivity of the land." This reference to exile, whether by Assyria (722 BCE) or Babylon (586 BCE), indicates that the book was crafted *after* monarchy had failed in Israel and Judah.[6] Furthermore, if Judges is part of the canonical corpus of the Former Prophets, which stretches through 2 Kings, there is again reason to believe that the author(s) of Judges knew of the failure of human kingship.[7] How could monarchy be presented as Israel's solution in the refrains across the conclusion of Judges when the institution of kingship had already failed them?

This leads to Dumbrell's interpretation of the refrain from an anti-monarchical vantage point. He takes the first part of the refrain ("In those days there was no king in Israel") as a testimony to Israel's continued existence during this tumultuous period, even without a king. Israel survived the period of the judges but did not survive the succeeding era of kingship, wherein misrule by kings led to the exile of both the Northern and Southern Kingdoms. In other words, Israel did not need a king to exist during the time of the judges, and they do not need a king to continue to exist during or after exile. The second part of the refrain ("all the people did what was right in their own eyes") captures the depraved moral and religious state of Israel during this time. So, without a king and without a religious or moral compass, Israel continued to exist due to "the pattern of direct divine intervention."[8] Or to

5. Dumbrell, "'In Those Days There Was No King in Israel,'" 28.
6. Dumbrell, "'In Those Days There Was No King in Israel,'" 29.
7. Dumbrell, "'In Those Days There Was No King in Israel,'" 29.
8. Dumbrell, "'In Those Days There Was No King in Israel,'" 29.

put it another way, "The ideal of Israel had been preserved throughout this period *in spite of* Israel."[9] With Israel now without a king and in exile due to sin, the refrain in the book of Judges encourages Israel that the nation's future rests *not* in the hands of a king but in the hands of a *God* who has chosen Israel to be his people.[10]

Daniel Block agrees with Dumbrell that contents elsewhere in the book and the time period of the audience lead to an unfavorable view of monarchical kingship in the book of Judges.[11] Block, however, interprets the refrain differently than Dumbrell. Since "the theme of the book is the *Canaanization of Israelite society during the period of settlement*,"[12] the aim of Judges is not political but is instead prophetic. It is "a call to return to the God of the covenant."[13] Since monarchs in later years prove to be unsuccessful at leading Israel into spiritual and moral faithfulness, the refrain that "there was no king in Israel" is a declaration regarding "Israel's rejection of the theocracy," a disregard for YHWH as their king.[14] The book of Judges points to the need for Israel to live under divine kingship as the answer to its moral, spiritual, and civil unraveling.

A challenge to this novel interpretation, however, is that reference to YHWH as king in Judg. 17:6, 18:1, 19:1, and 21:25 is far too cryptic to be credible, for the bald mention of "king" in application to God has not been sufficiently prepared for in the preceding narratives. As well, in the closing chapters of the book the nation is, in fact, depicted as assembling "to the LORD" (20:1; 21:5), designated "the people of God" (20:2), and described as repeatedly inquiring of YHWH for direction (20:18, 23, 27–28; 21:2, 3, 8).[15] Although other aspects of their behavior are clearly anarchical toward God's rule, it is at least worth acknowledging that the people are not as far removed from acknowledging YHWH as king as some assume.

Thus, for various reasons, some reject the view that "monarchy" is the solution to Israel's plight expressed by the refrain at the end of Judges; instead, YHWH's kingship is Israel's hope. Although, with Gideon, we agree

9. Dumbrell, "'In Those Days There Was No King in Israel,'" 31.

10. Dumbrell, "'In Those Days There Was No King in Israel,'" 31–32.

11. Daniel I. Block, *Judges, Ruth*, NAC 6 (Nashville: Broadman & Holman, 1999), 58–59, 483–84, 583n411.

12. Block, *Judges, Ruth*, 58.

13. Block, *Judges, Ruth*, 58.

14. Block, *Judges, Ruth*, 59. For an extended adaptation of Block's view, see Gregory T. K. Wong, *Compositional Strategy of the Book of Judges: An Inductive, Rhetorical Study*, VTSup 111 (Leiden: Brill, 2006), 200–223.

15. Brian Neil Peterson, *The Authors of the Deuteronomistic History: Locating a Tradition in Ancient Israel* (Minneapolis: Fortress, 2014), 180n58.

that Yhwh's reign is of utmost importance for Israel's well-being, the book of Judges can still be read as promonarchical without undermining a prioritization of Yhwh's kingship. This will become apparent below.

The Book of Judges as Promonarchical

The traditional interpretation of the refrain in Judg. 17:6, 18:1, 19:1, and 21:25 is that it supports the monarchy. According to Barry Webb, the refrain makes the point that "the institution of monarchy was needed to bring some kind of order out of the religious chaos of the judges period."[16] In order to establish that the book of Judges is "promonarchical," several challenges that were raised above must be addressed.

First, if Dumbrell and others are correct that Judges is written after the failure of the monarchy, how can the book of Judges present monarchy as a solution to Israel's religious and political unraveling? Would not this be like a dog returning to its vomit? Philip Satterthwaite provides a helpful response that clarifies in what way Judges can be "promonarchy." "Judges 17–21, so far from being unqualifiedly pro-monarchic, is intended to lead one towards a highly critical evaluation of much of what the kings described in Samuel and Kings actually do."[17] Judges is not suggesting that any old king will do; instead, the sort of kingship that chapters 17–21 endorse is a king who could remedy the problems in those chapters: household idols and a disregard for priestly order (17:1–5, 7–13); the abuse of power, stealing, murder, and false worship by a tribe (chap. 18); and sexual abuse, the murder of a woman, and a resulting civil war (chaps. 19–21). By presenting a "king" as a solution, Judges has in mind a king quite different from those in Samuel and Kings—a king who would uphold the worship of Yhwh through the proper priestly order, a king who would lead society toward justice and establish unity among the tribes.

Second, and related, does not the negative portrayal of Abimelech's kingship expose a bias against monarchy? If Deuteronomy serves as a lens for evaluating history in Judges, the specification in Deut. 17:15 that a king should be chosen by God contrasts with Abimelech's experience. Abimelech becomes king through self-assertion as he strikes a deal with the people. In this way,

16. Barry G. Webb, *The Book of Judges*, NICOT (Grand Rapids: Eerdmans, 2012), 426.
17. Philip Satterthwaite, "'No King in Israel': Narrative Criticism and Judges 17–21," *TynBul* 44 (1993): 75–88, esp. 88. Yairah Amit, *The Book of Judges: The Art of Editing*, trans. Jonathan Chipman, BIntS 38 (Leiden: Brill, 1999), 337–57, argues that in chaps. 17–18 kingship is a likely solution to Israel's problems, but the refrain does not seem to correspond with the problems in chaps. 19–21. Instead, the refrain was added in 19:1 and 21:25 in order to establish a façade that chaps. 19–21 belong with chaps. 17–18.

Abimelech is the choice of the people of Israel through his own political ma-
neuvering (Judg. 9:1–6), which mirrors how the later kings of the North would
become king.[18] The ideal, however, as is specified in Deut. 17:15 and reflected in
the experience of David's dynasty (1 Sam. 16), is for kingship to have its basis
in YHWH's choice. From this perspective, Brian P. Irwin helpfully qualifies what
it means to claim that Judges is pro-monarchy in light of its refrain: "While
the book of Judges endorses kingship as the replacement for the judges, it is
not an endorsement of *any* kingship."[19] The book of Judges advocates for a
kingship that is divinely endorsed, one which fits the pattern of Deut. 17 and
is capable of remedying the moral and religious problems in Judg. 17–21.

To what extent, then, can we say that the book of Judges views human
kingship as the solution to Israel's problems? Although we interpret the refrain as referring primarily to the need for human kingship within Israel,
one cannot forget Gideon's declaration earlier in the book: "The LORD will
rule over you" (Judg. 8:23). The sort of king Judges anticipates as a solution
to Israel's mess is one who orients the community around obeying and worshiping YHWH, Israel's King. This, of course, is what Deut. 17 already has in
mind when it calls for the king to devote himself to the instruction of Israel's
Suzerain, YHWH their King.

Conclusion

In *Lord of the Flies*, "savagery"—Golding's way of depicting corrupt human
nature—rages across the island like a wildfire. Yet even deliverance from tribal
life on an island into a world of grown-ups within British society does not
resolve the darkness within human nature; this is Golding's point. The book
of Judges offers a similar portrait of corruption, yet it goes further by pointing toward a solution—namely, a king who would rule in a way that guides
Israel to live under the rule of God.

Postlude: Canonical Reflections

If our interpretation of the refrain in Judges is correct, does the book of
Judges fall prey to Golding's critique that social change cannot remedy human
nature? In other words, can monarchy truly fix human nature? We must

18. See Brian P. Irwin, "Not Just Any King: Abimelech, the Northern Monarchy, and the
Final Form of Judges," *JBL* 131 (2012): 443–54.
19. Irwin, "Not Just Any King," 452.

remember that the author of Judges has a mature perspective on Israel's history; as he writes, he is looking back from exile or beyond. In many respects, 1–2 Samuel and 1–2 Kings capture how kingship—even kingship within the line of David—ultimately fails to bring about the sort of moral and spiritual leadership and transformation for which the book of Judges calls. Nonetheless, there are glimmers along the way of kings who could, with God's help, promote unity among the tribes, center the nation on God's presence, and summon obedience to Torah. This will become apparent in our chapters on Samuel, Kings, and Chronicles. With the failure of monarchy in view, it is at least possible that the author of Judges invites Israel not to give up on kingship but, rather, to hope for a king who aligns with what some of Judah's kings brought about, yet is far greater than any king the nation had known. From this angle, the book of Judges bears witness to Jesus—a king who promotes allegiance to God's kingdom, who welcomes and affirms women, who unites humanity with God, who transforms the human heart by the Spirit, who offers hope for a new creation through his resurrection, who will come again to do away with all idols and establish unending peace and harmony.

3

The Book of Ruth
and the House of David

The small-town story recounted in the book of Ruth is finally set within the context of God's grand purposes for Israel. It is a log-cabin-to-White-House kind of story, or it can be likened to a Hollywood tale of a struggling migrant mother whose family goes on to produce a president. The story of Ruth mirrors the history of Israel and is a theological explanation of that history that culminates in the house of David (see Ps. 78). Ruth comes out of the wilderness (Moab) into the promised land. The implication is that the promise of a blessed life in the land will be fulfilled in the house of David. Here is intimated the centrality of the royal house of David in God's good purposes for his people. This book can be read as an apology for the Davidic dynasty, a royal house that reaches its zenith with the birth of Jesus, who is the Christ (cf. the genealogy of Matt. 1).

The view that the book of Ruth is a late work, written to counteract the reforms of Ezra and Nehemiah banning marriages to foreign women (Ezra 9–10; Neh. 13), continues to find many supporters;[1] however, in this chapter,

---

Earlier versions of some of the material in this chapter can be found in Gregory Goswell, "The Book of Ruth and the House of David," *EQ* 86 (2014): 116–29, and in Peter H. W. Lau and Gregory Goswell, *Unceasing Kindness: A Biblical Theology of Ruth*, NSBT 41 (London: Apollos, 2016), 19–35. Used by permission.

1. E.g., Margo C. A. Korpel, *The Structure of the Book of Ruth*, Pericope 2 (Assen: Van Gorcum, 2001), 230–33; Tamara Cohn Eskenazi and Tikva Frymer-Kensky, *Ruth*, JPS Bible Commentary (Philadelphia: JPS, 2001), xxiv–xxv; Yairah Amit, *Hidden Polemics in Biblical*

we argue the case for an alternate way of reading the story of Ruth. Our aim is to show that the Ruth narrative can be read in relation to the house of David—namely, that its focus is the providential preservation of the family that produced King David and the implications for the Judean royal house. In this chapter we provide various arguments in favor of foregrounding the David connections when interpreting the story of Ruth.

The Differing Canonical Positions of the Book of Ruth

The position of the book of Ruth varies among canons.[2] In Hebrew canonical orders, Ruth is found in the third canonical division (Writings) and put either before Psalms (Talmud), as a kind of biography of the psalmist David, or after Prov. 31 (MT), making the heroine Ruth an example of "a good wife / worthy woman." In Greek canonical orders, Ruth comes after Judges, in an apparent effort to put it in its historical setting, because the story is set "in the days when the judges ruled" (Ruth 1:1).[3] In such a setting, it is a *third* Bethlehemite story after Judg. 17–18 and 19–21 (n.b. 17:7; 19:1) and forms a delightful contrast to the final chapters of Judges.[4] Ruth works well in all these canonical positions, but we need to look at the alternate canonical settings in a little more detail.

The order of the individual books within the Writings greatly fluctuates in the Jewish tradition.[5] According to the Babylonian Talmud (Baba Batra 14b), the book of Ruth comes at the beginning of the Writings, maybe due to the chronological principle that the events narrated belong to the time of the judges, but the presence of the ten-generation genealogy leading to

---

Narrative, trans. Jonathan Chipman, BIntS 25 (Leiden: Brill, 2000), 84–87; Victor H. Matthews, *Judges and Ruth*, New Cambridge Bible Commentary (Cambridge: Cambridge University Press, 2004).

2. L. B. Wolfenson, "Implications of the Place of the Book of Ruth in Editions, Manuscripts, and Canon of the Old Testament," *HUCA* 1 (1924): 171–75.

3. Jerome states that this is the reason for this placement (*Prologus Galeatus*); for a translation of this opinion of Jerome, see Roger Beckwith, *The Old Testament Canon of the New Testament Church and Its Background in Early Judaism* (Grand Rapids: Eerdmans, 1985), 119–20. In Josephus, *Jewish Antiquities* 5.318–37, the story of Ruth follows that of the judges. So too, in the list of Melito (Eusebius, *Ecclesiastical History* 4.26.13–14), Ruth follows Judges, and in Origen (Eusebius, *Ecclesiastical History* 6.25.2), Ruth is joined to Judges as one book.

4. Michael S. Moore, "To King or Not to King: A Canonical-Historical Approach to Ruth," *BBR* 11 (2001): 27–41; Warren Austin Gale, "Ruth upon the Threshing Floor and the Sin of Gibeah: A Biblical-Theological Study," *WTJ* 51 (1989): 369–75.

5. See the tabulation of eleven alternate orders provided by C. D. Ginsburg, *Introduction to the Massoretico-Critical Edition of the Hebrew Bible* (London: Trinitarian Bible Society, 1897; New York: Ktav, 1966), 7.

David (4:18–22) was probably another factor taken into account. In that baraita (preserving a pre–200 CE Tannaitic tradition), the relevant listing is "Ruth and the book of Psalms and Job and Proverbs" (coupled together in the way indicated), with Ruth (ending with the genealogy of David) positioned as a preface to Psalms. In line with this, the Psalter goes on to portray God helping David in his troubles and David as one who takes "refuge" (root ḥāsâ) in God (e.g., Pss. 2:12; 7:1 [7:2 MT]; 11:1; 16:1), just as Ruth herself does (Ruth 2:12: "under whose wings you have come to take refuge").[6]

Ruth, as the first of the five scrolls of the Megillot (a collection of smaller books read at Jewish festivals), follows immediately after Proverbs (in the Leningrad Codex), due to a link in their subject matter. Proverbs closes with a poem celebrating the "worthy woman" ('ēšet-ḥayil; 31:10–31), and the book of Ruth goes on to describe just such a woman. In Ruth 3:11, Boaz calls Ruth a "worthy woman" ('ēšet-ḥayil).[7] The description in Prov. 31:31 fits Ruth ("Let her works praise her in the gates"; cf. Ruth 3:12: "for all the gate of my people know . . ." [authors' trans.]), and Prov. 31:23 applies to Boaz ("Her husband is known in the gates when he sits among the elders of the land"), for both verses sound like allusions to the scene at the city gate in Ruth 4. This placement suggests a reading of Ruth as a wisdom piece, with Ruth the Moabitess a real-life example of the piety taught in Proverbs and embodied in the exemplary woman of Prov. 31.[8] In the Leningrad Codex's order of books—Proverbs, Ruth, Song of Songs—both Ruth and Song of Songs develop the picture of the virtuous and assertive woman pictured in Prov. 31.[9]

On the other hand, Ruth 1:1 locates the story in the period of the judges, and the Ruth narrative forms a sharp contrast with the story of the Levite from Bethlehem (Judg. 17:8–9) and that of the Levite's concubine who comes from Bethlehem (19:1–2) and with the drastic method used to provide wives for the surviving Benjaminites (Judg. 21). Judges 21:6 concerns the preservation of an Israelite tribe (Benjamin) threatened with extinction, and the book of Ruth depicts God's providence in preserving the Bethlehemite family that eventually produces David (Ruth 4:5, 10, 18–22). Notably, the idiom "to *take*

---

6. Jerome F. D. Creach, *Yahweh as Refuge and the Editing of the Hebrew Psalter*, JSOTSup 217 (Sheffield: Sheffield Academic, 1996).

7. Edward F. Campbell Jr., *Ruth: A New Translation with Introduction, Notes and Commentary*, AB 7 (Garden City, NY: Doubleday, 1975), 34–35.

8. See Gregory Goswell, "Is Ruth Also among the Wise?," in *Exploring Old Testament Wisdom: Literature and Themes*, ed. David G. Firth and Lindsay Wilson (London: Apollos, 2016), 115–33.

9. Cf. Tremper Longman III, *Song of Songs*, NICOT (Grand Rapids: Eerdmans, 2001), 2.

[*nāśāʾ*] wives," used in Judg. 21:23, recurs in Ruth 1:4.[10] Despite the variety in the Greek lists of Old Testament books,[11] what we can say is that the books Genesis–Ruth are a set grouping (Octateuch) and that Ruth is always placed after (or joined to) Judges. In other words, in the Greek Bible, Judges serves as a foil for the following book of Ruth.

In the other direction, there are connections between the figures of Ruth and Hannah, and, through Hannah's offspring, Samuel (the anointer of the first two kings) is also related to the coming monarchy (1 Sam. 1–2). The marriage of Boaz and Ruth and the birth of a son thematically prepare for Elkanah and Hannah and their (at first) childless relationship. The book of Ruth covers much the same ground as do the books of Samuel—namely, the period from "the days when the judges ruled" (Samuel being the last judge; see 1 Sam. 7:15) until the time of David and his rule. The book of Ruth may, therefore, be treated as a prehistory of the Davidic house, for, according to the genealogy provided by 4:18–22, Ruth and Boaz are the great-grandparents of David.[12] Without insisting that the *only and proper* position for Ruth is following Judges, our reading of the Ruth narrative takes that positioning of the book as its starting point and looks for various possible connections between the book and the house of David, all with the aim of better understanding the messianic theology of this portion of the Old Testament.

The David Connection

The interpretation of the book of Ruth in recent scholarship has made little of the link with David that is explicit in the final form of the book, but what we offer is a kind of *backward* reading, viewing the David connection as fundamental to elucidating the book's theme and purpose.[13] The uncovering of the link to David in the last verses of the book requires the reader to reread the story and to discover what might have been missed on the first reading. According to Frederic William Bush, the final resolution of a plot, and especially

10. Yair Zakovitch, *Das Buch Rut: Ein jüdischer Kommentar; Mit einem Geleitwort von Erich Zenger*, SBS 177 (Stuttgart: Katholisches Bibelwerk, 1999), 33, 79.

11. See the lists provided by H. B. Swete, *An Introduction to the Old Testament in Greek, with an Appendix Containing the Letter of Aristeas*, ed. H. St. J. Thackeray (Cambridge: Cambridge University Press, 1902; rev. R. R. Ottley; New York: Ktav, 1968), 226–27.

12. Jack M. Sasson, *Ruth: A New Translation with a Philological Commentary and a Formalist-Folkloric Interpretation* (Baltimore: Johns Hopkins University Press, 1979), 250–51.

13. Cf. Oscar Wilde, *Nothing . . . except My Genius*, compiled by Alastair Rolfe (London: Penguin, 1997), 27: "There is a great deal to be said in favour of reading a novel backwards. The last page is as a rule the most interesting, and when one begins with the catastrophe or the *dénouement* one feels on pleasant terms of equality with the author."

the dénouement (the outcome or consequences of the resolution) and any accompanying coda of a narrative, are important indicators of theme.[14] In the case of the narrative of Ruth, the plot centers on the filling of Naomi's emptiness (1:21). All the other characters—her husband, her sons, her two daughters-in-law, Boaz, even the son whom Ruth bears—stand in relation to Naomi (see 1:3, 5, 6; 2:1; 4:17).[15] All this tends to focus the story from Naomi's perspective. Her loss of family (husband and sons) at the beginning of the book (1:5b: "So that the woman was left without her two sons and her husband") is compensated by the provision of a son (through Ruth) at its end (4:13–17a). Though the son is born to Boaz and Ruth (v. 13), 4:17a stresses the significance of the son for Naomi ("A son has been born to Naomi"). This does not have to be taken as meaning that the issue of an heir for the line of Elimelech is only a secondary concern (*pace* Bush),[16] for the dénouement moves beyond the temporal needs of Naomi and shows that the son turned out to be an ancestor of illustrious David (v. 17b: "They named him Obed; he was the father of Jesse, the father of David"), and the connection with David is reinforced by the genealogy given in the coda (vv. 18–22).

Katharine Doob Sakenfeld would only see the David connection acting as "an imprimatur" on the implied ethic of the book about the need for the Israelite community to adopt a generous view of outsiders.[17] She states, "Because of David's stature in Judean tradition, just the mention of his name is sufficient to drive home the storyteller's point of view."[18] While by no means denying the canonical link to David, we counter that the effect of Sakenfeld's view is to minimize the David connection's significance for the message of the book, since that connection's only role is as *support* for the book's controversial implied ethic (combating xenophobia) rather than being part of the message of the book as such. Likewise, for André Lacocque, "the authority of the interpretation of the law presented in the book of Ruth finds its foundation in the person of David."[19] Again, on this interpretation, the unquestionable

---

14. Frederic William Bush, *Ruth, Esther*, WBC 9 (Dallas: Word, 1996), 48–49. Bush is dependent on John Beekman, John Callow, and Michael Kopesec, *The Semantic Structure of Written Communication*, 5th ed. (Dallas: SIL, 1981), 135, 137.

15. Adele Berlin, *Poetics and Interpretation of Biblical Narrative*, BLS 9 (Sheffield: Almond, 1983), 83–84. On the other hand, the mathematics of social network analysis indicates that Boaz is the most well-connected character; see John T. Dekker and Anthony H. Dekker, "Centrality in the Book of Ruth," *VT* 68 (2018): 41–50. It is Boaz who is in the line that leads to David (Ruth 4:18–22).

16. Bush, *Ruth, Esther*, 51: "His [Elimelech's] significance relates entirely to Naomi."

17. Katharine Doob Sakenfeld, *Ruth*, IBC (Louisville: John Knox, 1999), 4–5.

18. Sakenfeld, *Ruth*, 84.

19. André Lacocque, *Ruth: A Continental Commentary*, trans. K. C. Hanson, CC (Minneapolis: Fortress, 2004), 12.

prestige of David is used as support for the challenging message of the book but makes no further theological contribution. The connection with David is more significant than this, for, as noted by Adele Berlin, the canonical link to David not only "tends to elevate the status of the story"; it "tends to elevate David."[20]

The Genealogy Leading to David

An examination of the genealogy is necessary, for the originality of Ruth 4:17b–22 is commonly rejected in recent scholarship, with "all but universal agreement" that the verses are a later *appendix* to the story proper,[21] but the case is anything but decisive.[22] Ruth 4:17–22 reads:

> [17]And the women of the neighborhood gave him a name, saying, "A son has been born to Naomi." They named him Obed. He was the father of Jesse, the father of David. [18]Now these are the generations of Perez: Perez fathered Hezron, [19]Hezron fathered Ram, Ram fathered Amminadab, [20]Amminadab fathered Nahshon, Nahshon fathered Salmon, [21]Salmon fathered Boaz, Boaz fathered Obed, [22]Obed fathered Jesse, and Jesse fathered David.

We do not need to discount the genealogy as a later addition and, in so doing, to reject any *original* Davidic connection. The Ruth narrative has a symmetrical design, with a series of parallels found between chapters 2 and 3 and between chapters 1 and 4.[23] The chiastic balance of the story requires some kind of "family history" at the end, matching what is found at the beginning (1:1–5), and that is what the genealogy provides.[24] Shimon Bar-Efrat has commented on the chiastic structure of this book,[25] noting that the book opens with information about (three) people who died before the beginning of the main action (Elimelech, Mahlon, Chilion; vv. 1–5) and ends with a list of the (three) generations that were born after the conclusion of the main action (Obed, Jesse, David), with the matching numbers supporting the point made by Bar-Efrat.

20. Berlin, *Poetics and Interpretation*, 110.

21. Campbell, *Ruth*, 172.

22. See the detailed review and critique of the majority position provided by Robert L. Hubbard Jr., *The Book of Ruth*, NICOT (Grand Rapids: Eerdmans, 1988), 15–21.

23. Bezalel Porten, "The Scroll of Ruth: A Rhetorical Study," *Gratz College Annual of Jewish Studies* 7 (1978): 23.

24. Stephen Bertman, "Symmetrical Design in the Book of Ruth," *JBL* 84 (1965): 165–68.

25. Shimon Bar-Efrat, "Some Observations on the Analysis of Structure in Biblical Narrative," *VT* 30 (1980): 156–57.

The name of Perez begins the genealogy (Ruth 4:18: "Now these are descendants of Perez: Perez fathered . . ."), and he has already been named in
the body of the book (v. 12: "May your house be like the house of Perez").
The portrait of Perez as ancestral head is common to both verse 12 and the
genealogy, which, therefore, suits its context and was presumably tailored to fit
the narrative it caps. So, too, whatever the exact relation between the genealogy in Ruth 4 and the genealogy provided in 1 Chron. 2:5–16, both passages
give special prominence to the line of Perez, and the linear genealogy in Ruth
4 may be crafted to highlight the names of Boaz (seventh generation) and
David (tenth generation).[26] The effect of the genealogy is to link the story of
Ruth with the Bible's "main narrative" (= primary history)—namely, Genesis to Kings, in which kingship is a major concern.[27] In fact, the theme of
kingship is sounded immediately before the Ruth narrative in the refrain that
punctuates the last chapters of Judges: "In those days there was no king in
Israel" (Judg. 17:6; 18:1; 19:1; 21:25). The name Perez takes the reader back
into the patriarchal stories of Genesis (notably the circumstances of the birth
of Perez in chap. 38), then we move forward to David (whose final years are
recorded in 1 Kings 1–2), so that the genealogy helps to establish continuity
between earlier Israelite history and the beginning of the Davidic monarchy.

In other words, Ruth 4:17b and 4:18–22 show the wider significance of
the story. In support of this, the blessing provided by the family to Israel as a
whole has already been suggested by 4:11–12. The blessing uttered in 4:11–12
speaks of the future fame of the house (a name "renowned in Bethlehem"),
and this is picked up and widened in verse 14 ("May his name be renowned
in Israel"). The blessing of verse 12 speaks of multiple "offspring" (*zeraʿ* read
as a collective; RSV: "children"), and this finds its fulfillment in the family
genealogy leading to David. The blessing that likens Ruth to Rachel and Leah,
"who built up the house of Israel" (v. 11), and the hyperbolic commendation
of Ruth in 4:15b ("[She is] more to you than seven sons") also hint that she
will be ancestor of a famous figure with pan-Israelite significance.[28] Likewise,
the analogy of Tamar, who became a matriarch (v. 12; cf. Gen. 38)[29]—and we
might add a reference to Rahab (Josh. 2; cf. Matt. 1:5)[30]—supports the thesis
that Ruth's role will affect the destiny of the nation as a whole.

26. This is the thesis of Sasson in *Ruth*, 183–84, 186.
27. Berlin, *Poetics and Interpretation*, 110.
28. Hubbard, *Book of Ruth*, 21–22.
29. E.g., Ellen van Wolde, *Ruth and Naomi* (London: SCM, 1997), 127–31.
30. See Laura E. Donaldson, "The Sign of Orpah: Reading Ruth through Native Eyes," in
Ruth and Esther: A Feminist Companion to the Bible, ed. Athalya Brenner, 2nd series (Sheffield:
Sheffield Academic, 1999), 138–39.

Scholars have problems with Ruth 4:17b because there seems to be no connection between the name Obed (v. 17b) and "a son has been born to Naomi" (v. 17a), but the assigning of the name "Obed" (= he who serves) is appropriate for one who will serve the needs of Naomi in her old age, the role assigned to him in 4:15 by the Bethlehemite women who name him.[31] Robert L. Hubbard suggests that the importance of the birth of Obed is more than just signifying the survival and future of the threatened family, for the LORD's intervention strongly implies that the child has a special destiny (cf. Samson, Samuel).[32] This is supported by the fact that 4:13 is the only time *the narrator* describes God as active in events ("The LORD gave her [Ruth] conception, and she bore a son").[33] It is, therefore, valid to read the events of the book of Ruth as relevant to the fortunes of the house of David, for the final genealogy makes *explicit* the Davidic connection of the narrative (vv. 17b–22), and so the reader is invited to discern what the story says or implies about later Davidic rule.

Rereading the Book of Ruth

The connection of the family with David is hinted at as early as Ruth 1:2, which specifies the Ephrathite lineage of Elimelech and family ("They were Ephrathites from Bethlehem"), this being the clan name for a section of the population of Bethlehem (cf. 4:11).[34] From the start, therefore, the biblically literate reader of the narrative of Ruth would suspect that there is a link to the family of David, for in 1 Sam. 17:12 David is said to be the son of "an Ephrathite of Bethlehem in Judah."[35] The reader's suspicion that the story might have some connection with the family of David is confirmed at the close of the book (Ruth 4:17b, 18–22).

31. See Frederic William Bush, "Ruth 4:17: A Semantic Wordplay," in *"Go to the Land I Will Show You": Studies in Honor of Dwight W. Young*, ed. Joseph E. Coleson and Victor H. Matthews (Winona Lake, IN: Eisenbrauns, 1996), 13; D. R. G. Beattie, *The Targum of Ruth*, Aramaic Targums 19 (Edinburgh: T&T Clark, 1994), 32 (the targumic rendering of 4:21b connects the name Obed with his later wholehearted service of God); D. R. G. Beattie, *Jewish Exegesis of the Book of Ruth*, JSOTSup 2 (Sheffield: JSOT Press, 1977), 131.

32. Hubbard, *Book of Ruth*, 20, 97.

33. Ruth 1:6 is not, despite the assertion of some (e.g., Campbell, *Ruth*, 29), another instance of the storyteller directly asserting God's involvement, for it only states what Naomi *heard* (from whom? on whose authority?)—namely, "that the LORD had visited his people and given them food."

34. See the discussion provided by Bush, *Ruth*, 64–67.

35. Cf. Mic. 5:2 (5:1 MT): "But you, O Bethlehem Ephrathah, who are too little to be among the clans of Judah . . ."; Ps. 132:6: "Behold, we heard of it in Ephrathah."

Likewise, the refuge taken by Elimelech and family in neighboring Moab during the time of famine (Ruth 1:1–5) is later replicated when David leaves his parents in the safekeeping of the king of Moab during the period when he is on the run from Saul (1 Sam. 22:1–4). In other words, an episode in the early history of the family (the sojourn in Moab) foreshadows what will happen in the experience of its most famous descendant.[36] This is in line with Israelite storytelling generally, wherein typological parallels drawn between earlier and later historical events support a belief in the providential ordering of history (e.g., the description of what is, in effect, an Egyptian sojourn and exodus of Abram in Gen. 12:10–13:1).[37] The discovery of these intertextual links in the opening section of the book of Ruth encourages the reader to look for other connections with the later history of David.

Divine Providence

As noted already, God's direct involvement is stated by the narrator only once (Ruth 4:13), but God is repeatedly referred to by characters within the story (1:6, 9, 16–17, 20–21; 2:12, 20; 3:10, 13; 4:11, 12, 14).[38] This creates an expectation of how God will (or should) act to remedy problems or reward right behavior. More subtly, the apparently *chance* event of Ruth entering the field of Boaz (2:3) and the arrival of Boaz and of the unnamed close relation on the scene at just the right time (2:4; 4:1) support the same theology of God's superintendence of events.[39] As noted by Campbell, a striking feature of the story is the way in which each of the three main characters acts in the way that God is expected to act, the correspondence implying that they are divine agents. Naomi asks that God may provide her daughters-in-law with "rest" (1:9), but later it is she who seeks "rest" for Ruth (3:1; the related words are *mənûḥâ* and *mānôaḥ*). Boaz calls on God to recompense Ruth as one who has

36. Kirsten Nielson views the book of Ruth as written "to champion the right of David's family to the throne," such a *Realpolitik* defense being needed because of his dubious Moabite ancestry. See *Ruth: A Commentary*, trans. Edward Broadbridge, OTL (Louisville: Westminster John Knox, 1997), 23–29; cf. Murray D. Gow, *The Book of Ruth: Its Structure, Theme and Purpose* (Leicester, UK: Apollos, 1992), 130–39, 203–10. This view may find support in the repeated reference to Ruth's Moabite heritage (e.g., 1:22; 2:2, 6, 21); however, we have no other indicator in the Old Testament that the part-Moabite ancestry of David was an embarrassment to the ruling house of Judah.

37. See the discussion by Umberto Cassuto, *A Commentary on the Book of Genesis, Part II: From Noah to Abraham* (Jerusalem: Magnes Press, 1964), 334–37.

38. See Ronald M. Hals, *The Theology of the Book of Ruth*, FBBS 23 (Philadelphia: Fortress, 1969).

39. Campbell, *Ruth*, 29.

taken refuge under God's "wings" (*kānāp*; 2:12), but later Ruth, in effect, calls on Boaz to act as God's agent by spreading his "corner-garment" (= wing) over her (*kānāp*; 3:9). Above all, God's "kindness" (*ḥesed*) toward the family (2:20) is shown in part by Ruth's "kindness" (*ḥesed*) in thinking of the needs of the family and being willing to marry older Boaz (3:10).[40] It is significant that these examples of human characters as God's agents (3:1, 9, 10) are found in the lead-up to or within what might be viewed as the key scene in the book: the clandestine meeting between Ruth and Boaz on the threshing floor (vv. 7–13).

In line with this, the rise of David to the throne in the books of Samuel is shown to be providential (1 Sam. 16:13, 18; 18:12, 28; etc.). What is more, the term "wing" (*kānāp*) recurs in two important episodes in 1 Samuel concerning the rise of David to the throne.[41] In 1 Sam. 15, Saul's act of tearing the "hem" (*kānāp*) of Samuel's robe (15:27) is turned by Samuel into a prophetic sign (v. 28: "The LORD has torn the kingdom of Israel from you this day and has given it to a neighbor of yours, who is better than you"). Likewise, in 1 Sam. 24, David deftly cuts off the "hem" (*kānāp*) of Saul's robe (v. 5 [v. 6 MT]), with David's restraint in not slaying Saul acknowledged by Saul himself as proof that David is more righteous than he is and will receive the kingdom (vv. 16–22 [vv. 17–23 MT]). Another connection of the scene at the threshing floor in Ruth 3 with events in David's life is Ruth's deferential self-reference as Boaz's "handmaid" (3:9; *'āmâ* [2x]). Abigail repeatedly uses the same term about herself in her meeting with David in 1 Sam. 25 (vv. 24, 25, 28, 31, 41), and that meeting also leads to subsequent marriage (v. 42).[42] Just as Boaz invokes a divine blessing on Ruth (Ruth 3:10), David blesses Abigail, whom he views as God's agent, for her initiative in intercepting him on the way to kill Nabal saves him from bloodguilt, which would have imperiled his rise to the throne (1 Sam. 25:32–33). By their courage and resourcefulness, Ruth and Abigail, each in her own way, play a vital role in securing the welfare of the Davidic house.[43] In what amounts to a record

40. We have chosen the translation "kindness" for this admittedly difficult-to-translate Hebrew word, because, as demonstrated by Francis I. Andersen, *ḥesed* denotes nonobligatory, generous action. See "Yahweh, the Kind and Sensitive God," in *God Who Is Rich in Mercy: Essays Presented to Dr. D. B. Knox*, ed. Peter T. O'Brien and David G. Peterson (Homebush West, NSW: Lancer Books, 1986), 41–88. Andersen examines the three uses of the term in the book of Ruth on pp. 59–60.

41. Only the first connection is noted by Eskenazi and Frymer-Kensky, *Ruth*, xxiv.

42. Zakovitch, *Das Buch Rut*, 61. For further allusive links between Ruth 3 and 1 Samuel 25, see Yitzhak Berger, "Ruth and Inner-Biblical Allusion: The Case of 1 Samuel 25," *JBL* 128 (2009): 259, 267–69.

43. Cf. Gillian Feeley-Harnik, "Naomi and Ruth: Building Up the House of David," in *Text and Tradition: The Hebrew Bible and Folklore*, ed. Susan Niditch (Atlanta: Scholars Press, 1990), 179: "The book of Ruth depicts women's work as essential to creating the Davidic monarchy."

of the prehistory of the Davidic house, the author of Ruth shows that the workings of divine providence (through human agency) on behalf of David began during the lives of his ancestors.

Kindness, Human and Divine

It is widely recognized that the entwined themes of divine and human "kindness" (*ḥesed*) are important in the book of Ruth (1:8; 2:20; 3:10). In being willing to return with Naomi, the two daughters-in-law show "kindness" to their deceased husbands and to her (1:8), and this quality is confirmed in the case of Ruth by her adamant refusal to part from Naomi (vv. 16–17). In line with this, Boaz later blesses Ruth for her "kindness" (3:10). This verse actually speaks of her *two* acts of kindness ("You have made this last kindness greater than the first"). The first was her loyalty to Naomi and the family (cf. Boaz's praise of Ruth in 2:11–12), and the second is her willingness, for the sake of the family, to marry a relative of her deceased husband, though Boaz is an older man.[44] Naomi asks that God may repay the kindness of her daughters-in-law with kindness (1:8: "May the LORD deal kindly [*ḥesed*] with you"), and she sees in the new development reported by Ruth (Boaz's favor toward Ruth) a signal that God is acting in kindness toward the family (2:20). The sentence in 2:20 is ambiguous ("who has not forsaken *his* kindness to the living or the dead"), with the pronoun's antecedent either the LORD or Boaz ("Blessed be he [Boaz] by the LORD").[45] The second option is the one favored by scholars—namely, that it refers to Boaz's kindness—but if the ambiguity is deliberate (and we believe that it is), the reference is to God's kindness shown through that of Boaz.[46]

As noted by Sakenfeld, a scene remarkably similar to that in Ruth 1:8–18 is found in 2 Sam. 15:19–23, which depicts David leaving Jerusalem and attempting in vain to discourage someone from going with him.[47] What is more, foreign (Philistine) Ittai's forceful declaration in the form of an oath that he will be with David "whether for death or for life" (v. 21) is close to

---

44. See Katharine Doob Sakenfeld, *Faithfulness in Action: Loyalty in Biblical Perspective*, OBT (Philadelphia: Fortress, 1985), 32; Peter H. W. Lau, *Identity and Ethics in the Book of Ruth: A Social Identity Approach*, BZAW 416 (Berlin: de Gruyter, 2011), 107–9.

45. Translation of Ruth 2:20 is the authors'.

46. Mordechai Cohen, "Ḥesed: Divine or Human? The Syntactic Ambiguity of Ruth 2:20," in *Hazon Nahum: Studies in Jewish Law, Thought, and History Presented to Dr. Norman Lamm on the Occasion of His Seventieth Birthday*, ed. Yaakov Elman and Jeffrey S. Gurock (Hoboken, NJ: Ktav, 1997), 11–38; Nelson Glueck, Ḥesed *in the Bible*, trans. Alfred Gottschalk (Cincinnati: Hebrew Union College Press, 1967), 41–42.

47. The parallel is noted by Sakenfeld in *Faithfulness in Action*, 34.

that of Ruth (cf. Ruth 1:16–17).[48] David urges Ittai the Gittite, who has served him for only a short while, to go back and not go with him, concluding with an invocation of divine kindness (2 Sam. 15:20 MT: "And take back your brethren with you in kindness [ḥesed] and faithfulness," authors' trans.). This difficult text is commonly amended using the LXX (positing words that may have dropped out) to read: ". . . and take back your brethren with you; and may the LORD show kindness and faithfulness to you" (cf. RSV).[49] Even without textual repair, however, the reference must be to *divine* kindness (cf. David's use of the word pair "kindness and faithfulness" in 2 Sam. 2:5–6). The texts in Ruth 1 and 2 Sam. 15 both depict someone not in a position to repay kindness (Naomi, David) asking God to do what they cannot do themselves.

There is a close relation between God's "kindness" and the Davidic covenant tradition,[50] whose fountainhead is the dynastic oracle in 2 Sam. 7, wherein God promises (through Nathan) that he will not take his "kindness" (ḥesed) from David's son (v. 15; cf. 2 Sam. 22:51). Solomon said that God showed "great kindness" to David in giving him an heir to sit upon the throne (1 Kings 3:6; 2 Chron. 1:8). Behind the special position given to the house of David stands God's kindness. The word for "kindness" (ḥesed) is used seven times in Ps. 89 (vv. 1, 2, 14, 24, 28, 33, 49 [vv. 2, 3, 15, 25, 29, 34, 50 MT]).[51] The psalm opens with praise of the LORD's acts of kindness (v. 1 [v. 2 MT]), for God's kindness is firm and enduring (v. 2 [v. 3 MT]), as illustrated by his covenant with David (vv. 3–4 [vv. 4–5 MT]). God's kindness enabled David to defeat his enemies (vv. 22–23 [vv. 23–24 MT]). It is expected that the covenant will stand firm due to God's kindness (v. 28 [v. 29 MT]), even in the face of disloyalty by David's descendants (vv. 30–33 [vv. 31–34 MT]; cf. 2 Sam. 7:11b–16), but the unthinkable has happened and it appears that God has renounced the covenant (Ps. 89:38–51 [89:39–52 MT]). The Ruth narrative can be understood as giving hope for the future of the Davidic house. Despite the ancestors of David experiencing a time of extreme peril, God's kindness did not fail the family, and likewise (by implication) God's kindness will not fail the dynasty of David.

48. Eskenazi and Frymer-Kensky, *Ruth*, 18–19.

49. For repair of the text using the LXX, see S. R. Driver, *Notes on the Hebrew Text and the Topography of the Books of Samuel* (Oxford: Clarendon, 1913), 314.

50. For this paragraph, we acknowledge our dependence on Sakenfeld, *Faithfulness in Action*, 52–63; Sakenfeld, *The Meaning of Ḥesed in the Hebrew Bible: A New Inquiry*, HSM 17 (Missoula, MT: Scholars Press, 1978), 139–47.

51. See Marti J. Steussy, *David: Biblical Portraits of Power* (Columbia: University of South Carolina Press, 1999), 137–43.

Postlude: Canonical Reflections

We have provided a theological reading of the book of Ruth that interprets it within the wider story of God's purposes for Israel, with divine providence and kindness upholding the dynasty of David for the benefit of Israel as a whole. Several factors point to the conclusion that the book can legitimately be read as preparatory to God's dealings with David and his house. None of the canonical positions assigned to the book in the Hebrew and Greek canons (before Psalms, after Proverbs, or between Judges and Samuel) suggest that ancient readers viewed it as primarily written to promote a more generous view of foreigners. If its placement after Judges in the Greek Old Testament (and subsequent Christian canon) is allowed to have an impact on reading, the events in the book of Ruth are to be seen as preparing for David. The later history of David and his house is anticipated by the Ruth narrative's depiction of the workings of divine providence on behalf of the family that produced David and by the narrative's exploration of human and divine "kindness" in the lives of his forebears. The book of Ruth fits neatly within the trajectory of Davidic hope found in the Old Testament historical books. It is highly appropriate, therefore, to find that the one reference to the name of Ruth in the New Testament is as an ancestor of Jesus Christ in the genealogy in the opening chapter of Matthew's Gospel (1:5).

4

The Heart of Kingship
in 1–2 Samuel

During the final weeks of my Old Testament Literature class, I (Andrew) devote fifteen minutes each class period to Q&A. Questions range from the comical to the profound, but no student has ever asked, "Was kingship a good idea for Israel?" My students have decided already that Jesus is the king from the line of David, so of course kingship was a good idea. In ancient Israel, however, the question would have been unavoidable, and this tension is apparent throughout 1–2 Samuel. God is offended when Israel requests a king; Saul, Israel's first king, ultimately is rejected by God; David, the covenant king, closes 2 Samuel with a plethora of moral failures, resulting in upheaval within Israel.

So, does 1–2 Samuel agree with the book of Judges that a king is the answer to Israel's disarray? One can only offer a hesitant yes to this question because 1–2 Samuel's endorsement of kingship as the solution to Israel's dilemma involves three major qualifications:

1. Human kingship is subservient to God's kingship, Israel's ultimate hope.
2. The *office* of kingship is less important than the *heart* of the king who holds the office.
3. The book awaits a greater David, for no king in Samuel (and Kings) is able to remedy Israel's ills.

49

These points will become apparent as we walk through 1–2 Samuel's messianic expectations. We will find that the book directs our vision beyond the pages of Israel's history to a future Davidic king whose heart aligns with God as King and thereby brings great blessing and justice to Israel.

Hannah and Messianic Expectation

At first glance, a barren womb is a peculiar way to introduce the book that recounts Israel's transition to monarchy. On second thought, however, Hannah's barrenness links her with the matriarchs of Israel—Sarah, Rebekah, Rachel, and even Leah.[1] Throughout Israel's story, the barren womb gives occasion to place a spotlight on the God who brings life from lifeless wombs, a God who brings honor to the dishonored, a God who creates a fruitful nation out of an elderly couple. As it turns out, Hannah's experience (1 Sam. 1) and song (2:1–10) brilliantly introduce the messianic expectations within the book. This is apparent in three ways.

First, Hannah is a model of faithfulness. Although introducing the child Samuel is an important component in 1 Sam. 1, this chapter is also about the faithfulness of a barren woman who is willing to give away her long-awaited child to the Lord (vv. 26–28). Through distress-laced prayer and the fulfillment of a costly vow, Hannah comes to the fore as an example of faithfulness, preparing for a king whose heart also was faithful to the Lord (16:7).

Second, Hannah's story and song reflect an outlook that places its hopes primarily in God, not a human king.[2] It is God who brings life to a lifeless womb at the start of the book, and it is God whom Hannah praises:

My heart exults in the Lord. (1 Sam. 2:1)
There is no rock like our God. (v. 2)
The Lord kills and brings to life. (v. 6)

1. Joan E. Cook, *Hannah's Desire, God's Design: Early Interpretations of the Story of Hannah*, JSOTSup 282 (Sheffield: Sheffield Academic, 1999), 10–25, 49–51.
2. Walter Brueggemann, "I Samuel 1: A Sense of a Beginning," *ZAW* 102 (1990): 39. William J. Dumbrell advocates for the centrality of God's kingship not only in 1 Sam. 1 but throughout both books of Samuel. Taking his cues from the book opening in Shiloh and closing with David obtaining a place for the ark in Jerusalem, Dumbrell helpfully traces through the book to show how human kingship is not the ultimate focus of 1–2 Samuel; divine rule is. His argument, however, seems to swing the pendulum toward divine kingship to such an extent that he does not give enough emphasis to human kingship in the divine plan. See William J. Dumbrell, "The Content and Significance of the Books of Samuel: Their Place and Purpose within the Former Prophets," *JETS* 33 (1990): 49–62.

The LORD makes poor and makes rich. (v. 7)
He raises up the poor. (v. 8)
The pillars of the earth are the LORD's. (v. 8)
The LORD will judge the ends of the earth. (v. 10)
He will give strength to his king / and exalt the horn of his anointed. (v. 10)

Even if Hannah mentions a messiah figure ("his anointed") toward the end of her prayer, the overarching orientation of these opening chapters is upon the sovereign rule of God.

Third, Hannah expresses a messianic hope for Israel. In a prayer crafted for the entire community,[3] Hannah democratizes her experience of God and his ways and applies them to people in general throughout most of her song. She concludes, however, by focusing on God's ways with the anointed king:

> He will give strength to his king
> and exalt the horn of his anointed. (1 Sam. 2:10)

A few comments will illuminate this verse. To begin, there is a close connection between this verse and the start of the song. A more wooden, Hebraic translation captures this:

> My horn [*qeren*] is high [*rwm*, a *qal* verb form] in the LORD. (2:1, authors' trans.)

> He will raise high [*rûm*, a *hiphil* verb form] the horn [*qeren*] of his anointed. (2:10, authors' trans.)

Obviously, neither Hannah nor human kings have horns, but in ancient Israel a wild ox with a strong horn was a symbol of great power, confidence, and a high status (cf. Ps. 92:10). For this reason, Hannah can portray herself as having a horn that is high due to YHWH. As she looks to the future, she is confident that God will do the same for his anointed king. It may not be a coincidence that the next occurrence of "horn" in the book is the use of a horn (*qeren*) to anoint David in 1 Sam. 16.[4] God's first step in "raising up" the horn of "his anointed" is to have Hannah's son pour a horn of oil on

---

3. See Adele Berlin, "Hannah and Her Prayers," *Scriptura* 87 (2004): 227–32, who compares Hannah's prayer in the narrative (1 Sam. 1:11) with the poetic song in 2:1–10.

4. See Robert Polzin, *Samuel and the Deuteronomist: A Literary Study of the Deuteronomic History, Part Two: 1 Samuel* (Bloomington: Indiana University Press, 1993), 34–35, who exposes the significance of *qeren* ("horn") in 16:1 and 16:13 via association with 2:10, while noting that *pak* ("vial") is used for narrating the anointing of Saul (10:1). See Bernard Gosse, "Le salut et le messie en 1 Sam. 2,1–10, et Yahvé juge, à l'œuvre sur la terre et dans l'histoire, dans la tradition

David's head. Additionally, the phrase "his anointed" needs to be interpreted with caution. In 1–2 Samuel, Saul (1 Sam. 12:3, 5; 24:6 [24:7 MT]; 26:9, 11, 16; 2 Sam. 1:14) and David (2 Sam. 19:21 [19:22 MT]; 22:51) are referred to as "anointed" (*māšîaḥ*). The verb "to anoint" (root *mšḥ*) describes the anointing of Saul (1 Sam. 9:16; 10:1; 15:1, 17), David (1 Sam. 16:3, 12, 13; 2 Sam. 2:4, 7; 3:39; 5:3, 17; 12:7), Absalom (2 Sam. 19:10 [19:11 MT]), or even a shield (1:21). It is most likely that Hannah expects God to raise the horn of whoever holds the office of king. So, Hannah's "messianic" expectations pertain to how God will be faithful to future kings in Israel, not merely one particular king exclusively.

Thus, from the beginning, Hannah's story and prayer set the stage for the monumental move toward monarchy that 1–2 Samuel recounts. As Walter Brueggemann aptly states regarding the authors of the book: "They must have pondered long how to stage this narrative so that the subversive themes of fragility, surprise, and fidelity would not be lost either in the celebration of personality, or in the worldly impressive forms of power. . . . The real power in Israel's life and history belongs only to Yahweh, and not to the king or any other human agent."[5] Through the guidance of Hannah, the transition to monarchy in 1–2 Samuel is to be evaluated through the rubric of God's overarching rule, which prioritizes faithfulness and overturns common expectations pertaining to position and power.

Messianic Expectations Clarified: A Rough Start to Kingship

As Samuel's faithful tenure as judge winds down, the people of Israel request a king, and, although God approves their request, Samuel and the LORD are both dismayed (1 Sam. 8:6–7). This is not the response one might anticipate, especially with expectations for a king in the rearview mirror from Deut. 17, Judg. 21, and 1 Sam. 2. What we find is that 1 Sam. 8–15 introduces the jagged edges of human kingship in order to clarify YHWH's desires for the monarchy.

What Is Wrong with Requesting a King?

"Appoint for us a king to judge us like all the nations" (1 Sam. 8:5). What Israel hopes for in a king is not necessarily bad. As was common in the ancient world, the king's chief role was to ensure that there was justice across

---

des cantiques et du Psautier," *BN* 111 (2002): 18–22, who argues for close linguistic connections between Hannah's prayer, David's anointing in 1 Sam. 16, and David's song in 2 Sam. 22.

5. Brueggemann, "I Samuel 1," 43.

society.[6] At the end of chapter 7, it is clear that Samuel had devoted himself to the important task of judging all across Israel (7:15–17); now they want a new office to be in charge of this. Samuel's sons perverted justice (8:3), so Israel requests a king who will establish justice. Naturally, Samuel is offended; they are explicitly trashing the very institution he represents as insufficient for bringing about justice. God assures Samuel that this is not ultimately a rejection of Samuel; instead, this is a rejection of God "from being king over them" (v. 7).

What is it that makes Israel's request for a king problematic from God's perspective? The most common explanations bear down upon Israel's desire to be like other nations and/or state that God is king and that therefore a request for a human king is a rejection of God's sovereign rule.[7] These explanations, if correct, require serious qualifications. For one, there is nothing innately wrong with Israel modeling their institutions after the nations around them—the covenant treaty genre, Israel's law codes, and even the temple design all correspond with the nations around them, with modifications. So, a desire for a king like the surrounding nations is not automatically wrong. In fact, Israel's desire for a king to bring justice like other nations is upheld throughout the Old Testament (e.g., 2 Sam. 8:15; 1 Kings 10:9; Ps. 72; Isa. 11:2–3). The problem, then, is not that Israel was copying a neighboring institution. Additionally, God endorses the appointment of a king in Israel (1 Sam. 8:7, 9, 22) and had provided guidelines for kingship in Deut. 17, so the institution of monarchy is not in and of itself automatically forbidden under God's higher kingship.

It is useful to focus on the *timing* and *motivation* behind this request in answering our question about what makes the request for a king problematic. As for *timing*, this is a unique moment in Israel's history: up to this point God has had the exclusive title of king. By requesting a human king, the people rupture Yhwh's exclusive attribution as king. As Stephen Chapman states, "Henceforth, until the Exile, the Israelites will be unable to confess resolutely that God alone is king over Israel—apart from any human viceroy or partner."[8] At this moment when Israel gives voice to its desire for a monarch, gone are the days when Israel could claim that God alone was king. So,

6. See, for instance, the Code of Hammurabi.

7. E.g., P. Kyle McCarter Jr., *I Samuel: A New Translation with Introduction, Notes and Commentary*, AB 8 (Garden City, NY: Doubleday, 1980), 161; David Toshio Tsumura, *The First Book of Samuel*, NICOT (Grand Rapids: Eerdmans, 2007), 251–52; Bill T. Arnold, *1 & 2 Samuel*, NIVAC (Grand Rapids: Zondervan, 2003), 152–53.

8. Stephen B. Chapman, *1 Samuel as Christian Scripture: A Theological Commentary* (Grand Rapids: Eerdmans, 2016), 101.

just as Samuel is offended by Israel's rejection of the institution of judgeship, so God experiences rejection through Israel's dismissal of the institution of theocracy. This does not mean that God is entirely against the institution of human kingship; it just means that God sees elements of rejection within this request at this rupturing moment of transition.

As for *motivation*, God detects beneath their request a spirit of idolatry,[9] an act that corresponds with Israel's idolatrous ways since they came out of Egypt (1 Sam. 8:8). This becomes even more explicit in 1 Sam. 12 when Israel confesses their sin of "ask[ing] for [them]selves a king" (v. 19). Samuel responds by calling on them to not "turn aside after empty things that cannot profit or deliver, for they are empty" (v. 21). These descriptors pertain to gods, yet Samuel seems to include the request for a king in the same vein as idolatry when he addresses the problem of idolatry immediately after Israel confesses their sin of requesting a king. Repentance for Israel and its king will look like exclusive allegiance to YHWH. Their request for a monarch like the nations around them is problematic because it stems from Israel's rebellious heart, which seeks well-being in what is other than God.

God clarifies several matters for the people. First, the institution of monarchy will not automatically result in the establishment of justice; in fact, it will lead to the opposite (1 Sam. 8:10–18). Samuel warns Israel: Their children will be drafted into military service, some assigned to agriculture and others to fashioning war equipment. The king will confiscate their property, require produce from their lands and vineyards, and enlist them in slave labor. Instead of ensuring justice, God knows that the institution of monarchy will result in grave injustice.

The second clarification concerning kingship is that the welfare of the king and people depends on their obedience to the law of God, their ultimate king.[10] This is most apparent in Samuel's farewell address in 1 Sam. 12:14–15.

> [14]If you will fear the LORD and serve him and obey his voice and not rebel against the commandment of the LORD, and if both you and the king who reigns over you will follow the LORD your God, it will be well. [15]But if you will not obey the voice of the LORD, but rebel against the commandment of the LORD, then the hand of the LORD will be against you and your king.

Both people and king are to live in obedience to the commands of the LORD; the success of the monarchy depends on it. In a Sinai-like moment of fear

---

9. Robert P. Gordon, *I & II Samuel: A Commentary*, Library of Biblical Interpretation (Grand Rapids: Zondervan, 1999), 110.

10. See Dumbrell, "Content and Significance," 55–56.

before God, Israel acknowledges their sin in having requested a king (v. 19). Samuel responds by exhorting them to serve the LORD fully and not to turn away from him to "empty things that cannot profit or deliver, for they are empty" (v. 21). Samuel warns Israel and its monarch that they must live in fear of and faithful service to the LORD if the new institution is to be of any good to Israel (vv. 20–25). A successful move forward into monarchy will necessitate allegiance from Israel and king to YHWH's rule.

The Failure of King Saul

Amid the clarifications offered in 1 Sam. 8 and 12, the first king of Israel, Saul, comes into view. God identifies Saul as the king through revelation to Samuel (9:15) and to the people via lot (10:20–24). God also empowers Saul by the Spirit to bring a mighty salvation to Israel from the Ammonites (11:6–11). The initial impression of Saul's rule is quite positive. Yet Saul's disobedience to YHWH soon takes center stage across chapters 13–15. In chapter 13, Saul disobeys Samuel's instructions to wait for his arrival by taking the matters of battle sacrifice into his own hands (vv. 8–9). When Samuel confronts Saul, saying, "What have you done?" (v. 11), Saul attempts to excuse his behavior (vv. 11–12). Samuel then declares that the consequence of Saul's disobedience is that his dynasty will not continue (vv. 13–14). In chapter 15, Saul again disobeys Samuel's instructions—this time failing to devote all the Amalekites and their livestock to destruction. He preserves their king and the best of their livestock (vv. 8–9). When Saul encounters the prophet, he initially claims to have obeyed "the commandment of the LORD" (v. 13) and then again attempts to excuse his sparing of Agag and the animals (v. 15). Again, the prophet Samuel rebukes Saul and declares that the kingdom will be taken out of Saul's hands (v. 28). As soon as the office of king comes into being, the disobedience of the king displays the fragility of the office in terms of whether such a role can be carried out in obedience to the LORD.

The account of Saul does more than depict the first king's failures. By beginning with a king like Saul, the writer provides a foil to clarify what God desires in a king. The prophet Samuel says to Saul, "But now your kingdom shall not continue. The LORD has sought out a man after his own heart, and the LORD has commanded him to be prince over his people, because you have not kept what the LORD commanded you" (1 Sam. 13:14). Coming on the heels of Samuel's visionary speech in 1 Sam. 12, Samuel's message here makes it clear that Saul is not the sort of king God desires. God's king would act in unison with God's expectations, living under the rule of God himself as he leads the nation. Rolf P. Knierim captures this well: "As Yahweh's messiah, he stood under the commandment of absolute obedience. The messiah, even more than a prophet, must be perfect, if his work is to succeed and if he is to represent Yahweh exclusively."[11] God wishes for a king whose heart corresponds with his own.

By getting off on the wrong foot with YHWH by requesting a king and in the failures of Israel's first king, Israel developed expectations regarding their royal ideal: a king who will truly bring about justice, unlike most monarchs; a king who with his people will live obediently under the rule of YHWH their king.

The Blessing of a King after God's Heart

Although Saul remains on the throne until his death in 1 Sam. 31, God identifies Saul's replacement in chapter 16. God "has sought out a man after his own heart" (13:14), and Samuel identifies and anoints the future king: "Do not look on his appearance or on the height of his stature. . . . For the LORD sees not as man sees: man looks on the outward appearance, but the LORD looks on the heart" (16:7). Like Hannah, someone comes from the margins, from the realm of the unexpected; it is the youngest son, one not even included at the feast with the prophet, whom God chooses. Although it turns out that David is physically attractive (v. 12), the one God chooses to anoint is deemed by God to be markedly different from King Saul. In 1 Sam. 16–2 Sam. 10, a messianic picture emerges of what a king after God's heart looks like and the blessing such brings to Israel. Four features of the ideal king will occupy our attention.

A King with a Heart after God's Heart

The narratives about David reveal what it looks like to have a heart that corresponds to God's heart. In contrast to King Saul and the rest of Israel, who are overcome with fear at the threat of Goliath (1 Sam. 17:11, 24), David—who is not even old enough to enlist in the army—cannot sit back and allow the living God to be defied (vv. 26, 36). He steps forward, trusting that the LORD will deliver him from Goliath just as he has delivered him from lions and bears (v. 37). By placing the story of David and Goliath just after chapter 16, the writer shows that a heart that trusts God and desires the LORD's honor is central to what God looks for in his king.

11. Rolf P. Knierim, "The Messianic Concept in the First Book of Samuel," in *Jesus and the Historian: Written in Honor of Ernest Cadman Colwell*, ed. F. Thomas Trotter (Philadelphia: Westminster, 1968), 38.

Another aspect of David's character that 1–2 Samuel highlights is David's submission to God's sovereignty. An inordinate number of chapters depict the transition from Saul to David, but this provides insight into Saul's dissolution and David's character. David's devotion and dedication to Saul are unmistakable—David puts his life on the line to face Goliath (1 Sam. 17:32); David successfully leads Saul's troops in battle (18:5); David plays Saul songs to assuage the king's tormented soul (16:23; 18:10). Yet Saul is overcome with jealousy, hurls spears at David (18:11), and is so intent on murdering David that David is forced to live a life on the run in desolate regions, caves, and even Philistine territory. Given David's popularity (vv. 7, 16), it would have been natural for David to plot how he might overthrow Saul and take over the throne. David, however, has a different way of operating. Instead of overthrowing Saul, David flees. In fact, on two occasions—the first in a cave and the second while Saul lay asleep in camp—David had an opportunity to kill Saul. Indeed, those around him claimed that God had given Saul into his hand (24:4; 26:8). The urge to get revenge and claim the throne was so great that David sliced the corner of Saul's robe, but immediately "David's heart struck him" (24:5). He knew that this was not the way of God in this matter. Amid such suffering, why would David display mercy to Saul? David's conscience would not allow him to "put out [his] hand against the LORD's anointed" (26:11; cf. 24:6). David's choice of words, "the LORD's anointed," seems strategic. John Chrysostom offers a beautiful reflection on why David said "the LORD's anointed" rather than "the king": "Instead of calling him king, what did he say? 'Because he is the Lord's anointed,' lending him respect not on the basis of his position here-below but of the decision from on high."[12] God had not removed the anointed one (Saul) from the throne, so David dare not do so. To the frustration of those around him, and perhaps even readers, David waits and waits so that it is clear that David waits for God to establish his throne.

A final way David aligns with God's heart is apparent in how he regularly consults God. On many occasions, David seeks God's direct guidance in instances of danger and military decisions (1 Sam. 23:2, 4, 9–11; 30:7–8; 2 Sam. 2:1; 5:19, 23). Ironically, we are told that Saul—whose name in Hebrew derives from the verb meaning "to ask, inquire"—inquires of the LORD only twice (1 Sam. 14:37; 28:6; root *šʾl*), and in both instances the narrator tells us that the LORD did not answer. The recurring mention by the narrator that David has an open line of communication with the LORD contributes to the book's portrait of a king whose heart corresponds with God.

12. John Chrysostom, *Homilies on Hannah, David and Saul*, trans. Robert Charles Hill, *Old Testament Homilies*, vol. 1 (Brookline, MA: Holy Cross Orthodox, 2003), 23.

A King Centered on God's Kingship

As an outworking of David's heart, the king prioritizes God's rule. When Jerusalem becomes the capital of David's kingdom (2 Sam. 5:1–10), David summons the entire house of Israel to join him in bringing the ark of God into Jerusalem (6:1–2, 15). The ark of God symbolizes the throne of God,[13] so David is signifying before all of Israel that they are a nation and he is a king that live in the presence of and under the rule of God.[14] This is not merely a shrewd political move, whereby he can unify the religious and political establishments. No, by noting David's costly sacrifices (vv. 13, 17–18) and his "danc[ing] before the LORD with all of his might" (vv. 13–14, 16), the narrator wants us to see a king with a heart that genuinely delights in and reveres YHWH, the ultimate king of Israel. This establishes a pattern that the book of Kings develops, where the best Davidic kings are those who prioritize God's presence in the temple.

A King Who Implements Justice

We are told that "David reigned over all Israel. And David administered justice [*mišpāṭ*] and equity [*ṣədāqâ*] to all his people" (2 Sam. 8:15). Throughout the Old Testament, *mišpāṭ* and *ṣədāqâ* occur together as attributes and actions of YHWH (Job 37:23; Pss. 33:5; 36:6; 72:1; 99:4; 103:6; Prov. 8:20 [wisdom personified]; Isa. 5:16; 28:17; 33:5; Jer. 9:24; Mic. 7:9) and as characteristics desired in the king (2 Sam. 8:15; 1 Kings 10:9; 1 Chron. 18:14; 2 Chron. 9:8; Isa. 9:7; Jer. 22:3, 15; 23:5; 33:15) and people in general (Gen. 18:19 [Abraham's offspring]; Deut. 33:21 [Gad]; Ps. 106:3; Prov. 21:3; Isa. 1:27; 5:7; 56:1; 58:2; Ezek. 18:5, 19, 21, 27; Amos 5:24). For this reason, Graeme Auld describes this combination of terms as "godlike justice."[15] We will return to this feature of kingship in subsequent chapters, but it is sufficient for now to recognize that this echoes what Israel hoped for in a king— "Appoint for us a king to judge [*šāpaṭ*] us" (1 Sam. 8:5). This also prepares for 1–2 Kings and especially the prophets, who evaluate rulers in view of their commitment to or perversion of justice. Through the description of David in 2 Sam. 8:15, one ideal for God's king is to implement God's justice and righteousness across society.

---

13. The use of "LORD of Hosts" and the description of him as the one "who sits enthroned on the cherubim" (6:2) heighten this sense of divine rule. See Marc Zvi Brettler, *God Is King: Understanding an Israelite Metaphor*, JSOTSup 76 (Sheffield: Sheffield Academic, 1989), 83.

14. Dumbrell, "Content and Significance," 58.

15. A. Graeme Auld, *I & II Samuel*, rev. ed., OTL (Louisville: Westminster John Knox, 2011), 431.

A King Victorious in Battle for Israel

David has an impressive list of military accolades: smiter of the giant Goliath; killer of tens of thousands of Philistines (1 Sam. 18:7–8, 30; 23:5; 2 Sam. 5:17–25); plunderer of surrounding peoples (1 Sam. 27:8); avenger against the Amalekites (30:17); conqueror of Zion (2 Sam. 5:6–10); and subduer of the surrounding nations, Edom, Moab, Ammon, and Aram (8:11–12; chap. 10). Up to this point in Israel's history, there had never been military victory of this scale. Two features are noteworthy as one considers how military victory intersects with 1–2 Samuel's portrait of the ideal king. First, God is the one who enables David to be victorious. For this reason, the narrator provides statements throughout 1–2 Samuel that make it clear that God is responsible for David's military success:

> And David had success in all his undertakings, for the LORD was with him. (1 Sam. 18:14)

> And David became greater and greater, for the LORD, the God of hosts, was with him. (2 Sam. 5:10)

> And the LORD gave victory to David wherever he went. (8:6, 14)

In addition to statements by the narrator, communication between David and God offers a window into God's sovereignty over battle:

> I will give the Philistines into your hand. (1 Sam. 23:4)

> Go around to their rear. . . . When you hear the sound of marching in the tops of the balsam trees, then rouse yourself, for then the LORD has gone out before you to strike down the army of the Philistines. (2 Sam. 5:23–24)

The ideal king, then, has God fighting on his side and depends on the LORD for victory.

Second, David, as king, is not merely attaining victory for himself; instead, God has positioned the king to fight on behalf of and for the well-being of his people Israel. This is apparent when David fights Goliath as Israel's representative but also is obvious in that battles took place in order to ensure the security and well-being of Israel as a whole (e.g., 1 Sam. 23:5; 2 Sam. 10:19).[16] The expectation that a king would bring victory for the nation is also inherent

---

16. Knierim, "Messianic Concept," 34: "David fights as a representative for Israel and succeeds."

in Israel's request for a king: "But there shall be a king over us, that we also may be like all the nations, and that our king may judge us and go out before us and fight our battles" (1 Sam. 8:19–20).

The Davidic Covenant

God's covenant with David is monumental within the story line of Scripture.[17] We will begin by clarifying what is promised in 2 Sam. 7:1–17 as it pertains to a dynasty from David, and then attempt to situate these promises within the wider context of the Old Testament.[18]

A DYNASTY FOR DAVID'S FAMILY

Since King David's heart aligns with God's heart (1 Sam. 13:14; 16:7), isn't it safe to assume that God will be on board with what is now on David's heart, to build a temple for God?[19] Nathan thinks so: "Go, do all that is in your heart" (2 Sam. 7:3). Not so fast. That evening God reveals to Nathan that God does not wish for David to build him a house. Why? First Chronicles 22:8 highlights how David has shed too much blood in battle for God to allow him to build him a temple. In 2 Sam. 7, there is no explicit explanation such as one finds in 1 Chron. 22:8. Instead, the emphasis in 2 Sam. 7 is on how YHWH is the sovereign initiator of the Davidic dynasty, not the other way around. In other words, David is not responsible for YHWH's establishment in Israel; YHWH is responsible for the establishment of David's dynasty under YHWH's rulership.

Two lines of rhetoric make this focus on YHWH's sovereign initiative clear. First, the term for "house" (bayit) occurs eight times (2 Sam. 7:1, 2, 5, 6, 7, 11, 13, 16) at key junctures in the passage. David has a house (bayit) but recognizes that YHWH does not (vv. 1–2), and so he hopes to build him one. YHWH's first statement in this passage challenges why David would build him a house (vv. 5–6) when he has never asked for a house (bayit) throughout Israel's history (v. 7). Clearly, God does not need a house. Instead, God will make a house (bayit) for David (v. 11)—that is, a dynasty (v. 16). Nonetheless, David's son

---

17. For more on how one may refer to 2 Sam. 7 as a covenant, even if the Hebrew term bərît does not occur there, see Gregory Goswell, "What Makes the Arrangement of God with David in 2 Samuel 7 a Covenant?," ResQ 60 (2018): 87–97.

18. For an overview of scholarly debate on the composition of 2 Sam. 7:1–17, see P. Kyle McCarter Jr., II Samuel: A New Translation with Introduction, Notes and Commentary, AB 9 (New York: Doubleday, 1984), 210–24.

19. Among the few uses of lēbāb ("heart") in 1–2 Samuel, it is likely that Nathan's statement "Do all that is in your heart [lēbāb]" (2 Sam. 7:3) alludes to 1 Sam. 13:14 and 16:7, thereby indicating the rationale for Nathan's immediate endorsement.

will be the one who builds a house for YHWH (v. 13).[20] God, then, is not reject-ing a temple, but instead "seizes David's request for a temple as an opportunity to remake something threatening to the theocracy into something that can be incorporated within it."[21]

Second, the focus on the LORD asserting his sovereign priority is further evident in the mass of first-person verbs. Looking to the past, God states,

> I myself took you from the pasture. . . . I was with you. . . . I cut off all your enemies. (2 Sam. 7:8–9a)[22]

Looking to the future, God declares,

> I will make for you a great name. (v. 9b)
> I will make a place for my people. . . . I will plant them. (v. 10)
> I will give you rest from all your enemies. (v. 11)
> I will establish your offspring after you. . . . I will establish his kingdom. (v. 12)
> I will establish the throne of his kingdom forever. (v. 13)
> I myself will be his father. . . . I will reprove him. (v. 14)
> My steadfast love will not turn away from him just as I turned it away from Saul. (v. 15)

Make no mistake about it; YHWH is the one responsible for making a house for David, a dynasty that rests on the initiative of YHWH.

God's covenant with David has several noteworthy components. First, this covenant will be "forever" (2 Sam. 7:13, 16 [2x]). In Hebrew, the phrase translated as "forever" by the ESV is *ʿad-ʿôlām*. The phrase by itself does not automatically indicate an irrevocability,[23] as God revokes his promise to Eli's house that "[his] house and the house of [his] father should go in and out before [God] forever" (1 Sam. 2:30).[24] Although *ʿad-ʿôlām* does not automati-cally convey irrevocability, the contrast with God's treatment of Saul conveys permanence: "My steadfast love will not depart from [David's offspring], as I took it from Saul" (2 Sam. 7:15). As A. A. Anderson puts it, "The main fea-ture of this kingship will be its permanent stability."[25] Instead of erasing the

20. See Philip E. Satterthwaite, "David in the Books of Samuel: A Messianic Expectation?," in *The Lord's Anointed: Interpretation of Old Testament Messianic Texts*, ed. P. E. Satterthwaite, Richard S. Hess, and Gordon J. Wenham (Carlisle, UK: Paternoster, 1995), 54.

21. Lyle Eslinger, *House of God or House of David: The Rhetoric of 2 Samuel 7*, JSOTSup 164 (Sheffield: Sheffield Academic, 1994), 64.

22. Our own translation, which highlights the first-person pronoun that brings emphasis.

23. See a list of uses in Eslinger, *House of God or House of David*, 46–48.

24. McCarter, *II Samuel*, 206.

25. A. A. Anderson, *2 Samuel*, WBC 11 (Dallas: Word, 1989), 122.

dynasty of David due to the sin of its kings, God promises discipline rather than extermination (v. 14).

Second, God's relationship with the Davidic dynasty can be understood as a father relating to his sons. For Christians, an initial instinct may be to interpret God's pledge, "I will be to him a father, and he shall be to me a son" (2 Sam. 7:14), as a promise about Jesus, who is ontologically the Son of God. That is, until they read the rest of the verse: "When he commits iniquity, I will discipline him." Clearly, the "father-son" relationship in view is not an ontological description of God as divine Father relating to a divine Son. Instead, the "father-son" relationship is a metaphor that captures the covenantal nature of how God will relate to the king. More precisely, this statement focuses not on David himself but on David's offspring who succeed him. As Lyle Eslinger puts it, "Yahweh steps in as the orphaned Davidide's father and sonship is transferred from David."[26] For this reason, in covenantal contexts, the king is called God's son in Pss. 2:7–8 ("You are my son") and 89:26–27 ("He shall cry to me, 'You are my Father.' . . . I will make him the firstborn").[27] This, of course, does not mean that God in his providence did not use this metaphor in order to prepare God's people to comprehend the divine-Father/divine-Son relationship when that would be made manifest later in redemptive history.[28] Thus, the core of God's promise to David is God's long-standing commitment to David's dynasty, a commitment that will be evident in God's fatherly relationship toward the king as an adopted son.

PROMISES TO DAVID IN THE CONTEXT OF GOD'S PROMISES TO ISRAEL

The promise of dynasty to David cannot be abstracted from God's promises to Abraham. For one, when God says, "I will make for you a great name" (2 Sam. 7:9), this calls to mind God's word to Abraham: "I will . . . make your name great" (Gen. 12:2). These two verses are the only occasions in the Hebrew Bible where *gādal* ("to make great" [*piel*]) or *gādôl* ("great") and *šēm* ("name") combine to refer to the greatness of a human name. Additionally, when God refers to offspring *"who shall come from your* [David's] *body"* (2 Sam. 7:12b), this resembles a similar assurance to Abraham: *"One who will come from your own body shall be your heir"* (Gen. 15:4 NKJV). It is only

26. Eslinger, *House of God or House of David*, 59.

27. Petri Kasari claims that this is an adoption formula that is common throughout the ANE between a god and a king upon the king's succession to the throne. Petri Kasari, *Nathan's Promise in 2 Samuel 7 and Related Texts*, Publications of the Finnish Exegetical Society 97 (Helsinki: Finnish Exegetical Society, University of Helsinki, 2009), 38.

28. This insight comes from a conversation with Daniel Treier, a colleague in systematic theology at Wheaton College.

in reference to David's offspring (2 Sam. 7:12; 16:11) and Abraham's (Gen. 15:4) that the verb *yāṣāʾ* ("to come out") coordinates with *mēʿeh* ("body") in reference to offspring in the entire Hebrew Bible. Finally, the use of "offspring" (*zeraʿ*; 2 Sam. 7:12; cf. Gen. 15:5; 17:7, 19) certainly calls to mind Abrahamic traditions that we unpacked in our chapter on the Pentateuch. These numerous associations with Abrahamic promises make it clear that from this point forward the Davidic king would be a channel through which God would fulfill his promises to Abraham.[29] In light of Genesis's expectations of a royal offspring from Abraham's line, one can now say that the Davidic dynasty is the royal strand of Abraham's seed that is expected to play a role in God's plans to redeem the world through Israel.[30]

Not only does the Davidic covenant call to mind Abrahamic promises, but it also alludes to the national covenant established at Sinai. Under David, God says, "I will establish a place for my people" (2 Sam. 7:10, authors' trans.). The phrase "my people" reverberates especially with the Exodus and Sinai traditions (e.g., Exod. 6:7; Lev. 26:12). Additionally, the prospect of God giving David "rest from all [his] enemies" (2 Sam. 7:11) corresponds with a similarly phrased promise in Deut. 12:10 and 25:19 ("when he gives you rest from all your enemies"; cf. Josh. 23:1). Although the expectations that Israel would dwell peacefully in the land soon after conquest under Joshua do not come about, there is renewed hope that now under a Davidic king God's promised rest will be fulfilled. As will become apparent in 1–2 Kings, the realization of these promises through a Davidic king is contingent upon the king's willingness, along with the people, to live obediently under God's law as set forth at Sinai.

Summary

First Samuel 16–2 Sam. 10 presents an idyllic portrayal of David and what life could be like under such a king. The ideal king has a heart that corresponds with God, and this is especially apparent in how the king trusts God, administers justice, manifests restraint, seeks God, and centers the community on God as Israel's supreme king. As a result, God enables the Davidic king to be victorious in battle and brings great blessing through the king to the people. God's commitment to David culminates in God's covenantal promises that David's

29. Psalm 72:17 expresses hope that the promise to Abraham that all clans/nations on the earth will be blessed through Abraham's offspring (Gen. 12:3; 22:18) will find a dimension of fulfillment in the Davidic King ("May people be blessed in him").

30. Paul R. Williamson, *Sealed with an Oath: Covenant in God's Unfolding Purpose*, NSBT 23 (Downers Grove, IL: IVP Academic, 2007), 124.

dynasty will endure, unlike Saul's, and that the Davidic king will become a siphon through which God's earlier promises to Israel can find realization.

David's Unraveling and God's Faithfulness

Although 1–2 Samuel highlights the blessings of a Davidic king who is in tune with God, it also makes clear that the ideal can only hold for so long, even in the case of David. Beginning with 2 Sam. 11 and continuing through to the end of the book, David's kingdom begins to unravel amid David's personal unraveling. David abuses his power and sleeps with another man's wife, Bathsheba (2 Sam. 11). He misuses his power over the military and makes arrangements to have Bathsheba's husband murdered in battle. As punishment, David's child through Bathsheba dies (12:14). Soon thereafter one of David's sons, Amnon, rapes his half-sister, Tamar, but David refrains from doing anything about it (13:22).[31] Further bloodshed ensues, as another son of David, Absalom, avenges his sister by murdering his half-brother Amnon. Later, Absalom usurps his father, forcing David to flee from Jerusalem, and then sleeps with David's concubines to show that there is a new king in town (16:22). Absalom is killed soon after, and even when David resumes his role as king in Jerusalem, his reign remains in turmoil. The book concludes with another account of David's sin—taking a census, which God and those around him interpret as a shameful act (24:3). This results in the death of many within Jerusalem. Sinful behavior in David and his children and the unraveling of tranquility and blessing in Israel mark the final stretch of David's reign as king (2 Sam. 11–24).

The negative appraisal of David's reign in 2 Sam. 11–24 accomplishes significant purposes within the book. First, these chapters highlight God's mercy for and commitment to David. With God's rejection of Saul looming in the background, it is striking how God's promise that he would remain committed to David and his offspring (7:15) is on full display. Following the adultery or the murder or David's passivity toward rape or the pride of a census, God in his freedom has many reasons to revoke the promises made to David, just as he had with Eli and later Saul. However, since God promises to discipline without eliminating the line of the Davidic king, the dynasty of David will continue. It will continue solely due to the mercy and promise keeping of God himself.

Second, 1–2 Samuel is written with an awareness of the failure of future Davidic kings. The author certainly would have been aware of Solomon's

---

31. This resembles Eli's inability to properly respond to the sin of his own children (1 Sam. 2:29).

failure, and perhaps also of the failures of all the kings whose reigns are narrated in 1–2 Kings.[32] This reframes how we look at these books. The failure of David prepares for the continuing failure of one Davidic king after another in 1–2 Kings. This cuts in several directions. On the one hand, it contributes to the unfolding story of how the failure of Davidic kings to live according to God's commands is what ultimately leads to the exile of Judah. On the other hand, the idealization of David in 1 Sam. 16–2 Sam. 10 highlights the positive dimensions of God's choice to work through a Davidic king, even if the benefit of such an arrangement is based on the fragile contingency of the king's obedience. The good and the bad of David give birth to an expectation that perhaps a greater David—a Davidic king who will not fall into sin like David—will arise through whom God will fulfill his promises to Abraham, Moses, and David.

Thus, the failure of David reminds Israel that God is the one who is supremely dependable as Israel's king. Yet God remains faithful to David's line, so the expectation is that the longevity of the Davidic dynasty will be anchored in the commitment of God himself. As God's commitment remains, hope emerges for a greater David, one without sin to plague God's plans to bless the entire world through Israel.

Conclusion

We began this chapter by asking whether 1–2 Samuel would affirm the epilogue of Judges. Would a monarch be the remedy for Israel's religious and social ills? Whether it is Hannah's story and song, Israel's request for a king, or the reigns of Saul and David, the answer has repeatedly been that Israel's well-being depends supremely on living faithfully before God as their King. God chooses to utilize human kingship, yet the most important feature of kingship is not the office of monarch but the heart of the king. God pledges himself in covenant to the dynasty of David, a king whose heart aligns with God's, yet even David fails. Due to God's faithfulness to his promise and his merciful nature, hopes surface that perhaps a king greater than David will arise through whom God will fulfill his promises to Abraham. The positive part of David's reign offers a window into the sort of king 1–2 Samuel idealizes: a king centered on

32. See David G. Firth, *1 & 2 Samuel*, ApOTC 8 (London: Apollos, 2009), 22–33, who dates the final form of the book as preexilic. We tend to view 1–2 Samuel and 1–2 Kings as mutually informing one another, yet composed by different authors. For instance, the ideals of kingship in David's life find echoes and development in the ideals seen in Solomon, Hezekiah, and Josiah. An account of David's failures seems necessary to prepare for the failure of Davidic kings in 1–2 Kings, yet 1–2 Kings usually hangs on to the more positive outlook on David.

God as King; a king who brings Israel rest from their enemies; a king whose heart aligns with God's; a king who institutes justice.

Postlude: Canonical Reflections

In many respects, Jesus can be seen as a greater David. Like David, Jesus holds a primary concern that God be at the center of the community (John 2:17). Like David, Jesus regularly responds with mercy toward enemies due to a trust in God's sovereignty (Luke 23:34). Just as David did not pursue the throne for himself through an overthrow, so Jesus's exaltation as king rested in the hands of God alone (Phil. 2:5–11). Just as David desired the implementation of justice, so Jesus was an advocate for justice (Matt. 23:23). Many other parallels between Jesus and David can surely be made.

Two major differences, however, between Jesus and David are evident. First, although a "son of David," Jesus is also the Son of God. As both the Divine King and the messianic king, Jesus was able to accomplish something King David and other Davidic kings were unable to attain. Jesus was completely sinless, as he submitted to the Father's will perfectly. In fact, Jesus did not simply have a heart that corresponded with God's; Jesus is one with the Father. As a divine Davidic king, Jesus is indeed a greater David. A second significant difference is that Jesus did not rule as king in a geopolitical fashion, as King David had. Even though he could bear the title "son of David," the plot of his earthly mission as it related to political office was largely influenced by the vision of the suffering servant from Isa. 53. When Christ comes again, however, the fullness of Christ's rule as the Davidic king will become far more evident.

5

Failure and the Royal Ideal in 1–2 Kings

No book has had a greater impact on Western higher education, especially within liberal arts colleges, than John Henry Newman's *The Idea of a University* (1852).[1] In it, Newman expresses a vision for a new, Catholic university in Ireland—a vision aimed at investors and inscribing the DNA of the prospective college. The book's success, however, contrasts with Newman's demise as president and the withering of the newly founded university. Within four years of its opening Newman resigned, and the university never came close to attaining its vision and was defunct within a few decades.[2] If ideals never materialize, is there something wrong with those ideals? Not automatically. The ideals may be valid, yet circumstances may prohibit their attainment. Such is the case in the book of Kings. Despite recounting the failure of kingship in Israel and Judah and the resulting exile of these nations, the book of Kings also portrays an ideal for Davidic kingship that transcends its failed history. We will make a case for this by considering three vantage points on the *ideal of kingship* in Kings: the Solomonic ideal, the Josianic ideal, and the exilic perspective.

1. John Henry Newman, *The Idea of a University*, ed. Frank M. Turner (New Haven: Yale University Press, 1996).
2. The school was open from 1854–57. On the social and ecclesial factors in the failure of the college, see Colin Barr, "The Failure of Newman's Catholic University of Ireland," *Archivum hibernicum* 55 (2001): 126–39.

The Solomonic Ideal

Solomon is a mixed bag. He is "the first good and bad king" in the book of Kings.[3] Can an idolater and the reason for a nation's split still be a vehicle for conveying what kingship should or could be in Israel? Yes. As we will see, 1 Kings 1–11 presents Solomon as a "greater David," in at least four ways—though we will not gloss over the negatives.

Extensive Dominion Ideal

David's success in defeating enemies and extending Israel's borders serves as a backdrop for idealizing the extent of the kingdom at the time of Solomon. David has had remarkable military success, subduing the Philistines to the west; Edom, Moab, and Ammon to the east; and Aram to the north (2 Sam. 8:12; chap. 10). David succeeds because "the LORD gave victory to David wherever he went" (8:6, 14). Although it is clear that God grants David rest from his surrounding enemies (2 Sam. 7:1), no statements about David's reign compare to the heightened language that describes Solomon's dominion. First Kings 4:20–21 and 4:25 read:

> [20]Judah and Israel were as many as the sand by the sea. They ate and drank and were happy. [21]Solomon ruled over all the kingdoms from the Euphrates to the land of the Philistines and to the border of Egypt. . . . [25]And Judah and Israel lived in safety, from Dan even to Beersheba, every man under his vine and under his fig tree, all the days of Solomon.

These descriptions resonate with previous promises given to Abraham. Israel has now become like the sand of the sea (cf. Gen. 22:17; 32:12). Their borders now extend from Egypt to the Euphrates (15:18).[4] To enhance the impression, the writer utilizes the prophetic motif of dwelling under the vine and fig tree (Mic. 4:4; Zech. 3:10; cf. Isa. 36:16) to capture how idyllic life can be under a king like Solomon. By characterizing the extent of Solomon's reign in this way, the writer gives the impression that the extension of dominion over the Levant beginning under King David reaches a culmination of Abrahamic and prophetic proportions under King Solomon.

In addition to the extent of the land, there is also a development from tribute received by David to that received by King Solomon. We are told

---

3. Alison L. Joseph, *Portrait of the Kings: The Davidic Prototype in Deuteronomistic Poetics* (Minneapolis: Fortress, 2015), 98.

4. Iain Provan, "The Messiah in the Books of Kings," in *The Lord's Anointed: Interpretation of Old Testament Messianic Texts*, ed. P. E. Satterthwaite, Richard S. Hess, and Gordon J. Wenham (Carlisle, UK: Paternoster, 1995), 76–77.

that Moab (2 Sam. 8:2) and Aram (v. 6) "brought tribute [*minḥâ*]" to David. King Solomon also receives tribute, but the depictions of it differ from the account of tribute brought to David in two ways. First, the *extent* of nations that bring Solomon tribute is significant. From the Euphrates to Egypt, nations "brought tribute [*minḥâ*]" to Solomon (1 Kings 4:21 [5:1 MT]); in fact, "the entire earth was seeking the presence of Solomon . . . and they were each bringing their own gift [*minḥâ*]" (10:24–25, authors' trans.). Second, the *amount* of tribute Solomon receives is important in 1 Kings, whereas the amount brought to David is not specified in 2 Samuel. Annually, Solomon would receive 666 talents of gold (approximately fifty thousand pounds) that would detail Israel's shields, Solomon's throne ("the like of it was never made in any kingdom," v. 20), and his drinking vessels (vv. 14–21). In addition to gold, he received "silver . . . , garments, myrrh, spices, horses, and mules" (v. 25; cf. 4:22–28 [5:2–8 MT]; 10:26–29). If David's reception of tribute was a sign of the dominion God had granted him, the portrayal of Solomon's wealth through tribute reaches idealized proportions. It appears, then, that 1 Kings 1–11 depicts Solomon so as to express the benefits of extensive dominion and security under the Davidic king—a Davidic king whose success exceeded David's.

Justice and Wisdom Ideal

Another aspect of the Solomonic ideal pertains to justice and wisdom;[5] as we will see, justice and wisdom are intertwined in 1 Kings 1–11. Again, David's reign provides a backdrop to help readers see how this extends in the reign of Solomon. In 2 Sam. 8:15, the narrator states: "So David reigned over all Israel. And David administered justice [*mišpāṭ*] and righteousness[6] to all his people." This aligns with the people of Israel's request for a king to "judge" [*šāpaṭ*] them (1 Sam. 8:5), although previously Samuel had been filling that role in Israel (7:15–17). What appears as a summary statement about David in 2 Sam. 8:15 develops in relationship to wisdom in the narratives about Solomon.

First Kings 3 is perhaps the most well-known chapter from Kings within churches. There Solomon requests of God: "Give your servant therefore an understanding mind" (v. 9a). What is less known, however, is *why* Solomon requests wisdom. The second half of the verse reveals Solomon's purpose behind

5. On Solomon as "a prototype of God's ideal, wise king," see Nathan Lovell, "The Shape of Hope in the Book of Kings: The Resolution of Davidic Blessing and Mosaic Curse," *JESOT* 3 (2014): 11.

6. Here we modify the ESV, which has "equity."

the request: "To judge [*šāpaṭ*] your people in order to discern between right and wrong. For who is able to judge [*šāpaṭ*] this great people of yours?" (v. 9b, authors' trans.). Solomon knows that he is in over his head—how is he supposed to ensure justice for the nation of Israel? He requests wisdom from God to enable him to judge the people with wisdom.

King Solomon's wisdom-endowed justice is on fullest display in the second half of 1 Kings 3 and in chapter 10. Immediately after the dream where God grants his request, Solomon's wisdom is put to the test: two prostitutes come, each claiming that a dead child is the other woman's and the living child is her own (3:16–27). Solomon remarkably exposes the truth, and, as a result, Israel is in awe. The narrator's statement at the end of the chapter is integral to understanding the account: "And all Israel heard of the judgment [*mišpāṭ*] that the king had rendered [*šāpaṭ*], and they stood in awe of the king, because they perceived that the wisdom of God was in him to do justice [*mišpāṭ*]" (v. 28). Israel marvels at Solomon's wisdom because of how it expresses itself in justice.

In 1 Kings 10, the queen of Sheba responds similarly to her encounter with Solomon's wisdom: "Happy are your servants, who continually stand before you and hear your wisdom! Blessed be the LORD your God, who has delighted in you and set you on the throne of Israel! Because the LORD loved Israel forever, he has made you king, that you may execute justice [*mišpāṭ*] and righteousness" (vv. 8–9). What is striking to the queen of Sheba is how Solomon's God-given wisdom enables him to execute justice for the good of Israel. Yes, David executed justice, but 1 Kings amplifies this ideal for Davidic kingship through the account of Solomon and clarifies that justice through a king becomes possible through divinely endowed wisdom.

Temple Commitment Ideal

David's concern for centralizing Israel around God's royal presence is prominent in 2 Sam. 6–7. David brings the ark of God into Jerusalem, sacrificing, dancing, and blessing the people along the way (6:5–19). In the next chapter, he expresses to the prophet Nathan his desire to build a house for God (7:2). Although it would be David's son who would build the temple (v. 13), the author of Samuel presents David as one who is keen for God's throne (i.e., the ark) to be central within David's kingdom.

The bulk of the Solomon narrative revolves around the temple, as preparations are made (1 Kings 5), the temple is built (chap. 6) and furnished (7:13–51), the ark enters (8:1–11), Solomon dedicates the temple (vv. 12–66), and God responds by appearing to Solomon (9:1–9). The king spares no expense in the process. He decks out the temple with cedar and cypress from Lebanon (5:10), costly stones (v. 17), and gold. He enlists a work force of 183,000 people to harvest and transport timber, cut stone, bear burdens, build, and serve as officials (vv. 13–16). This temple construction is associated with David, as the narrator specifies that "Solomon brought in the things that David his father had dedicated, the silver, the gold, and the vessels" (7:51). Furthermore, along with sacrificing before the ark as it is transported to the temple (8:5), like David had done (2 Sam. 6:13), Solomon "offered as peace offerings to the LORD 22,000 oxen and 120,000 sheep" (1 Kings 8:63). By offering sacrifices that could be eaten by nonpriests, Solomon provided meat that all of Israel could feast on at this moment of dedication (8:65–66). The extravagance, perhaps exaggerated,[7] aims to impress an ideal through Solomon—namely, an ideal whereby the king's chief priority is to uphold and promote the centrality of the LORD's presence among the people at the temple.

Exclusive Faithfulness Ideal

Although the previous three ideals find positive expression in Solomon's life, this final ideal, the most important one for the rest of Kings,[8] expresses itself in an unfortunate fashion through the negative example of Solomon. David's only address to Solomon in 1 Kings comes in his dying words. David's message opens by establishing the Sinai covenant as the lens by which he and future Davidic kings will be evaluated. First Kings 2:2–4 reads:

> [2]I am about to go the way of all the earth. Be strong, and show yourself a man, [3]and keep the charge of the LORD your God, walking in his ways and keeping his statutes, his commandments, his rules, and his testimonies, as it is written in the Law of Moses, that you may prosper in all that you do and wherever you turn, [4]that the LORD may establish his word that he spoke concerning me, saying, "If your sons pay close attention to their way, to walk before me

---

7. This would have been consistent with hyperbolic rhetorical devices of the time. So, e.g., James A. Montgomery, *The Book of Kings*, ed. Henry Snyder Gehman, ICC (Edinburgh: T&T Clark, 1950), 200; John Gray, *I and II Kings: A Commentary*, 2nd ed., OTL (Philadelphia: Westminster John Knox, 1964), 233; Burke O. Long, *1 Kings*, FOTL 9 (Grand Rapids: Eerdmans, 1984), 107; Mordechai Cogan, *I Kings*, AB 10 (New Haven: Yale University Press, 2001), 289. On the other hand, Marvin Sweeney estimates that the quantity of sacrifices over the fourteen days could feed 100,000–200,000 people and that the population of Jerusalem was between 100,000 and 400,000 by the eighth century BCE. Marvin A. Sweeney, *I & II Kings*, OTL (Louisville: Westminster John Knox, 2007), 136.

8. See Joseph, *Portrait of the Kings*, 98–104, on how the commands given to Solomon and his failure contribute to the construction of a Davidic ideal revolving around exclusive faithfulness to the LORD. Joseph does not, however, explore other ways Solomon may contribute to the ideal.

in faithfulness with all their heart and with all their soul, you shall not lack a man on the throne of Israel."

What is striking here is how the Davidic covenant comes to be viewed through the conditional lens of the Sinai covenant. The longevity of the Davidic dynasty depends on whether Solomon and subsequent kings obey the law of Moses.[9]

The emphasis on obedience to the Sinai covenant develops when the LORD appears to Solomon after the temple's dedication. As God reiterates how the continuation of the Davidic dynasty depends on obedience to God's commands, several unique elements surface (1 Kings 9:4–9). First, David serves as the paradigm for obedience: "If you will walk before me, as David your father walked, with integrity of heart and uprightness." (v. 4). This is perplexing in view of David's sins of adultery and murder, sins that 1 Kings 15:5 acknowledges. It is unlikely that the author of Kings is trying to whitewash David's checkered history. Instead, he is drawing on the positive aspects of David's faithfulness to the LORD—in particular, there is no indication that David fell into idolatry. Second, and related, God specifies in 9:4–9 a key aspect of not keeping God's commandments: "If you . . . do not keep my commandments . . . but go and serve other gods and worship them . . ." (v. 6). The consequences for disobedience will be explained to those passing through as follows: "Because they abandoned the LORD their God . . . and laid hold on other gods and worshiped them" (v. 9).[10] Third, the consequences in this passage extend beyond the absence of an heir of David upon the throne. Israel will be exiled (v. 7) and the temple will be in ruins (v. 8), consequences that call to mind curses from Deut. 28 (vv. 36–37, 49–52) for disobeying God's instructions. Thus, the book of Kings opens by presenting obedience to Mosaic law from Sinai—particularly exclusive faithfulness to the LORD as typified by David—as an essential requirement in the longevity of the Davidic dynasty.

As it turns out, Solomon's failure is epic. The king who had God appear to him twice, who was divinely endowed with wisdom, who built a temple for God, who was rich beyond comparison, and who led Israel during a time of incredible peace, ends up as the king who not only worships but also builds high places for the gods of his hundreds of foreign wives (1 Kings 11:1–8). In fact, Solomon fails in regard to every prohibition that Deut. 17 directs

9. Gregory Goswell, "King and Cultus: The Image of David in the Book of Kings," *JESOT* 5 (2016–17): 174.

10. On the central concern with cultic faithfulness in the Davidic king, see Goswell, "King and Cultus," 175.

toward the king: acquiring many wives (Deut. 17:17a; cf. 1 Kings 11:1–3), excessive amounts of gold (Deut. 17:17b; cf. 1 Kings 10:14), and many horses (Deut. 17:16; cf. 1 Kings 10:26–29). In these respects, Solomon's "heart was not wholly true to the LORD his God, as was the heart of David his father" (1 Kings 11:4).

If the success of the Davidic dynasty depends on obedience to Mosaic law, Solomon's disobedience gives little hope for the dynasty's future. In fact, if obedience to the Sinai covenant were the only grounds for a future, God would have every right to bring the Davidic dynasty to an end. It is at this moment that another component in the longevity of the Davidic dynasty shines through: "I will not tear away all the kingdom, but I will give one tribe to your son, for the sake of David my servant and for the sake of Jerusalem that I have chosen" (1 Kings 11:13). As the united nation will soon divide into Israel and Judah, God's faithful commitment to David is unmistakable. There is only one dynasty in Judah throughout its history, regardless of a king's corruption, but in Israel there are nine dynasties. The "lamp of David" will continue to burn in Jerusalem due to God's unconditional commitment to uphold his promise to David.[11]

Thus, there is an ideal that God's king is to be faithful to the LORD within the framework of the Mosaic law. There is also, however, an unmatched faithfulness evident in the LORD's long-suffering commitment to the promises he made to David, even amid his own anger with Solomon (1 Kings 11:9).

Summary

In Kings, Solomon emerges as a "greater David." On the one hand, he is *greater* than David in several ways: (1) the idyllic nature of his dominion extends beyond David's; (2) his divinely endowed wisdom enables him to display justice that surpasses the statements about David executing justice; (3) though David desired it, Solomon is the one who builds a temple for the LORD. On the other hand, Solomon is also a greater *sinner* than David. Although David and then God urge Solomon to obey the commands of Moses (e.g., 1 Kings 2:2–4; 3:14; 9:4–9), Solomon fails by worshiping other gods, by establishing high places for them, and by violating all of the prohibitions in Deut. 17:14–20. In this respect, Solomon was not like his father, David (1 Kings 11:4), yet this contrast with David highlights how obedience to Torah is a central ideal in the author's conception of the ideal king. Thus, through the positive and negative portrayals of Solomon, the following elements contribute to the book's royal

---

11. For a helpful exploration of the tension between God's faithfulness to David and expectations of covenant obedience, see Lovell, "Shape of Hope."

ideal: extensive dominion, justice through wisdom, temple-centeredness, and obedience to Torah.

The Josianic Ideal

In the aftermath of Solomon's failure, Kings narrows its focus. Its primary aim is to evaluate whether subsequent kings in Israel and Judah did what was "evil" or "right" (*yāšār*) in the eyes of the LORD. Through these evaluations, it is possible to construct another dimension of the book's ideal king.

What Makes a King "Evil"?

The prominent "sin of interest" after Solomon is idolatry. After all, if Solomon failed due to idolatry and the nation divides because of it, idolatry should be of utmost concern. The first king of the North, Jeroboam, receives this message from God: "If you . . . do what is right in my eyes by keeping my statutes and my commandments, as David my servant did, I will be with you and will build you a sure house, as I built for David" (1 Kings 11:38). This is an astounding promise: God is willing to do for Jeroboam what he did for David if Jeroboam obeys the commands of God. Jeroboam's first move as king, however, is to set up golden calves in Dan and Bethel (12:26–29), so it is clear that Jeroboam is disobeying the chief of God's commands by worshiping through idols. Jeroboam's line swiftly ends, and over the course of Israel's 208-year existence, not one of its nineteen kings receives a positive evaluation.[12] The primary reason these kings of Israel are evil is that they follow the idolatrous course set by Jeroboam.[13] Even shifts in rulership through nine different dynasties do not change the idolatrous ways of Israel and its kings. Eventually, Israel ends up in exile, and the narrator's lengthy justification (2 Kings 17:7–23) of such punishment can be boiled down to one reason: idolatry. It is not the fact that these kings were not from the line of David that made them "evil"; God was willing to give Jeroboam the same destiny as David. What makes a king of Israel "evil" is his perpetual idolatry.

---

12. One possible exception is Jehu, who is affirmed for doing right in killing Ahab's family, but he too walked in the sins of Jeroboam (2 Kings 10:30–31).

13. Immediately after stating that a king "did what was evil in the sight of the LORD," the author nearly always mentions how that king followed or did not depart from "the sins of Jeroboam" (Nadab [1 Kings 15:30]; Baasha [15:34]; Zimri [16:19]; Omri [16:26]; Ahab [16:31]; Jehoram [2 Kings 3:3]; Jehu [10:31]; Jehoahaz [13:2]; Jehoash [13:11]; Jeroboam II [14:24]; Zechariah [15:9]; Menahem [15:18]; Pekahiah [15:24]; Pekah [15:28]).

Among the nineteen kings of Judah, all from the line of David, eleven are deemed "evil."[14] It is idolatry and the worship of other gods that makes these eleven "evil." Rehoboam builds high places, sets up Asherim, and establishes cult prostitutes (1 Kings 14:22–24), and his son Abijam follows suit (15:3). Next, Jehoram (2 Kings 8:18) and Ahaziah (v. 27) follow the idolatrous ways of the kings of Israel, including Ahab, who promotes the worship of Baal. Ahaz (16:3–4) too follows the kings of the North, but he even stoops to child sacrifice. The worst of them all is Manasseh (21:2–9), who rebuilds altars for Baal (like Ahab) and worships all the host of heaven. What is more, although the writer targets only idolatry and worshiping other gods when evaluating the other kings, Manasseh's involvement in shedding innocent blood across Jerusalem is mentioned twice (21:16; 24:4). Amon (21:20–22) is idolatrous like his father. Judah's four final kings are said to be evil like their fathers. Since all their fathers violated the command requiring exclusive, nonidolatrous worship, Jehoahaz (23:32), Jehoiakim (v. 37), Jehoiachin (24:9), and Zedekiah (v. 19) must have done the same. As with the kings of Israel, so with the kings of Judah: idolatry and the worship of other gods is the key factor in what makes a king "evil." If we look at this from the inverse, these negative portrayals, as was the case with Solomon, teach that exclusive faithfulness to YHWH is an essential component in the ideal king of 1–2 Kings.

What Makes a King "Right"?

As for the positive assessments of kings in the book of Kings, there is a single common denominator between all eight of the kings who are deemed to "do right in the eyes of the LORD" (1 Kings 15:11; 22:43; 2 Kings 12:2; 14:3; 15:3, 34; 18:3; 22:2): nonidolatrous, exclusive faithfulness to YHWH. Asa's heart was "wholly true to the LORD" (1 Kings 15:14), as was that of his son Jehoshaphat (22:43). Through the instruction of the priest Jehoiada, Joash (Jehoash) was faithful to YHWH (2 Kings 12:2–3), with three generations of kings "doing what was right in the eyes of the LORD like their father": Amaziah (14:3), Azariah (15:3), and Jotham (15:34). Hezekiah "held fast to the LORD" (18:6), and Josiah "turned to the LORD with all of his heart" (23:25). Although there are other characteristics that figure in what makes a king "good" in Kings, the common denominator is that the king shows exclusive

---

14. Ten kings of Judah are said to "do evil in the eyes of the LORD": Rehoboam (1 Kings 14:22), Jehoram (2 Kings 8:18); Ahaziah (8:27); Ahaz (16:2); Manasseh (21:2); Amon (21:20); Jehoahaz (23:32); Jehoiakim (23:37); Jehoiachin (24:9); Zedekiah (24:19). Abijam is not directly described as "evil," but one may presume he was because he is said to be like his father Rehoboam.

allegiance to YHWH. The reason for such an emphasis on this factor makes good sense in a book that begins with Solomon succumbing to the entrapments of idolatry and worship of other gods. According to the outlook of Kings, the linchpin—the foundation for kingship—is exclusive faithfulness to the LORD; all else unravels if a king is idolatrous or worships other gods.

The *common denominator* approach to deciphering the ideal king of 1–2 Kings is just a start. In Josiah, one finds a more complete picture of the ideal king.[15] Several observations support this notion. First, at the conclusion of the account of Josiah's reign, the narrator states: "Before him there was no king like him, who turned to the LORD with all his heart and with all his soul and with all his might, according to all the Law of Moses, nor did any like him arise after him" (2 Kings 23:25). With this statement, it is apparent that the author of Kings wishes readers to interpret Josiah as the pinnacle of the kingship ideal. Second, a comparison of Josiah with the descriptions of the other "good" kings supports viewing Josiah as offering the most complete portrait of the book's ideal king. As the following chart displays, nothing positive is affirmed in another "good" king that cannot also be said of Josiah, yet only Josiah has all these qualities. King Josiah is the total package.

Figure 5.1

Characteristics of the "Good" Kings of Judah

Good King	Explicit Reference to Torah Obedience	Temple Focus	Religious Reform	
			Remove high places	*Remove idols and other gods*
Asa		1 Kings 15:15		1 Kings 15:12–13
Jehoshaphat		like Asa (1 Kings 22:43)		like Asa (1 Kings 22:43)
Jehoash		2 Kings 12:4–16		
Amaziah	2 Kings 14:5–6			
Azariah (Uzziah)	like Amaziah (2 Kings 15:3)			
Jotham	like Azariah (2 Kings 15:34)	2 Kings 15:35		
Hezekiah	2 Kings 18:6		2 Kings 18:4	2 Kings 18:4
Josiah	2 Kings 23:2–3	2 Kings 22–23	2 Kings 23:8, 19–20	2 Kings 23:4–20

There are three predominant characteristics in the Josianic ideal. First, the king is to obey the instructions of Moses. Sure, Amaziah is said to have obeyed Torah by not putting children to death for the sins of their parents

15. Lovell, "Shape of Hope," 13–14.

(2 Kings 14:5–6), and even Hezekiah is said to have not "depart[ed] from following [the LORD], but kept the commandments" (18:6). Of Josiah, however, we read of his dramatic response of contrition upon hearing God's word (22:11–13), which God acknowledges ("because your heart was penitent, and you humbled yourself before the LORD, . . . and you have torn your clothes and wept," v. 19). Josiah then institutes a renewal of the covenant between the nation and God, with a promise to keep all of God's commandments (23:1–3). He even reinstitutes the Passover "as it is written in this Book of the Covenant" (vv. 21–23). In light of David opening Kings by commanding Solomon to obey God's commands given through Moses (1 Kings 2:2–3), Josiah is the culmination of the book's desire for royal obedience to Torah.

Second, the king is to prioritize the temple, acknowledging that God's royal presence within Israel is of utmost importance. Yes, Asa brings gifts to the temple, only later to have to draw upon those resources to pay off invading Arameans (2 Kings 15:15, 18). Jehoash, who was mentored by a priest, took steps toward ensuring that money collected at the temple would be used for its repairs, but he too would use the temple treasury to appease Aram (12:4–18). Jotham built an upper gate for the temple (15:35). Josiah exceeds them all. He not only makes repairs to the temple (22:3–7); he also prioritizes the word of the One who dwells in the temple. Josiah gathers the entire community at "the house of the LORD" to renew the covenant as they read from the book found "in the house of the LORD" (23:2). Furthermore, he purges foreign gods from the temple and dismisses corrupt priests in response to the Torah (vv. 4–5). Josiah exemplifies the ideal that a king should order the nation around the LORD's presence in the temple and summon their response to the instruction deriving from the temple.

Third, the ideal king will lead the way in religious reform, often in conjunction with the priests. The first six "good" kings did not remove the "high places" from Judah (1 Kings 15:14; 22:43; 2 Kings 12:3; 14:4; 15:4, 35), but finally Hezekiah (2 Kings 18:4) and Josiah (23:8, 19–20) do. Hezekiah's reforms led him to remove high places, breaking down their pillars and cutting down the Asherah. Apparently, in Judah, people were committing idolatry with the bronze snake of Moses, so he destroyed that too. Although Hezekiah's religious reforms were more extensive than those before him, they pale in comparison to Josiah's. Josiah pursues a wide-ranging reform. Positively, he leads Judah in covenant renewal with YHWH (vv. 1–3) and promotes the celebration of Passover at the temple in Jerusalem (vv. 21–23). Negatively, he eradicates anything tainted by deviant worship. Cultic objects and high places associated with Asherah, Baal, and the host of heaven are destroyed, including those established by previous kings (Ahaz, Manasseh, and Solomon; vv. 12–14). Horses dedicated to the sun were removed (v. 11). Josiah even dismisses faithless priests (v. 5). Indeed, the purge reaches even into Israel (vv. 15–20). As exemplified in the account of Josiah, an ideal king will pursue religious reform that directs the community toward pure worship in Jerusalem, summons the people to obedience to Torah, and eliminates any hint of worship that deviates from nonidolatrous, exclusive worship of YHWH.

The Josianic Ideal and Messianic Expectation

After the reign of Solomon, the book's litmus test is whether a king upholds or deviates from the nonidolatrous, exclusive worship of YHWH. In the cases of all nineteen kings of the North and eleven kings of Judah, deviation from the norm is the reason they are said to "do evil in the eyes of the LORD." Those eight Davidic kings who do what is "right in the eyes of the LORD" share a common feature: they worship the LORD alone, in a nonidolatrous fashion. Although this is what qualifies a king as "upright," the portrayal of King Josiah extends this ideal in three further ways. The ideal king (1) is obedient to the law of Moses, (2) prioritizes the temple, and (3) institutes religious reform across the nation.

To what extent is this Josianic ideal "messianic"? First, clearly the book of Kings is crafted with the ideal of Josiah in mind, as the depiction of prior kings prepares for a culmination of the book's ideals in Josiah. Whoever wrote Kings—with its final form certainly exilic or early postexilic—wanted to portray what kingship should be and did so during a time when there was no king. The book does not merely provide a narrative of why Israel and Judah fell; it also presents the ideals of what kingship should be. Second, Josiah's premature death at Megiddo at the age of thirty-nine is jarring. David's and Solomon's reigns of forty years were each longer than the entire life of Josiah. In an account that depicts the wonders of his reign, the abrupt end to Josiah, who dies in a battle that was not his own, is disorienting for the reader. Could the shock of his death promote hope for a greater Josiah? Third, Josiah is unable to alter God's anger against Judah; exile became irrevocable prior to his reign, and even Josiah's faithfulness could not alter this (2 Kings 23:26–27). Yet there may have been hope that after God's anger was appeased through exile, a Josiah-like king would reign without the threat of judgment looming on the horizon.[16]

---

16. See Lovell, who thinks this leads to hope in a king who would be able to remedy Judah's sin ("Shape of Hope," 15–20). Although this is a possibility, there is a tendency in the Bible to view exile as the means by which Judah's sins would be dealt with (cf. Lev. 26:42–43; Isa. 40:1–2).

Coordinating the Josianic Ideal with the Solomonic Ideal

How do Solomon and Josiah coordinate across the book? Due to Solomon's unraveling through false worship, the nearly exclusive interest in the remainder of the book is upon the religious character of the king. Countering Solomon's failure is what occupies the Josianic ideal; the ideal king will worship the LORD exclusively, obey his commands, promote religious reform, and prioritize the temple. These ideals found in Josiah correspond with some of the ideals evident in the Solomon narrative: obedience to the commandments and prioritization of God's temple. So, there is substantial overlap in terms of what the Solomon and Josiah narratives convey regarding the royal ideal.

In Solomon, however, features emerge that receive virtually no attention in the remainder of Kings—namely, the notion of a wise king who establishes justice. As one moves beyond 1 Kings 1–11, key terms for wisdom and justice do not occur in the rest of the book. Wisdom terms, such as the words for "wisdom" (*ḥokmâ*; 3:28; 4:29, 30, 34; 5:12; 10:4, 6–8, 23–24; 11:41), "wise" (*ḥākām*; 2:9; 3:12; 5:7), "to be wise" (*ḥākam*; 4:31), and "to understand" (*bîn*; 3:9, 11, 12), do not occur in association with any other king in 1–2 Kings. Furthermore, it is quite a surprise that the verb "to judge" (*šāpaṭ*; 1 Kings 3:9, 28; 7:7) and the nouns "justice" (*mišpāṭ*; 3:11; 7:7; 10:9) and "righteousness" (*ṣədāqâ*; 3:6; 10:9) are virtually absent from the rest of Kings in reference to the king's role in bringing about justice. The only exception is a brief statement in 2 Kings 15:5: "And Jotham the king's [Azariah's] son was over the household, governing [*šāpaṭ*] the people of the land."

If the emphasis on the "wisdom" and "justice" exemplified by Solomon is part of the royal ideal of Kings, why is it missing in the portrayals and evaluations of the bad and good kings in the rest of the book? First, this shows how the fundamental priority for a king in the outlook of the entire book is nonidolatrous, exclusive worship of the LORD. Given that Solomon failed in this regard, with immense consequences, it is understandable that the rest of Kings will focus on this criterion when assessing subsequent kings. All else unravels if faithfulness to the LORD is missing. Second, the brief mention of Jotham "governing" (*šāpaṭ*) the people (2 Kings 15:5) suggests that the book of Kings presumes that establishing a just society continues to be an important role of the king. Third, the Solomonic ideal of a wise king who establishes justice contributes to royal messianic expectations elsewhere in the Old Testament, as we will see in our chapters on Isaiah and Jeremiah. Books such as Proverbs and Ecclesiastes also affirm this ideal by associating wisdom with the Davidic king. Thus, it is best to view the Solomonic and Josianic ideals as complementary rather than conflicting. Although the most important tasks of the ideal king are to worship the LORD exclusively, prioritize the temple, and promote obedience to the commandments, there is also a desire for God to endow a king with wisdom to establish justice across an expansive dominion.

Exilic Perspective

Along with the Solomonic and Josianic ideals, the vantage point from exile at the conclusion of the book is significant in any construal of the nature of messianic expectation in Kings. The final story in Kings is brief and obscure, lending itself to various interpretations. After thirty-seven years in exile, Jehoiachin is set free from prison, is elevated above all other captive kings, receives new garments, and dines at the table of Babylon's new king, Evil-Merodoch (2 Kings 25:27–30). For Gerhard von Rad, by ending with this story, the author leaves the door of history open to the hope that God will yet continue to work through Davidic kingship.[17] For others, the story merely enables the book to end on a positive note, without providing any anticipation of restoration.[18] By itself, this passage is ambiguous, yet, when read in light of the narrative unfolding across the book, the passage holds out a flicker of hope that God will remain faithful to the line of David.[19] Several brief reflections below will clarify the sort of hope the passage promotes in light of the tension between the conditional and unconditional promises to the house of David in the book.[20]

Throughout the book, the predominant issue is the need for a king who will live faithfully toward the LORD and obey the Sinai covenant. As David said to Solomon, "Keep the charge of the LORD your God, walking in his ways and keeping his statutes, his commandments, his rules, and his testimonies, as it is written in the Law of Moses . . . that the LORD may establish his word

17. Gerhard von Rad, *Old Testament Theology*, trans. D. M. G. Stalker (Peabody, MA: Hendrickson, 2005), 1:343.

18. Mordechai Cogan and Hayim Tadmor, *II Kings*, AB 11 (Garden City, NY: Doubleday, 1988), 330. For others such as Jon D. Levenson, "The Last Four Verses in Kings," *JBL* 103 (1984): 353–61, the passage affirms hope in God's promises to David while also developing an outlook of assimilation within the new reality of exercising rule while subservient amid a more dominant nation. Similarly, see Long, *1 Kings*, 289, who interprets the passage as endorsing the need for exiles to get along with Babylon and cooperate. Walter Brueggemann, *1 & 2 Kings*, SHBC 8 (Macon, GA: Smyth & Helwys, 2000), 608–9, states: "Hope, elusive and emancipatory, is a refusal to accept an end, a refusal to give Nebuchadnezzar the final word, a refusal to think that our defeats have in them the defeat of holiness, a refusal as it is more recently, to give Hitler a posthumous victory. And so the boy king, now middle-aged, eats and waits, not knowing. The scene is so Jewish."

19. Provan, "Messiah in the Books of Kings," 72.

20. Provan, "Messiah in the Books of Kings," 73–74.

that he spoke concerning me, saying, 'If your sons pay close attention to their way . . . you shall not lack a man on the throne of Israel'" (1 Kings 2:3–4; cf. 9:4–9). Solomon, eleven kings of Judah, and all nineteen kings of Israel fail in this respect, and this failure results in the exile of Israel and Judah. There is no longer a Davidic king on the throne in Jerusalem when the book ends. Given such an emphasis on the necessity of obedience, it is jarring that the book ends with a favorable mention of Jehoiachin, a king who was said to have done "what was evil in the sight of the LORD" (2 Kings 24:9). Whatever sort of hope the story of Jehoiachin dining at table with Babylon's king might offer, it is certainly not that Jehoiachin is a royal exemplar of obedience who experiences favor from God.

Although the conditional nature of God's relationship with kings is predominant in 1–2 Kings, God's unwavering, merciful commitment to the line of David is a subtheme throughout the book. This is apparent in several ways. First, although there are nine dynasties in the North, there is only one—the Davidic—in the South. Second, God reiterates his commitment to his promises to David throughout the checkered history of Davidic kings. After God announces that Jeroboam will soon reign, God does not give Judah over to him, telling him, "Yet to [Solomon's] son I will give one tribe, that David my servant may always have a lamp before me in Jerusalem" (1 Kings 11:36). Although Solomon's successors Rehoboam and then Abijam do evil like Solomon, God gives Abijam a lamp in Jerusalem "for David's sake" (15:4). Indeed, even after Jotham plunges into the great sins of Ahab, we are told: "Yet the LORD was not willing to destroy Judah, for the sake of David his servant, since he promised to give a lamp to him and to his sons forever" (2 Kings 8:19).

God's faithfulness to the line of David seems unwavering throughout Kings, even when Davidic kings worship other gods. God seems committed to having a lamp of David in Jerusalem forever! Yet after countless warnings about the consequences of disobedience, the unfathomable happens. God irrevocably commits to destroying Judah due to Manasseh's depravity (2 Kings 21:11–14)—even Josiah cannot avert God's anger (23:26–27). How can we reconcile God's unwavering commitment to the Davidic dynasty with his decision to wipe Jerusalem clean? The answer to this tension comes through the Jehoiachin story, which closes the book. The conditional elements in God's relationship with Davidic kings, as David expressed in 1 Kings 2:2–3, explain how it is that God can remove the lamp of David from Jerusalem through Babylon.[21] Yet the subtheme of God's enduring commitment to David

---

21. Lovell, "Shape of Hope," helpfully explores the tensions between the conditional and unconditional aspects of coordination of the Davidic and Sinai covenants in Kings. See also

is not extinguished with exile. Even when there is no king on the throne in Jerusalem, God's merciful commitment to the line of David extends to an evil king in exile (Jehoiachin) from the line of David. God's merciful commitment will triumph over the failures of the Davidic kings. Lissa Wray Beal captures the sentiment here well: "In the change of Jehoiachin's fortunes, might the promise of an eternal dynasty granted to David remain (2 Sam. 7:15–16; 1 Kings 8:25–26)? Will the punishment leveled against the Davidic house truly not last forever (1 Kings 11:39)? Will the Davidic lamp (1 Kings 11:36; 15:4; 2 Kings 8:19) burn once again in Jerusalem? The openness of Jehoiachin's story to the future keeps these possibilities alive."[22] As we look to Jehoiachin, we see a dim ember, a slight signal that God's commitment to the line of David has not ended.

If the story of Jehoiachin keeps alive hope in God's *unconditional* faithfulness toward the house of David, what about God's *conditional* expectations for a Davidic king? Negatively, the failure of the kings to uphold God's expectations results in exile and the absence of a king on the throne in Jerusalem. Positively, however, Josiah is an example of faithfulness, an example of what could be. His premature death and inability to alter God's plans of exiling Judah create a dissatisfaction and discontent in a reader, a desire for godly kings like Josiah to reign for length of days for the good of the nation. Josiah's actions and fate prompt an expectation that a king like Josiah will again reign in Judah. Thus, the conditional and unconditional dynamics in promises associated with David in Kings continue through the figure of Josiah and the story of Jehoiachin. In Jehoiachin, we find God's enduring commitment to the line of David in spite of disobedience (unconditional), while the Josiah narrative invites hope for a king who is faithful to God's (conditional) expectations. The hope remains that through God's faithfulness, a Davidic king will again reign in Jerusalem, a king whose heart fully aligns with God.[23]

Conclusion

We began this chapter by pondering whether ideals can endure amid failure. In 1–2 Kings, human kingship ultimately leads both Israel and Judah into exile. Through stories of failure and glimmers of success, a portrait of an

---

Joseph, *Portrait of the Kings*, 77–105, where she looks at the conditional overlay upon the unconditional promises to David within 1–2 Kings.

22. Lissa M. Wray Beal, *1 & 2 Kings*, ApOTC 9 (Nottingham: Apollos, 2014), 530–31.

23. For a less optimistic view of the book's conclusion, see Goswell, "King and Cultus," 170–71.

ideal king emerges. With regard to wisely administering justice, prioritizing the temple, and extending Israel's dominion, Solomon is a greater David. Negatively, however, Solomon's failure to obey the commands of Moses, particularly in his worship of other gods, makes him a greater sinner than David. Due to the consequences of Solomon's false worship, the rest of Kings uses nonidolatrous, exclusive faithfulness to YHWH as the litmus test for whether a king is evil or upright in God's sight. In Josiah, the fullest manifestation of faithfulness to YHWH is seen in his centralization of worship and his enactment of religious reforms across Judah, leading the nation to renew its covenant commitment to obey the law of Moses. Although Josiah is an exemplar in faithfulness, exile is Judah's fate. Without a king on the throne in Jerusalem, a glimmer of hope emerges at the close of the book when Jehoiachin experiences favor in exile. What is the ideal that endures beyond the failure plotted across the book? For one, Davidic kingship can only survive due to the unfailing, merciful commitment of the LORD to the house of David. Second, God's ideal king will worship the LORD exclusively, prioritize the temple, and promote obedience to the commandments, while establishing justice through divinely endowed wisdom across the kingdom.

Postlude: Canonical Reflections

A genealogy introduces Matthew's account of Jesus Christ, the son of David. The kings within Jesus's lineage conclude with Jehoiachin (a.k.a. "Jechoniah," 1:11), and then Jehoiachin serves as the transitional ancestor to an exilic lineage that ends in Jesus, "who is called Christ" (v. 16). Although there are "good" kings in the lineage, such as David, Hezekiah, and Josiah, there are wicked kings as well, such as Jotham, Ahaz, and Manasseh. At the end of Kings, Jehoiachin's elevation by Evil-Merodoch is no guarantee that God will reestablish the line of David upon the throne. By selecting Jehoiachin as the transitional king in Matthew's genealogy, rather than Zedekiah, Matthew could be indicating that God's faithfulness to the line of David in the story of Jehoiachin has been proven. Hope in God's faithfulness to David, even throughout the darkness of exile, is vindicated in the birth of Christ.

Along with bearing witness to the faithfulness of God to his promises to David in Christ, the book of Kings bears witness to the Solomonic and Josianic ideals as manifest in Jesus Christ. As for obedience to the Torah of Moses and the promotion of obedience toward it, Jesus both embodies and demands a righteousness that exceeds that of the Pharisees (Matt. 5:20). From his consecration as a child (Luke 2:39) to his victory over Satan's temptations in the wilderness (4:1–13) and to his prominence as a teacher of the law of Moses (Matt. 7:28–29), Jesus is a messiah whose obedience to Torah, instruction of Torah, and summoning of others toward obedience is unmatched. What is more, his wisdom is unmatched (13:54), and his zeal for the temple of the LORD is unrivaled, as he cleanses the temple and presents his own body as the temple of God (John 2:13–22). Although Jesus does not assume a throne in Jerusalem, his life and ministry certainly accord with and fulfill the ideal king projected by 1–2 Kings.

6

Royal Messianic Expectations
in Isaiah

Many Christians expect there to be countless promises of a royal Messiah in Isaiah. After all, passages from Isaiah figure prominently in the New Testament, in Handel's *Messiah*, and in Christmas cantatas. This creates the impression that Isaiah must be full of messianic promises. The truth of the matter, however, is that only nineteen out of 1,292 verses qualify as promises of a future king from the line of David: 9:1–7, 11:1–10, 16:5, 32:1.[1] Although these passages are extremely important, this reminds us that foretelling a Davidic king fits within a larger aim of the book of Isaiah—namely, the primary role of the future Davidic king is to be an agent of the Divine King to implement and uphold justice within society amid the establishment of God's kingdom.

The Big Picture of Isaiah

Across Isa. 1–66, three lead agents play important roles in the establishment of God's kingdom. While Christians profess that ultimately Jesus embodies what

---

This chapter draws heavily on Andrew T. Abernethy, *The Book of Isaiah and God's Kingdom: A Thematic-Theological Approach*, NSBT 40 (Downers Grove, IL: IVP Academic, 2016), chap. 4. Used by permission. See the final two-thirds of that chapter for a more extensive treatment of messianic hopes that includes the servant and anointed messenger in Isaiah.

1. The contrast between faithless Ahaz and faithful Hezekiah in Isa. 7 and 36–37 could warrant further attention. We will only note here that the verse specification of 9:1–7 in English Bibles is 8:23–9:6 in the MT. Below, it will become apparent why we do not include Isa. 7:14; 42:1–9; 49:1–6; 50:4–9; 52:13–53:12; or 61:1–3 as anticipating royal messianic figures.

the book of Isaiah envisions for all three of these lead agents, we are not certain that these agents were known to be the same individual throughout Isaiah. By maintaining the distinct vocation of each agent, a reader can appreciate the wide range of ministries Jesus fulfills in his first and second comings. In Isa. 1–39, the primary era in view is preexile, during the time of Assyria. Judah's kings and communities are corrupt, so the Holy Divine King will bring forth a purging judgment. Out of the ashes of judgment, hope arises for a brand of Davidic kingship that differs drastically from that of the Judean rulers of the time—the hope is for a king who will ensure justice across society (9:6–7; 11:2–5; 16:5; 32:1). In Isa. 40–55, the scene shifts to exile.[2] The central hope of this section of the book is that exiles will return to Zion to rebuild the temple and that God will return as the saving King (40:9–11; 52:7). An important question, however, is how a persistently sinful nation can remain in the presence of this saving God. The lead agent of Isa. 40–55 is a prophetic, priestly servant who will reconcile Israel and the nations back to God through the servant's suffering (49:1–6; 50:4–9; 52:13–53:12). In Isa. 56–66, the setting is back in the land, with temple rebuilding underway (66:1–2). The message of this section is eschatological, centering on the climactic coming of God to Zion as the international King in both judgment and salvation. The lead agent in this final part of the book is an eschatological messenger (61:1–3), whom God empowers to declare the good news of the in-breaking of God's kingdom.

Due to similarities between these lead agents and due to Jesus's fulfillment of all of these, some evangelical scholars tend to conflate the three lead agents as if the book of Isaiah had only one lead agent, the Messiah, in mind.[3] The problem with this is that the unique vocation of each agent becomes obscured. It seems better to retain distinctions between the roles of these agents. To remedy the social ills of preexilic corruption, promises that God will use a king to establish justice are fitting. To restore exiled Israel and the nations to God, God empowers a suffering servant to atone for their sins amid calls to repentance. To comfort the weary who await a greater restoration for Zion, God will mobilize a messenger to declare the freeing news of God's kingdom. The following diagram illustrates this schema:

2. There is, of course, debate over the authorship and composition of Isaiah. The best path in reading the book is to read it in view of the particular setting a given part of the book invites one to adopt. Due to the recurring mention of Assyria in chaps. 1–39, of Babylon in chaps. 40–55, and of postexilic concerns amid the rebuilding of the temple (66:1–2), the book has clearly been formed to address eras in Israel's history that stretch from preexile to exile to postexile to the new heavens and new earth.

3. E.g., J. Alec Motyer, *The Prophecy of Isaiah: An Introduction and Commentary* (Downers Grove, IL: InterVarsity Press, 1993); Gary V. Smith, *Isaiah 1–39*, NAC 15A (Nashville: B&H, 2007); Gary V. Smith, *Isaiah 40–66*, NAC 15B (Nashville: B&H, 2009).

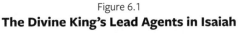

Figure 6.1
The Divine King's Lead Agents in Isaiah

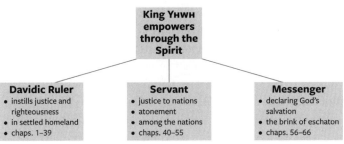

Depending on how one defines "messianic," all these lead agents could be worthy of attention. Since our study focuses on *royal* messianic expectations, our attention below will be limited to the Davidic ruler from Isa. 1–39.

Is Immanuel a Davidic Ruler?

Since Matt. 1:23 quotes Isa. 7:14, many expect the "Immanuel" passage to speak directly of a future Davidic king. Upon reading 7:1–17, however, one realizes that the primary time frame is the 730s BCE, when Aram and Israel threaten Judah. By the time the woman Isaiah speaks of has given birth and named her son "Immanuel" and he has grown old enough to discern good from evil, two things will take place: (1) the lands of the threatening nations will be laid waste (v. 16), and (2) the child will be living in the aftermath of desolation in the land, as indicated by his eating a nomadic diet of curds and honey (vv. 15, 17; cf. vv. 22–25).

The question arises whether this child is one of Ahaz's, of Davidic lineage.[4] If so, Isaiah refers to a woman in Ahaz's harem as the "virgin" or "young woman" who will conceive and give birth to this child. If the child is Davidic, the promise indicates that God will remain faithful to uphold the line of David during a time of threat and raise up a faithful king who knows right from wrong, unlike Ahaz.[5] The problem with conclusively identifying the child in

---

4. For those who interpret the child as a descendant of Ahaz, see Joseph Blenkinsopp, *Isaiah 1–39: A New Translation with Commentary*, AB 19 (New York: Doubleday, 2000), 232–34; G. Smith, *Isaiah 1–39*, 206–14; H. G. M. Williamson, *Variations on a Theme: King, Messiah and Servant in the Book of Isaiah*, Didsbury Lectures 1997 (Carlisle, UK: Paternoster, 1998), 104–9.

5. Some appeal to editorial placement of 9:1–7 in this context as inviting a reading of 7:14 as Davidic. See Ronald E. Clements, "The Immanuel Prophecy of Isa. 7:10–17 and Its Messianic Interpretation," in *Die Hebräische Bibel und ihre zweifache Nachgeschichte: Festschrift für Rolf*

7:14 with the house of David is the impossibility of reconciling the date of this child's birth (ca. 733 BCE) with that of Hezekiah's, as Hezekiah would have already been nine years old at the time of this event (2 Kings 16:2; 18:2). Additionally, since 7:1–17 deals with the king and the nation, the sign in 7:14–16 need not be limited to God's plans with the house of David—"Immanuel" is a sign of God's action within that international crisis. Furthermore, we find out virtually nothing about who this child is or what he will do;[6] what is most significant is the child's role as a temporal marker that points to the acts of God. Since chronology based on 1 and 2 Kings is extremely complicated, we cannot rule out that 7:14 has a child from the line of David in view (i.e., Hezekiah),[7] but the primary emphasis is on "Immanuel," *God with us* in judgment and deliverance (cf. 8:8, 10) instead of on qualities inherent in the child itself.[8] The name Immanuel contributes to the larger aims of Isa. 6–8: showing how God, the Holy King, can be trusted to be "Immanuel"—God with us—as he brings about judgment and deliverance, initially in the context of the Assyrian crisis.[9]

How does the interpretation offered above of Isa. 7:14 correspond with its use in Matt. 1:23? Some suggest a "double-fulfillment" model,[10] but "prediction-fulfillment" does not quite capture what is happening in Isaiah and Matthew. With Paul Wegner and James Hamilton, we prefer the concept of

---

Rendtorff zum 65. Geburtstag, ed. Christian Macholz and Ekkehard Stegemann (Neukirchen-Vluyn: Neukirchener Verlag, 1990), 230–35. Williamson, *Variations on a Theme*, 104, however, critiques Clements's view.

6. John Goldingay, *Isaiah*, NIBC (Peabody, MA: Hendrickson, 2001), 64; John H. Walton, "Isa. 7:14: What's in a Name?," *JETS* 30 (1987): 296; Rikk E. Watts, "Immanuel: Virgin Birth Proof Text or Programmatic Warning of Things to Come (Isa. 7:14 in Matt 1:23)?," in *From Prophecy to Testament: The Function of the Old Testament in the New*, ed. Craig Evans (Peabody, MA: Hendrickson, 2004), 96; Paul Wegner, "A Re-examination of Isaiah IX 1–6" *VT* 42 (1992): 127.

7. Another prominent view is that "Immanuel" is one of the children of the prophet; see John Oswalt, *The Book of Isaiah: Chapters 1–39*, NICOT (Grand Rapids: Eerdmans, 1986), 213; Craig Blomberg, "Interpreting Old Testament Prophetic Literature in Matthew: Double Fulfillment," *TJ* 23 (2002): 21; James Hamilton, "'The Virgin Will Conceive': Typological Fulfillment in Matthew 1:18–23," in *Built upon the Rock: Studies in the Gospel of Matthew*, ed. Daniel Gurtner and John Nolland (Grand Rapids: Eerdmans, 2008), 236–38. Williamson, *Variations on a Theme*, 103, points out, however, that the ʿalmâ (virgin) is unlikely to be called such if she had already given birth (Shear-Yashub). Christopher Seitz, *Isaiah 1–39*, IBC (Louisville: Westminster John Knox, 1993), 62–63, rules out the option that Immanuel is one of Isaiah's children by observing a number of crucial differences between Immanuel and Isaiah's children.

8. Similar sentiments are expressed throughout Gregory Goswell, "Royal Names: Naming and Wordplay in Isaiah 7," *WTJ* 75 (2013): 97–105.

9. Walton, "Isa. 7:14," 295.

10. Blomberg, "Interpreting Old Testament Prophetic Literature in Matthew."

"patterning."[11] The pattern evident in Isa. 7:14 of God being with his people in both judgment and salvation corresponds with and escalates climactically at the incarnation of Jesus Christ.[12] It is not necessary for 7:14 to refer in its original context to a coming Davidic king in this understanding, for it is the pattern of God being with his people that is most prominent, though as it turns out God chooses to show himself to be "with us" in an escalating fashion through an actual virgin birth,[13] taking on flesh, and being born into the line of David.

Characteristics of the Davidic Ruler

While human rulers are failing to bring about justice (Isa. 1:23) and kings are dying (6:1), wavering in faith (7:11–17), and even faltering and being warned of exile (chap. 39), the prophet holds forth hope that God will establish a better Davidic king. There are four main passages in Isaiah that speak of a future Davidic ruler (9:6–7; 11:1–10; 16:5; 32:1). Instead of working through each passage, we will identify several key characteristics in Isaiah's depiction of this lead agent.

The Davidic Ruler Is God's Agent

Isaiah 9:1–7 and Isa. 11 make it abundantly clear that the Davidic ruler is an extension of God's own plan and work.[14] In 9:1–7, the centrality of God is evident in several ways. To begin, throughout the passage, God is the primary actor.[15] In verse 1, it is God who will reverse Galilee's fortunes; he brought contempt to the area in the past but will make it glorious in the

---

11. Wegner, "Re-examination of Isaiah IX 1–6," 134–35; Hamilton, "Virgin Will Conceive," 232–34, 239–46. Hamilton primarily uses the term "typology," but he often coordinates this with patterning.

12. For an emphasis on judgment in the Immanuel sign and its outworking in Matthew, see Watts, "Immanuel."

13. Debate revolves around how to understand the term translated as "virgin" ('almâ). While the term can refer to a "virgin," it has the broader meaning of a girl who is mature enough to marry and have children. Even if the 'almâ in 7:14 were a virgin at the time of Isaiah's message, her ensuing pregnancy would certainly have been understood as stemming from intercourse with a man. For an overview, see Wegner, "A Re-examination of Isaiah IX 1–6," 106–15; Gordon Wenham, "Bĕtûlāh, 'A Girl of Marriageable Age,'" VT 22 (1972): 326–47.

14. God's primacy is also apparent in 16:5 (divine passive: "A throne will be established") and in 32:1.

15. For similar reflections, see Gregory Goswell, "The Shape of Messianism in Isaiah 9," WTJ 77 (2015): 102–6.

future. In verses 3–4, the uses of the second person in addressing God place
a spotlight on God:

> You have multiplied the nation;
>   you have increased its joy;
> they rejoice before you
>   as with joy at the harvest.
> . . . .
> For the yoke of his burden,
>   and the staff for his shoulder,
>   the rod of his oppressor,
>   you have broken as on the day of Midian.

God is the reason behind the great increase in joy that the people are
experiencing,[16] and the first among three reasons (9:4, 5, 6) for such joy is
the recognition that God himself has delivered them from the oppressor (v. 4).
What is more, when verses 6–7 reflect on the joy the Davidic ruler brings to
the nation, the focus on God continues with the use of passive verbs:

> For to us a child is born,
>   to us a son is given. (v. 6a)

This is surely an instance of the divine passive; God is the one who has given
this child.[17] The final clause in verse 7 crystallizes this theocentric emphasis by
stating: "The zeal of the LORD of hosts will do this." God is the chief actor
throughout verses 1–7, and he is the one who will provide the Davidic ruler.

Additionally, the primacy of God is apparent in Isa. 9:1–7 when we consider
the names that the ruler will bear: "Wonderful Counselor, Mighty God, Everlasting Father, Prince of Peace" (v. 6b). There are two ways of understanding
these names. One position holds that these names describe the Davidic king.
At the crux of this position is the interpretation of the second name: "Mighty
God." Since "mighty God" refers to God in 10:21, interpreters like John
Oswalt and J. Alec Motyer understand "mighty God" to be indicating that
the Davidic ruler will be divine.[18] Since this king is divine, the other titles
make sense, for this divine-human king will naturally have counsel far beyond
human counsel, be everlasting in fatherly care, and establish peace. There are,
however, a few challenges with this view. For one, it seems unlikely that Isaiah

---

16. Goswell, "Shape of Messianism," 103, displays how the hymnlike nature of this passage
exposes that "it is the deeds of YHWH that are celebrated."

17. Goswell, "Shape of Messianism," 105; Williamson, *Variations on a Theme*, 33.

18. Oswalt, *Book of Isaiah*, 245–47; Motyer, *Prophecy of Isaiah*, 102–5.

would conceptualize a Davidic ruler as being divine. While a king can be described as a "son" of God (2 Sam. 7:14; Ps. 2:7), the language of "sonship" does not describe the ontological essence of the king as divine but rather the nature of God's covenantal relationship with that king. As J. J. M. Roberts argues, "divine sonship" is metaphorical, even mythological, language that highlights how a human king could take up an office so dear to God and carry out God's plans in the world.[19] Another challenge with this position is that it overlooks how names work, which leads to the second way of understanding these names.

An increasingly favored view is that these names primarily describe God rather than the human king. The foundation of this position is recognizing how names work in Isaiah and the Old Testament.[20] Names often point to realities beyond the person bearing them. The names of Isaiah's children, Shear-Yashub ("a remnant shall return," 7:3) and Maher-Shalal-Hash-Baz ("swift is the plunder; fast is the pillage," 8:1), describe what Israel's experience will be, as do the names of Hosea's children—Lo-Ammi ("not my people"; Hosea 1:9) and Lo-Ruhamah ("no compassion," 1:6). Among these kinds of names are theophoric names, for they have a divine name in them, usually "el" or "yah." Eliezer ("God of help"), Elkanah ("God of grace"), Hezekiah ("YHWH is strong"), Isaiah ("YHWH saves"), Immanuel ("God with us"), and Ishmael ("God is hearing") are examples of names with a divine element in them. These names do not claim that the human bearing them is divine; instead, they say something about God. Similarly, it is probable that the names in Isa. 9:6 point to God, not to the essence of the human ruler. During this era of radical reversal from gloom to joyful glory (vv. 1–2), from oppression to freedom (v. 4), and from warfare to peace (v. 5), it is fitting for the Davidic king who rules during this peaceful time to bear these names; they point to the God who has brought about this glorious situation. The sight of an upright king ruling in Zion bears witness to God as the unsurpassable

19. J. J. M. Roberts, "Whose Child Is This? Reflections on the Speaking Voice in Isaiah 9:5," *HTR* 90 (1997): 115–29.

20. Paul Wegner, *An Examination of Kingship and Messianic Expectation in Isaiah 1–35* (Lewiston, NY: Mellen, 1992); John Goldingay, "The Compound Name in Isaiah 9:5(6)," *CBQ* 61 (1999): 239–44. Both Wegner and Goldingay divide these titles into two names. Wegner, *Examination of Kingship*, 111, suggests "wonderful planner [is] the mighty God; the Father of eternity [is] a prince of peace [or well-being]." Goldingay, "Compound Name," 243, advocates for "One who plans a wonder is the warrior God; the father forever is a commander who brings peace." Both are influenced by William L. Holladay, *Isaiah: Scroll of a Prophetic Heritage* (Grand Rapids: Eerdmans, 1978), 108–9, who advocates for three names, with the first and last describing the king and the middle being theophoric: "Planner of Wonders; God the war hero (is) Father forever; prince of well-being."

planner who has worked out his own plans wonderfully, while foiling the plans of the nations (cf. 8:10; 25:1; 29:14), as the mighty God who can save a remnant from the fiercest foe (10:21), as an everlasting father who has shown that his fatherly care and rule never cease (cf. 63:16; 64:8 [64:7 MT]), as the "prince (ruler) of peace" who brings about lasting peace, unlike those rulers at the time of Isaiah (cf. 3:14; 31:9; 34:12).[21] The names of this Davidic ruler, then, point beyond the human office to King YHWH, who has wondrously saved his people and established a Davidic ruler in their midst. Mighty indeed is God.

Thus, in Isa. 9:1–7, the prospect of a Davidic ruler fulfilling his office is something only God himself can make happen, as is evident in God serving as the chief actor in these verses. What is more, the very names that the Davidic ruler bears point beyond the human ruler to the Divine King who in his wisdom, might, fatherly care, and governance has put an end to war, brought joy to the nation, and placed a Davidic ruler on the throne. God, in his zeal, will bring this about.

Isaiah 11 also emphasizes God's involvement with an anticipated Davidic ruler. This is apparent in the imagery that opens this passage. While debate surrounds how best to understand the term often translated as "stump,"[22] the arboreal imagery unmistakably points to a reality when all that exists is a small sign of potential, for only a stump remains with a small sprout emerging from it. Just as God unexpectedly selects Jesse's youngest son, so Jesse's stump, which will be destroyed through imperial threat, will again bear fruit. God will again raise up a ruler from the line of Jesse. Additionally, the role of God's Spirit in 11:2 exposes how the Davidic king is God's agent:

> And the Spirit of the LORD shall rest upon him,
>   the Spirit of wisdom and understanding,
>   the Spirit of counsel and might,
>   the Spirit of knowledge and the fear of the LORD.

The term "Spirit" occurs four times in this verse. Just as God's Spirit is an indication of God's validation of David's rule (1 Sam. 16:13–14), so God's Spirit will do the same with the future ruler from Jesse's line.[23] What is more, God's Spirit is an extension of God himself that empowers and equips his agents for his purposes, such as when God grants his Spirit to builders of the

---

21. Goldingay, "Compound Name," 241–43; Wegner, *Examination of Kingship*, 112.

22. See Wegner, "Re-examination of Isaiah IX 1–6," 231–32.

23. Hilary Marlow, "The Spirit of Yahweh in Isaiah 11:1–9," in *Presence, Power and Promise: The Role of the Spirit of God in the Old Testament*, ed. David Firth and Paul Wegner (Downers Grove, IL: InterVarsity, 2011), 225.

tabernacle (Exod. 28:3) or judges (Judg. 3:10; 6:34; 11:29; 13:25; 14:6, 19). In Isa. 11, God's Spirit will endow the Davidic ruler with wisdom, which is vital for the task of ruling, as Solomon recognized and as is indicated by the final three uses of "the Spirit" here and by its correlation with wisdom. Thus, as in Isa. 9, so also in Isa. 11 the Davidic ruler is God's agent. These texts demand that we not place our hope in a human king; rather, hope resides in God, the Divine King. If there ever would be a ruler from Jesse's line to reign, it would only be through the work of God and his empowering wisdom.

The Davidic Ruler and a Context of Deliverance

Another prominent feature of the Davidic king is that he will rule *after* deliverance from disaster. It is unclear, though, whether the future Davidic ruler is a deliverer in Isaiah. In Isa. 9:1–7, God is the one who has saved his nation from their enemies:

> For the yoke of his burden,
> and the staff for his shoulder,
> the rod of his oppressor,
> *you* have broken as on the day of Midian. (v. 4)

Coming to this passage after Isa. 6–8, we understand these oppressors to be Assyria. God will break his people free from their burden, as light shining in the darkness. What is not clear is whether Yhwh uses the Davidic ruler as an agent to bring about God's salvation. This is ambiguous because verses 6–7 are the last of three (vv. 4, 5, 6–7) explanations ("for" [*kî*]) given to clarify why joy has overtaken the nation (v. 3). Does the final explanatory clause, where a Davidic ruler is given by God, illumine the previous explanations, conveying the idea that it is through the Davidic ruler that God broke the rod of the oppressor (v. 4) and destroyed every garment of war (v. 5)? Or, is God's giving of a Davidic ruler one among three reasons given for the nation's joy? If the latter, the Davidic ruler is not understood as a savior figure, but instead is an agent for God in the aftermath of salvation.[24] What is certain in this passage is that God is receiving the glory for the nation's salvation (whether this was accomplished through a Davidic agent or not), and the description of the Davidic ruler emphasizes his role in the aftermath of salvation, as he promotes a peaceful, just kingdom.

24. See Gregory Goswell, "Isaiah 16: A Forgotten Chapter in the History of Messianism," *SJOT* 28 (2014): 96; Goswell, "Shape of Messianism," 101–10; Williamson, *Variations on a Theme*, 33–34.

In Isa. 11, it is only in verse 4b where there is the faintest suggestion that the Davidic ruler might be a deliverer:

> And he shall strike the earth with the rod of his mouth
> and with the breath of his lips he shall kill the wicked.

The parallel verses suggest the focus is upon the fair treatment of the powerless instead of delivering Israel from their enemies. The weapons in verse 4, "rod of his mouth" and "breath of his lips," are instruments of speech, so the upright decrees of this ruler will stand against the wicked. As Gary V. Smith puts it, "The aim is not to present a negative view of uncontrolled slaughter of wicked people, but to emphasize that everything will be guided by principles of justice."[25]

The literary placement of Isa. 9:1–7 and 11:1–9 further emphasizes the focus being upon a Davidic ruler who reigns in the aftermath of deliverance. As for 9:1–7, it comes just after gloomy reflections on life under judgment through Assyria (8:19–22). By placing after chapter 8 a passage full of hope in God's deliverance (9:1–5), capped off with a vision of a Davidic ruler reigning in peace (vv. 6–7), the prophet offers hope that an ideal ruler will emerge when judgment passes. As for 11:1–9, its placement after Isa. 10 develops further the vision for a Davidic ruler reigning in the wake of Assyria's demise. The mighty Assyria and its king will be cut down, just like the branches of a mighty tree are cut down with an ax (10:33–34), but a humble sprout will sprout from a stump (11:1) after Assyria falls.[26] Through arranging these texts in this way, the prophet offers a vision of the Davidic ruler that differs from J. R. R. Tolkien's vision set forth in *The Return of the King*. There Strider's (Aragorn) kingship becomes evident when he leads his forces victoriously and bravely against Sauron. In the book of Isaiah, God is the saving, warrior figure, and the Davidic king will reign in the aftermath of God's salvation.[27]

The Davidic Ruler Will Establish Justice and Righteousness

The chief task of the Davidic ruler in Isaiah is to be an agent of justice and righteousness. This feature appears in all four of the passages that speak

25. G. Smith, *Isaiah 1–39*, 273.
26. Willem Beuken, "'Lebanon with Its Majesty Shall Fall. A Sprout Shall Come Forth from the Stump of Jesse' (Isa. 10:34–11:1): Interfacing the Story of Assyria and the Image of Israel's Future in Isaiah 10–11," in *The New Things: Eschatology in Old Testament Prophecy; Fss. for Henk Leene*, ed. J. W. Dyk et al. (Maastricht: Uitgeverij Shaker, 2002), 17–33; Wegner, "Reexamination of Isaiah IX 1–6," 229–30; Williamson, *Variations on a Theme*, 52.
27. See Goswell, "Isaiah 16," 95–96.

explicitly of the Davidic agent. In Isa. 9:7 (9:6 MT), we read of the Davidic agent's purpose:

> Of the increase of his government and of peace
> > there will be no end,
> on the throne of David and over his kingdom,
> > to establish it and to uphold it
> *with justice and with righteousness*
> > from this time forth and forevermore.
> The zeal of the LORD of hosts will do this.

David's kingdom will be anchored in justice and righteousness. Isaiah 11:3–5 shares this vision.

> ³And his delight shall be in the fear of the LORD.
> He shall not *judge* by what his eyes see,
> > or decide disputes by what his ears hear,
> ⁴but *with righteousness* he shall judge the poor,
> > and decide *with equity* for the meek of the earth;
> and he shall strike the earth with the rod of his mouth,
> > and with the breath of his lips he shall kill the wicked.
> ⁵*Righteousness* shall be the belt of his waist,
> > and faithfulness the belt of his loins.

Isaiah 11 looks for a time when even those with no economic, political, and social capital will receive a fair hearing due to this king. The community at Isaiah's time was not "seeing" or "hearing" (6:10), but this king will have a perception of a different order, not being influenced by any deception or temptations that would thwart justice.[28]

Brief statements concerning the king in 16:5 and 32:1 display this same focus on justice:[29]

> Then a throne will be established in steadfast love,
> > and on it will sit in faithfulness
> > in the tent of David
> one who judges and seeks *justice*
> > and is swift *to do righteousness*. (16:5)

> Behold, a king will reign *in righteousness*,
> > and princes will rule *in justice*. (32:1)

---

28. Wegner, "Re-examination of Isaiah IX 1–6," 255; Williamson, *Variations on a Theme*, 49.

29. Goswell, "Isaiah 16," 97. See Williamson, *Variations on a Theme*, 62–72, who argues that the statement in 32:1 is more proverbial.

All four of these passages emphasize the Davidic ruler's role in establishing justice. "This role is bound up as closely as it is possible to imagine with the maintenance of 'justice' and 'righteousness,' terms which . . . stand as a sort of shorthand for the ordering of society as a whole in accordance with God's will."[30]

The emphasis on the Davidic ruler's role in establishing justice and righteousness is not surprising, for this is one of God's chief concerns in the book of Isaiah. The book opens in Isa. 1 with a summons for the audience to do justice and righteousness (1:16–17), a vision of God transforming an unrighteous city of corrupt leaders into a city of righteousness (vv. 21–26), and the promise to redeem Zion in righteousness and justice (v. 27). In Isa. 5, God laments how his vineyard, Judah and Israel, has not produced the justice and righteousness he had hoped for (v. 7). The powerful are squeezing out poor inhabitants and amassing houses and fields (vv. 8–9), are drunkards (v. 11), and ignore God's works (v. 12). Though injustice seems to be prevailing, an alternative destiny is stated in verses 15–16:

> [15]Man is humbled, and each one is brought low,
>   and the eyes of the haughty are brought low.
> [16]But the LORD of hosts is exalted in justice,
>   and the Holy God shows himself holy in righteousness.

In language reminiscent of Isa. 2, these verses assert that the tables will be turned, for there is no room for the pride of unjust humans when YHWH as king assumes his rightful place of exaltation. Significantly, it is in justice and righteousness that YHWH will be exalted. Scholars are divided between whether the "justice" and "righteousness" in view in 5:16 belong to YHWH or to humanity. In other words, will God be exalted when he acts in righteous judgment toward the unjust, or will God be exalted when his people act in justice and righteousness? The strength of the former position is the parallel with verse 15, where the contrast is between sinful humanity and God—God will be exalted in justice when he righteously levels prideful, unjust humanity.[31] The strength of the latter position is that "righteousness" and "justice" in verse 7 clearly refer to human behavior, so this might entail that the use of the terms in verse 16 refers to human action (cf. 1:17).[32] Actually, it may

---

30. Williamson, *Variations on a Theme*, 70.

31. H. G. M. Williamson, *A Critical and Exegetical Commentary on Isaiah 1–5*, ICC (London: T&T Clark, 2006), 375–76.

32. R. W. L. Moberly, "Whose Justice? Which Righteousness? The Interpretation of Isaiah v 16," *VT* 51 (2001): 55–68; Thomas L. Leclerc, *Yahweh Is Exalted in Justice: Solidarity and Conflict in Isaiah* (Minneapolis: Fortress, 2001), 61.

be unnecessary to bifurcate the two options: God may choose to enact his justice and righteousness through his agents. As R. W. L. Moberly puts it, "It is a basic prophetic axiom that YHWH acts in and through the actions of his servants. . . . Thus YHWH's actions of justice and righteousness may be seen precisely in the actions of justice and righteousness performed by those accountable to him."[33] God is committed to responding to injustice with his own justice and righteousness, and since the chief role of the Davidic ruler is to ensure justice and righteousness in 9:7 and 11:3–5, it is possible that we are to view him as an avenue through which God expresses his righteousness and justice amid his quest to set the world right.

As we have seen in chapters across this volume, God's plans to use human rule to establish justice and righteousness accord with the role David and his progeny undertook.[34] In 2 Sam. 8:15, we are told: "So David reigned over all Israel; and David administered justice and righteousness for all his people" (NASB).

After David (cf. 2 Sam. 15:6), King Solomon is also extolled in light of how God's wisdom enabled him to do "justice" (1 Kings 3:28). The queen of Sheba praises God for providing a king like Solomon to Israel to "execute justice and righteousness" (10:9). Even in a song of Israel, perhaps by Solomon, requests are made that God grant the king justice:[35]

> [1]Give the king your justice, O God,
>   and your righteousness to the royal son!
> [2]May he judge your people with righteousness,
>   and your poor with justice!
> [3]Let the mountains bear prosperity for the people,
>   and the hills, in righteousness!
> [4]May he defend the cause of the poor of the people,
>   give deliverance to the children of the needy,
>   and crush the oppressor! (Ps. 72:1–4)

While Jerusalem's kings consistently abuse their power and do not practice justice, Isaiah, along with Jeremiah (Jer. 23:5; 33:15), holds forth a vision of promise that is anchored deeply in Israel's history. During eras of injustice, the hope is that God will again use the office of David, as he has in the past, to bring about a just and righteous order to God's society. The result of the

---

33. Moberly, "Whose Justice?," 63.

34. Daniel Schibler, "Messianism and Messianic Prophecy in Isaiah 1–12 and 28–33," in *The Lord's Anointed: Interpretation of Old Testament Messianic Texts*, ed. P. E. Satterthwait, Richard S. Hess, and Gordon J. Wenham (Grand Rapids: Baker, 1995), 97–98.

35. Williamson, *Variations on a Theme*, 37–38.

just and righteous reign of the Davidic agent will be an era of great peace
(Isa. 9:7).

Conclusion

The hoped-for Davidic ruler in Isaiah has several characteristics. First, God
will establish and empower the Davidic king. Second, the Davidic agent will
rule during the era of salvation, when oppression and judgment have passed.
Third, the Davidic ruler will primarily serve as a vessel for establishing God's
justice and righteousness across society. While the church may tend to obsess
about messianic figures in the Old Testament and which passages do or do not
qualify, the book of Isaiah reminds us that such figures must be understood in
light of the purposes, reign, and person of God the King. The Davidic ruler
is chiefly an agent of God who establishes justice and righteousness through
God's Spirit during the era of salvation.

Postlude: Canonical Reflections

Who is the referent of these hopes (Isa. 9:1–7; 11:1–9; 16:5; 32:1)? Most of
these passages originally were understood in association with existing kings.[36]
As anchored as Isa. 1–12 is in the realities of the Assyrian era, it would be
quite possible to understand 9:1–7 and 11:1–9 to be applying to Hezekiah,
who ruled during a time when Sennacherib's armies were defeated, and later
to Josiah, who reigned during a time when Assyrian dominance was fading.
We find, however, that even within the book of Isaiah, Hezekiah introduces
a transition away from human kingship (Isa. 39).[37] Though Hezekiah does
not fulfill these expectations, Josiah emerges later as a strong candidate as he
pushes for reform, but he dies unexpectedly, resulting in a chain of kings who
fail in their task of promoting justice and righteousness (Jer. 22:11–17). With

36. For a chart of views, see Antti Laato, *Who Is Immanuel? The Rise and the Foundering of
Isaiah's Messianic Expectations* (Åbo: Åbo Academy Press, 1988), 2. Randall Heskett, *Messianism within the Scriptural Scrolls of Isaiah*, LHBOTS 456 (London: T&T Clark, 2007), 58–60,
83–132, does not think that 7:14, 9:1–17, or 11:1–9 were originally messianic, though he thinks
that they all take on a messianic flavor due to their placement in the book.

37. See Gregory Goswell, "Farewell to Davidic Kingship: The Meaning and Significance of
Isaiah 39," *ResQ* 61 (2019): 87–106. Some scholars emphasize the idealized portrayal of Hezekiah in Isaiah (e.g., Christopher Seitz, *Zion's Final Destiny: The Development of the Book of
Isaiah; A Reassessment of Isaiah 36–39* [Minneapolis: Fortress, 1991], 47–118), and others are
more scathing (James Kennedy, "Yahweh's Strongman? The Characterization of Hezekiah in
the Book of Isaiah," *PRSt* 31 [2004]: 383–97).

Isaiah's hopes that a Davidic ruler will arise in the aftermath of Assyria's rule dissolving and with the prospect of the exile of the house of David to Babylon concluding Isa. 1–39, there is a level of uncertainty concerning what to do with God's promises concerning a Davidic ruler. Just as Hezekiah and Josiah did not fulfill the expectations of Isaiah's Davidic promises, the postexilic era offers little clarity as well.

Jesus Christ offers an "amen" to these promises from Isaiah, though in an unexpected fashion. The New Testament opens by stating that Jesus is the Christ, "the son of David" (Matt. 1:1; cf. Luke 1:69; 2:4; 3:31), and he is referred to as "son of David" repeatedly (Matt. 9:27; 12:23; 15:22; 20:30, 31; 21:9, 15; Mark 10:47, 48; Luke 18:38, 39; Rom. 1:3). This connection between Jesus and David in the New Testament sits awkwardly, however, with the expectations of Isaiah. It was not during an era of salvation from political foes that Jesus came as a Davidic king, for Rome still was sovereign over Palestine before, during, and after Jesus came. Jesus did not sit on any throne in Jerusalem. It was likely for this reason that Jesus was mocked as "king" throughout his trial even to his final breath on the cross (Matt. 27:29, 37, 42). He did not fit the mold of the expected Davidic ruler, as cross and crown were irreconcilable. Jesus did, however, embody the Davidic king's commitment to justice and righteousness, as he confronted systems of injustice, particularly religious ones (Matt. 23:23; Luke 11:42), and as he astounded people with his wisdom (Matt. 13:54; Mark 6:2; Luke 2:40, 52). He was the light to the desolate areas around Galilee (Matt. 4:15). Though his rule during his first coming did not manifest itself as one might expect, Jesus's rule as the heavenly king is as the "Root of David" that has conquered, so Jesus, the Davidic king, issues decrees (Rev. 3:7) and unleashes God's justice into the world through the unfolding of the scroll (5:5; 22:16; cf. Isa. 11:1). In fact, when Jesus comes again, he will come as the ruler who will issue justice (Rev. 19:11) on behalf of his saints. So, in his resurrection and ascension, he indeed reigns upon the throne of David as the conquering king (Luke 1:32–33), and the realization of his mission for justice and righteousness will culminate when he comes again. Thus, the hopes for a Davidic ruler offer a canonical witness to Jesus's first and second comings as king, but his rule is realized in an unexpected fashion, which we believe stems from the unexpected fusion in the New Testament between Isaiah's expectations regarding the Davidic ruler and his expectations regarding the suffering servant.

7

The Death and Rebirth
of Kingship in Jeremiah

The darkest moment in the story line of the Old Testament is Jerusalem's
fall to Babylon. The land is ravaged. Those in the city starve. Jerusalem's
walls crumble. The temple burns to the ground. Women are raped. Priests
are killed. Survivors are exiled. The poor are left behind. No Davidic king
is on the throne. Imagine the spiritual and psychological turmoil of God's
people. Hadn't God chosen this city? Shouldn't God's glorious presence be
in the temple? Didn't God promise this land to our offspring? What benefit
is there in being God's covenant people if we end up starved, abused, and
slain? Didn't God promise that someone from David's line would always
reign upon the throne? The book of Jeremiah, along with Lamentations, is
the Old Testament's rawest window into the people's experiences and God's
involvement in this cauldron of suffering. The book of Jeremiah offers a divine
perspective on the ashes and aims to stoke remaining embers of faith in the
wake of Babylonian captivity.[1] In this chapter, we explore one of the crises
that the book of Jeremiah addresses—faith when there is no Davidic king.
This chapter begins with how the book of Jeremiah construes the death of

1. Many parts of the book of Jeremiah derive from before Jerusalem's fall, but Jeremiah's
ministry extends beyond the fall (chaps. 40–45), and the book reaches its final form in the exilic
or postexilic era. A recent trend in scholarship on prophetic literature is to grasp how books like
Jeremiah function as disaster and survival literature. See Louis Stulman and Hyun Chul Paul
Kim, *You Are My People: An Introduction to Prophetic Literature* (Nashville: Abingdon, 2010).

Davidic kingship before moving on to the book's promises of life beyond death for Davidic kingship. Davidic kingship is buried in unrighteousness through exile with the hope that it will be raised to life for righteousness.

The Death of Unrighteous Kingship

The book's opening chapter prepares for much of what will transpire as it relates to Davidic kingship throughout the book.[2] Three observations capture the royal dynamics at work within chapter 1. First, the opening three verses set Jeremiah's ministry during the reigns of Josiah, Jehoiakim, and Zedekiah. Throughout the book, Jeremiah speaks about, between, or during the reigns of these kings—Josiah (3:6), Jehoahaz (22:11–17), Jehoiakim (22:18–23; 25–26; 35–36), Jehoiachin (22:24–30; 24), and Zedekiah (27–29; 32–34; 37–39). Jeremiah's message is political, intersecting continually with these notorious kings. Second, chapter 1 states that Jeremiah will stand against these kings. God appoints Jeremiah "over nations and over kingdoms," and the programmatic words in the rest of the verse make the combative nature of his appointment clear:

> to pluck up and to break down,
> to destroy and to overthrow,
> to build and to plant. (1:10)

Primarily, Jeremiah will speak words that bring the nations and kingdoms—especially Judah—to ruin. Later in the chapter, God pictures Jeremiah like a fortified city, standing against Judah's kings, officials, priests, and people (v. 18). Although Jeremiah is assailed by Judah's leaders, God will ensure that the prophet and the word proclaimed will prevail (v. 19; cf. v. 12). Third, Judah's undoing comes at the hands of "kingdoms of the north," whose kings will "set [their] throne[s] at the entrance of the gates of Jerusalem" (v. 15). Thus, chapter 1 casts a shadow of incumbent doom for Davidic kingship that spreads throughout the book—Jeremiah will stand against those on the throne of David, and eventually foreign kings will displace Judah and its kings.

Jeremiah's indictments against Judah's kings paint a picture of their corruption. They are unjust, not ensuring justice for the orphan or the poor (5:28; 22:3). Even when they take steps to release Hebrew slaves, it does not

---

2. On the role of Jer. 1 as part of the book's scaffolding, see Martin Kessler, "The Scaffolding of the Book of Jeremiah," in *Reading the Book of Jeremiah: A Search for Coherence*, ed. Martin Kessler (Winona Lake, IN: Eisenbrauns, 2004), 57–66.

stick—it was more expedient for the powerful to maintain a system of injustice (34:8–16). They violate the Sabbath (17:22–27). They are shepherds who lack care for their flock (22:22; 23:1). Most damning is the Davidic kings' unwillingness to heed God's word spoken through Jeremiah. The nadir of this motif is when King Jehoiakim slowly shreds the scroll of Jeremiah's words, burning it piece by piece in the fire (chap. 36). During Zedekiah's time, the narrator tells us, "Neither [Zedekiah] nor his servants nor the people of the land listened to the words of the LORD that he spoke through Jeremiah the prophet" (37:2). This becomes apparent as King Zedekiah keeps Jeremiah around, hoping that God's pronouncement will change; Zedekiah will only heed the prophetic word if the prophet tells him what he wants to hear (chaps. 37–38).[3] Thus, Jeremiah is God's mouthpiece, confronting Judah's wayward kings;[4] their only hope "is that they bow to [God's sovereign] word and respond to the prophet."[5]

Due to this level of rebellion against God and his word, Jeremiah announces that Davidic kingship will crumble. As disgrace awaits a caught thief, so disgrace awaits the kings, officials, priests, and prophets of Judah due to their idolatry (Jer. 2:26). Judah's king will lose heart as Babylon, the ravenous lion, comes (4:6–9). The bones of dead kings will be unearthed (8:1), and Jehoiakim's burial will be like that of a donkey (22:19). They will become drunk from the wine of God's wrath (13:12–14). Just as livestock await their time of slaughter, so Judah's shepherds have a time of slaughter awaiting them (25:34). This judgment will bring an end to the Davidic dynasty in Jerusalem. We are told that both Jehoiakim (36:30) and Jehoiachin (22:30) will not have any offspring to sit upon the throne of David. Indeed, as Zedekiah flees Jerusalem, is captured, sees his heirs slaughtered, and has his eyes torn out (39:5–7), the five-hundred-year history of a Davidic king ruling in Jerusalem comes to an end.

The shocking condemnation and fall of the house of David in Jeremiah figures importantly within what Louis Stulman describes as "the dismantling of Judah's cherished beliefs and social structures."[6] Judah wrongly presumes

---

3. See, however, Robert P. Carroll, *From Chaos to Covenant: Prophecy in the Book of Jeremiah* (New York: Crossroad, 1981), 153–54, who offers a more positive appraisal of Zedekiah than the book's narrator offers (Jer. 37:2).

4. For more on how the depiction of failing kings corresponds with the failure of people and leader alike in Jeremiah, see Andrew T. Abernethy, "Theological Patterning in Jeremiah: A Vital Word through an Ancient Book," *BBR* 24 (2014): 149–61, esp. 157–61.

5. Carroll, *From Chaos to Covenant*, 157.

6. Louis Stulman, *Jeremiah*, AOTC (Nashville: Abingdon, 2005), 15. For more on the aim of Jeremiah to unravel Israel's symbolic world, see Louis Stulman, "The Prose Sermons as Hermeneutical Guide to Jeremiah 1–25: The Deconstruction of Judah's Symbolic World," in

that they are immune from divine punishment due to having a Davidic king. As Walter Brueggemann states, "The royal-temple ideology, embodied in temple liturgy and royal claims of legitimacy, asserted and imagined that it was an indispensable vehicle for God's way and blessing in the world. It was therefore assumed that the royal-temple apparatus was immune to covenant sanctions and to God's judgment."[7] This outlook can appropriately be referred to as "sociolatry."[8] An idolatrous, unjust, God-ignoring era of Davidic kingship ends with no one on the throne for David in Jerusalem. Instead, the rulers of Babylon are now sitting in the gates of Jerusalem (Jer. 39:3; cf. 1:15).

Hope for Righteous Kingship

The bleak backdrop across Jeremiah enables promises of hope to shine forth with stunning radiance.[9] Among a wider orbit of promises, the book of Jeremiah looks forward to a time when Davidic kingship will resume. Jeremiah uses two prominent metaphors to depict a future for Davidic kingship: "shepherds" and a "sprout."[10] As we look at each of these, it will become apparent that at the center of these hopes is YHWH himself, who will bring about his purposes for his people through a new era of Davidic kingship.

Shepherds

The use of the shepherding motif to refer to kingship is not new with Jeremiah. Some twelve hundred years earlier King Hammurabi describes himself as "the shepherd, called by Enlil."[11] Within the Old Testament, Ps. 78 recounts how God calls a shepherd boy, David, to shepherd Israel with integrity of heart

---

Troubling Jeremiah, ed. A. R. Diamond and K. M. O'Connor, JSOTSup 260 (Sheffield: Sheffield Academic, 1999), 34–63.

7. Walter Brueggemann, *A Commentary on Jeremiah: Exile and Homecoming* (Grand Rapids: Eerdmans, 1998), 6.

8. On this terminology, adopted from Peter Ivan Kaufman, see David J. Reimer, "Redeeming Politics in Jeremiah," in *Prophecy in the Book of Jeremiah*, ed. Hans M. Barstad and Reinhard G. Kratz, BZAW 388 (Berlin: de Gruyter, 2009), 121–36.

9. Marvin A. Sweeney, "Jeremiah's Reflection on the Isaian Royal Promise: Jeremiah 23:1–8 in Context," in *Uprooting and Planting: Essays on Jeremiah for Leslie Allen*, ed. John Goldingay, LHBOTS 459 (New York: T&T Clark, 2007), 309.

10. There are other promises of the restoration of Davidic kingship in Jeremiah that will not be dealt with in this chapter: Jer. 17:25; 30:9, 21.

11. Theophile J. Meek, trans., "The Code of Hammurabi," in *Ancient Near Eastern Texts relating to the Old Testament*, ed. James B. Pritchard, 3rd ed. (Princeton: Princeton University Press, 1969), 164. For more on the background of the shepherd metaphor for rulers in the ancient world, see Timothy Laniak, *Shepherds after My Own Heart: Pastoral Traditions and Leadership in the Bible*, NSBT 15 (Downers Grove, IL: IVP Academic, 2006), 42–74.

(vv. 71–72). Since shepherds have the responsibility of guiding, protecting, feeding, and caring for the flock, "shepherd" is a ripe metaphor for rulers in the ancient world. Two passages use the shepherd metaphor to envision the renewal of Davidic kingship: Jer. 3:15 and 23:1–4.

JEREMIAH 3:15

In the first promise of hope in the book, God declares, "Return, O faithless children. . . . And I will give you shepherds after my own heart, who will feed you with knowledge and understanding" (3:14–15). Several observations unveil the message of this verse. First, the verb translated as "feed" by the ESV should be translated as "shepherd":[12] "I will give you shepherds after my own heart who will *shepherd* [r'h] you with knowledge and understanding." The verb r'h uses the same root as the noun "shepherd" earlier in the verse, and shepherding involves more than feeding, as guidance, protection, and care can be connoted too. By translating the verb more broadly, one enables the verb to call to mind other aspects important to a ruler's task. Also, the adjusted translation makes it clearer that "with knowledge and understanding" modifies the nature of the shepherding, not what the flock will eat.[13] So, what will it look like for these shepherds to shepherd with knowledge and understanding? The answer will become apparent below.

Second, the shepherds will be in alignment with God. God will give shepherds after his own heart (Jer. 3:15). This, of course, calls to mind 1 Sam. 13:14, where Samuel conveys God's intention to seek a king "after his own heart"; Saul did not listen to God's word, so a king after God's heart would be one that does obey. Similarly, here, the shepherds, who are "after [God's] own heart," signal that being in tune with God and his will is fundamental to kingship under God. The literary context within Jer. 2–3 reinforces this interest in allegiance to the LORD. God's once-devoted bride left him for worthless idols (2:5), and Judah's and Israel's "shepherds" contributed to this idolatry: "The shepherds transgressed against me" (v. 8). Since "shepherds" in verse 8 is the nearest reference to the term in 3:15, the contrast between shepherds who rebel against God (2:8) and shepherds who are "after my own heart" (3:15) is stark. Judah has been doing something unheard of—changing their gods (2:10–11). They have forsaken a fountain of living waters for broken cisterns (v. 13). They are playing the whore with the gods under every tree

12. William L. Holladay, *Jeremiah 1: A Commentary on the Book of the Prophet Jeremiah, Chapters 1–25*, Hermeneia (Philadelphia: Fortress, 1986), 60; J. A. Thompson, *The Book of Jeremiah*, NICOT (Grand Rapids: Eerdmans, 1980), 202.

13. In Hebrew, "understanding" is an infinitive absolute. The LXX interprets "knowledge" (*dēʻâ*) as if it were an infinitive absolute.

(v. 20), like a donkey in heat lusting after the gods (v. 24). Their kings, officials, priests, and prophets turn to trees and stones as gods (2:26–27; 3:6). Jeremiah 3:15 offers hope of a time when Judah will be led by shepherds whose hearts align with God. What is more, in verse 17, these shepherds will rule during a new era of God's expanded presence in Jerusalem. The era of the ark will be over, and Jerusalem will be called "the throne of the LORD" (v. 17). With the LORD as King, these shepherds' hearts will align with God, their King, carrying out his will and leading the people to align with God.

Third (and related), exclusive devotion to the LORD leads the shepherds to uphold justice and righteousness. When read in isolation, it is unclear what Jeremiah means by describing the shepherds as shepherding "with knowledge and understanding" in 3:15. Similar phraseology, however, occurs in 9:24: "Let him who boasts boast in this, that he *understands* and *knows* me, that I am the LORD who practices steadfast love, justice, and righteousness in the earth." In 9:24, knowledge and understanding of God pertain to recognizing God's nature as one who does (ʿśh) steadfast love (ḥesed), justice (mišpāṭ), and righteousness (ṣədāqâ). If 9:24 illumines what "with knowledge and understanding" means in 3:15, these shepherds will carry out their task of shepherding in light of God's commitment to steadfast love, justice, and righteousness.

Fourth, these shepherds are simply one feature among several within the era of restoration. Repentance will usher in a new era for Zion, where God will bring many to dwell (Jer. 3:14). Just as God promised to the patriarchs (Gen. 28:3; 35:11; 48:4; Lev. 26:9), those in Zion will be fruitful and multiply (Jer. 3:16). As noted above, God's throne will be there (v. 17). God, then, is establishing these shepherds to shepherd those in Zion during an era of abundant blessing.

In summary, after a dark era when shepherds were sinning against God (Jer. 2:8), 3:15 expects a time when the Divine King will designate shepherds who will care for the people by maintaining justice and by guiding them to live before God as their King.

JEREMIAH 23:1–4

Jeremiah 21:11–23:8 is the book's lengthiest discourse on the topic of Davidic kingship. After criticizing numerous Judean kings for injustice (more on this under "A Righteous Sprout" below), the prophet writes,

> [1]"Woe to the shepherds who destroy and scatter the sheep of my pasture!" declares the LORD. [2]Therefore thus says the LORD, the God of Israel, concerning

the shepherds who care for my people: "You have scattered my flock and have driven them away, and you have not attended to them. Behold, I will attend to you for your evil deeds, declares the LORD. ³Then I will gather the remnant of my flock out of all the countries where I have driven them, and I will bring them back to their fold, and they shall be fruitful and multiply. ⁴I will set shepherds over them who will care for them, and they shall fear no more, nor be dismayed, neither shall any be missing, declares the LORD." (23:1–4)

The rhetoric within these verses is potent. To begin, the flock that the shepherds mistreat is God's flock. The kings of Judah—the "shepherds"—are not autonomous figures that exercise dominion over their own people. Instead, these shepherds are appointees, designated to care for the flock of another, God's flock. "Yahweh is the shepherd to whom undershepherds report."[14] These shepherds have destroyed "the sheep of *my* pasture, declares the LORD" (23:1). Those responsible for "*my* people . . . have scattered *my* flock" (v. 2). Make no mistake about it; God will not stand to the side and allow leaders to abuse his people.

Additionally, God supervenes as the sovereign shepherd. On the one hand, God never ceases to be shepherd, even when the woeful shepherds are in charge. The people remain God's flock all along, and God drove (*ndḥ*) his flock to exile as the shepherds were driving (*ndḥ*) them away (Jer. 23:2, 3). On the other hand, God takes over exclusively as shepherd to reverse the impact of those other shepherds who have scattered and destroyed God's flock. From exile, God will gather his flock, restore it to its pasture, and enable it to be fruitful and multiply (v. 3). Although the shepherds did not "attend" (*pqd*) to the flock, God takes on this characteristic when he "attends" (*pqd*) to the evil deeds of the shepherds in judgment (v. 2).

Finally, having punished the first round of shepherds and supervened as chief shepherd to return his flock from exile, God will establish a new era of shepherds over his people. Under the care of these shepherds, God's flock will neither fear nor be unprotected (Jer. 23:4).

Thus, in Jer. 23:1–4, God intervenes to reverse the circumstances of his flock. Gone will be the days of oppression, fear, and scattering. God will punish the wicked shepherds, regather his flock from among the nations, and establish a new order of shepherds who will shepherd with care.

As we look at the next metaphor of kingship, it will become apparent that the preeminent quality of these shepherds is a commitment to justice and righteousness.

14. Leslie Allen, *Jeremiah*, OTL (Louisville: Westminster John Knox, 2008), 257.

A Righteous Sprout

Two passages in Jeremiah use the image of a "righteous sprout." We will consider each in turn.

JEREMIAH 23:5–6

Flowing directly out of the promises about a new era of shepherds in Jer. 23:1–4, there is hope for a new king, a "righteous sprout":

> [5]Behold, the days are coming, declares the LORD, when I will raise up for David a righteous Branch, and he shall reign as king and deal wisely, and shall execute justice and righteousness in the land. [6]In his days Judah will be saved, and Israel will dwell securely. And this is the name by which he will be called: "The LORD is our righteousness." (23:5–6)

In view of our aims, we will dig into several items from these verses to illumine the passage's meaning. First, "the days are coming" is not eschatological in the fullest sense of the term. Instead, as is the case throughout the prophets, the expression "the days are coming" looks primarily to the time when a new era will begin after exile. As J. A. Thompson puts it, "The forthcoming era was not seen as something reserved for the eschatological era, but as coming at the end of a particular era that had been marked by a failure in the functioning of the kingship in the context of the covenant."[15] For instance, "the days are coming" in verses 7–8 refers to a time when people will take oaths in view of God being the one who brought them out of the lands he had scattered them to in exile (cf. 30:3; 31:27; 48:12; 49:2).

Second, "righteous Branch" is a common translation of *ṣemaḥ ṣaddîq* in English Bibles (ESV, NIV, NASB, HCSB, and KJV). The major problem with translating *ṣemaḥ* as "branch" is that a *ṣemaḥ* often springs from the ground (Gen. 19:25; Ps. 65:9–10; Isa. 4:2; 61:11; Ezek. 16:6–7).[16] So, it does not refer to a branch growing from a tree, as a noun like *ḥōṭer* does in Isa. 11:1 ("A Sprout will come forth from the stump of Jesse," authors' trans.).[17] The noun

---

15. Thompson, *Book of Jeremiah*, 491; see also Allen, *Jeremiah*, 259; William McKane, *Jeremiah*, ICC (Edinburgh: T&T Clark, 1986), 1:561.

16. For a survey of the uses of the noun, see Wolter H. Rose, *Zemah and Zerubbabel: Messianic Expectations in the Early Postexilic Period*, JSOTSup 304 (Sheffield: Sheffield Academic, 2000), 94–99.

17. E.g., Brueggemann, *Commentary on Jeremiah*, 207; Elmer A. Martens, *Jeremiah* (Scottdale, PA: Herald, 1986), 149. See Sweeney, who argues that Jeremiah wrote 23:1–8 via conscious reflection on Isa. 11:1–16. He notes many thematic correspondences between these texts, yet he does not explore what the differences between "Sprout" (Isa. 11:1) and "sprout" (Jer. 23:5) entail. Sweeney, "Jeremiah's Reflection," 308–21.

ṣemaḥ refers more generally to vegetative growth. This leads Wolter Rose to translate the phrase *ṣemaḥ ṣaddîq* in Jer. 23:5 as "righteous growth."[18] In our opinion, "growth" is too generic since it can connote nonvegetative growth, so we prefer the term "sprout" as it captures the idea of vegetative growth that is not limited to a tree and thus is preferable here.[19]

The question, then, is what the metaphor of "sprout" accomplishes in this context. Insight into the function of "sprout" comes from the end of Jer. 22, where the LORD declares:

> Write [Jehoiachin] down as childless,
>   a man who shall not succeed in his days,
> for none of his offspring shall succeed
>   in sitting on the throne of David
>   and ruling again in Judah. (22:30)

Jehoiachin, who is dethroned by Nebuchadnezzar and led into exile, will not have a child who sits on the throne of David; there is no hope that Jehoiachin's family will return to the throne (cf. 36:30). Even though Zedekiah son of Josiah, from the line of David, takes over as king, the slaughtering of Zedekiah's sons removes any trace of David's seed from the book of Jeremiah (39:6). The Davidic lineage appears dead in promise and reality. Yet the metaphor of the "sprout" signals that "out of devastation, life would sprout, albeit barely."[20] Just as vegetation grows from an unseen seed beneath the surface of the ground, so God's promise to David will spring to life when all seems lost.

Third, some scholars translate *ṣaddîq* as "legitimate" or "rightful" over against "righteous." William Holladay supports this view because a Phoenician inscription, dating to 273–272 BCE, uses the phrase to mean "legitimate branch" to assert the legitimacy of a king. According to him, then, Jeremiah is drawing upon "a general Northwest Semitic term for the legitimate king."[21] By reconstructing a historical context where people questioned the legitimacy of Zedekiah, Holladay concludes that the play on Zedekiah's name with *ṣaddîq* points to a time when there will be no ambiguity as to the legitimacy of the "legitimate *ṣemaḥ*."[22]

---

18. Rose, *Zemah and Zerubbabel*, 119.

19. So, William R. Osborne, *Trees and Kings: A Comparative Analysis of Tree Imagery in Israel's Prophetic Tradition and the Ancient Near East*, BBRSup 18 (University Park, PA: Eisenbrauns, 2018), 142.

20. Stulman, *Jeremiah*, 214.

21. Holladay, *Jeremiah 1*, 618.

22. Holladay, *Jeremiah 1*, 617–18; Thompson, *Book of Jeremiah*, 489–90.

Although Holladay's view is possible, the literary context strongly supports interpreting *ṣaddîq* as "righteous."[23] In the following line, "righteous sprout" is the subject of verbs clearly pertaining to establishing justice across society. "He shall . . . deal wisely [*śkl* in *hiphil*]" (Jer. 23:5) corresponds with the expectation in 3:15 that shepherds after God's heart will shepherd with "knowledge and understanding [*śkl* in *hiphil*]."[24] The relationship we identified between wisdom and righteousness in 3:15 (cf. 9:24) is apparent in the rest of 23:5: "He . . . shall execute ['*śh*] justice [*mišpāṭ*] and righteousness [*ṣədāqâ*] in the land." The linguistic correspondence between the adjective *ṣaddîq* and the noun *ṣədāqâ* indicates that the "sprout" is *ṣaddîq* because he will establish *ṣədāqâ* across the land. In fact, the promise of the "righteous sprout" in 23:5–6 is the culmination of a focus on justice and righteousness across chapters 21–22. God has been calling on unrighteous kings to "do ['*śh*] justice [*mišpāṭ*] and righteousness [*ṣədāqâ*]" (22:3; cf. *mišpāṭ* in 21:12), just as Josiah had "[done; '*śh*] justice [*mišpāṭ*] and righteousness [*ṣədāqâ*]" (22:15).[25] Shallum (22:11–17), Jehoiakim (22:18–23), Jehoiachin (22:24–30), and Zedekiah (21:11–22:10) all stand condemned for oppression, greed, and not defending the poor and needy. Having "buried" Judah's kings due to their unrighteousness in chapters 21–22, Jeremiah "resuscitates" Davidic kingship in 23:5–6.[26] Jeremiah 23:5–6 declares that there will be a "righteous sprout" who will be and do what God desires from Davidic kings—instill justice and righteousness across society. In this view, the play on Zedekiah's name suggests that "Zedekiah is not the righteous king; another will come in the future."[27] Within this literary context, the primary sense of *ṣaddîq* calls to mind "righteousness," and, if legitimacy is also called to mind through the term, it would be secondary.

23. Some scholars argue that it calls both legitimacy and social righteousness to mind through intentional ambiguity. See Peter C. Craigie, Page H. Kelley, and Joel F. Drinkard Jr., *Jeremiah 1–25*, WBC 26 (Dallas: Word, 1991), 330.

24. Bernard Gosse, "La nouvelle alliance et les promesses d'avenir se référant à David dans les libres de Jérémie, Ezéchiel, et Isaie," *VT* 41 (1991): 422, also observes the association between Jer. 3:15 and 23:5.

25. It is striking how this is the only positive mention of Josiah in Jeremiah. For reflections on how differently 2 Kings portrays Josiah in comparison to Jeremiah, see J. G. McConville, *Judgment and Promise: An Interpretation of the Book of Jeremiah* (Leicester, UK: Apollos, 1993), 54–58.

26. The language of burial and resuscitation in this context derives from McConville, *Judgment and Promise*, 58.

27. Tremper Longman III, *Jeremiah, Lamentations*, NIBC (Peabody, MA: Hendrickson, 2008), 160. For an insightful reflection on similarities between Jer. 23:5–6 and Isaiah's servant songs, see Christopher Begg, "Zedekiah and the Servant," *ETL* 62 (1986): 393–98. He argues that Zedekiah serves as a foil to the servant of the LORD. On the other hand, some argue that 23:5–6 was written to present Zedekiah as the "righteous sprout." See Reimer, "Redeeming Politics in Jeremiah," 127–35; Sweeney, "Jeremiah's Reflection," 308–21.

Fourth, the theme of "righteousness" emerges at the end of verse 6 when we learn the king's name: "The LORD is our righteousness [ṣədāqâ]." As with "Immanuel" in Isa. 7:14 and the titles in 9:6, this is a theophoric name, a personal name that conveys something about God.[28] In other words, this is not a statement about the nature of the king (i.e., that the king will be YHWH). This becomes clear in Jer. 33:16, where the same name applies to the city of Jerusalem. Just as Jerusalem is not considered to be divine when called "the LORD is our righteousness," so it is with the "righteous sprout." By bearing this name, the "righteous sprout" will point to YHWH as the one who vindicates his people and establishes righteousness across the land through the Davidic king.

In summary, Jer. 23:5–6 offers hope beyond the apparent death of the line of unrighteous Davidic kings in exile; David's dynasty would emerge as a "righteous sprout," as God's vehicle for promoting justice and righteousness across the land.

JEREMIAH 33:14–26

Although Jer. 33:15–16 is nearly identical to 23:5–6, its function within 33:14–26 enriches our understanding of the promise of a "righteous sprout" in several ways.[29] For one, the restoration of Davidic kingship is part of God's restoration of other forms of leadership. Jeremiah 33:17–18 explicates the promise of the "righteous sprout": "David shall never lack a man to sit on the throne of the house of Israel, and the Levitical priests shall never lack a man in my presence." The restoration of the priests is also included in 33:21. As God promises a new era for Israel after exile, both Davidic kings and Levitical priests are important fixtures in the era of renewed leadership, as we will see in books like Zechariah and 1–2 Chronicles. An implication of this is that the "righteous sprout" should be understood not as an individual messianic figure but as the institution of kingship itself; Jeremiah 23:5–6 and 33:15–16 promise a renewal of the office of Davidic kings. This does not mean that God could not in his providence fulfill this expectation with a singular Davidic king, but one must be cautious not to impose such an expectation upon the original author and readers of the text.

Additionally, Jer. 33 offers one of the strongest commitments by God to the Davidic covenant. In verses 19–26, God appeals twice to his commitment to creation to underscore his faithfulness to the line of David. With a tone of

---

28. Thompson, *Book of Jeremiah*, 490–91; Holladay, *Jeremiah 1*, 619.

29. The LXX does not include Jer. 33:14–26. McConville, *Judgment and Promise*, 101–2, observes that the theology of 33:14–26 is already part of chaps. 30–32, so its absence would not have a major impact if one prioritized the LXX tradition. For the unique coordination of theological strands in 33:14–26, see Dane Ortlund, "Is Jeremiah 33:14–26 a 'Centre' to the Bible? A Test Case in Inter-canonical Hermeneutics," *EQ* 84 (2012): 119–38.

irony, God says that when he breaks his covenant with day and night, along with heaven and earth, then he will break his covenant with David (vv. 20–21, 25–26). Since he will never do the former, the implication is that he will never break his covenant with David. A challenge emerges, however, since it seems like God indeed breaks his covenant with David when the throne of David is empty after Zedekiah. Had not God promised through Nathan that David would always have a descendant upon the throne (2 Sam. 7:13, 16)? On this point, Hayyim Angel offers a helpful insight: "Psalm 89, and many people in Jeremiah's generation, understood Nathan's prophecy that the Davidic kingdom would last 'forever' to mean 'always.' However, Jeremiah prophetically explains that no other dynasty ever will supplant the Davidic kingship, even if there is no king on the throne."[30] When one considers how Jer. 22 ends with an indictment of childlessness for the Davidic line and then develops into hope for the renewal of the Davidic dynasty as shepherd and a righteous sprout in chapter 23, Angel's statement captures Jeremiah's attempt to frame the tension surrounding the absence of a Davidic king upon the throne. The throne remains established and reserved for the Davidic dynasty, even when the dynasty seems to have run its course. As long as day and night and heaven and earth continue, God's people can be sure that God's commitment to the line of David endures. Someday the dynasty of David will sprout to life.

Summary

In Jeremiah, the two most prominent metaphors for encapsulating a rebirth of the Davidic dynasty are shepherds and a sprout. By using the metaphor of the "shepherd," Jeremiah captures the absence of care by Judah's kings and promises an era when God as the chief shepherd will install new shepherds to care for his flock (3:15; 23:1–4). The metaphor of the "sprout" unearths a promise that seems buried; a "righteous sprout" will grow out of the lifeless ground of a decimated line of Davidic kings. In both metaphors, the chief purpose of these Davidic kings will be to serve as God's agents in promoting justice and righteousness.

Conclusion

After a class session on the prophets, a Sudanese refugee approached me (Andrew) with a smile on his face. He said: "That will be great." He just smiled

---

30. Hayyim Angel, "The Eternal Davidic Covenant in II Samuel Chapter 7 and Its Later Manifestations in the Bible," *Jewish Biblical Quarterly* 44 (2016): 86.

after he said this, as if his soul was in the midst of a utopia. I said: "What will be great?" He responded: "When there will be a king who can bring about justice for everyone." "Ah," I said. "You know what it is like to have bad kings, don't you." He said: "Yes, I do." Then he walked away with a smile.

We suspect that after eras of unjust Judean kings and exile, the readers and hearers of Jeremiah had a response similar to that of the Sudanese student. There would be great comfort in knowing that God brought an end to the idolatrous and unrighteous rule of Davidic kings. No other prophet gives such an up-close look at the corruption and fall of the Davidic kings as Jeremiah. Jeremiah's consolation goes beyond announcing the fall of David's house, however. There is hope that God will reestablish the dynasty of David after exile. A "sprout" will arise out of an apparently dead lineage. There will be a new era of Davidic kings, and they will care for God's flock and uphold justice and righteousness.

Since Jeremiah's prophecies offer hope regarding a restoration of the dynasty of Davidic kings—not merely promising a singular king—can we speak of these prophecies about shepherds and a "righteous sprout" as messianic?[31] It is best to understand these passages as contributing to a set of messianic expectations rather than being messianic oracles in and of themselves. Odds are that the book of Jeremiah, both in its MT and LXX forms, did not take its final shape until well after the return from exile. With no Davidic king upon the throne during the Persian era, it is at least possible that hope would begin to centralize around an individual who would inaugurate the new era of Davidic kingship. Even if it is probable that the expectation was that subsequent Davidic kings would reign after the inaugurator, hope would likely focus on the individual at the beginning of the new era. In fact, the book of Zechariah uses Jeremiah's metaphor of "sprout" as a title for a messianic figure who will come after Zerubbabel to build an even greater temple (Zech. 3:8; 6:12–13).[32] An increasingly individualized reading becomes apparent in the Targum of Jeremiah, which replaces "righteous Sprout" with Messiah: "Behold the days are coming, says the Lord, when I shall raise up for David *an Anointed One* of righteousness" (23:5).[33]

---

31. See Joyce Baldwin, who unconvincingly argues that "righteous sprout" is a technical term for a singular Messiah. Joyce G. Baldwin, "Ṣemaḥ as a Technical Term in the Prophets," *VT* 14 (1964): 93–97. Her conclusions are mainly conjectures. For instance, she identifies the "righteous Sprout" as a Messiah because God gave the "righteous Sprout" righteousness. It is not clear to us how this qualifies the Sprout to be a Messiah when God gives Solomon wisdom to carry out righteousness.

32. See Rose, *Zemah and Zerubbabel*, 130–41. He argues convincingly against viewing the "Sprout" as Zerubbabel.

33. Robert Hayward, trans., *The Targum of Jeremiah*, ArBib 12 (Collegeville, MN: Liturgical Press, 1987), 111.

Postlude: Canonical Reflections

How does Jeremiah's message regarding Davidic kingship figure into the two-testament canon's witness to Christ? First, Jeremiah speaks into the abyss of many years without a Davidic king. God's faithfulness to his promises to David did not depend on there being a king perpetually upon the throne in Jerusalem. God's faithfulness would be proven within history, when God would resuscitate David's line. The announcement that Jesus, son of David, is king is testimony to God's faithfulness to his promise to David. Second, Jeremiah was not privy to knowing that there would be only one Davidic king who would rule from the throne of David forever. So, Christ's first coming, ascension, and second coming clarify that what Jeremiah envisages as an era of multiple shepherds from the line of David is subsumed within the lens of a singular king.

As one considers the portrait of Jeremiah's ideal king, Jesus certainly corresponds. Jesus emerges as a "son of David" from a virgin womb after a long period without a Davidic king ruling in Jerusalem, like a "sprout" emerging from the ground. The angel declared to Mary: "And the Lord God will give to him the throne of his father David, and he will reign over the house of Jacob forever, and of his kingdom there will be no end" (Luke 1:32–33). Yet in the Gospel narratives we do not see Jesus's reign upon the throne of David as one might expect. On the one hand, Jesus's "righteousness" in his earthly life is readily apparent when one contrasts him with Jehoiakim, Jehoiachin, and Zedekiah. It could never be said of Jesus that he oppressed the poor, built fancy palaces, or neglected the rights of the orphan and the widow as these kings had (Jer. 21:11–22:30). Instead, in Jesus's earthly life, he cared for the poor, advocated for justice for the vulnerable, and demanded that his disciples do the same (cf. Matt. 23:23; 25:31–46). It is not a surprise, then, that the body of Jesus, his church, carries forth this mission (e.g., Gal. 2:10; James 1:27). On the other hand, the "righteous sprout" who would instill justice across the land from the throne of David will become more evident in Christ's second coming. We have every reason to believe that Jesus is a shepherd whose heart aligns with God's (Jer. 3:15) and who will instill justice and righteousness throughout the social fabric of the world when he comes again.

8

The Prince Forecast in Ezekiel

Sometimes bigger is not better. One would have thought that the size of the prophecy of Ezekiel made it too large to be ignored, but, in fact, its great bulk is probably one reason for its comparative neglect in Christian preaching and teaching. As with the other large prophetic books (Isaiah and Jeremiah), preachers appear to find its size daunting. In studying and then preaching on the book of Ezekiel, too many pastors are not sure where to start, and so they do not start at all. Preachers should adopt the motto, "Impossible, difficult, done." What at first looks *impossible* (devising a preaching series on Ezekiel) is discovered to be *difficult* when attempted, but, before long, with persever-ance, the job is *done*. In the case of our theme of messianism, Ezekiel has an essential contribution to make.

The picture of the future shape of Israelite rule in the prophecy of Ezekiel continues to fascinate scholars, who generally explain the portrait of the "prince" (*nāśîʾ*) in Ezek. 40–48 as a reaction to royal abuse of authority in the past (see, e.g., 22:6, 27), or they see it as necessitated by the radically theocentric nature of the prophecy, and there is a measure of truth in both explanations.[1] The figure of the "prince" is not confined to Ezek. 40–48, and

---

An earlier version of material in this chapter was published as Gregory Goswell, "The Prince Forecast by Ezekiel and Its Relation to Other Old Testament Messianic Portraits," *BN* 178 (2018): 53–73. Used by permission.

1. For the first approach, see, e.g., Jon D. Levenson, *Theology of the Program of Restoration of Ezekiel 40–48*, HSM 10 (Missoula, MT: Scholars Press, 1976), 113–14; for the second ap-proach, see, e.g., Joachim Becker, *Messianic Expectation in the Old Testament*, trans. David E. Green (Philadelphia: Fortress, 1980), 62–63.

so in this chapter we will also examine Ezek. 34 and 37. As is the case for many other features of this prophetic book, Ezekiel's portrait of the new temple in the vision of Ezek. 40–48 and the prince's place within it is in many ways unique. We will argue that once the role of the prince is understood in its Ezekielian setting and its key components identified, several close analogies can be found in a wide range of biblical literature, such that Ezekiel's species of eschatology represents an established strand in Old Testament expectation.

The Divine and the Human Shepherd (Ezekiel 34)

The "shepherd" (rō'eh) is a standard image for kingship in the ANE,[2] and this metaphor dominates Ezek. 34:1–16, which is an oracle outlining the failures of the preexilic kings and saying what God will do about this dire situation. In response to these failures, verse 11 anticipates that YHWH himself will act as the true shepherd for the welfare of his covenant people ("I myself will search for my sheep and will seek them out"). YHWH will search for, rescue, and regather the flock that was scattered on the day that he had to judge his people for their sin (v. 12).[3] God will do what the false shepherds failed to do (v. 16; cf. v. 4). There will also be a judgment among the flock (vv. 17–22), with God discriminating between oppressive and oppressed sheep. In this context, God promises that a Davidic figure will be placed over the flock as the "one shepherd," implying a North-South reunification (vv. 23–24),[4] and this new "David" is the symbol and guarantee of that unity. Ezekiel expands on this notion in 37:15–24, where the reunion of the kingdoms is made explicit and the term "one" ('eḥād) occurs no fewer than eleven times and the "one shepherd" designation is repeated (v. 24). A careful reading of the passage reveals that YHWH the Shepherd plays a much greater role in chapter 34 than does the Davidic shepherd, with YHWH insisting, "I myself will be the shepherd of my sheep. . . . You are my sheep" (vv. 15, 31). Ezekiel 34:23–24 reads:

> [23]And I will set up over them one shepherd, my servant David, and he shall feed them: he shall feed them and be their shepherd. [24]And I, the LORD, will be their God, and my servant David shall be prince among them. I am the LORD; I have spoken.

2. See, e.g., Daniel I. Block, *The Book of Ezekiel: Chapters 25–48*, NICOT (Grand Rapids: Eerdmans, 1998), 279–81; Jack W. Vancil, "Sheep, Shepherd," *ABD* 5:1187–90; J. J. Glück, "Nagid-Shepherd," *VT* 13 (1963): 144–50.

3. The same focus on God as the one who will rescue is found in Ezek. 20:33–38 (n.b. v. 33: "I [= God] will be king over you").

4. Kenneth E. Pomykala, *The Davidic Dynasty Tradition in Early Judaism: Its History and Significance for Messianism*, SBLEJL 7 (Atlanta: Scholars Press, 1995), 27.

The future royal figure is said to be a Davidide (v. 23), but the term "king" (*melek*) seems to be avoided. The substitute term of *nāśî'* (usually rendered in English versions as "prince") does not need to suggest a lower rank than king but may hint at a different way of carrying out the royal role than was the experience in the preexilic period, when many kings misused their authority, dishonored God, and oppressed their people.[5] The shepherd here is called "David."[6] There is nothing in Ezek. 34 to imply a *line* of kings, and the specification of "one" could be read as precluding the thought of a dynasty (though a hereditary position appears to be in view in 45:8–9 and 46:16–18).[7] The ruler will be appointed by Yhwh himself, as is consistent with Ezekiel's theocratic emphasis, and this ruler's installation only takes place *after* the rescue has been achieved by the Divine Shepherd.[8] The "my servant" designation used here is another feature that stresses the figure's subordination to Yhwh. The use of "prince" (34:24) is consistent with Ezekiel's earlier efforts to downplay Israel's monarchy (e.g., 7:27; 12:12; and 19:1, all of which use "prince").[9]

In Ezek. 34:23, the prince is simply described as carrying out the role of a shepherd (ESV: "feed"; the root *rāʿâ* from which *rōʿeh*, "shepherd," is formed), and, as noted by Walther Zimmerli, "The active function of this shepherd is not in any way more closely defined."[10] Zimmerli attributes this feature to an exclusive focus on God's holy dwelling place and so God's presence (as King) among his people. However, a hint that this shepherd's function may include the typical social justice role of the ANE king is found in verse 16 as part of the description of what *God* will do for his flock ("I will strengthen the weak, . . . I will feed [root *rāʿâ*] them in justice").[11] So also, as noted by Iain M. Duguid, the strategic positioning of verse 23 straight after the notice of God's intervention to "judge between sheep and sheep" (vv. 20–22) may be

5. See Daniel I. Block, "Bringing Back David: Ezekiel's Messianic Hope," in *The Lord's Anointed: Interpretation of Old Testament Messianic Texts*, ed. P. E. Satterthwaite, Richard S. Hess, and Gordon J. Wenham (Carlisle, UK: Paternoster, 1995), 168–69.

6. For the earlier application of the metaphor to David, see, e.g., 2 Sam. 5:2; Ps. 78:70–72.

7. André Caquot, "Le Messianisme d'Ézéchiel," *Semitica* 14 (1964): 22.

8. As noted by Block, "Bringing Back David," 177; cf. Iain M. Duguid, *Ezekiel and the Leaders of Israel*, VTSup 56 (Leiden: Brill, 1994), 55; Caquot, "Le Messianisme d'Ézéchiel," 18–19, esp. 19: "His role commences after the recovery" (*son rôle commence après le rétablissement*).

9. According to Paul M. Joyce, "King and Messiah in Ezekiel," in *King and Messiah in Israel and the Ancient Near East: Proceedings of the Oxford Old Testament Seminar*, ed. John Day, JSOTSup 270 (Sheffield: Sheffield Academic, 1998), 331.

10. Walther Zimmerli, *Ezekiel 2: A Commentary on the Book of the Prophet Ezekiel, Chapters 25–48*, trans. James D. Martin, Hermeneia (Philadelphia: Fortress, 1983), 278–79.

11. For the widespread expectation on ANE kings to uphold social justice, see Moshe Weinfeld, *Social Justice in Ancient Israel and in the Ancient Near East* (Jerusalem: Magnes Press, 1995), 45–56. This aspect is explicit in the parallel passage in Jer. 23:1–8 (esp. v. 5: "And [he] shall execute justice and righteousness in the land").

taken as implying that God's servant will use his authority ("over them") to exercise judgment and protect the flock,[12] and Duguid's observation corrects a scholarly tendency to view the prince in Ezekiel as without any authority.

Likewise, it is said that God will feed them "on the mountains of Israel . . . on the mountain heights of Israel" (Ezek. 34:13–14),[13] and presumably this is also the location of the human shepherd in his subordinate role (cf. 17:22–23). If that is the case, this feature presages the presence of the prince in the temple vision of chapters 40–48. The phrase "mountains of Israel" appears frequently in the prophecy of Ezekiel and at times is associated with pagan cultic activity (e.g., 6:2–5; 18:6) and typified as the location of (deviant) cultic activity. We are not suggesting that the "mountains of Israel" is as such a reference to Zion/Jerusalem, though 37:22 does explicitly connect the phrase in question with the promised future ruler and immediately states that idolatry will no longer be present (v. 23). In other words, this text brings together the three significant themes of mountains, king, and cultus and, by so doing, prepares readers for the contents of the vision of Ezekiel in chapters 40–48.

The Oracle of the Two Sticks (Ezekiel 37:15–28)

The fifth night message of Ezekiel centers on a symbolic act in which the joining of two sticks represents the reunion of the two formerly divided kingdoms of Judah and Israel. There will be one "nation" in the land and one "kingdom" under "one king" (37:22),[14] and God announces, "My servant David shall be king [*melek*] over them" (v. 24). The term "king" in application to the promised leader in verse 24 picks up the use of "king" in verse 22,[15] but contrasts with Ezekiel's preferred designation for Israel's rulers, "prince." Ezekiel 37:22–24 reads:

> [22]And I will make them one nation in the land, on the mountains of Israel. And one king shall be king over them all, and they shall be no longer two nations, and no longer divided into two kingdoms. [23]They shall not defile themselves anymore with their idols and their detestable things, or with any of their transgressions. But I will save them from all the backslidings in which they have sinned, and

12. Duguid, *Ezekiel and the Leaders of Israel*, 47–49.

13. The motif of "the mountains of Israel" is more than a mundane geographical descriptor of Palestine in Ezekiel; see Walther Zimmerli, *Ezekiel 1: A Commentary on the Book of the Prophet Ezekiel, Chapters 1–24*, trans. Ronald E. Clements, Hermeneia (Philadelphia: Fortress, 1979), 185–86.

14. With the "one king" guaranteeing their unity as a national state, see Walter Gross, "Israel's Hope for the Renewal of the State," *JNSL* 14 (1988): 129–30.

15. It is just possible that the "one king" in 37:22 is Yʜᴡʜ, but this interpretation is considered and finally discounted by Joyce ("King and Messiah in Ezekiel," 328, 335).

will cleanse them; and they shall be my people, and I will be their God. [24]My servant David shall be king over them, and they shall all have one shepherd. They shall walk in my rules and be careful to obey my statutes.

According to Daniel Block, the uncharacteristic use of "king" in this passage may be due to the discussion of the restoration of united Israel as a "nation" (*gôy*), such that the concern is the prophetic affirmation of Israel's reconstitution as a nation in its own right.[16] In other words, the use of "king" over "prince" in this passage highlights the restoration of Israel's national status in line with the general ANE expectation that an independent nation has its own king.[17] The language of 37:24 recalls 34:24, except for the use of the term "king," which has just been explained ("My servant David shall be king [prince] over [among] them"), but the text of Ezekiel reverts to the use of "prince" in 37:25. The verses that immediately follow (vv. 26–28) anticipate the sanctuary focus of chapters 40–48, and on that basis, as noted by Kenneth E. Pomykala, "the prophecy of a new David is only a component part of Ezekiel's visions of an ideal future for Israel, where the emphasis is on the LORD's relationship with his people and the presence of his sanctuary among them."[18] None of this says or implies that messianic expectation is unimportant in the prophecy, but it would be true to say that the promise of a future leader is put in a context that in various ways places the focus on God's own rule.

The fivefold recurrence of "forever" (using various constructions with *'ôlām*) in Ezek. 37:24–28 points to the definitive nature of the coming salvation, and especially important is the promise that "their children's children shall dwell there [in the land] forever" (v. 25b). Their possession of the land in the future will be perpetual, and the unsuccessful attack by Gog in chapters 38–39 will reaffirm this promise.[19] God's arrangement with David is part of this lasting state of affairs (37:25: "David my servant shall be their prince forever"). The climax is found in the mention of the *sanctuary* in their midst "forevermore" (vv. 26b–28), which looks forward to Ezek. 40–48, with its detailed picture of the temple and its rituals. The prominence of the new temple in the final vision of the canonical book is a way of emphasizing God's kingship—namely, his presence as King in his palace (= temple; see 43:7: "Son

16. Block, "Bringing Back David," 178. Zimmerli, likewise, sees the reference to Israel as a "nation" and "kingdom" as the trigger for the use of "king." Zimmerli, *Ezekiel 2*, 277–78.

17. There is no need to amend the text to "prince" (following the LXX "ruler" [*archōn*]).

18. Pomykala, *Davidic Dynasty Tradition*, 29.

19. Thomas Renz, *The Rhetorical Function of the Book of Ezekiel*, VTSup 76 (Leiden: Brill, 1999), 117.

of man, this is the place of my throne and the place of the soles of my feet, where I will dwell in the midst of the people of Israel forever"),[20] and the role of the prince is set within that overarching theocratic framework.

The Prince in Ezekiel 40–48

The term "prince" (nāśî')is also used in Ezek. 40–48 to denote the human ruler (44:1–4; 46:1–3, 8–10, 12), and "king" (melek) is scarcely used, except retrospectively of earlier "kings" (43:7–9). Zimmerli says that there is no Davidic hope in these chapters,[21] but his view of the matter does not need to be accepted as fact,[22] for what is said in these chapters is consistent with the limited form of Davidic kingship on view in chapters 34 and 37.[23] Various scholars recognize the identity of Davidic kingship in these chapters, and, as noted by Christophe Nihan, this is supported by 17:22–24, which announces that YHWH will plant on "a high mountain" (har-gābōah) a "sprig" from the Davidic tree.[24] The expression is only found elsewhere in Ezekiel in 40:2 ("a very high mountain" [har gābōah mə'ōd]), where the new temple complex is introduced, such that chapter 17 anticipates the presence of the prince in the temple on the "very high mountain." This is not to deny that there are differences—for example, in Ezek. 40–48 the prince is not explicitly identified as a Davidide; he is not designated YHWH's "servant" ('ebed); there is no use of "king" in application to him, and no shepherding (rō'eh) role is specified. Absence, however, is not the same as a positive denial and therefore does not require the explanation that a different figure is in view in the final chapters of the canonical book.

Joachim Becker believes that the title "prince" has "an antimonarchic coloration" (einen antimonarchischen Anstrich),[25] but this is probably going too far.[26] After the acceptance of human kingship within the theocratic

20. There may be an allusion to the ark as God's throne or footstool (cf. 1 Sam. 4:4; 2 Sam. 6:2; Pss. 99:5; 132:7; 1 Chron. 28:2; Isa. 6:1–2); see Walther Zimmerli, "Planungen für den Wiederaufbau nach der Katastrophe von 587," VT 18 (1968): 242.

21. Zimmerli, "Planungen für den Wiederaufbau," 245.

22. For the question of whether to equate the two figures, see Levenson, Program of Restoration, 57–62; Steven Shawn Tuell, The Law of the Temple in Ezekiel 40–48, HSM 49 (Atlanta: Scholars Press, 1992), 105–8.

23. Levenson, Program of Restoration, 57, 62–69.

24. Christophe Nihan, "The nāśî' and the Future of Royalty in Ezekiel," in History, Memory, Hebrew Scriptures: A Festschrift for Ehud Ben Zvi, ed. Ian Douglas Wilson and Diana V. Edelman (Winona Lake, IN: Eisenbrauns, 2015), 235.

25. Becker, Messianic Expectation, 63.

26. For a more nuanced evaluation, see Kalinda Rose Stevenson, The Vision of Transformation: The Territorial Rhetoric of Ezekiel 40–48, SBLDS 154 (Atlanta: Scholars Press, 1996), 119–23.

framework of God's relationship with Israel as his covenant people at the time of Samuel and Saul (1 Sam. 8–12), human rule and God's kingship are never again set in direct opposition to each other or viewed as fundamentally contradictory. The term "prince" goes back to the officers who represented the Israelite tribes,[27] and Duguid concurs with E. A. Speiser that outside the book of Ezekiel, the term usually denotes a tribal representative,[28] so that Ezekiel is thought by some scholars to be paring down the royal office to premonarchic proportions,[29] with the role modeled on the "prince" of each tribe in Num. 2 and 7. However, the term is used of Solomon in 1 Kings 11:34, and in Ezekiel it can designate an Israelite royal head of state (12:10, 12; 19:1; 21:12, 25 [21:17, 30 MT]; 22:6),[30] as well as other foreign rulers in a vassal role (26:16; 27:21; 32:29).[31] The term does not at all conflict, therefore, with the Davidic designation of its bearer, and too much significance is not to be read into this choice of terminology,[32] though its use is consistent with a royal individual stripped of the structural temptations to abuse his position, which is probably why Ezekiel chose to use it. In other words, kingship is not so much discarded as reconfigured in a way that limits possible abuse of power,[33] for it operates naturally within the framework of "Ezekiel's distinctive radical theocentricity" wherein God is chief shepherd (34:15, 24).[34] In line with this, the covenant relationship of Yhwh with his people is prioritized over that of the prince and people, with the Covenant Formulary ("They shall be my

27. The classic study is that of E. A. Speiser, "Background and Function of the Biblical *Nasi'*," in *Oriental and Biblical Studies: Collected Writings of E. A. Speiser*, ed. J. J. Finkelstein and Moshe Greenberg (Philadelphia: University of Pennsylvania Press, 1967), 113–22, who opts for the translation "chieftain." Cf. the more recent comprehensive survey of the term provided by Duguid, *Ezekiel and the Leaders of Israel*, 10–18.

28. Duguid, *Ezekiel and the Leaders of Israel*, 18.

29. E.g., Joyce, *King and Messiah in Ezekiel*, 331.

30. Pomykala, *Davidic Dynasty Tradition*, 28n61.

31. An extensive discussion is provided by Nihan, "Future of Royalty," 230–34.

32. Warns Duguid, *Ezekiel and the Leaders of Israel*, 25–26, 31–33.

33. Perhaps under the influence of the Deuteronomic critique of kingship, says Karl-Martin Beyse, *Serubbabel und die Königserwartungen der Propheten Haggai und Sacharja: Eine historische und traditionsgeschichtliche Untersuchung*, AzTh 1.48 (Stuttgart: Calver, 1972), 61–62. For similarities to the law of the king in Deut. 17, see J. Gordon McConville, "Law and Monarchy in the Old Testament," in *A Royal Priesthood? The Use of the Bible Ethically and Politically: A Dialogue with Oliver O'Donovan*, ed. Craig Bartholomew, Jonathan Chaplin, Robert Song, and Al Wolters, Scripture & Hermeneutics Series 3 (Carlisle, UK: Paternoster, 2002), 85; Bernard M. Levinson, "The Reconceptualization of Kingship in Deuteronomy and the Deuteronomistic History's Transformation of Torah," *VT* 51 (2001): 533n55.

34. Cf. Joyce, *King and Messiah in Ezekiel*, 335, who sees the exaltation of the one (Yhwh) requiring a concomitant diminution of the other (the prince).

people, and I will be their God") surrounding the description of the role of the prince in chapter 37 (vv. 23b, 27b).[35]

The office of prince has little independence, and the limitations imposed on him accentuate the kingship of Yʜᴡʜ, such that it may not be *strictly* accurate to speak of a messianic reign. According to Becker, "One should have no illusions about the status accorded the king in the book's expectations: He stands in the shadow [*Schatten*] of theocracy and privileged priesthood."[36] Minimal administrative organization is in view in Ezek. 40–48; after all, in a theocracy scant attention need be given to the mechanics of government, for God himself does most things, or at least he does the most important things.[37] However, the following features are to be noted: the temple no longer abuts the palace (43:7–8); the city is in no sense "the city of David" but now "shall belong to the whole house of Israel," not just Judah and Benjamin (45:6); the city has inhabitants drawn from all tribes (48:19); its gates give equal access to all tribes (vv. 30–34); and the prince is not associated with any particular tribe but is a pantribal figure who has his own portion of land. In other words, the future of God's kingdom is so constituted as to prevent the recurrence of the earlier royal abuses witnessed in Israelite history.

On the other hand, the prince has unique privileges in the new temple of the vision (Ezek. 44:1–4; 46:1–3, 8–10, 12), such that certain sacred spaces are open to him alone. He alone may sit in the outer east gate (the entryway of the divine presence) and eat his sacrificial meals there (v. 3). Taking his stand at the inner east gate, he is the sole lay observer of the ministrations of the priests in the inner court (46:2, 8, 12).[38] He joins (maybe even leads) the sacral procession of the people on festival days (v. 10). He has a special allotment of land on either side of the sacred reserve (45:7; 48:21–22). He supplies what is needed for sacrifices in the temple (e.g., 45:22: "On that day the prince shall provide [*waʿāśâ*] for himself and all the people of the land a young bull for a sin offering"; cf. 46:4, 12–17),[39] which may explain why he needs an extensive portion of land.[40] The prince is the leader and

---

35. Cf. Leslie C. Allen, *Ezekiel 20–48*, WBC 29 (Waco: Word, 1990), 194: "[The designation] underlines the monarch's subordination to Yahweh . . . [and] emphasizes the king's links with the people."

36. Becker, *Messianic Expectation*, 62.

37. Levenson, *Program of Restoration*, 113.

38. Tuell, *Law of the Temple*, 108.

39. Charles R. Biggs, "The Role of the *Nasi* in the Programme for Restoration in Ezekiel 40–48," *Colloquium* 16 (1983): 49. Nihan reads 45:17b ("It is he who shall *perform* [*hûʾ-yaʿāśeh*] the sin offering"; RSV: "provide") as meaning that the prince is the one ultimately responsible for the offering's performance (by the agency of priests). Nihan, "Future of Royalty," 239.

40. Suggests Block, *Book of Ezekiel*, 659–60.

representative of the worshiping community described in Ezekiel's vison (45:16–17), in regard to the presentation of the offering prescribed in the preceding verses (vv. 13–15), such that the people hand over what is required for the offering to the prince, and he is then responsible for supplying what is needed for all the festivals.[41]

According to Jon D. Levenson, "Clearly the *nāśî'* is here a figure of great honour, however impotent,"[42] though that undoubtedly puts things too strongly. The reader of the prophecy of Ezekiel is repeatedly reminded of the excesses of the prince's royal predecessors (43:6–11; 45:8–12; 46:16–18), such that a role devoid of defined governmental responsibilities seems justified.[43] On that basis, some scholars posit that the use of the term "prince" reflects a downgrading justified by a sustained critique of royalty.[44] Others maintain that the prince retains various Davidic prerogatives,[45] for he owns tracts of land and servants (45:7–8; 48:21–22), and he may even have a role in maintaining a just social order (see 45:9–12, addressed to the "princes of Israel"; cf. the condemnation of judicial crimes of former kings in 22:25).[46] This is not contradicted by 44:24, where the priests are assigned the role of judges to any dispute.[47] It is plain that the prince has responsibilities to fulfill.

In summary, therefore, the picture of the future provided by Ezekiel is of a reunited Israelite kingdom ruled by Yʜwʜ, and the centerpiece of the divine kingdom is the new temple in a rejuvenated paradisial land. In this theocratic context, the restricted position of the Davidic prince is of one who has responsibility for seeing that the cult is supplied and performed. The prince may also have a (less prominent) judicial role in maintaining social equity and the care of the vulnerable (in line with Jeremiah's portrait of the future Davidic ruler in Jer. 23:5).[48]

---

41. Cf. Zimmerli, *Ezekiel 2*, 478.

42. Levenson, *Program of Restoration*, 113.

43. Cf. Levenson, *Program of Restoration*, 113–14; Joyce, "King and Messiah in Ezekiel," 331: "His is certainly a limited role, albeit one of prestige and influence."

44. E.g., Joyce, "King and Messiah in Ezekiel," 323–26 (also 332: "Thus *nāśî'* replaces *melek*, so as to undo the damage done in the past by royal leaders").

45. See, e.g., Klaus Seybold, *Das davidische Königtum im Zeugnis der Propheten*, FRLANT 107 (Göttingen: Vandenhoeck & Ruprecht, 1972), 145–46; Duguid, *Ezekiel and the Leaders of Israel*, 10–57; Michael Konkel, *Architektonik des Heiligen: Studien zur zweiten Tempelvision Ezechiels (Ez 40–48)*, BBB 129 (Berlin: Philo, 2001), 270–86, who says that the "prince" of chaps. 40–48 is "the Davidide of the time of salvation" ("der Davidide der Heilszeit") (273, 285).

46. As noted by Nihan, "Future of Royalty," 238.

47. Duguid, *Ezekiel and the Leaders of Israel*, 54, 131.

48. See chap. 7 in the present volume.

Postlude: Canonical Reflections

Regarding Ezekiel's picture of the future, insufficient notice has been taken of many close analogies found elsewhere in the Old Testament. Ezekiel's prince is the head of a "liturgical kingdom,"[49] and this model of future royalty is not as anomalous as it may at first seem, for essentially the same picture of David as a cultic leader is found in the prophecy of Amos (6:5), for example.[50] As we will see, as in the vision of Ezekiel (esp. 47:1–12), Amos prophesies that the rebuilt sanctuary-city of Jerusalem (9:11) will be the rejuvenating source for the restored land (vv. 13–15). The portrait of David in 6:5 may carry with it the implication of the presence of a Davidic figure in the restored sanctuary-city of Jerusalem ("the booth of David"), with this Davidide acting as chief worshiper in the cult. In the theology of the Chronicler, if the return of the Davidic house is to be contemplated (though this hope is not explicit in Chronicles), the chief role of the Davidic king would be to support temple worship, just as David and Solomon did in their lifetime.[51] Similarly, in a reading of the Psalter as a connected whole, like the vision of Ezekiel, the prospect is held out of a united Israel whose life focuses on the temple, and "David" in book 5 of the Psalter is portrayed as a model of true devotion to God the King.[52]

49. Levenson, *Program of Restoration*, 129.
50. See chap. 10 in the present volume.
51. See chap. 15 in the present volume.
52. See chap. 13 in the present volume.

9

Kingship for a United Nation
in Hosea

Stories of romance have universal appeal (e.g., the phenomenal popularity of Jane Austen's *Pride and Prejudice*, both the book and the television adaptations). The prophecy of Hosea is a well-known example of the Bible's use of the marriage metaphor for the relationship between God and his people.[1] The heart of the prophecy is a story of love gone wrong. The turbulent marriage of Hosea and Gomer (Hosea 1 and 3) reflects the history of the covenant relationship between God and Israel from the exodus to the exile and to the return (chap. 2). Gomer's sin, punishment, and restoration become a symbol of God's dealings with Israel. After the merited punishment of the exile, there will be a new exodus, a new wilderness journey, a new entry into the land, and a renewing of the covenant that involves the restoration of monarchic rule in Israel.

Recent appreciation of the Book of the Twelve (= Minor Prophets) as a literary whole provides an opportunity to revisit the contested issue of the attitude to kingship in the prophecy of Hosea and, in particular, its mention

An earlier version of material in this chapter was published as Gregory Goswell, "'David Their King': Kingship in the Prophecy of Hosea," *JSOT* 42, no. 2 (2017): 213–31. Copyright © 2017 (Gregory Goswell), reprinted by permission of SAGE Publications, DOI: 10.1177/030908921 6677671.

1. Gerlinde Baumann, *Love and Violence: Marriage as Metaphor for the Relationship between YHWH and Israel in the Prophetic Books* (Collegeville, MN: Liturgical Press, 2003), chap. 6.

of the prospect of Davidic rule (Hosea 3:5). Reading Hosea in light of the Book of the Twelve will impact our interpretation of the promise found in 3:5. Davidic kingship is a recurrent theme in the Twelve, though its prominence is not to be exaggerated.[2] If the prophecy of Hosea, and Hosea 1–3 in particular, is viewed as strategically placed in premier position and functioning as an *introduction* to the Twelve,[3] the expectation is that it may provide indications of the view of kingship on show in the Book of the Twelve as a canonical unit, and we believe that this is the case. In fact, two key texts on the future shape of Israelite kingship occur in this section of Hosea's prophecy (1:11 [2:2 MT]; 3:5).

Hosea among the Twelve

The order of the books in the Twelve in the Dead Sea Scrolls fragments consistently agrees with the masoretic tradition, always with the positioning of Hosea as the head book.[4] The order within the Twelve may be chronological in design, moving from the Assyrian period (e.g., Hosea, Amos) through to the Persian period (Haggai, Zechariah, and Malachi), though the dating of several of the books is a matter of dispute (e.g., Joel and Obadiah).[5] Part of the explanation of their placement among or alongside the eighth-century prophets may be an editorial desire to achieve an alternation of prophets who ministered in Israel and Judah: Hosea (Israel), Joel (Judah), Amos (Israel), Obadiah (Judah), Jonah (Israel), and Micah (Judah).[6] According to C. F. Keil, this oscillating North-South sequence might continue a little further in the Book of the Twelve if Nahum were shown to be a northerner and Habakkuk a southerner. The gentilic adjective "the Elkoshite" attached to the name

2. James D. Nogalski, "Recurring Themes in the Book of the Twelve: Creating Points of Contact for a Theological Reading," *Int* 61 (2007): 131.

3. The suggestion is that of Paul R. House, *The Unity of the Twelve*, JSOTSup 97 (Sheffield: Almond, 1990), 74–76.

4. The relevant materials are 4Q76, 4Q77, 4Q78, 4Q80, 4Q82, Mur 88, and 8H9ev 1. This list is provided in James VanderKam and Peter Flint, *The Meaning of the Dead Sea Scrolls: Their Significance for Understanding the Bible, Judaism, Jesus and Christianity* (San Francisco: Harper, 2002), 138–39.

5. See the discussion provided by Marvin A. Sweeney, *Hosea, Joel, Amos, Obadiah, Jonah*, vol. 1 of *The Twelve Prophets*, Berit Olam (Collegeville, MN: Liturgical Press, 2000), xxvii–xxviii.

6. Raymond C. Van Leeuwen, "Scribal Wisdom and Theodicy in the Book of the Twelve," in *In Search of Wisdom: Essays in Memory of John G. Gammie*, ed. L. G. Perdue, B. Scott, and W. Wiseman (Louisville: Westminster John Knox, 1993), 34. The idea goes back to C. F. Keil, *The Minor Prophets*, trans. J. Martin, vol. 10 of *Commentary on the Old Testament* (1869; repr., Grand Rapids: Eerdmans, 1980), 3.

of Nahum presumably refers to his hometown of Elkosh (Nah. 1:1), whose location is unknown, but is possibly a village in Galilee (maybe Capernaum, meaning "the city of Nahum"),[7] and the anti-Nineveh orientation of his prophecy is consistent with a concern about the threat that Assyria posed to Israel (though Nah. 1:15 [2:1 MT] addresses Judah). The prophet Habakkuk is occupied with the Chaldean threat to Judah (1:6), and so presumably he is to be classified as a southern prophet. This geographical schema encourages a hermeneutic that reads the prophetic threats and promises in the various booklets that make up the Twelve as applying to *both* kingdoms and, even more widely, to God's people generally, irrespective of time and place. The schematic ordering of the prophetic books, with its implied loosening of the tie between the prophecy and an original temporal or geographical location (as far as that can be determined), makes the issue of the possible Judean updating of Hosea's prophecies less significant than scholarly interest in the question may have supposed.

The Integrity of the Prophecy of Hosea

Many who study the prophecy of Hosea have discerned what they view as signs of later Judean editing (after the time of Hosea himself)—for example, in 1:7, where Judah is exempted from the threat of certain judgment leveled at Israel ("But I will have mercy on the house of Judah"), or in 5:5, with its condemnation of Judah along with Israel ("Judah also shall stumble with them"). As these two examples show, oracles both of judgment and hope would have to be included in any theory of extensive Judean redaction (or redactions) of this prophetic book.[8] Hosean prophecy is mostly addressed to the Northern Kingdom, yet at times it refers to the Southern Kingdom. Given that the superscription at 1:1 mentions by name four southern kings (Uzziah, Jotham, Ahaz, and Hezekiah) as well as Jeroboam II, king of Israel, it is no surprise to find a united-kingdom stance in the final form of the prophecy. As well, in the superscription, Judean kings are listed *before* Israelite kings (as also in Amos 1:1), so that some relation of the contents of the prophecy to the situation of Judah is assumed from the outset in the canonical form of the book.

7. It seems impossible, however, to be certain of its location; see Duane L. Christensen, *Nahum: A New Translation with Introduction and Commentary*, AB 24F (New Haven: Yale University Press, 2009), 159–61.

8. On this topic, see the detailed study of Grace I. Emmerson, *Hosea: An Israelite Prophet in Judean Perspective*, JSOTSup 28 (Sheffield: Sheffield Academic, 1987), 56–116. She refuses to assume that Hosea as a northerner must have had an anti-Judean stance (95).

There are, in fact, *many* references to Judah in the prophecy, some fifteen by name in total (Hosea 1:1, 7, 11 [2:2 MT]; 4:15; 5:5, 10, 12, 13, 14; 6:4, 11; 8:14; 10:11; 11:12 [12:1 MT]; 12:2 [12:3 MT]). This stands in contrast to the prophecy of Amos, in which Judah is mentioned only three times (1:1; 2:4; 7:12). Are *all* the Hosean references to Judah obviously later and redactional? Was the original scope of Hosea's message extended to include Judah within the impending judgment? Were Hosea's words to Israel later updated for (and circulated in) Judah? Were these verses added when Hosea and/or his disciples fled south after the fall of Samaria in 722 BCE? There is no need to discount the theological value of what may be, in terms of the chronology of production, secondary material,[9] for if such material were proved to be present, this would indicate that Hosea's message was revered and viewed as having ongoing relevance. Such updating should be accorded prophetic status, for the prophetic books depict the community as recipients, not makers, of the books.[10] Certainly, Hosea's prophecy is not one-sidedly pro-Judah (see 5:5, 10, 12, 14; 6:4, 11; 12:2 [12:3 MT]) and may be read as a warning to Judah not to go the way of her sister kingdom, lest she be punished similarly (4:15: "Let not Judah become guilty"). Given Hosea's position at the head of the Book of the Twelve, the plethora of Hosean references to Judah suggests a reading strategy wherein the Twelve as a canonical unit is to be interpreted as addressed to God's people generally, whether in the North or South, whether at home or in exile.

Hosea's Attitude toward the Monarchy

As is commonly pointed out, Hosea is highly critical of the Israelite kings of his day (5:1, 2, 8–12; 7:3–7; 8:4; 9:15; 10:3, 7, 8, 9, 15; 13:10, 11).[11] The prominence of this critique in the prophecy is such that André Caquot labels it a "leitmotive."[12] The leadership terms used in these indictments, "king" (*melek*) and "prince" (*śar*),[13] are those also found in 3:4, so that Hosea's prediction

9. Emmerson, *Judean Perspective*, 59.

10. See E. Earle Ellis, "The Old Testament Canon in the Early Church," in *Mikra: Text, Translation, Reading and Interpretation of the Hebrew Bible in Ancient Judaism and Early Christianity*, ed. Martin Jan Mulder (Peabody, MA: Hendrickson, 2004), 688n158.

11. The references in 5:13, 8:10, and 10:6 are best explained as pertaining to the Assyrian king (as is explicit in 11:5); see Anthony Gelston, "Kingship in the Book of Hosea," in *Language and Meaning: Studies in Hebrew Language and Biblical Exegesis; Papers Read at the Joint British-Dutch Old Testament Conference held at London, 1973*, ed. A. S. van der Woude, OTS 19 (Leiden: Brill, 1974), 73–74.

12. André Caquot, "Osée et la Royauté," *RHPR* 41 (1961): 126.

13. E.g., the pairing of "king" and "prince" in Hosea 7:3.

about being deprived of government in 3:4 ("For the children of Israel shall dwell many days without king or prince") is to be interpreted in this wider context. Did Hosea favor Davidic rule, or did he reject kingship in principle? The latter would rule out the former; however, on closer investigation, most of the references listed above are at best ambivalent on the subject of kingship.

A negative view of the institution of kingship is evident in Hosea 8:4 ("They made kings, / but not through me. / They set up princes,[14] / but I knew it not") and 13:11 ("I gave you a king in my anger, / and I took him away in my wrath"). In the first text, the Israelites are accused of making kings independently of YHWH, which seems to make "Hosea's criticism of the kingship . . . quite fundamental,"[15] but the follow-up allusion to idols (8:4b) and the calf image in particular (v. 5) suggests a rejection of the schismatic kingship (and its associated idolatry) set up by Jeroboam I.[16] This would allow the possibility, even the likelihood, that Hosea contemplated a restoration of Davidic rule in the near or distant future.[17] The second text depicts the political instability of Israel (its rapid turnover of kings) as a judgment by God, making the relative stability of hereditary (David-style) monarchy an attractive alternative in the eyes of the prophet Hosea.

The repeated phrase "the days of Gibeah" (Hosea 9:9; 10:9) may mean that Israelite monarchy from the very beginning (from the time of its establishment by Saul at Gibeah) was displeasing to God (cf. 1 Sam. 11:4: "Gibeah of Saul"),[18] though it is more likely that these verses allude to the outrage at Gibeah in the days of the judges as setting the tone for the rebellion of the Israelite nation (cf. Judg. 19–21).[19] Likewise, the statement "every evil of theirs is in Gilgal" in Hosea 9:15 may allude to Saul's inauguration (1 Sam. 11:15), but the two other references to Gilgal in Hosea have cultic connections (4:15; 12:11 [12:12 MT]), and Hosea's anti-Baal stance makes it more probable that 9:15 looks back to the cult of Baal-peor (cf. v. 10), which is linked to Gilgal (and Shittim) in Mic. 6:5 (cf. Num. 25:1).[20]

The cryptic expressions in Hosea 7:7 ("They devour their rulers [root šāpaṭ]. / All their kings have fallen") may refer to (and condemn) the series of coups d'état that destabilized the final years of the Northern Kingdom (cf. 2 Kings 15:10–30). There is the apparent repudiation of Jehu's revolu-

---

14. Assuming the derivation of the Hebrew verb from the geminate root śārar, for there are repeated references to the office of "prince" (śar) in Hosea (3:4; 7:3, 5, 16; 8:10; 9:15; 13:10).

15. James M. Ward, "The Message of the Prophet Hosea," *Int* 23 (1969): 398.

16. Emmerson, *Judean Perspective*, 106–7.

17. So also Emmerson, *Judean Perspective*, 110.

18. Ward, "Message of the Prophet Hosea," 398.

19. G. I. Davies, *Hosea*, NCB (Grand Rapids: Eerdmans, 1992), 223.

20. As noted by Gelston, "Kingship in the Book of Hosea," 81.

tion (2 Kings 9–10), involving as it did a royal bloodbath of Omrides and Davidides (Hosea 1:4: "the blood of Jezreel") and leading to the divine threat of the abolition of kingship in the North ("I will put an end to the kingdom of the house of Israel," 1:4b). A number of references depict the disastrous ineffectiveness of the kings in times of crisis (10:3, 7, 15). It cannot be established, however, that Hosea finds fault with the northern kings due to the sole legitimacy (in his eyes) of the Davidic dynasty,[21] nor is it clear that he disapproved in principle of the institution of kingship as a form of government. Hosea has not a good word to say about the contemporary exercise of kingship, but he can also make strong anti-prophet (9:7–8) and anti-priest statements (5:1; 6:9; 10:5). He is critical of *all* the main authority figures in the Israelite nation and therefore cannot be read as singling out kingship for special criticism. What this means is that an announcement by Hosea of a restoration of kingship in the future does not have to be viewed as out of place in a record of his proclamation.

"They Shall Appoint for Themselves One Head" (Hosea 1:11)

As reflected and supported by the chapter division in the Hebrew Bible, Hosea 1:10–11 (2:1–2 MT) is best seen as a new unit of thought, focused on hopeful future prospects for God's people. Hosea 2:1 (2:3 MT) belongs with the preceding two verses, despite the change from prophetic announcement in the third person to a second-person plural command ("Say to your brothers . . . and to your sisters"). Hosea 2:1 continues the theme of a future restoration,[22] and it picks up (and reverses) the judgment embodied in the earlier sign-names given to Hosea's children (1:6, 9, 10 [2:1 MT]). Hosea 1:11 reads, "And the children of Judah and the children of Israel shall be gathered together, and they shall appoint for themselves one head. And they shall go up from the land, for great shall be the day of Jezreel."

The name "David" is mentioned in Hosea 3:5, this being its sole use in the prophecy of Hosea, but in 1:11 the prophet envisions a reunited nation under a single leader whom he does not call king but "head" (*rōʾš*), and, according to Anthony Gelston, the choice of "head" is odd if a Davidide is in mind.[23] Grace I. Emmerson labels "head" a "neutral term" that suggests a northern rather than a southern provenance, and on that basis she argues that 1:11

21. Ward, "Message of the Prophet Hosea," 397–98.

22. For 2:1–3 (MT) as a subunit, see Brad E. Kelle, *Hosea 2: Metaphor and Rhetoric in Historical Perspective*, AcBib 20 (Atlanta: Society of Biblical Literature, 2005), 169–79.

23. Gelston, "Kingship in the Book of Hosea," 78.

may be original to Hosea's proclamation.[24] Wider biblical usage shows that the designation "head" is a premonarchic (Judg. 10:18; 11:8, 9, 11) and early monarchic (1 Sam. 15:17) term for a pantribal leader (Jephthah and Saul, respectively) that has no necessary connection to Davidic-style kingship.[25] What connects these two early appointments of leaders is that they are the result of agreement between different tribal groups,[26] and such a conceptual feature suits the use of this leadership term in the Hosean context of a joint head of North and South and does not, as such, rule out a Davidic candidate.

This restoration of the nation's fortunes will be brought about by divine initiative, as made plain by the series of divine statements of intent found in the parallel text (Hosea 2:23: "I will sow . . . I will have mercy . . . I will say . . ."; cf. Jer. 31:27).[27] Nothing is said about the involvement of the promised "head" as military leader or deliverer, despite the presence in Hosea 1:11 of military terminology referring to the day of battle ("the day of Jezreel")—namely, a battle fought in the valley of Jezreel (1:5; cf. the analogous phrases in Isaiah and the Psalter: "the day of Midian" [Isa. 9:4; 9:3 MT]; "the day of Jerusalem" [Ps. 137:7]).[28] The context implies that the restoration (requiring the defeat of enemies) is effected by the action of God himself as the Divine Warrior, with this verse picking up the language of divinely effected defeat and deliverance in 1:5 and 1:7 (both of which mention weaponry). By contrast, the "one head" appears to have a purely governmental function within the reunited nation.

According to A. A. Macintosh, the Hebrew verb translated "they shall be gathered" (root *qābaṣ*) has the concrete sense of an assembly gathered for the purpose of choosing a single leader, so it is the language of convocation (cf. Gen. 49:1–2; Deut. 33:5; 1 Sam. 7:6).[29] Especially relevant is 1 Sam. 8:4, which uses the root *qābaṣ* of the gathering of the elders of the people wherein request is made for the appointment of a king.[30] On this understanding, the verse states that at a common assembly the separate kingdoms will *agree*

24. Emmerson, *Judean Perspective*, 97.

25. J. R. Bartlett, "The Use of the Word *rōʾš* as a Title in the Old Testament," *VT* 19 (1969): 1–3.

26. Cf. Num. 14:4, which uses the term "head" for a replacement for Moses.

27. Emmerson, *Judean Perspective*, 28–30.

28. Hans W. Wolff, *Hosea: A Commentary on the Book of the Prophet Hosea*, trans. Gary Stansell, Hermeneia (Philadelphia: Fortress, 1974), 28.

29. A. A. Macintosh, *Hosea*, ICC (Edinburgh: T&T Clark, 1997), 30; so too Davies, *Hosea*, 61 (who notes the 1 Sam. 7:6 parallel).

30. The references are provided by Francis I. Andersen and David Noel Freedman, *Hosea: A New Translation with Introduction and Commentary*, AB 24 (Garden City, NY: Doubleday, 1980), 207.

about who will become their governmental head ("They shall appoint for themselves one head"). In Job 29:25 and 1 Sam. 15:17, "head" is found in parallel with "king" (*melek*), so it is a term that can be applied to a king,[31] and it is not anti-royal as such, despite the strictures against kings later in the prophecy of Hosea.

Although Hosea 1:11 does not explicitly state that the "head" will be a Davidide, a Davidide is the most likely candidate for the role, given earlier historical experience under the united monarchy (cf. 2 Sam. 5:1–5; 19:41–43). Judahites would be unlikely to accept a non-Davidic ruler, and Israelites might well recall that they had once lived under the rule of the Davidic house in the persons of David and Solomon. The priority given to "the children of Judah" in this verse (preceding "the children of Israel") does not necessarily prove its Judean redactional origin (*pace* Davies[32]), but, if instead it depicts Judah as the dominant partner in the union, this implies that a Davidic head is indeed in mind. Understood in this way, what is said subsequently in Hosea 3:5 only makes explicit what is *implied* in the more general wording of 1:11.[33] At the very least, nothing in the wording of 1:11 excludes the possibility that Hosea expects a Davidic leader over a reunited Israelite kingdom embracing North and South.

"David Their King" (Hosea 3:5)

The marital history of Hosea and Gomer (3:1–3) is explicitly said to symbolically reflect God's dealings with Israel elaborated in verses 4 and 5 (with the link forged by verse 4a ["For . . ."]).[34] Hosea 3:1–5 reads:

> [1]And the LORD said to me, "Go again, love a woman who is loved by another man and is an adulteress, even as the LORD loves the children of Israel, though they turn to other gods and love cakes of raisins." [2]So I bought her for fifteen shekels of silver and a homer and a lethech of barley. [3]And I said to her, "You must dwell as mine for many days. You shall not play the whore, or belong to

31. Cf. Ps. 18:43 (18:44 MT); Isa. 7:8–9. For these references, see Kelle, *Hosea 2*, 217.

32. Davies, *Hosea*, 61.

33. So also Douglas K. Stuart, *Hosea–Jonah*, WBC 31 (Waco: Word, 1987), 68, and Peter Machinist, "Hosea and the Ambiguity of Kingship in Ancient Israel," in *Constituting the Community: Studies on the Polity of Ancient Israel in Honor of S. Dean McBride Jr.*, ed. John T. Strong and Steven S. Tuell (Winona Lake, IN: Eisenbrauns, 2005), 153–81.

34. For the cohesion of 3:1–5 as a unitary text, whether as an original or redactional whole, see Ehud Ben Zvi, *Hosea*, FOTL 21A/1 (Grand Rapids: Eerdmans, 2005), 78–87; cf. Gale A. Yee, *Composition and Tradition in the Book of Hosea: A Redaction Critical Investigation*, SBLDS 102 (Atlanta: Scholars Press, 1987), 57–64.

another man; so will I also be to you." ⁴For the children of Israel shall dwell many days without king or prince, without sacrifice or pillar, without ephod or household gods. ⁵Afterward the children of Israel shall return and seek the Lᴏʀᴅ their God, and David their king, and they shall come in fear to the Lᴏʀᴅ and to his goodness in the latter days.

The mention by Hosea of "David their king" in 3:5 is not to be ignored or explained away, but on the other hand, it cannot be said that Hosea places any *emphasis* on a Davidic hope, for this is the only Hosean text that mentions David, and the focus is completely on the people's response to Yʜᴡʜ in the last part of the verse. The way in which punishment is depicted by Hosea in 3:4 ("For the children of Israel shall dwell *many days* without king [*melek*] or prince [*śar*], . . .") envisages a temporary rather than a permanent deprivation of kingship,[35] and, therefore, 3:5 is not easily detached from what precedes, for some such expression of hope appears to be required by the provisional situation set up in 3:4.[36] As noted by Emmerson,[37] the deprivation envisaged in verse 4 is both political and cultic, so that the promised restoration also must involve both cultic and political spheres: they will "again seek [*bāqaś*] Yʜᴡʜ their God and David their king."[38] Jeremiah 30:9 also features the Hosean pairing of God and king but uses "serve" (*'ābad*), which, like "seek" (see below), is a term that can have both cultic and noncultic senses ("But they shall *serve* the Lᴏʀᴅ their God and David their king"). Many scholars see the parallel in Jeremiah as supporting an exilic or postexilic dating of the Hosean reference to David, though it is just as likely that Jeremiah took up and developed this theme from Hosea (cf. Jer. 23:5; 33:17, 21, 22, 26). Given the political instability of his day, it is not impossible to conceive of the prophet Hosea favoring a Davidic restoration as the antidote.[39] Of course, for Ehud Ben Zvi, who interprets this prophetic composition as one read by the lite-rati of postexilic Yehud, the Davidic connection is not at all surprising and

---

35. The pairing of king and prince is also found in 7:3, 8:10, and 13:10.

36. Emmerson, *Judean Perspective*, 12–14.

37. Emmerson, *Judean Perspective*, 102–3; noted also by Caquot, "Osée et la Royauté," 132–34; cf. Alexander Rofé, "David Their King (Whom God Will Raise): Hosea 3:5 and the Onset of Messianic Expectation in the Prophetic Books," in *Leshon Limmudim: Essays on the Language and Literature of the Hebrew Bible in Honour of A. A. Macintosh*, ed. David A. Baer and Robert P. Gordon, LHBOTS 593 (London: Bloomsbury T&T Clark, 2013), 130–35.

38. Authors' trans., understanding the Hebrew verb (root *śûb*) as adverbial in force ("again") (BDB 998).

39. See Gerald G. Swaim, "Hosea the Statesman," in *Biblical and Near Eastern Studies: Essays in Honor of William Sanford LaSor*, ed. Gary A. Tuttle (Grand Rapids: Eerdmans, 1978), 180.

represents no problem.[40] This approach is developed further by James M. Trotter, who reads Hosea 3:5 as supporting the Persian period ideal of "a Davidic descendant ruling over Yehud as part of a Persian provincial administration."[41] Trotter is right in arguing for the absence of messianic fervor or of efforts to foment rebellion against the Persian overlords in Isa. 40–55, Ezra-Nehemiah, Chronicles, Ezekiel, Haggai, and Zechariah, but he fails to note the hope of the dawning of God's kingdom on display in these books, and the presence of this hope discounts his suggestion that the books promote (or can be used to promote) loyalty to the Persian imperium.[42]

Returning to the text of Hosea 3:5, for the regular use of the verb *bāqaš* (*piel*, "to seek") in the sense of cultic approach to God, see 5:6, 15; 7:10 (cf. Deut. 4:29; Pss. 24:6; 27:8; Amos 5:4–6). The people's seeking YHWH contrasts with their earlier crime of seeking lovers (Hosea 2:7 [2:9 MT]), being a metaphor for idolatrous worship. For its noncultic application to kingship, and specifically the desire of the northern tribes to live under Davidic rule, see the parallel provided by 2 Sam. 3:17 ("For some time past you have been seeking [root *bāqaš*] David as king over you").[43] Such usage shows that the words "and David their king" in Hosea 3:5 need not be viewed as an editorial supplement (*Nachtrag*), identifiable due to the circumstance that the redactor did not notice that the object did not exactly suit the verb used.[44]

There is a clear connection and correlation between Hosea 3:4 and 3:5—namely, (1) the "many days" are a limited period of deprivation, and "afterward" (*'aḥar*) comes restoration; (2) in 3:5 the reference to Israel's return to "seek the LORD their God" implies a future reestablishment of the Israelite cult and is parallel to the sacrifice, pillar, and so on in 3:4; (3) the reference to the removal of king and prince in verse 4 finds a parallel in the mention of the people's seeking "David their king." Although the prediction of Israel's voluntary seeking God in verse 5 has no analogy in the preceding prophetic symbolic action in 3:1–3, as noted by Jörg Jeremias, the ominous threat to Israel of cultic deprivation in verse 4 runs exactly parallel to the speech of

40. Ben Zvi, *Hosea*, 87–94.

41. James M. Trotter, *Reading Hosea in Achaemenid Yehud*, JSOTSup 328 (London: Sheffield Academic, 2001), 113.

42. See Gregory Goswell, "The Fate and Future of Zerubbabel in the Prophecy of Haggai," *Bib* 91 (2010): 77–90; Gregory Goswell, "The Attitude to the Persians in Ezra-Nehemiah," *TJ* 32 (2011): 191–203.

43. Emmerson, *Judean Perspective*, 103. Likewise, in 2 Sam. 19:41–43, some northerners claim an equal share in David as their king.

44. *Pace* Susanne Rudnig-Zelt, "Vom Propheten und seiner Frau, einem Ephod und einem Teraphim—Anmerkungen zu Hos 3:1–4:5," *VT* 60 (2010): 393.

the prophet against the adulterous woman in verse 3 ("You shall not play the harlot, or belong to another man"),[45] which can be related to what was stated earlier—namely, that Israel will not turn back to God until their idolatrous worship has become impossible (2:11 [2:13 MT]). The reason for Hosea's action (3:3) is revealed in the next verse (v. 4a: "For . . ."), with the connection supported by the repetition of the phrase "many days" (vv. 3, 4). The action of Hosea toward his wife (v. 3) and those of God toward Israel (v. 4) are both aiming at reclamation. In other words, Israel's seeking in verse 5 is motivated by their deprivation spoken of in verse 4. The sentiments in these two verses suit the contents of the wider Hosean context, as noted by Jeremias (who finds an analogous thought in 5:15), though he still does not see 3:5 as a credible continuation of verse 4. Hosea 3:1–4 fits with the early preaching of Hosea in 2:6–7 and is in harmony with (what Jeremias identifies as) his post–733 BCE preaching as recorded in 10:1–8. Though Jeremias fails to note it, the announced judgment in Hosea 10 includes the removal of kingship (10:7a: "As for Samaria, her king is cut off," authors' trans.), so that this again leaves open the possibility that, according to Hosea, the restoration of kingship will be a feature of Israel's experience beyond the time of imposed divine judgment (such as found in 3:5).

The hopeful prospects depicted in 3:5 are set to take place "in the latter days," with this phrase picking up and matching the adverb "afterward" (*'aḥar*) at the beginning of the verse.[46] A fully eschatological reading is supported by the fact that, as noted by Andrew Dearman, "the quality of life depicted in 3:5 is such that nothing else in the book of Hosea would supersede it."[47] Dearman finds a parallel in Deut. 4:29–30, which also shares common vocabulary ("seek," "in the latter days," "return" [*šûb*]), and there, likewise, the final state of God's people is described in glowing terms that allow no further historical development beyond the promised endpoint.[48] In other words, the presence of a Davidic ruler over the reunited people of God has a secure position in Hosea's vision of the ultimate future in the plan of God.

---

45. Jörg Jeremias, *Hosea und Amos: Studien zu den Anfängen des Dodekapropheton*, FAT 13 (Tübingen: Mohr Siebeck, 1996), 75–76. In this paragraph we acknowledge our dependence on Jeremias, though we do not agree with all his arguments.

46. Walter Gisin, *Hosea: Ein literarisches Netzwerk beweist seine Authentizität*, BBB 139 (Berlin: Philo, 2002), 95.

47. J. Andrew Dearman, *The Book of Hosea*, NICOT (Grand Rapids: Eerdmans, 2010), 139.

48. Cf. Dwight R. Daniels, *Hosea and Salvation History: The Early Traditions of Israel in the Prophecy of Hosea*, BZAW 191 (Berlin: de Gruyter, 1990), 119, who notes what is said in 2:19 (2:21 MT): "And I will betroth you to me *forever.*"

Postlude: Canonical Reflections

A Davidic hope is on show in the Book of the Twelve, as we have just demonstrated in the case of the prophecy of Hosea (Hosea 3:5; cf. Mic. 5:2–4 [5:1–3 MT]; Zech. 3:8; 6:12–13), but without suggesting that divine and human kingship are at loggerheads in biblical thinking, it should be noted that this prophetic corpus gives only a modest place to a revival of Davidic rule in the future as promised by God. The prospect of a future Davidide does not feature at all in seven out of twelve booklets (Joel, Obadiah, Jonah, Nahum, Habakkuk, Zephaniah, Malachi). However, if the Book of the Twelve is viewed as a connected whole, the absence of this theme in any one booklet does not need to be understood as a denial of any Davidic component to the future.[49] The anticipation of a future Davidide is present but not prominent in this prophetic corpus.

The vital issue is not whether a Davidic hope is present in the Book of the Twelve—for it clearly is—but what form this expectation takes. We will discover that nothing subsequent to the prophecy of Hosea in the Twelve amends or corrects the key features of the Hosean portrait of kingship—namely, kingship is a viable model for Israelite government, both now and in the future; restored kingship is Davidic in character; the future king does not play the role of deliverer; and Davidic rule over the nations is not mentioned. Our argument will be that in the Book of the Twelve, the Davidic king has an important, but circumscribed, role in the dawning kingdom of God (implementing justice and righteousness), for it is Yhwh who will deliver his people and rule the nations from Jerusalem.

---

49. As properly pointed out by Anthony R. Petterson, "The Shape of the Davidic Hope across the Book of the Twelve," *JSOT* 35 (2010): 226.

10

David's Booth in Amos

It would be a mistake to read the Old Testament prophets only for predictions about the coming of Jesus, for that would be to use them in a highly selective fashion and to impose a foreign agenda on their productions. A passage like Amos 9:11–15 (quoted in Acts 15) might attract our attention for this reason (v. 11a: "In that day I will raise up / the booth of David that is fallen"), but then what use would we make of the preceding eight and a half chapters? Presumably, the prophets spoke for their own day, as well as for future days, and so they spoke in a historical and religious context, and they spoke on a whole range of important subjects. In the present study we are focusing on texts in the Old Testament of a royal messianic nature, not because we consider such verses to be the only things of worth in what the prophets wrote, but because this is the theme we have chosen to explore and explain. In fact, we will discover that Amos 9:11–15 is not a messianic prophecy in the way commonly understood.

David is mentioned twice by name in Amos (6:5; 9:11), and it is commonly supposed that the final oracle of the prophecy of Amos includes a message of hope for the house of David.[1] The authenticity of the message of salvation found in Amos's prophecy, especially in the closing verses of Amos 9,

---

An earlier version of material in this chapter is found in Gregory Goswell, "David in the Prophecy of Amos," *VT* 61 (2011): 243–57. Used by permission.

1. See, e.g., Max E. Polley, *Amos and the Davidic Empire: A Socio-Historical Approach* (New York: Oxford University Press, 1989).

is assumed in this study of the Old Testament in canonical form,[2] but the focus of our concern is whether the revealed plan of God for his people in the proclamation of Amos includes some form of Davidic revival. To that end, it will be necessary to give close attention to the opening of the prophecy, to the allusion to the historical figure of David in Amos 6, and to the phrase "the booth of David" (9:11). We will try to interpret this key phrase in the context of the teaching of Amos as a whole and in the wider setting provided by the Book of the Twelve.

A Southern Prophet in the North

As indicated by the superscription of the book (1:1), Amos comes from the Southern Kingdom (Tekoa in Judah) but is residing in and speaking to the North (Israel). This demonstrates that both kingdoms were viewed by the prophets as part of the one people of God, irrespective of the political divide, but does it hint at the original Davidic unity that embraced both North and South, as we saw in our study of Hosea?[3] The mention of both a southern and northern king in the superscription to the book is also relevant ("Uzziah . . . Jeroboam"). Significantly, despite the northern target of Amos's words, the order of the mention of names of kings in 1:1 gives priority to the southern king (Uzziah). The superscription of Hosea also lists southern and northern kings (Hosea 1:1), with southern kings again given priority, both in terms of initial position in the sentence (as in Amos 1:1) and number (four southern kings versus one northern). Subsequently, the titles attached to the prophetic books Micah (1:1) and Zephaniah (1:1) mention only southern kings. The Book of the Twelve certainly has a Judah (Jerusalem) focus, but that is not necessarily the same as a Davidic focus, for though David captured Jerusalem and made it his capital, more often in the prophets Jerusalem/Zion is pictured as God's capital (see below).

Early references to the canon count the Book of the Twelve as one book.[4] The order of the books *within* the Twelve remains constant in the masoretic tradition,[5] and the evidence of the Dead Sea Scrolls fragments of the Twelve

2. The passage is both frequently viewed as secondary and frequently defended as original; for an example of each approach, see Robert B. Coote, *Amos among the Prophets: Composition and Theology* (Philadelphia: Fortress, 1981), who attributes 9:7–15 to the postexilic C editor; and Shalom M. Paul, *Amos*, Hermeneia (Minneapolis: Fortress, 1991), 288–90.

3. E.g., Polley, *Amos and the Davidic Empire*, 3.

4. 4 Ezra 14:45; Josephus, *Against Apion* 1.38–41; Sirach 49:10; Baba Batra 14b/15a.

5. By contrast, the LXX order is Hosea, Amos, Micah, Joel, Obadiah, Jonah, Nahum (and from then on it coincides with the MT order).

indicates that these twelve prophetic booklets were copied on one scroll in ancient times. The order within the Twelve in the masoretic tradition may well be intended to be chronological, though the temporal location of several of the prophets is uncertain—notably, Joel and Obadiah. Their placement among the eighth-century prophets may be, in part, due to a desire to have an alternation of prophets who ministered in Israel and Judah: Hosea (Israel), Joel (Judah), Amos (Israel), Obadiah (Judah), Jonah (Israel), and Micah (Judah). Such a schematic ordering encourages a hermeneutic that reads the threats and promises in the different prophecies as applying to *both* kingdoms,[6] and this ordering suggests that an interest in North/South unity is not unique to the teaching of Amos and, therefore, may not be connected to an underlying Davidic frame of reference. The schema is also a reminder that any feature of the prophetic booklet labeled "Amos" is to be read within the context of the Book of the Twelve as a whole.

Jerusalem/Zion as God's Capital

In Amos's opening words, the Hebrew word order gives a prominent position to "from Zion . . . from Jerusalem" in the two clauses of Amos 1:2 ("*From Zion* the LORD roars, / and *from Jerusalem* he utters his voice," ESV alt.). This highlights the Jerusalem sanctuary as the point of origin of the revelation communicated through Amos to Israel.[7] It is commonly argued that this feature recalls the theological ideal of a reunited Davidic kingdom centered in Jerusalem (the old Davidic capital), so that Amos is addressing "the scandal of the divided kingdom."[8] Along those lines, G. Henton Davies says that the refrain of 4:6, 8, 9, 10, and 11 ("Yet you did not return to me") involves the moral requirement that northerners return to Zion, which 1:2 has designated the true source of divine revelation. However, the fact is that most references to Zion/Jerusalem in Amos and in the Twelve generally have no explicit Davidic connection. To assist an accurate appraisal of what is intended, we should note that what Amos 1:2 says about Zion corresponds with what is found in a link verse in Joel (the preceding prophecy),[9] implying that the message of Amos is not to be read in isolation from the other prophetic voices in the Twelve.

6. For more detail, see the previous chapter on Hosea.
7. As noted by G. Henton Davies, "Amos—The Prophet of Re-Union," *ExpTim* 92 (1981): 197.
8. Davies, "Amos—The Prophet of Re-Union," 198.
9. As noted and made much of by James D. Nogalski, *Literary Precursors to the Book of the Twelve*, BZAW 217 (Berlin: de Gruyter, 1993), 97–122.

Joel 3:16 reads:

> The LORD roars from Zion,
>   and utters his voice from Jerusalem,
>   and the heavens and the earth quake.
> But the LORD is a refuge to his people,
>   a stronghold to the people of Israel.

Amos 1:2 reads:

> And he said:
>
>> "The LORD roars from Zion
>>   and utters his voice from Jerusalem;
>> the pastures of the shepherds mourn,
>>   and the top of Carmel withers."

As noted by Hans Wolff, another verbal link with the prophecy of Joel is "the catchword expression" of restored fortunes in Amos 9:14a that is found earlier in Joel 3:1 (4:1 MT).[10] According to James D. Nogalski, "The way in which Joel and Amos are related through quotations indicates an intentional association."[11] Like Amos, Joel 3 (4 MT) combines descriptions of the paradisial renewal of the land and of judgment on foreign nations (esp. Egypt and Edom). Specifically, it could be argued that Joel 3:16–21 (4:16–21 MT) provides a theological framework for the prophecy of Amos that follows, with Joel 3:16 (4:16 MT; // Amos 1:2) and Joel 3:18a (4:18a MT; // Amos 9:13) in effect bracketing the beginning and end of Amos, implying that the prophecy of Amos is to be interpreted within that frame of reference.[12]

What is most significant for our present purpose is that Amos 1:2a picks up and reuses the description of divine roaring from Zion/Jerusalem in Joel 3:16a (4:16a MT); however, no Davidic allusion is to be found in the prophecy of Joel. Whatever happened to the empire of David? The concern of our question is not the issue of the historical demise and disintegration of David's

10. H. W. Wolff, *Joel and Amos*, trans. Waldemar Janzen, S. Dean McBride Jr., and Charles A. Muenchow, Hermeneia (Philadelphia: Fortress, 1977), 354.

11. James D. Nogalski, "Joel as 'Literary Anchor' for the Book of the Twelve," in *Reading and Hearing the Book of the Twelve*, ed. James D. Nogalski and Marvin A. Sweeney, SBL Symposium Series 15 (Atlanta: Society of Biblical Literature, 2000), 95, 99.

12. Aaron Schart, *Die Entstehung des Zwölfprophetenbuchs: Neubearbeitungen von Amos im Rahmen schriftübergreifender Redaktionsprozesse*, BZAW 260 (Berlin: de Gruyter, 1998), 261–74. Schart argues that Joel and Obadiah were incorporated into the Twelve to frame Amos (261).

empire after his death, but the history of the *concept* of his empire as an ideal and a future hope. It may well be that the Zion tradition arose from David's choice of Jerusalem and the experience of empire under David and Solomon,[13] but that tradition as developed and preserved in the Psalter, the prophecy of Isaiah, and the Book of the Twelve (including Amos) depicts Zion/Jerusalem (both present and future) as primarily *God's* capital, from which he rules the world. In other words, we cannot simply see in every reference to Jerusalem/Zion an allusion to David and his kingdom.

Zion as God's International Capital

The book opens with oracles against foreign nations (Amos 1–2). Michael L. Barré and others argue that what these eight nations have in common is that they were all once part of the Davidic empire and that this was the criterion for their selection.[14] In apparent support of this view, the canonical book ends with what is often viewed as the promise of a restored Davidic empire (9:11–12), forming an *inclusio* around the book as a whole. In line with this evaluation, Barré understands the formula "I will not cause *it* to return" (RSV margin; ESV: "I will not revoke the punishment"), wherein "it" is not specified (1:3, 6, etc.), as meaning "I will not let him return (to me)." YHWH will not take the guilty party back as a vassal in good standing, the theory of Barré being that the condemned nations as members of the Davidic empire were vassals of YHWH.[15] Needless to say, this is only one possible answer to the disputed question of the identity of the object of the verb.[16]

Paul Noble is right to critique Barré for making too much of terms like "brother(s)" (ESV: "brother[hood]" [1:9, 11]), "his allies" (ESV: "his pity" [1:11]), and "acts of rebellion" (ESV: "transgressions" [e.g., 1:13; 2:1]), which,

---

13. As favored by J. J. M. Roberts, "The Davidic Origin of the Zion Tradition," *JBL* 92 (1973): 329–44.

14. Michael L. Barré, "The Meaning of *l' 'šybnw* in Amos 1:3–2:6," *JBL* 105 (1986): 611–31. The arguments of Barré are subjected to thorough criticism by Paul R. Noble, "Israel among the Nations," *HBT* 15 (1993): 56–62. We acknowledge our substantial dependence on Noble.

15. Barré, "Meaning of *l' 'šybnw*," 622–23. Cf. Polley, *Amos and the Davidic Empire*, 69: "By revolting against the Davidic ruler, these nations, including Israel, had rejected the authority of Yahweh."

16. See, for example, Paul R. Noble, "'I Will Not Bring "It" Back' (Amos 1:3): A Deliberately Ambiguous Oracle?," *ExpTim* 106 (1994–95): 105–9; James R. Linville, "What Does 'It' Mean? Interpretation at the Point of No Return in Amos 1–2," *BibInt* 8 (2000): 400–424. Both authors explore what they see as the inherent ambiguity in the expression.

apart from the last, occur in just two oracles, those directed at Tyre and Edom (Amos 1:9–10, 11–12), and these words are not by any means exclusively treaty terms. Unlike the other foreign nations listed, Tyre was not conquered or subjugated by David and is specifically said to be a treaty partner and therefore is accused of treaty violation (v. 9: "They . . . did not remember the covenant of brotherhood"). This recalls the close links between Tyre and Israel since the days of David and Solomon. Solomon and Hiram make a covenant in 1 Kings 5:12 (5:26 MT), and Hiram refers to Solomon as his "brother" in 9:13. A reference to Israel as "his [Edom's] brother" (Amos 1:11) most likely refers to their ethnic kinship, not to a connection by way of treaty (cf. Obad. 10, 12). However, most of the oracles in Amos 1–2 have no possible covenant/treaty links at all. As well, 3:9 (mentioning Egypt) and 9:7 (mentioning the Ethiopians) show that God's sovereignty over the nations is unconnected to whether they were once constituents of the Davidic empire. The nations selected for mention in Amos 1–2 appear to be chosen simply due to their geographical proximity to either Israel or Judah.[17] They represent all the nations of the world. The picture, then, is of God's sovereignty over the nations generally, exercised from his international capital, Zion/Jerusalem (1:2).

Like David—Not (Amos 6:5)

The first actual mention of David in Amos is in the phrase "like David" (6:5), which provides an ironic comparison of contemporary Israelite leaders with David, the point being that these unworthy leaders are really not like David at all. Amos 6:4–7 reads:

> [4]Woe to those who lie on beds of ivory
>   and stretch themselves out on their couches,
> and eat lambs from the flock
>   and calves from the midst of the stall,
> [5]who sing idle songs to the sound of the harp
>   and like David invent for themselves instruments of music,
> [6]who drink wine in bowls
>   and anoint themselves with the finest oils,
>   but are not grieved over the ruin of Joseph!
> [7]Therefore they shall now be the first of those who go into exile,
>   and the revelry of those who stretch themselves out shall pass away.

17. See, e.g., the schema of Andrew E. Steinmann, "The Oracle of Amos's Oracles against the Nations: 1:3–2:16," *JBL* 111 (1992): 687.

Some Old Testament texts credit David with making (= inventing) certain stringed instruments for sacred song,[18] and the same notion may be present here (6:5b: "Like David [they] *invent* [*ḥāšab*] for themselves instruments of music"). For the sense of "invent," see Exod. 31:4, though its interpretation in Amos 6 is a matter of dispute. The Hebrew preposition in verse 5a ("who sing idle songs *to* [*'al*] the sound of the harp") may do double duty for the second-half of the parallel poetic line, resulting in this alternate translation: "They improvise [*ḥāšab*] for themselves *upon* instruments like David" (v. 5b).[19] However, irrespective of the exact translation, the condemned leaders of Zion and Samaria are sarcastically likened to David, who enjoyed lasting fame for his role as a singer of sacred songs such as are preserved in the Psalter, and possibly as the inventor of several musical instruments used in worship.

The oracle containing Amos 6:5 is bound together by an *inclusio*: "those who stretch themselves . . . stretch themselves" (vv. 4a, 7b), with the section describing the leaders' self-indulgent apathy (vv. 4–6) and their punishment (v. 7). The offending leaders eat lambs and calves, which otherwise might be offered in sacrifices (v. 4). The allusion to "bowls" (*mizrāq*; v. 6) is elsewhere only used in sacrificial ritual (e.g., Num. 7:13, 25; 2 Chron. 4:8; ESV: "basins"), but here the leading men misuse sacred bowls as drinking vessels for the feasting. So too, the expression "[they] anoint themselves" (*māšaḥ*) usually has sacred associations. Wine and oil are also used in offerings (Exod. 29:40; Lev. 2:4, 15; 23:13). Feasting and anointing the body were suspended in periods of mourning and crisis (2 Sam. 14:2; Dan. 10:3), but what is depicted is the criminal apathy of the leaders about the perilous state of the nation that faces the judgment of God (Amos 6:6b). By contrast, David as the singer of sacred song is a model of piety. David used music and song for worship, whereas those indicted in verse 5 use them for carousing. The allusion to David in Amos 6, however, has no messianic coloring,[20] and David is simply depicted as a worshiper and cultic figure. This raises the possibility that the phrase "the booth of David" (9:11) may also have a cultic nuance, and that is what we will now proceed to argue.

18. See 1 Chron. 23:5; 2 Chron. 29:26–27; Neh. 12:36; 11Q5 151A ("My hands made an instrument and my fingers a lyre"); cf. Ps. 151:2 in the LXX.

19. Cf. the translation of Francis I. Andersen and David Noel Freedman, *Amos: A New Translation with Introduction and Commentary*, AB 24A (New York: Doubleday, 1989), 544; also, David Noel Freedman, "But Did King David Invent Musical Instruments?," *Bible Review* 1 (1985): 49–51.

20. As noted by James R. Linville, "[David] is not imagined as a king, but rather the model musician." James R. Linville, *Amos and the Cosmic Imagination*, SOTSMS (Aldershot, UK: Ashgate, 2008), 123.

The Booth of David

The most significant passage pertaining to messianic expectations in Amos is 9:11–15. After articulating the standard interpretation, we will present an alternative understanding that emphasizes the restoration of God's reign in Jerusalem. Amos 9:11–12 reads:

> [11]"In that day I will raise up
>   the booth of David that is fallen
> and repair its breaches,
>   and raise up its ruins
>   and rebuild it as in the days of old,
> [12]that they may possess the remnant of Edom
>   and all the nations who are called by my name,"
>   declares the LORD who does this.

The most common interpretation of the cryptic phrase "the *booth* of David" is that it is a metaphor for the "house" of David—namely, the Davidic dynasty and kingdom (cf. targum: "the kingdom of the house of David"; see 2 Sam. 7:5, 11; 1 Kings 11:38).[21] That house is now only a fallen "booth," and the restoration of the divided kingdom and lost empire is promised. God's promise in Amos 9:11 to "raise [it] up" (2x) and "rebuild it as in the days of old" may possibly be connected to 2 Sam. 7:12 and 7:27, respectively. This, anyway, is the commonly rehearsed argument by scholars. However, the other terms used in Amos 9:11 ("repair," "breaches," "ruins") do not particularly suit the flimsy structure of a "booth," but rather refer to the object to which the metaphor points (see below).[22] Possible support for the interpretation that sees the booth as a metaphor for David's kingdom may be an implied contrast between "the booth of David" (= the dissolved empire of David) and "all the nations" in verse 12. The phrase "as in the days of old" is used in Mic. 7:14 and Mal. 3:4, though in these cross-references it has no Davidic connection, so that Shalom Paul's judgment that Amos 9:11b is "a nostalgic reflection upon the ideal period of the Davidic Empire" is not supported by the phrase itself.[23] Our main criticism of the view that the "booth" refers to David's line and kingdom, however, is that other views have stronger exegetical supports.

---

21. See the survey of research on the phrase since 1860 in Sabine Nägele, *Laubhütte Davids und Wolkensohn: Eine auslegungsgeschichtliche Studie zu Amos 9,11 in der jüdischen und christlichen Exegese*, AGJU 24 (Leiden: Brill, 1995), 150–58.

22. In response to this problem, Coote wants to see reference in v. 11 to Israel as God's vineyard (cf. Isa. 5:1–7). Coote, *Amos among the Prophets*, 124–25.

23. Paul, *Amos*, 290–91.

A second view, promoted by Kenneth Pomykala, is that "the booth of David" refers to the city of Jerusalem and the oracle concerns the restoration of Jerusalem.[24] As noted by Pomykala, the term "booth" is applied to forlorn Jerusalem in Isa. 1:8 ("And the daughter of Zion is left / like a booth in a vineyard"). On this understanding, God promises in Amos 9:11 to repair the "breaches" (*pirṣîm*) in the city's walls, this being the most common sense of the term (e.g., 1 Kings 11:27; Neh. 6:1; Isa. 58:12).[25] The verb "to repair" (*gādar*) means building with stone or putting up a stone wall (Lam. 3:7–9; Ezek. 22:30; Hosea 2:6 [2:8 MT]), so that this term also suits application to a city.[26] The repairing of "its breaches" (Amos 9:11) picks up 4:3, where the women of Samaria are threatened that they will "go out through the breaches [of the city walls]" (both verses using the noun *pereṣ* in plural form). The juxtaposed prophecy of the rebuilding and reoccupation of ruined cities in 9:14 implies that verse 11 is also about the rebuilding and reoccupation of a city. The noun "ruins" (*hărisōt*) in verse 11 is only found here in the Hebrew Bible but is used in Sirach 49:13 of Nehemiah's repair work on the city wall.[27] The cognate verb *hāras* ("to tear down") is often used in the Bible.[28] In summary, the terminology of Amos 9:11 ("breaches," "ruins," "rebuild") points to a city as the object of reference. As well, if verse 11 does refer to Jerusalem, this provides an *inclusio* with Jerusalem in 1:2 around the book of Amos.

As noted by Pomykala, the terminology of the booth of David that is "fallen" can apply to destroyed cities (e.g., "Fallen, fallen is Babylon," Isa. 21:9). On this reading, the key phrase in Amos 9:11 is a parody on "the city of David," so named because Jerusalem was captured and rebuilt by David (cf. 2 Sam. 5:6–10). Vital for interpretation is the recognition that Amos 9:11–15 echoes and reverses earlier prophecies of judgment in the book of Amos.[29] In the present case, verse 11 recalls both "Fallen, no more to rise, / is virgin Israel" (5:2) and "They [= those involved in degenerate cults] shall fall, / and never

24. Kenneth E. Pomykala, "Jerusalem as the Fallen Booth of David in Amos 9:11," in *Biblical Studies in Honor of Simon John De Vries*, vol. 1 of *God's Word for Our World*, ed. J. Harold Ellens, Deborah L. Ellens, Rolf P. Knierim, and Isaac Kalimi, JSOTSup 388 (London: T&T Clark International, 2004), 275–93; Kenneth E. Pomykala, *The Davidic Dynasty Tradition in Early Judaism: Its History and Significance for Messianism*, SBLEJL 7 (Atlanta: Scholars Press, 1995), 61–63.

25. For the similarities between Amos 9:11 and Isa. 58:12, see Joseph W. Groves, *Actualization and Interpretation in the Old Testament*, SBLDS 86 (Atlanta: Scholars Press, 1987), 182–83.

26. Pomykala, "Fallen Booth of David," 284.

27. BDB 249; *DCH* 2:593.

28. BDB 248.

29. See Groves, *Actualization and Interpretation*, 179–91.

rise again" (8:14).[30] Given the cultic context of the lament in 5:2 (n.b. 5:4–6) and the cultic content of 8:14, the parallels raise the possibility that 9:11 also has a cultic focus—that is, it refers to Jerusalem as a cultic center, with the temple as its focal point.

This leads to the third (and preferred) interpretation, which is really a refinement of the second interpretation. This emphasizes the sanctuary character of Zion/Jerusalem, to which the phrase "the booth [sukkâ] of David" points—namely, the temple and Jerusalem as a unit.[31] A possible parallel is found in Isa. 4:6, where the word "booth" is used of the cloud, smoke, and fire that will cover future Zion:"It will be for a pavilion [sukkâ], a shade by day from the heat, and for a refuge and a shelter from the storm and rain" (RSV alt.; following MT versification). The mention of cloud, smoke, and fire recalls the wilderness wanderings of the exodus period, denoting God's presence and protection (e.g., Ps. 105:39). As well, cloud and fire are connected to God's presence in the tabernacle (Exod. 40:38), and the theophanic cloud filled the newly dedicated temple (1 Kings 8:10–11). As has often been noted, Isa. 4:2–6 is a companion passage to 2:1–4 about "the mountain of the house of the LORD,"[32] and this suggests that the temple is also in view in Isa. 4 (though not explicitly mentioned). This supposition is supported by the reference to "her [Zion's] assemblies" (4:5)—namely, festal gatherings (cf. 1:13), and Joseph Blenkinsopp says that this alludes to "ceremonies carried out in the temple."[33] Here, then, is a passage in the prophets that depicts the eschatological state of salvation and relates the term "booth" to God's protection of Zion as a cultic center.

David brought the ark to Jerusalem and put it in a tent ('ōhel; 2 Sam. 6:17; 7:2), which 2 Sam. 11:11 speaks of as a "booth" (sukkâ). According to Francis I. Andersen and David Noel Freedman, "[The booth of David] could stand for one or more of the buildings of the capital city that had symbolic significance," and they opt for the tent housing the ark "because that is the one structure presumably erected by David for which we do not have a name."[34] As noted by H. G. M. Williamson, God's sanctuary is regularly referred to as a tent ('ōhel), and, by extension, this is applied to the later temple, "especially in connection

30. All three verses use the Hebrew roots meaning "to rise" (qûm) and "to fall" (nāpal). On the complementary nature of the passages in Amos 5 and 9, see Cullen I. K. Story, "Amos—Prophet of Praise," VT 30 (1980): 71n13.

31. Nägele also comes to this conclusion (Laubhütte Davids und Wolkensohn, 211–14); cf. Jason Radine, The Book of Amos in Emergent Judah, FAT 2.45 (Tübingen: Mohr Siebeck, 2010), 199–211.

32. E.g., Christopher Seitz, Isaiah 1–39, IBC (Louisville: Westminster John Knox, 1993), 41.

33. Joseph Blenkinsopp, Isaiah 1–39: A New Translation with Commentary, AB 19 (New York: Doubleday, 2000), 204.

34. Andersen and Freedman, Amos, 914.

with the idea of asylum (Pss. 27:5 [also uses *sukkâ*]; 61:4 [61:5 MT]; cf. 15:1; 78:60)."[35] Such usage is explained by a knowledge of the tent erected by David for the ark (2 Sam. 6:17), the same "tent of the LORD" to which Joab fled for asylum (because it housed the altar with horns; see 1 Kings 2:28–34). In the book of Isaiah, when the focus is upon the security of Zion-Jerusalem, "the city of our appointed feasts" is called "an immovable tent [*'ōhel*]" (33:20), and this is another probable allusion to YHWH's tent.[36] These references in the Psalter and Isaiah show that the "tent/booth" that was used by David to house the ark and that was later transferred to the temple (1 Kings 8:4) became a metaphor applied to Jerusalem as the site of the temple.

A parallel to Amos 9:11 is found in Isa. 16:5 that speaks of "the tent [*'ōhel*] of David."[37] This is another text that may preserve a reminiscence of the Davidic tent that (pre-temple) was the cultic center of the nation.[38] In line with the idea of the temple as a place of asylum (see above), Isa. 16:1–4 describes Moabite emissaries seeking asylum under the protection of the Davidic ruler who sits enthroned (*yāšab*) "in the tent of David" (16:5). The same blend of associations is at play in Amos 9:11, and in both passages David's "tent/booth" is best understood as a reference to Jerusalem as a cultic center. David is referred to because he is depicted in 2 Sam. 6 as the one responsible for bringing the ark (= God's throne or footstool, 6:2) to Jerusalem and housing it in a tent (6:17). In the next chapter, we are told that David "tarried [*yāšab*] before YHWH" to pray (2 Sam. 7:18),[39] presumably in the tent-shrine he had erected for the ark. It was through David's initiative that the captured city of Jerusalem became not simply his own capital (2 Sam. 5:9: "the city of David") but YHWH's capital as well. The focus in Amos 9 is on Zion's cultic restoration, yet this may imply that the restoration will include a pious Davidic king (see below).

In line with this understanding, Zion in Joel is called "my [God's] holy mountain" (3:17 [4:17 MT]). According to Terence Collins, "The preoccupation with the status of Zion and its temple is a major feature of Joel . . . [and] serves to ensure that the same preoccupation is a key note for the whole of *The Twelve*."[40]

---

35. H. G. M. Williamson, *Variations on a Theme: King, Messiah and Servant in the Book of Isaiah*, Didsbury Lectures 1997 (Carlisle, UK: Paternoster, 1998), 61, citing Klaus Koch, "*'ohel*," *TDOT* 1:127.

36. According to Willem A. M. Beuken, *Isaiah, Part II, Volume 2: Isaiah Chapters 28–39*, HCOT (Leuven: Peeters, 2000), 273.

37. See Gregory Goswell, "Isaiah 16: A Forgotten Chapter in the History of Messianism," *SJOT* 28 (2014): 91–103.

38. F. M. Cross, "The Priestly Tabernacle in the Light of Recent Research," in *Temples and High Places in Biblical Times*, ed. A. Biran (Jerusalem: Keter, 1981), 177n31.

39. The translation is provided by A. A. Anderson, *2 Samuel*, WBC 11 (Dallas: Word, 1989), 126.

40. Terence Collins, *The Mantle of Elijah: The Redaction Criticism of the Prophetical Books*, Biblical Seminar 20 (Sheffield: JSOT Press, 1993), 68.

The Zion/temple theme is found in verses such as Joel 1:13–16; 2:1, 15–17, 23, 32 (3:5 MT); 3:16–21 (4:16–21 MT), and Zion is viewed as God's capital, the fructifying center of the land/earth, and the place of refuge of God's people. Consequently, according to Rolf Rendtorff, "those who are at ease in Zion" (Amos 6:1) may be those who drew the wrong conclusion from the picture of Zion as a place of escape and refuge in Joel.[41] If the context provided for Amos in the Twelve is deemed significant, the presentation in Joel shapes the interpretation of Amos in a certain direction. In Obadiah, the "vision" that follows straight after the visions of Amos (chaps. 7–9), Zion is "my [= God's] holy mountain" (Obad. 16) and the capital of a kingdom that the Lord rules (Obad. 21).

As well, Amos 9:11 is the thematic inverse of the earlier announced judgment on Bethel, the "king's sanctuary . . . the house [ESV: "a temple"] of the kingdom," which, therefore, might be nicknamed "the booth [ESV: "house"] of Jeroboam" (7:9, 13 ESV alt.). In Amos's third vision, the prophet sees Yhwh standing on or by ('al) a wall (v. 7), and the succeeding verses imply that it is the wall of the Bethel sanctuary (vv. 9, 10, 13). In a further development of the same theme, in the fifth vision (9:1–4), Amos sees Yhwh standing on or by ('al) "the altar." If the collapse of the temple structure (capitals/thresholds) refers to the destruction of the Bethel sanctuary, as is most likely,[42] "maybe Amos could envisage a future hope for Israel under the Jerusalem cult,"[43] which, we argue, is what is contemplated in v. 11. James R. Linville has noted the allusive but persistent references to architectural structures in 7:7–17 and chapter 9, including a description of the created order as a cosmic temple built by God (9:6; cf. Ps. 78:69).[44] Therefore, the destruction of the false sanctuary at Bethel finds its positive counterpart in the restoration of the Jerusalem sanctuary (9:11).

That They May Possess

The anticipated extension of authority over all the nations in Amos 9:12 complements the judgments pronounced upon the nations in Amos 1–2 (*inclusio*) but need not refer to a restoration of the Davidic/Solomonic kingdom. In 9:12,

41. Rolf Rendtorff, "How to Read the Book of the Twelve as a Theological Unity," in *Reading and Hearing the Book of the Twelve*, ed. James D. Nogalski and Marvin A. Sweeney, SBL Symposium Series 15 (Atlanta: Society of Biblical Literature, 2000), 82.

42. E.g., Gary V. Smith, *Amos*, Mentor (Fearn, Scotland: Christian Focus, 1998), 359; Joyce Rilett Wood, *Amos in Song and Book Culture*, JSOTSup 337 (London: Sheffield Academic, 2002), 82–85.

43. As suggested by M. E. W. Thompson, "Amos—A Prophet of Hope?," *ExpTim* 104 (1992): 75.

44. James R. Linville, "Visions and Voices: Amos 7–9," *Bib* 80 (1999): 38.

Edom is used as a synecdoche for "all the nations," which is best understood as an equivalent object of the verb "to possess" in the parallel structure of verse 12.[45] Significantly, Edom has the same representative role in the book of Obadiah that immediately follows (Obad. 15: "all the nations"). The expression "[all the nations] who are called by my name" denotes ownership, but this does not need to be limited to former national constituents of the Davidic empire.

The Hebrew plural verb "*they* may possess" (root *yāraš*), which is not supplied with an explicit subject (Amos 9:12a), could possibly refer to future rulers of the Davidic dynasty who reassert their authority over national members of the former Davidic empire,[46] but certainly no individual royal figure is in view in this passage. It is more likely, given the use of the same plural verb in Obadiah, that Davidic prerogatives are democratized and that it is the people of Zion/Jerusalem who will "possess" (*yāraš*) the nations (Philistia, Edom) and areas of the North (Ephraim, Samaria, Gilead; cf. Obad. 17, 19 [3x], 20).[47] As in Amos 9, in Obadiah no individual Davidide is in view, so that it is best to see "they shall possess" as a democratization of Davidic promises. So too, Mic. 4:8 democratizes the promise of a renewed kingdom of David and speaks of "kingship for the daughter of Zion," and in 4:13 it is the people of the city (not a Davidide) who will be victorious over the nations ("You [= the daughter of Zion] shall beat in pieces many peoples.")

In summary, Zion/Jerusalem in the prophecy of Amos is portrayed as God's capital from which he rules the entire world (1:2). The criterion of selection of the condemned foreign nations in Amos 1–2 is not membership of the former Davidic empire but the fact that they are neighboring nations of Israel or Judah. They represent God's rulership over *all* nations. The allusion to David in 6:5 is as a liturgical figure, and the rebuilt "booth of David"

---

45. Cf. the rendering of this verse in the LXX and New Testament as human race (= *'ādām*) instead of Edom (*'ĕdōm*). For explanations of the differences between MT and LXX that do not have to be put down to accidental misreading of the Hebrew text, see W. Edward Glenny, *Finding Meaning in the Text: Translation Technique and Theology in the Septuagint of Amos*, VTSup 126 (Leiden: Brill, 2009), 224–28. The same applies to the form of the Old Testament text found in Acts 15; see Nägele, *Laubhütte Davids und Wolkensohn*, 71–107. The LXX form of Amos 9:12 ("that the remnant of the human race may seek"), as noted by Arie van der Kooij, implies an understanding of 9:11 as referring to the rebuilt city of David, including the temple, as the goal of the eschatological pilgrimage of the nations. Arie van der Kooij, "The Septuagint of Zechariah as Witness to an Early Interpretation of the Book," in *The Book of Zechariah and Its Influence*, ed. Christopher Tuckett (Aldershot, UK: Ashgate, 2003), 60.

46. According to Paul, *Amos*, 291.

47. So too Nägele, *Laubhütte Davids und Wolkensohn*, 213; cf. Paul L. Redditt, "The Production and Reading of the Book of the Twelve," *SBL 1997 Seminar Papers* (Atlanta: Scholars Press, 1997), 404: "The redactors [responsible for 9:12a] are pro-Jerusalem but the Davidic house seems no longer to have been an issue."

in 9:11 is Jerusalem thought of as the site of the temple. What this means is that there is no individual messianic figure in view in Amos 9, and it is best to see the final prophecy of hope as democratizing Davidic promises. However, if the presence of a Davidic leader is to be contemplated in Amos's picture of the end time, the portrait of David in Amos 6 suggests that such a future "David" will be the leader of worship in the renewed city of Jerusalem (such as is found in the vision of Ezek. 40–48).[48] Indeed, if one reads Amos in the context of the Twelve, in which there is a recurring Davidic hope, the logic of the prophecy of Amos *implies* the presence in restored Jerusalem of a Davidic figure as worshiper and patron of the cult.

Postlude: Canonical Reflections

The use of Amos 9 by James in Acts 15 confirms the interpretation we have offered. The singling out of Edom (Amos 9:12) is not surprising when it is noticed that this nation is highlighted in Amos 1–2 as well. Edom is the *fourth* (3 + 1) nation in the three/four pattern used by the prophet ("For three transgressions of Edom, and for four . . . ," 1:11–12), which draws attention to Edom in the series of nations condemned. As well, Edom is mentioned in 1:6, 9, and 2:1, due to its involvement in the sins of other nations (whether as partner or victim),[49] so that Edom is placed before the reader several times. This certainly favors the view that 9:11–15 is an original part of the literary design of the book of Amos. What is more, there are hints of Edom's *spiritual* incorporation in a restored kingdom of God together with all the nations "who are called by my name" (cf. Deut. 28:10, where God's name is called over Israel as a sign of their being chosen by God). This shows the credibility of James's reference to this prophecy in Acts 15:16–21 in relation to the gentile mission initiated by Peter and carried forward by Paul.[50]

Acts 15:12–16 reads:

> [12]And all the assembly fell silent, and they listened to Barnabas and Paul as they related what signs and wonders God had done through them among the Gentiles. [13]After they finished speaking, James replied, "Brothers, listen to me. [14]Simeon has related how God first visited the Gentiles, to take from them a people for his name. [15]And with this the words of the prophets agree, just as it is written,

---

48. See chap. 8 in the present volume.

49. As noted by M. Daniel Carroll R., "God and His People in the Nations' History: A Contextualised Reading of Amos 1–2," *TynBul* 47 (1996): 61.

50. John H. Sailhamer, *Introduction to Old Testament Theology: A Canonical Approach* (Grand Rapids: Zondervan, 1995), 250–52.

[16]"After this I will return,
and I will rebuild the tent of David that has fallen;
I will rebuild its ruins,
    and I will restore it."

Something more profound is predicted in Amos 9 than simply a reimposition of Israel's rule and influence over surrounding nations. James, quoting these verses at the Council of Jerusalem, asserts that God has taken "a people [*laos*] for his name" (Acts 15:14), so that believing gentiles are part of the people of God (now more widely defined) in the same way as believing Jews are (for the word "people" [*'am*] in the Old Testament is almost exclusively applied to Israel), and James shows that this interpretation of what is happening through the gentile mission has prophetic warrant. There is nothing in Amos 9 about gentiles having to become Jews, so what is contemplated is the incorporation of gentiles as gentiles into the people of God.

The rebuilt "tent of David" is the Christian community (= the new temple) being formed through the worldwide preaching of the gospel. The use of Amos 9:11–12 in the theology of the book of Acts shows that the gentile mission fulfills Old Testament prophecy. The preaching of the gospel begins in the Jerusalem temple (Acts 2–5) and fans out from there. So too, the first Christian community gathers in the temple courts (2:46; 3:1; 5:12; 6:7).[51] Consistent with this Lukan focus, the rebuilt "dwelling of David" (15:16 RSV) is understood by James as the reconstituted temple, which consists of believing Jews and gentiles and which is forming through the worldwide preaching of the gospel.[52] Luke's account of the council in Acts 15 is a major turning point of Luke's story, and the prophecy of Amos 9 plays a crucial part in the proceedings. A potential threat to the continued expansion of the gospel to the gentile nations is dealt with by recourse to Old Testament prophecy. Immediately after this is the beginning of the extension of the gospel into Europe (Acts 16). Once the decision of the Council of Jerusalem is made, the focus of the rest of the book of Acts is on the unstoppable progress of the gospel to the "ends of the earth" through the Pauline mission.[53]

---

51. Ron C. Fay, "The Narrative Function of the Temple in Luke-Acts," *TJ* 27 (2006): 255–70.

52. Cf. Richard Bauckham, "James and the Jerusalem Church," in *The Book of Acts in its Palestinian Setting*, ed. Richard Bauckham (Grand Rapids: Eerdmans, 1995), 452–55; Craig R. Koester, *The Dwelling of God: The Tabernacle in the Old Testament, Intertestamental Jewish Literature, and the New Testament*, CBQMS 22 (Washington, DC: Catholic Biblical Association of America, 1989), 85–87.

53. Andreas J. Köstenberger and Peter T. O'Brien, *Salvation to the Ends of the Earth: A Biblical Theology of Mission* (Downers Grove, IL: IVP Academic, 2001), 150–51.

11

Davidic Rule in Micah

What sets the artist apart from others is the gift of seeing familiar things with fresh eyes and then, whether on a canvas, in a symphony, or in a literary work, enabling others to see what they saw. The contrast between art and science is often exaggerated, for the scientist has the same gift, only differently directed, and the result of scientific endeavor is the discovery and sharing of new knowledge via scientific papers. Is the process of interpreting Scripture an art or a science? Probably a bit of both. In this book, our efforts are aimed at helping believers to see familiar messianic texts afresh, for our routine way of looking at well-known texts sometimes needs a little revision.

The metaphor of shepherd and sheep is used several times in the prophecy of Micah to describe the relationship between God and his people (2:12–13; 4:6–8; 7:14). The shepherd image is also applied to the promised human ruler in 5:4 (5:3 MT),[1] and it is the role of this messianic figure in Mic. 5 that we are seeking to clarify. Though Mic. 5 has been frequently studied and is of special interest to the Christian reader due to its use in the New Testament and application to Jesus (see Matt. 2:6), the role of the Davidic ruler in Mic. 5 is often inflated beyond what is indicated in the prophetic text. Despite what

An earlier version of material in this chapter was published as Gregory Goswell, "Davidic Rule in the Prophecy of Micah," *JSOT* 44, no. 1 (2019): 153–65. Copyright © 2019 (Gregory Goswell), reprinted by permission of SAGE Publications, DOI: 10.1177/309089218772577.

1. The versification of Mic. 5 differs by one between the Hebrew and English versions: 5:1–15 in the English, 4:14–5:14 in the MT.

is regularly asserted,[2] the future messianic figure is not depicted by Micah as the deliverer of God's people; rather, he is assigned the more modest role of dispenser of justice within the divine economy.

The Messianic Heart of the Prophecy

The messianic section at Mic. 5:1–4 (4:14–5:3 MT) can be viewed as strategically placed in the middle of the book. This textual unit comprises four verses, with its starting point coinciding with and supported by the Latin/English chapter division (5:1 [4:14 MT]).[3] Micah 5:1–4 reads:

> [1]Now muster your troops, O daughter of troops;
>   siege is laid against us;
> with a rod they strike the judge of Israel
>   on the cheek.
> [2]But you, O Bethlehem Ephrathah,
>   who are too little to be among the clans of Judah,
> from you shall come forth for me
>   one who is to be ruler in Israel,
> whose coming forth is from of old,
>   from ancient days.
> [3]Therefore he shall give them up until the time
>   when she who is in labor has given birth;
> then the rest of his brothers shall return
>   to the people of Israel.
> [4]And he shall stand and shepherd his flock in the strength of the LORD,
>   in the majesty of the name of the LORD his God.
> And they shall dwell secure, for now he shall be great
>   to the ends of the earth.

The crisis pictured in 5:1 provides the necessary context for the verses that follow, for their message of hope responds to the picture of the humiliation of "the judge [*šōpēṭ*] of Israel" in the first verse of the unit by depicting a future Davidic figure provided by God.[4] This supposition is supported by the disjunctive "But you . . ." at verse 2a, indicating that a contrast is drawn with

2. E.g., Ralph L. Smith, *Micah–Malachi*, Word Biblical Themes (Dallas: Word, 1990), 19; Ehud Ben Zvi, *Micah*, FOTL 21B (Grand Rapids: Eerdmans, 2000), 121, 128; Bruce K. Waltke, *A Commentary on Micah* (Grand Rapids: Eerdmans, 2007), 294.

3. See John T. Willis, "Micah 4:14–5:5, a Unit," *VT* 18 (1968): 532–35.

4. David Gerald Hagstrom, *The Coherence of the Book of Micah: A Literary Analysis*, SBLDS 89 (Atlanta: Scholars Press, 1988), 63.

what immediately precedes. Also relevant is the Hebrew wordplay of striking the "cheek" (*halləḥî*) and mention of "Bethlehem" (*bêt-leḥem*), which ties together problem and solution (vv. 1–2). The context of the messianic oracle is the portrayal of a city (= Jerusalem) under siege (v. 1; cf. 4:9, 11),[5] with a foreign invader humiliating its ruler.

The choice of the designation *šōpēṭ* (ESV: "judge") for the city's ruler (Mic. 5:1), who is undoubtedly the Judean king,[6] is explained, at least in part, by the Hebrew alliterative wordplay with the preceding clause: "With a *rod* [*šēbeṭ*] they strike upon the cheek the *ruler* [*šōpēṭ*] of Israel" (authors' trans.).[7] The same wordplay is present in Isa. 11:4, where it is said that the promised ruler "shall *judge* with righteousness the poor" and "shall smite the earth with the *rod* [*šēbeṭ*] of his mouth" (authors' trans.). Furthermore, the titular use of *šōpēṭ* alludes to the essential role of the Israelite king as the enforcer of "justice" (*mišpāṭ*) and the nation's chief legal officer (e.g., 2 Sam. 14:1–7; 15:1–6), so that the future ruler will also presumably fit this mold—that is, he will administer justice (cf. Ps. 72:1–2; Isa. 9:7 [9:6 MT]; 11:3–5; 16:5; 32:1; Jer. 23:5).[8] The failure of leaders to uphold "justice" (*mišpāṭ*) was earlier exposed and condemned (Mic. 3:1, 9, 11),[9] and this messianic unit in Mic. 5 is framed in terms that address the present problems of the Judean state.

Though the Davidism is implicit rather than explicit, the promised ruler is pictured as coming from the small village of "Bethlehem Ephrathah" (Mic. 5:2),[10] the birthplace of David (1 Sam. 16:18; 17:12), so there is no doubt that the arrival of a future Davidide is in prospect. The text goes on to speak of this figure's "origins," this being an abstract noun based on the same Hebrew root just used for his "coming forth" (*yāṣā'*) from the town of Bethlehem, and so what is referred to is his ancient lineage—to be specific, his ancestral Davidic origins ("from of old, from ancient days"). Like Isa. 9 and 11, Mic. 5 does not designate the coming ruler under the title "king," even though all three passages clearly indicate that he is a Davidide (Isa. 9:7: "on the throne

5. Charles S. Shaw, *The Speeches of Micah: A Rhetorical-Historical Analysis*, JSOTSup 145 (Sheffield: Sheffield Academic, 1993), 139.

6. E.g., Keith W. Whitelam, *The Just King: Monarchical Judicial Authority in Ancient Israel*, JSOTSup 12 (Sheffield: JSOT Press, 1979), 53–54.

7. J. M. Povis Smith, *Micah, Zephaniah and Nahum*, ICC (Edinburgh: T&T Clark, 1911), 101.

8. Gregory Goswell, "Isaiah 16: A Forgotten Chapter in the History of Messianism," *SJOT* 28 (2014): 97.

9. Mignon R. Jacobs, *The Conceptual Coherence of the Book of Micah*, JSOTSup 322 (Sheffield: Sheffield Academic, 2001), 197–202.

10. The two place-names stand in apposition and are identified. For their identification, see also Gen. 35:19; 48:7; Ruth 4:11.

of David"; 11:1: "from the stump of Jesse"). In each case the human ruler is subordinated to the Divine King.[11] The subservience of the figure to Yhwh is underlined in Mic. 5:2 in two ways: (1) his place of origin is relatively insignificant ("[you] who are too little to be among the clans of Judah"), so that his promotion to the position of ruler must be due to God's enabling; (2) he comes forth "for me" (God speaking)—that is, to serve God's purposes. This expression may be intended by Micah to pick up what is said about the choice of David in 1 Sam. 16:1: "I [God] will send you [Samuel] to Jesse the Bethlehemite, for I have provided *for myself* a king among his sons."[12] In line with this, the clause that follows in Mic. 5 expresses the divine purpose for which the figure comes forth ("to be ruler in Israel").[13]

It seems the more exalted title of "king" (*melek*) is deliberately withheld from the ruler of the city, because of his present humiliated state at the hand of foreign nations (Mic. 5:1) and, more importantly, because in the prophecy of Micah this royal title is mostly applied to Yhwh (cf. 2:13; 4:7). Instead, 5:2 uses the term "ruler" (*môšēl*). This may be a wordplay on the name of Solomon (cf. 1 Kings 4:21: "Solomon [*šəlōmōh*] was ruling [*môšēl*] over all the kingdoms . . . ," authors' trans.). What looks like an intentional substitution of leadership terms can be compared to the preference for "leader" (*nāgîd*) in the books of Samuel (ESV: "prince"; see 1 Sam. 9:16; 2 Sam. 5:2; 7:8)[14] and the predilection for "prince" (*nāśîʾ*) in the prophecy of Ezekiel (e.g., 34:24; 37:25),[15] with the substitutions preventing any possible appearance of rivalry between the human ruler (so designated) and God the supreme King.[16]

God Will Deliver His People

Whatever the exact meaning of Mic. 5:3 ("when she who is in labor has given birth"), it concerns the *timing* of the birth of the promised ruler just announced. The first part of the verse may be reminiscent of Isa. 7:14; that is, God is preparing a child, to be born of an unnamed woman, but closer to home, this cryptic expression picks up the metaphor of Daughter Zion as a pregnant mother in agony (Mic. 4:9–10), so that the one giving birth

---

11. Cf. Gregory Goswell, "The Shape of Messianism in Isaiah 9," *WTJ* 77 (2015): 101–10.

12. J. Smith, *Micah, Zephaniah and Nahum*, 104.

13. J. Smith, *Micah, Zephaniah and Nahum*, 106.

14. Lyle M. Eslinger, *Kingship of God in Crisis: A Close Reading of 1 Samuel 1–12*, BLS 10 (Sheffield: Almond, 1985), 302–9.

15. E.g., Ashley S. Crane, *Israel's Restoration: A Textual-Comparative Exploration of Ezekiel 36–39*, VTSup 122 (Leiden: Brill, 2008), 119–26.

16. See H. Gross, "*māšal* II," *TDOT* 9:70.

in the present passage is likely the same.[17] The point is that there will be an intervening period of affliction for God's people.[18] The second half of 5:3 alludes either to a return from exile (4:10) or to the reunification of Northern and Southern Kingdoms (2:12) as a second indicator of the time of the arrival of the Messiah. Note the connection of 5:3 with the preceding verse ("Therefore . . ."), with the two chronological indicators stating that a period of distress is a necessary part of the fulfillment of the divine plan that will certainly culminate in the arrival of the divinely promised ruler.

Of course, nothing in the verse says or implies that the one to be born is responsible for reversing the defeat of God's people or for enabling the return of "his [the Messiah's] brothers [= Judeans or Israelites more generally]." This human shepherd is not said to gather the scattered flock (if that is what Mic. 5:3b in fact alludes to),[19] for that is something done by YHWH himself without mention of human mediation (cf. 2:12; 4:6).[20] It is only in the next verse that the role of the messianic figure is specified (5:4). James L. Mays is correct, therefore, when he says, "The expected ruler has no part in their deliverance; that is the work of YHWH. . . . But their return sets the stage for the beginning of his reign as described in v. 4."[21] The people are given up (by God) until the return (v. 3), which means that the events of verse 4 are subsequent to YHWH delivering his people from exile and/or reunifying Judah and Israel,[22] so that it is only *after* the divinely effected deliverance has occurred that the messianic ruler arrives on the scene (cf. Isa. 8:23; 10:33–34; 16:4–5).[23] The wider context of Mic. 4–5 supports the view that God is the agent of the restoration of his people, for it is God who assembles "the lame" (= the remnant; 4:7–8) and redeems his exiled people from Babylon (v. 10b), and the placing of the booty under the ban is an acknowledgment that the victory over the nations is brought about by YHWH, "the Lord of the whole earth" (v. 13). In other words, in the preceding units, any mention of messianic agency in the rescue of God's people is entirely lacking.

17. B. Renaud, *La Formation du Livre de Michée: Tradition et Actualisation*, Études Bibliques (Paris: J. Gabalda, 1977), 247–48, 273–74, 281–83.

18. Shaw, *Speeches of Micah*, 153: "The prophet is proclaiming that the defeat of some within Israel will continue until the time that Jerusalem's labor has ended; that is, until she has defeated her enemies."

19. *Pace* Philip Peter Jenson, *Obadiah, Jonah, Micah: A Theological Commentary*, LHBOTS 496 (New York: T&T Clark International, 2008), 158.

20. The focus on divine action is noted by Daniel L. Smith-Christopher, *Micah: A Commentary*, OTL (Louisville: Westminster John Knox, 2015), 168.

21. James L. Mays, *Micah: A Commentary*, OTL (London: SCM, 1976), 117.

22. Hagstrom, *Coherence of the Book of Micah*, 66.

23. See Goswell, "Isaiah 16," 95–96.

The Domestic Role of the Messianic Figure

The royal figure will appear on the scene (ESV: "stand" ['*āmad*][24]), and "he shall . . . shepherd" (*rā'â*) God's people; thus the prophet applies the metaphor of the flock (Mic. 5:4). We have seen the shepherd metaphor for future Davidic rulers in our chapters on Jeremiah and Ezekiel. The role of this shepherd is compatible with and explained by the Davidic ideal of the shepherd-king (cf. 2 Sam. 5:2; 7:7; Ps. 78:70–72) and by what is, in fact, a standard ANE understanding of kingship. Only here in the Bible does the verb for "to act as shepherd" lack an expressed object (cf. Mic. 5:6a below: "And they shall shepherd [root *rā'â*] the land of Assyria with the sword"), so the ancient and modern versions resort to interpretive expansion (e.g., RSV: "[He shall] feed *his flock*"; in line with the LXX). In the wider context of Micah's prophecy, the meaning must be that YHWH, the royal shepherd (see 2:12–13; 4:6–7; 7:14), will rule his people through this human agent, whom he empowers and to whom he gives authority ("in the strength of the LORD, / in the majesty of the name of the LORD his God," 5:4).[25] The close relation of dependence of this human figure on YHWH is also alluded to by use of the appositive epithet "his God" (v. 4; cf. 1 Sam. 30:6), so that the promised ruler in no sense usurps God's kingship.[26] The messianic figure, in dependence on YHWH for power and authority, will tend the flock, though the passage does not go into detail about what is involved in this task. The only hint is provided by Mic. 5:1—namely, the ruler's domestic role of upholding justice. Before rushing to adopt a maximalist view of what the Davidic shepherd may do, it is well to note that subsequent verses say nothing to justify attributing to this human ruler anything but the highly circumscribed role of establishing justice across society, as was the case in the use of the shepherd metaphor in Jer. 23:1–5.

Commentators often find fault with the brevity of the pregnant expression that opens the second half of Mic. 5:4: "And they shall dwell *secure*" (adverb added in the ESV). Usually when this verb (*yāšab*) has such a meaning, it is accompanied by adverbial modifiers meaning "forever" (Ps. 125:1; Joel 3:20) or "in safety" (1 Kings 4:25; Ezek. 34:28).[27] In the present case

24. Cf. the use of this verb in Dan. 8:23 and 11:2–3 for the historical rise of kings. The alternative is to find a pictorial representation of the stance of the shepherd supervising his flock (cf. Isa. 61:5: "Aliens shall stand [root *'āmad*] and feed [root *rā'â*] your flocks," RSV).

25. *Pace* Francis I. Andersen and David Noel Freedman, it is not clear that "strength" and "majesty" need to imply military achievement. *Micah: A New Translation with Introduction and Commentary*, AB24E (New York: Doubleday, 2000), 469.

26. Mays, *Micah*, 117.

27. But M. Görg finds a regular nuance of stability of location (e.g., Deut. 12:10). See Görg, "*yāšab*," TDOT 6:426–29.

this meaning is implied by the causal clause that follows, which furnishes the reason for the future security of Israel ("For now he shall be great / to the ends of the earth"). To whom does this clause refer? There are, in fact, two options. The usual view is that it forecasts the spread of the renown and the universal recognition of the messianic ruler (Mic. 5:4: "He shall be great" [*yigdal*]),[28] which ensures that no foreign nation will dare attack or oppress God's people (cf. what is said of Solomon in 1 Kings 10:23–25; Ps. 72:8–11). It is not said explicitly that the pacification of the nations of the world is the result of the ruler's personal military exploits, though such an idea is often read into this passage.[29] The portrait of the future Davidide in Mic. 5 is more nuanced than that, for Solomonic peace is what is expected, and like Solomon, this figure inherits a pacific realm. To find an allusion to Solomon is supported by what is earlier said in 4:4, with 5:4 and 4:4 linked by way of catchword ("But they shall sit [root *yāšab*] every man under his vine and under his fig tree," 4:4).[30] Micah 4:4 appears to contain an excerpt from 1 Kings 4:25 (5:5 MT): "Judah and Israel lived [root *yāšab*] in safety, from Dan even to Beersheba, every man under his vine and under his fig tree, all the days of Solomon."

Of course, the positioning of Mic. 4:4 indicates that the security enjoyed is the result of God's rule over the nations and the consequent end of all wars (vv. 1–3), with a description of YHWH using the typology of a wise Solomon-like king who teaches the nations "his ways" and "his paths" (v. 2),[31] and so the alternate interpretation is that 5:3b in fact describes YHWH and the extension of his rule over the nations in the eschaton (cf. Mal. 1:5, 11, 14, each verse using the root *gādal*, "to be great"),[32] with the result that mention of the promised messianic ruler in Mic. 5 is confined to verses 2 and 4a. The same idea expressed by the term for "great" (*gādôl*) occurs in the Psalter (95:3; 96:4;

28. The imperfective verb has ingressive force in future time (Waltke, *Commentary on Micah*, 285); cf. the great name of Abram and David (Gen. 12:2; 2 Sam. 7:9).

29. E.g., Waltke, *Commentary on Micah*, 286.

30. Hans W. Wolff, *Micah: A Commentary*, trans. Gary Stansell, CC (Minneapolis: Augsburg, 1990), 146.

31. Note the use of "ways/paths" in wisdom material (e.g., Ps. 1:6; Prov. 2:8); see William J. Dumbrell, *The Faith of Israel: A Theological Survey of the Old Testament*, 2nd ed. (Leicester, UK: Apollos, 2002), 94, 110, for the significance of the visit of the queen of Sheba in shaping the eschatology of the prophets (1 Kings 10:1–10).

32. So also, Hans Strauß, *Messianisch ohne Messias: Zur Überlieferungsgeschichte und Interpretation der sogenannten messianischen Texte im Alten Testament*, Europäische Hochschulschriften XXIII/232 (Frankfurt am Main: Peter Lang, 1984), 58. For the Malachi passages, see Gregory Goswell, "The Eschatology of Malachi after Zechariah 14," *JBL* 132 (2013): 629. For God as "great," see 2 Sam. 7:22, 26; Pss. 35:27; 40:16; 70:4; 104:1 (references provided by Ben Zvi, *Micah*, 127).

99:3),[33] so that in describing the universal reign of God, Mic. 5 is drawing on Psalmic exemplars. Sudden switches in the person referred to are something of a feature in Mic. 5, and the nonspecified third-person subject in verse 4b ("*he* shall be great") could be understood as picking up the double mention of God that immediately precedes ("the LORD . . . the LORD his God"). As well, finding a picture of God's universal rule fits with the earlier reference to YHWH as "the Lord of the whole earth" (4:13).

Israel's Protection against Invasion

The messianic unit is followed by what might be viewed as three supplementary units (Mic. 5:5–6, 7–9, and 10–15), each beginning with "And it shall be . . ." (*wəhāyâ*). Micah 5:5–6 reads:

> [5]And he shall be their peace.
>
> When the Assyrian comes into our land
>   and treads in our palaces,
> then we will raise against him seven shepherds
>   and eight princes of men;
> [6]they shall shepherd the land of Assyria with the sword,
>   and the land of Nimrod at its entrances;
> and he shall deliver us from the Assyrian
>   when he comes into our land
>   and treads within our border.

The first line of verse 5 is difficult for at least a couple of reasons. First, "And this shall be peace" (RSV) may go with what follows or with what precedes, or the clause may be viewed as a hinge between the two units. Second, there is the question of translation, for the demonstrative "this" may be the archaic determinant or nominalizer ("[And he will be] the One of Peace [*šālôm*]),"[34] and, if so, this quasi-titular expression could imply, by means of wordplay, that the messianic figure is Solomon-like (*šəlōmōh*; cf. 1 Chron. 22:9; Ps. 72:7),[35] so that a warlike figure is not contemplated in this passage (cf. 1 Kings 4:24:

---

33. See Jörg Jeremias, *Das Königtum Gottes in den Psalmen: Israels Begegnung mit dem kanaanäischen Mythos in den Jahwe-König-Psalmen*, FRLANT 141 (Göttingen: Vandenhoeck & Ruprecht, 1987), 110.

34. *IBHS* §19.5d.

35. Walter Brueggemann, *Solomon: Israel's Ironic Icon of Human Achievement*, Studies on Personalities of the Old Testament (Columbia: University of South Carolina Press, 2005), 132, 136.

"And he [= Solomon] had peace [*šālôm*] on all sides around him").[36] In line with this interpretation, nothing is said in the preceding three verses about the coming ruler delivering Israel.[37] Again, the alternate view is that the title in verse 5a refers to Yнwн, just as in Isa. 9 the theophoric name assigned to the Davidic child extols God (not the promised Davidic child) as "prince of peace," due to the peace and security that God has provided for his people.[38]

In what may be phrased as a "communal response" to the preceding verses,[39] a possible future scenario is now sketched (Mic. 5:5: "If/when the Assyrian comes into our land . . ."). As correctly noted by Smith, "Instead of the one great leader, there are here seven or eight, and these are not raised up by the Messiah but by the populace."[40] They are *popular* leaders ("then *we will raise up* against him seven shepherds"), and nothing says or implies that they are "the king's generals and subordinates."[41] The picture is of the citizenry (or elders) of Israel taking the initiative of appointing leaders in a military emergency (cf. Judg. 11:1–11).[42] A perceived lack of coordination with what was said in the previous verse leads many scholars to delete Mic. 5:5–6a as an intrusive gloss.[43] Of course, any clash of perspectives is substantially reduced if verse 4b is understood to refer to God's greatness. There are several significant differences: the verses shift to a first-person plural mode of expression ("we/our"),[44] now "Assyria" is pictured as invading the land of Israel, and its defense is placed in the hands of seven/eight leaders, presumably clan or tribal chiefs, with any messianic figure nowhere to be seen, for he would appear to be superfluous in such a situation.[45] The military leaders are designated "shepherds" and "princes of [= appointed by and representing] humans."[46]

---

36. For other examples of punning on Solomon's name, see Moshe Garsiel, *Biblical Names: A Literary Study of Midrashic Derivations and Puns*, rev. ed. (Ramat Gan: Bar-Ilan University Press, 1991), 190–92, 204–6.

37. As correctly noted by Hagstrom in *Coherence of the Book of Micah*, 66.

38. Paul Wegner, "A Re-examination of Isaiah IX 1–6," *VT* 42 (1992): 109–12.

39. According to Hagstrom, *Coherence of the Book of Micah*, 66–67.

40. J. Smith, *Micah, Zephaniah and Nahum*, 107.

41. *Pace* Jenson, *Obadiah, Jonah, Micah*, 160.

42. As correctly noted by Andersen and Freedman, *Micah*, 478.

43. But see the arguments of Willis, "Micah 4:14–5:5, a Unit," 537–42.

44. This is a return to the point of view in 5:1 ("Siege is laid against *us*"). As noted by Waltke, "By the end of the oracles the tables are completely turned from *their attack against us* to *our attack against them*" (*Commentary on Micah*, 294). The numerical graduation 7/8 probably expresses "a considerable number" (*GKC* §134s; cf. Eccles. 11:2).

45. W. Nowack, *Die kleinen Propheten*, Göttingen Handkommentar zum Alten Testament (Göttingen: Vandenhoeck & Ruprecht, 1903), 230.

46. With Ben Zvi, we read it as a genitive of agency (*Micah*, 130; cf. *IBHS* §9.5.1). The term "princes" (*nāśî'*) is used of chiefs of federated foreign Trans-Jordanian tribes (Josh. 13:21; Ps. 83:11 [83:12 MT]) and "the princes of the north" (Ezek. 32:30).

The reappearance of the vocational term "shepherd" that was used shortly before of the messianic figure (cf. v. 4 RSV, with "feed") may imply that these appointed leaders replace him or that they do what he might otherwise have been expected to do in such a situation.

It is not clear that the subject of the verb in Mic. 5:6—"*He* shall deliver us"—is the messianic figure (*pace* Bruce Waltke),[47] for that is to ignore the context provided by verses 5–6a, wherein other military leaders are to the fore. As a result, some scholars (e.g., J. M. P. Smith) see the progression of thought requiring the plural ("They will deliver"), but if we retain the text without emendation, another possibility is that God is the subject of this verb.[48] A sudden switch to a third-person reference to God finds a precedent in verse 3a ("He shall give them up"), where it is said that God will give his people into the hands of their enemies (cf. 2 Sam. 5:19; 1 Kings 22:6).[49] If their defeat is attributed to God, it is indeed appropriate that God (using agents) is said to be the one who delivers his people. In this way, both defeat and deliverance are under providential control. In line with this, the root meaning "to deliver" or "to rescue" (*nāṣal*) was used earlier of the divinely effected rescue from Babylon in Mic. 4:10 ("There you [= Daughter of Zion] shall be *rescued*"), with the next line clarifying that this is indeed God's doing ("There the LORD will redeem you / from the hand of your enemies").

Waltke's main argument in favor of the messianic figure doing the rescuing is that the literary device of *inclusio* connects "He is the one of peace" (Mic. 5:5a, authors' trans.) and "He shall deliver" (v. 6b),[50] both referring to the Messiah, with verses 5–6 exhibiting an ABA structure. However, the relation of the two clauses could just as well be one of *contrast* rather than of equation, depicting the Messiah as a Solomon-like figure of peace versus God as the one who effects the needed deliverance, or else (and more likely, as far as we can see) both clauses refer to God, who is the source of both peace and deliverance for his people.

YHWH Cuts Off His People's Enemies

In support of the position for which we are arguing, the victory over enemies in Mic. 5:7–9 is ascribed to YHWH through the agency of "the remnant of Jacob." Micah 5:7–9 reads:

47. Waltke, *Commentary on Micah*, 292. Waltke is right, however, in classifying the clause as summarizing the situation just described.
48. So also, e.g., Ralph L. Smith, *Micah–Malachi*, WBC 32 (Waco: Word, 1984), 45, though he supplies no reasons.
49. The references are provided by Wolff (*Micah*, 145).
50. Waltke, *Commentary on Micah*, 286, 304.

> ⁷Then the remnant of Jacob shall be
>   in the midst of many peoples
> like dew from the LORD,
>   like showers on the grass,
> which delay not for a man
>   nor wait for the children of man.
> ⁸And the remnant of Jacob shall be among the nations,
>   in the midst of many peoples,
> like a lion among the beasts of the forest,
>   like a young lion among the flocks of sheep,
> which, when it goes through, treads down
>   and tears in pieces, and there is none to deliver.
> ⁹Your hand shall be lifted up over your adversaries,
>   and all your enemies shall be cut off.

This can be compared with what is found in 4:8, a verse that democratizes the promise of a renewed kingdom of David and speaks of "kingship for the daughter of Zion," just as in verses 11–13 it is the people of the city of Zion (not a Davidide) who will be victorious over the nations ("You [the daughter of Zion] shall beat in pieces many peoples"). True enough, the situation in the previous two verses of Mic. 5 is one of military threat on home soil ("if he [the Assyrian] comes into our land" [stated in both verses]), whereas verses 7–8 concern the invincible might of the Israelite remnant ("in the midst of many peoples . . . among the nations, in the midst of many peoples"),[51] but the anticipated rule over "Assyria" (v. 6a) forges a thematic bridge between the two units if Assyria is viewed as typifying foreign aggressor nations.[52] The choice of Assyria (*'aššûr*) also creates a wordplay with "remnant" (*šǝ'ērît*) in the verses that follow.[53] According to Wolff, the parallel expression "the land of Nimrod" (v. 6a; = Mesopotamia) supports reading Assyria as a cipher for oppressive foreign rule in general (cf. Gen. 10:8–12).[54]

Whatever the exact force of the comparisons with dew and lion (Mic. 5:7–8),[55] they refer to "the remnant of Jacob," providing a democratized

---

51. This may refer to a Jewish diaspora or to regathered Israel as the center of the world (Jenson, *Obadiah, Jonah, Micah*, 161).

52. As, for example, it appears to do in Ezra 6:22; Ps. 83:8; Lam. 5:6; Nah. 3:18; Zech. 10:10–11; see Jörg Jeremias, *Kultprophetie und Gerichtsverkündigung in der späten Königszeit Israels*, WMANT 35 (Neukirchen-Vluyn: Neukirchener Verlag, 1970), 51n1.

53. Lamontte M. Luker, "Beyond Form Criticism: The Relation of Doom and Hope in Micah 2–6," *HAR* 11 (1987): 296.

54. Wolff, *Micah*, 147.

55. For the exegetical alternatives, see David J. Bryant, "Micah 4:14–5:14: An Exegesis," *ResQ* 21 (1978): 226. The image of falling dew does not have to be benign; see 2 Sam. 17:12.

reapplication of comparisons from nature found in proverbial material describing the favor and wrath of kings (cf. Prov. 16:14, 15; 19:12; 20:2).[56] The two lines at the end of Mic. 5:7, "which delay not for a man / nor wait for the children of man," encourage God's people to trust entirely in God's help. So too, the expression "there is none to deliver [nāṣal]" at the close of verse 8 is, as noted by Leslie Allen, usually connected to God's defeat of his people's enemies (Deut. 32:39; Job 10:7; Ps. 50:22; Hosea 5:14),[57] suggesting that the anticipated victory of the remnant is God ordained or God enabled. The Hebrew text of Mic. 5:9 expresses a wish (the verb is jussive; "May your hand be lifted up over your adversaries," authors' trans.), but interpreters differ over whether the person addressed is God (a request) or the remnant (an exhortation or benefaction). We favor the former alternative—namely, that it is a prayer, asking that God's hand be raised in military action (cf. Ps. 89:13; Isa. 26:11), with this verse revealing that God is the ultimate source of the triumph enjoyed by "the remnant of Jacob." This interpretation finds support by reference to what is found in the parallel half-line (Mic. 5:9b), which should be understood as a divine passive ("May all your enemies be cut off," authors' trans.),[58] for subsequent verses repeatedly feature God as the subject of the verb "to cut off" (kārat; vv. 10a, 11a, 12a, 13a: "I [God speaking] will cut off . . ."), and in verse 15 the object of God's anger is the nations "that did not obey," just as they bear the brunt of his attack in verse 9.

Micah 5:10–15 reads:

> [10]And in that day, declares the LORD,
>   I will cut off your horses from among you
>   and will destroy your chariots;
> [11]and I will cut off the cities of your land
>   and throw down all your strongholds;
> [12]and I will cut off sorceries from your hand,
>   and you shall have no more tellers of fortunes;
> [13]and I will cut off your carved images
>   and your pillars from among you,
> and you shall bow down no more
>   to the work of your hands;
> [14]and I will root out your Asherah images from among you
>   and destroy your cities.

56. As noted by Burkard M. Zapff, *Redaktionsgeschichtliche Studien zum Michabuch im Kontext des Dodekapropheton*, BZAW 256 (Berlin: de Gruyter, 1997), 99–104.

57. Leslie C. Allen, *The Books of Joel, Obadiah, Jonah and Micah*, NICOT (Grand Rapids: Eerdmans, 1976), 354n72.

58. Hagstrom, *Coherence of the Book of Micah*, 67.

[15]And in anger and wrath I will execute vengeance
on the nations that did not obey.

Following the lead of John Willis,[59] we believe that the purpose of this pericope is to announce that in this time of military threat, God will cut off all other possible objects of Israel's trust (armaments, fortresses, magic arts, idolatrous practices), so that she must rely on Yhwh alone to defeat the foreign aggressor nations (v. 15). Our main point, however, is that nothing in verses 7–15 indicates any involvement of the messianic figure in the triumph of God's people over the nations of the world.

Postlude: Canonical Reflections

The picture that emerges in the prophecy of Mic. 5 is similar to that found in Isa. 9, 11, and 16, wherein the promised Davidide is styled a domestic ruler and not a conquering deliverer. The role of the Davidide as shepherd is stated but receives no elaboration, though the implication is that his chief task is to promote social justice. He is the divinely designated ruler of God's people, but he is not accorded the title "king." With regard to the subjugation of the nations, the role of David as the warrior (e.g., in the book of Samuel) is transferred to the remnant. Though the Davidic ruler is the centerpiece of Micah's picture of the consummated kingdom of God, he is not said to be responsible for the peace or deliverance enjoyed by God's people. The result is that in the prophecy of Micah, God is the undisputed King and Deliverer.

In the application of the prophecy of Mic. 5 found in the New Testament, it is seen as fulfilled in the birth of Jesus as "the Christ" (Matt. 2:6). In this Matthean passage, the visit of the Magi bearing gifts serves to recall the story of the queen of Sheba (Matt. 2:11; cf. 1 Kings 10:2, 10; Ps. 72:10–11, 15), and therefore, consistent with the presentation of Mic. 5, the messianic theology of the First Evangelist features the typology of the birth of a Solomonic ruler who receives international recognition.[60] Of course, in line with the high Christology of the evangelist, Jesus, being God in the flesh, is also the Divine Shepherd-King who seeks, saves, and refines his flock (Matt. 10:6; 14:14; 15:24, 32; 25:31–46),[61] so that reading

59. John T. Willis, "The Authenticity and Meaning of Micah 5:9–14," *ZAW* 81 (1969): 368.

60. R. T. France, *The Gospel of Matthew*, NICNT (Grand Rapids: Eerdmans, 2007), 62; W. D. Davies and Dale C. Allison Jr., *The Gospel according to Saint Matthew*, ICC (Edinburgh: T&T Clark, 1988), 1:250–51.

61. As recognized by John Paul Heil, "Ezekiel 34 and the Narrative Strategy of the Shepherd and Sheep Metaphor in Matthew," *CBQ* 55 (1993): 698–708.

Mic. 5 in this biblical-theological framework means that Jesus also carries out what is predicated of God in the prophecy of Micah. The New Testament writers are, in fact, regularly reading the Old Testament in this manner, applying what is said about God in the Old Testament not just to the Father but to Jesus himself.

12

The Sprout, the Divine Shepherd, and the Messenger in Zechariah and Malachi

We humans are good at avoiding things we find difficult. This "avoidance syndrome" gets us into trouble if it means that we never get around to doing what our boss at work has asked us to do, or if we need to have that awkward conversation with a friend about bad behavior (theirs or ours) but are scared to broach the subject. I (Greg) have often joked with a couple of scholarly friends who are experts in the prophecy of Zechariah (and on whose expertise we draw in this chapter) that I will leave this difficult-to-understand part of the Bible to them, but the present book on messiahship requires an examination of this book. The challenge in understanding the prophecy of Zechariah, both its visions and oracles, is universally acknowledged, but that does not give us permission to avoid these texts. Despite the difficulty of the material, its importance is signaled by the fact that it is picked up in the Gospel passion narratives and applied to Jesus (something we will come back to at the end of this chapter).

An earlier version of material in this chapter was published in Gregory Goswell, "A Theocratic Reading of Zechariah 9:9," *BBR* 26 (2016): 7–19. Copyright © The Pennsylvania State University, University Park, PA, 2016. This article is used by permission of The Pennsylvania State University Press.

Zerubbabel and the "Sprout"

In Zech. 1–8, we find the term *ṣemaḥ*, which also appeared in our discussion of Jer. 23:5. Although the term is often translated as "Branch," we argued in chapter 7 that it is best to translate it as "Sprout," and we will retain this translation here. Here it is used to predict the arrival of a *future* agent of God (Zech. 3:8),[1] who cannot be identified with Zerubbabel, for the simple fact that Zerubbabel is already on the scene, whereas God says, "I am about to bring [using *hinneh* plus participle] my servant, the Sprout" (authors' trans.).[2] This figure is provided by God, as is also stated of the similarly named figure in Jer. 23:5 and 33:15. Though the figure of Zech. 3:8 is not said to be a Davidide as such, the association with the earlier prophecy of Jeremiah strongly implies that he is, and so this hope is to be classified as messianic (and Zech. 6 will make explicit his royal status).[3] As God's "servant," he comes to fulfill some (as yet unspecified) divine purpose. No function for the Sprout is revealed, but this lack will be supplied in chapter 6.

Zechariah 6:11–14 reads:

> [11]Take from them silver and gold, and make a crown, and set it on the head of Joshua, the son of Jehozadak, the high priest. [12]And say to him, "Thus says the LORD of hosts, 'Behold, the man whose name is the Sprout: for he shall branch out from his place, and he shall build the temple of the LORD. [13]It is he who shall build the temple of the LORD and shall bear royal honor, and shall sit and rule on his throne. And there shall be a priest on his throne, and the counsel of peace shall be between them both.'" [14]And the crown shall be in the temple of the LORD as a reminder to Helem, Tobijah, Jedaiah, and Hen the son of Zephaniah.

Just as there is in the prophecy of Haggai a regular pairing of leaders, Zerubbabel and Joshua (1:1, 12, 14; 2:2, 4), so also Zech. 6:9–15 envisions

---

1. There is no link to the plant imagery of Isa. 11:1, where different terminology and different imagery are used (Wolter H. Rose, *Zemah and Zerubbabel: Messianic Expectations in the Early Postexilic Period*, JSOTSup 304 [Sheffield: Sheffield Academic, 2000], 91–120). Rose demonstrates that the word *ṣemaḥ* means "vegetation, greenery, growth"—that is, plants as a whole—and in Zech. 6:12 the cognate verb is also used ("For he shall grow up [*yiṣmaḥ*] in his place," RSV).

2. As demonstrated by Rose, *Zemah and Zerubbabel*, 121–41; see also Anthony R. Petterson, *Behold Your King: The Hope for the House of David in the Book of Zechariah*, LHBOTS 513 (New York: T&T Clark International, 2009), 98–100, 114–20; Anthony R. Petterson, "The Eschatology of Zechariah's Night Visions," in *"I Lifted My Eyes and Saw": Reading Dream and Vision Reports in the Hebrew Bible*, ed. Elizabeth R. Hayes and Lena-Sofia Tiemeyer, LHBOTS 584 (London: Bloomsbury T&T Clark, 2014), 119–34.

3. As rightly pointed out by Petterson (*Behold Your King*, 125), who builds on Janet E. Tollington, *Tradition and Innovation in Haggai and Zechariah 1–8*, JSOTSup 150 (Sheffield: JSOT Press, 1993), 171.

a priestly-royal duo consisting of Joshua and "the Sprout," who will build the temple. This role is stated twice in the text (vv. 12–13), and the second occurrence is more emphatic ("It is he [*hû'*] who shall build the temple of the LORD"). This was a responsibility assigned to Zerubbabel in 4:6–10, and therefore many scholars view the parallel as proving that Zerubbabel is the Sprout,[4] but the reference in Zech. 6 must be to the building of a future (and more glorious?) temple in the consummated kingdom of God (cf. Ezek. 40–42; Hag. 2:9). A royal personage is envisaged, though he is not to be identified with Zerubbabel, for, again, a *future* figure is in mind (Zech. 6:12b–13), such that this passage cannot be indicating the imminent restoration of the monarchy in the person of Zerubbabel.[5] As pointed out by Wolter H. Rose, the absence of a definite article before "man" in 6:12b ("Behold, *a man* [*'îš*] whose name is Sprout . . ." [not following the RSV or ESV]) indicates that the prophet is not talking about the one to whom he is speaking, nor about anyone present.[6]

Some gifts for the temple are used to make an *impressive* crown (the probable sense of the Hebrew plural in Zech. 6:11).[7] Only one crown is in view in this passage, for only "the head of Joshua" is mentioned (v. 11), and the crown is then placed in the temple (v. 14), presumably in readiness for the coming Sprout.[8] The fact that the crown is put on Joshua's head, not Zerubbabel's, again shows that the latter is not to be identified with the Sprout. The second-to-last clause of verse 13 is difficult but is best translated (similarly to the RSV), "There will be a priest beside [*'al*] his throne," such that the picture is similar to the king-and-priest pairing predicted in Jer. 33:17–22 (cf. 1 Sam. 2:35).[9] The Sprout will "sit and rule [*māšal*] upon [*'al*] his throne," and the harmony of the duo, or the resultant peaceful condition due to their joint

---

4. E.g., Michael H. Floyd, *Minor Prophets, Part 2*, FOTL 22 (Grand Rapids: Eerdmans, 2000), 405.

5. See Anthony R. Petterson, "A New Form-Critical Approach to Zechariah's Crowning of the High Priest Joshua and the Identity of 'Shoot' (Zechariah 6:9–15)," in *The Book of the Twelve and the New Form Criticism*, ed. Mark J. Boda, Michael H. Floyd, and Colin M. Toffelmire, SBL Ancient Near East Monographs 10 (Atlanta: SBL Press, 2015), 285–304.

6. Rose, *Zemah and Zerubbabel*, 125–26.

7. E.g., Joyce G. Baldwin, *Haggai, Zechariah, Malachi: An Introduction and Commentary*, TOTC (Leicester, UK: Inter-Varsity, 1988), 133.

8. Suggests Petterson, *Behold Your King*, 115, 117.

9. In Jer. 33:17–22 and 1 Sam. 2:35, the priestly figure is certainly not in a seated posture. It may seem odd that the identical Hebrew phrase (*'al-kis'ô*) in the same passage has two different meanings ("upon/beside his throne"), and the ESV translates them identically, but priests never sit on thrones in the Old Testament. First Samuel 1:9; 4:13, 18, depicting Eli, are not really exceptions, for this is in the premonarchic situation, and his seated posture may reflect his authority as a judge as well as his position as priest. The Hebrew preposition (*'al*) has the same sense in Zech. 4:14 ("who *stand by* the Lord of the whole earth"), where the phrase "stand by" refers to those who are attendants to a king. The LXX may not represent a deviant text but

counsel, is expressed by way of further wordplay on the name of "Solomon" (*šəlōmōh*; cf. "Peaceful counsel [*'ăṣat šālôm*] shall be between them"). A comparison can be made with the idyllic picture provided by Zech. 3:10 ("Every one of you will invite his neighbor under his vine and under his fig tree"), a verse that is reminiscent of the picture of the reign of Solomon as a golden period in Israelite history (cf. 1 Kings 4:25 [5:5 MT]; Mic. 4:4). As in Mic. 5, the implication is that a Solomon-like ruler is in view, and here his roles are temple building and domestic rule. This differentiates Zechariah's vision from what is found in the prophecy of Haggai, wherein the future transformation of the temple is due to the action of God himself (Hag. 1:8: "And I will fill my house with glory," authors' trans.). Haggai mentions no messianic agency, but this is an omission on his part rather than a direct contradiction of what is said by Zechariah.

A Theocratic Reading of Zechariah 9:9

Zechariah 9:9 reads:

> Rejoice greatly, O daughter of Zion!
>> Shout aloud, O daughter of Jerusalem!
> Behold, your king is coming to you;
>> righteous and having salvation is he,
> humble and mounted on a donkey,
>> on a colt, the foal of a donkey.

The meaning of Zech. 9:9 is contested, with a point of disagreement being whether the one depicted entering Jerusalem "riding on an ass" is a messianic figure or Yhwh himself. The majority view is that the figure is human rather than divine, but we argue that this verse is better understood as a metaphorical depiction of the entry of Yhwh.[10] Terence Collins has highlighted the importance of the motif of the coming of Yhwh in the prophecy generally—for instance, in both halves of the book (chaps. 1–8, 9–14), references to Yhwh's arrival are found near the beginning (2:10 [2:14 MT]; 9:14) and the end (8:3;

---

provides a paraphrastic rendering that supports the interpretation offered here ("And a priest will be on his right hand").

10. A recent advocate for this position is Wolter H. Rose, "Zechariah and the Ambiguity of Kingship in Postexilic Israel," in *Let Us Go Up to Zion: Essays in Honour of H. G. M. Williamson on the Occasion of His Sixty-Fifth Birthday*, ed. Iain Provan and Mark J. Boda, VTSup 153 (Leiden: Brill, 2012), 219–31.

14:5) of these major sections.[11] We follow Paul D. Hanson, who classifies Zech. 9 as a "divine warrior hymn."[12] He argues that 9:1–17 is a unity and that 9:1–8 depicts the march of God as the Divine Warrior from the north to the temple, and so God says, "I will *encamp* [root *ḥānâ*] at my house" (v. 8a), meaning God will "station troops" (cf. Isa. 29:3; 1 Sam. 11:1; 13:5), doing so with the aim of ensuring the protection of the temple from foreign attack.

The resolution of the disputed reading of Zech. 9:9 is also assisted by noting how the book concludes—namely, with a final vision of the eschatological reign of God (esp. 14:9: "And the LORD will be king over all the earth"). There are clear similarities between chapters 9 and 14,[13] such that they frame the second half of the book. Both chapters feature the action of the Divine Warrior in the eschatological battle that leads to the defeat and subjugation of the nations (9:1–7, 10a, 14–17; 14:1–3, 12–15), YHWH's defense of Jerusalem (9:8; 14:2), his entry into the city (9:9; 14:4–5), and his universal rule (9:10b; 14:9), and both chapters focus on the "house" of God (9:8; 14:20). The fact that no messianic agency is in sight in Zech. 14 adds weight to the suggestion that 9:9 is best understood as a picture of the Divine Warrior. How does this theocratic focus fit with the prophecies of the Sprout in earlier chapters? Anthony R. Petterson is right to warn interpreters of Zechariah that "the coming of the future king and the coming of YHWH are not to be pitted against each other,"[14] but how exactly are the two strands of expectation to be integrated? We will take up this crucial issue after all the relevant Zecharian materials have been examined.

In the Old Testament, especially in poetry, whether the Psalter or prophetic oracles, there can be sudden, unannounced changes of person, such that one moment God is speaking in the first person (I or me) and the next he is being referred to in the third person (he).[15] Likewise, the references to one or more key figures in Zech. 9 involve unannounced switches of person,[16] so that the abrupt change of person at the start of verse 9 (from first-person singular to third-person singular) and the reverse change at the start of verse 10 (from

---

11. The motif is found in Zech. 1:16; 2:10 [2:14 MT]; 8:3; 9:14; 14:3, 5; see Terence Collins, "The Literary Contexts of Zechariah 9:9," in *The Book of Zechariah and Its Influence*, ed. Christopher Tuckett (Aldershot, UK: Ashgate, 2003), 38.

12. Paul D. Hanson, *The Dawn of Apocalyptic: The Historical and Sociological Roots of Jewish Apocalyptic Eschatology*, rev. ed. (Philadelphia: Fortress, 1979), 286–324.

13. E.g., Adrian M. Leske, "Context and Meaning of Zechariah 9:9," *CBQ* 62 (2000): 669–70.

14. Petterson, *Behold Your King*, 244.

15. Referring to oneself in third person rather than first person is a rhetorical device called illeism. See Roderick Elledge, *Use of the Third Person for Self-Reference by Jesus and Yahweh: A Study of Illeism in the Bible and Ancient Near Eastern Texts and Its Implications for Christology*, LNTS 575 (London: Bloomsbury T&T Clark, 2017), 67–83.

16. See the table provided by Rose, "Ambiguity of Kingship," 228.

third-person singular to first-person singular) are by no means unprecedented. These changes of person do not require the supposition that someone other than Yhwh is featured—that is to say, in verse 9 the same divine figure may be depicted as in verses 1–8.

Zechariah 9:8, 10 reads:

> Then I will encamp at my house as a guard,
>   so that none shall march to and fro;
> no oppressor shall again march over them,
>   for now I see with my own eyes. (v. 8)

> I will cut off the chariot from Ephraim
>   and the war horse from Jerusalem;
> and the battle bow shall be cut off,
>   and he shall speak peace to the nations;
> his rule shall be from sea to sea,
>   and from the River to the ends of the earth. (v. 10)

It is commonly assumed that if God is the speaker of 9:9, then the one of whom he speaks in the third person ("your king") must be someone other than himself, but this is not the case, for in the following chapter, third-person references to God are found within a divine speech (10:3–12; see vv. 3b, 7b, 12),[17] including the speech attribution at the end of verse 12 ("declares the Lord"). In Zechariah, therefore, it is perfectly possible for Yhwh to speak about himself in the third person.[18]

The Analogy with Zechariah 2:10

Terence Collins argues that Zech. 2:10 (2:14 MT) conforms to a distinct literary form, the "proclamation of arrival" (other examples being Isa. 30:27; 35:4; 40:9–11; 62:11; Zeph. 3:14–17),[19] and Helmer Ringgren stresses that it is Yhwh's coming *as king* that is the usual focus.[20] The striking similarities of Zech. 9:9 and 2:10 (2:14 MT) favor the notion that 9:9 depicts the entrance of God into the city of Jerusalem.

17. Carol L. Meyers and Eric M. Meyers note the frequent shift between first and third person for Yhwh in Zech. 10. Carol L. Meyers and Eric M. Meyers, *Zechariah 9–14*, AB 25C (New York: Doubleday, 1993), 195.

18. See the discussion of the issue provided by David L. Petersen, *Zechariah 9–14 and Malachi*, OTL (Louisville: Westminster John Knox, 1995), 78. Petersen cites Hosea 1:7 as another example of the same phenomenon ("I will save them by the Lord their God").

19. Collins provides a table for ease of comparison. See Collins, "Literary Contexts," 36.

20. Helmer Ringgren, "Behold Your King Comes," *VT* 24 (1974): 207–11.

Zechariah 2:10	Zechariah 9:9
Sing and rejoice, O daughter of Zion, for behold, I come and I will dwell in your midst, declares the LORD.	Rejoice greatly, O daughter of Zion! Shout aloud, O daughter of Jerusalem! Behold, your king is coming to you; righteous and having salvation is he, humble and mounted on a donkey, on a colt, the foal of a donkey.

Both verses have three main constituents: (1) a call to rejoice, (2) an address to the city of Jerusalem in the second-person singular ("O daughter of Zion" in both cases), and (3) an announcement of the arrival of some significant personage.[21] In Zech. 2:10 (2:14 MT), it is plain that YHWH's arrival is announced (by YHWH himself), given that God is explicitly stated to be the speaker ("Behold, I come and I will dwell in your midst, declares the LORD"). In a holistic reading of the book of Zechariah, the similarities between the two verses are of such a nature as to compel the conclusion that the noted points of correspondence are deliberate (a literary convention is being followed), and this suggests that the reader is meant to view them as describing the same event.

The Figure on the Ass

Despite the striking similarities between Zech. 9:9 and 2:10 (2:14 MT), the mode of entry depicted in 9:9 leads Collins to posit a fundamental distinction between these verses, excluding the possibility that YHWH could be described in anthropological terms as riding an ass, such that 9:9b, according to him, surprises the reader by subverting the literary form.[22] But if God can be depicted in thoroughly human terms as fighting and despoiling his enemies (9:4) and encamping at Jerusalem (v. 8), it is hard to see why he cannot be pictured, like any other warrior-king, as riding victoriously into the city he has secured (v. 9). Certainly, the anthropomorphic image is a bold one, and some would see it as too corporeal and constrictive for deity (insofar as it depicts dependence on a beast of burden for mobility); however, a Zecharian parallel is found in the depiction of the Divine Warrior in 14:4, which says that "[YHWH's] feet shall stand on the Mount of Olives."

The figure in Zech. 9:9 is described as "triumphant" (ṣaddîq; cf. RSV), and this multivalent term can have a military sense and probably does here, given the context provided by verses 1–8. A comparison can be made with

21. For this paragraph we acknowledge our dependence on Rose, "Ambiguity of Kingship," 229–30.
22. Collins, "Literary Contexts," 37.

the description of YHWH in Isa. 45:21: "a righteous [ṣaddîq] God and a Savior" (RSV), so that the use of ṣaddîq in Zech. 9:9 supports the view that a warrior-king is depicted, presumably the Divine Warrior of the preceding verses.

The second term applied to the figure in Zech. 9:9 is the *niphal* participle of the root *yāšaʿ*, which occurs only twice elsewhere in the Old Testament and is used (it is commonly claimed) of someone saved by someone else: in Deut. 33:29 of Israel ("a people saved [nôšāʿ] by the LORD") and in Ps. 33:16 of the Davidic king ("the king is not saved [nôšāʿ] by his great army"). On this understanding, the figure in Zech. 9:9 is "saved by divine help" (*victorieux de par le secours divin*).[23] On the other hand, the Vulgate (the noun *salvator*) and LXX (the active participle *sōzōn*) read the *niphal* participle in the active voice.[24] The *niphal* participle can have reflexive force, and Ps. 33:16 may be translated thus: "The king doth not *gain a victory* by his great army,"[25] or "the king does not *deliver himself* by his great army." A closely related possibility is that Zech. 9:9 is an example of the use of the *niphal* participle with resultative force (= "victorious," RSV). The Latin and Greek versions, therefore, provide a credible reading of the Hebrew text as a reference to the victory enjoyed by the royal figure depicted (cf. NEB: "His victory gained").

The royal figure is described as "humble" (*ʿānî*). This is an odd epithet to find employed in relation to a royal figure, so that the difficulty is not greatly relieved if it is applied to a human king as opposed to God as King. Given the regular connection in the theology of the Old Testament between being afflicted, humble, or poor and being (subsequently) saved/exalted,[26] the implication may be that the one referred to is *set to be exalted*. In line with this, Michael Widmer has argued that the related term *ʿānāyw* (used of Moses in Num. 12:3) speaks of the *expectation of being vindicated*.[27] Consistent with this understanding, the designation in Zech. 9:9 is followed by a description of the royal figure on his way to his enthronement (see below).[28]

23. Paul LaMarche, *Zacharie IX–XIV: Structure littéraire et messianisme* (Paris: Gabalda, 1961), 43.
24. According to Anthony Gelston, this is a perfectly possible rendering of the Hebrew text; see *The Twelve Minor Prophets*, vol. 13 of *BHQ*, 142*.
25. This translation is provided by Charles Augustus Briggs and Emilie Grace Briggs, *The Book of Psalms*, 2 vols., ICC (Edinburgh: T&T Clark, 1906), 1:285.
26. E.g., Ps. 34:6 (34:7 MT: "This poor man [ʿānî] cried, and the LORD . . . saved him out of all his troubles").
27. Michael Widmer, *Moses, God, and the Dynamics of Intercessory Prayer*, FAT 2.8 (Tübingen: Mohr Siebeck, 2004), 268–69.
28. In terms of syntax, *ʿānî* is closely related to what follows (reading the conjunction as a *waw-explicativum*: "that is, [and so] riding on . . .").

The motif of a figure "riding on a he-ass, on a donkey, the offspring of she-asses" (Zech. 9:9, authors' trans.) does not need to indicate humility or a rejection of militarism (in implied contrast to arriving on horse or in a chariot).[29] According to Frans Laubscher, it can be viewed as an appropriate royal mount, being the traditional riding animal prior to the importation of horses.[30] As clarified by Kenneth Way, the point of the involved description of the animal is the purity of the royal mount ("a purebred jackass"). Due to its rarity and expense, it is a prestigious animal appropriate for use by a king,[31] and is therefore an image that may be used in application of the royal metaphor to YHWH. Significantly, the coronation of Solomon at Gihon (outside the city of Jerusalem) involved a ride on the royal mule, with his crowning followed by his triumphant entrance into the city and his enthronement (1 Kings 1:34–40). As suggested by Gerhard von Rad, Zech. 9:9 alludes to what was an ancient tradition and pictures the king on his way to being enthroned.[32] All in all, close examination of the terms used indicates that nothing in the wording of 9:9 excludes the idea that the enthronement of YHWH, the Warrior-King, is being described.

Zechariah 9:10 and Psalm 72:8

The last difficulty for a theocratic reading of Zech. 9:9 is the clear allusion to Ps. 72:8 in Zech. 9:10b.

Zechariah 9:10b reads:

> His rule shall be from sea to sea,
> and from the River to the ends of the earth.

Psalm 72:8 reads:

> May he have dominion from sea to sea,
> and from the River to the ends of the earth!

This intertextual connection is widely understood as proving that Davidic rule is in prospect in this half-verse. It is identical to the picture given of the

29. For a thorough discussion of the various terms used, see Kenneth C. Way, "Donkey Domain: Zechariah 9:9 and Lexical Semantics," *JBL* 129 (2010): 105–14.

30. Frans du T. Laubscher, "The King's Humbleness in Zechariah 9:9: A Paradox?," *JNSL* 18 (1992): 126–27, 130.

31. Way, "Donkey Domain," 113–14.

32. Gerhard von Rad, "The Royal Ritual in Judah," in *The Problem of the Hexateuch, and Other Essays*, trans. E. W. Trueman Dicken (Edinburgh: Oliver & Boyd, 1966), 222–23.

hoped-for universal realm of the Davidic king (Solomon?) in Ps. 72:8–11. But in Zech. 9:10a, it is YHWH who cuts off the chariot, war horse, and battle bow ("I [YHWH] will cut off the chariot from Ephraim . . . and the battle bow shall be cut off [by YHWH]"),[33] in line with the picture of future world demilitarization through divine action given in Ps. 46:9, Isa. 9:2–7, and Hosea 2:18, so that, despite the change in person in Zech. 9:10aβ (from first person to third person), it is God's pacification and rule of the nations that is in view. There is no reason to exclude the possibility that language in the Psalter used to describe the global rule of the Davidic king is taken up in Zech. 9 and reapplied to the global dominion of the Divine King. Regarding God's use of human agents, what might be thought to be Davidic prerogatives are democratized in Zech. 9, for the Divine Warrior says that he will use Judah, Ephraim, and the citizenry of Zion ("your sons, O Zion") as his weapons (v. 13). Nothing is said in verse 13 about Davidic agency in the anticipated defeat of foreign powers. The shift in pronoun (especially in v. 10b) and parallels with Ps. 72:8 allow for the possibility that a ruler, perhaps from David's line, is in view in Zech. 9:9, although we have offered plausible explanations of the theocratic view.

The Figure of the Shepherd in Zechariah

The people's troubles are due to their "lack of a shepherd" (Zech. 10:2)—that is, the right kind of leader—and God promises to punish the false "shepherds," who here appear to be oppressive foreign kings (10:3; 11:1–3), with God using the community to bring this about, and no messianic leader is in view in the battle described (10:4–7). Then, in 11:4–14, the prophet is commissioned to act the role of a good shepherd (= king), but he is unable to improve the situation (vv. 4, 7–9), and he offers his resignation and is given a wage of "thirty shekels of silver" (vv. 9, 12).

Zechariah 11:4, 7, and 12 read:

> Thus said the LORD my God: "Become shepherd of the flock doomed to slaughter." (v. 4)

> So I became the shepherd of the flock doomed to be slaughtered by the sheep traders. And I took two staffs, one I named Favor, the other I named Union. And I tended the sheep. (v. 7)

---

33. Reading the passive voice as implying divine agency. Collins acknowledges that v. 10aα describes God's actions. Collins, "Literary Contexts," 39.

Then I said to them, "If it seems good to you, give me my wages; but if not, keep them." And they weighed out as my wages thirty pieces of silver. (v. 12)

Matthew 27:9 reads:

Then was fulfilled what had been spoken by the prophet Jeremiah, saying, "And they took the thirty pieces of silver, the price of him on whom a price had been set by some of the sons of Israel."

The First Evangelist's use of this passage does not help illuminate this cryptic material,[34] and when it is applied to Jesus, for example, it is unclear whether he is being depicted as the rejected prophet or the rejected shepherd (= king)—for the prophet is mimicking a shepherd—though it is probably the latter. In a second sign-act, the prophet plays the role of the worthless shepherd, who deserves and receives God's judgment (Zech. 11:15–17).[35]

In Zech. 12:1–3, the nations come against Jerusalem, but the LORD strikes panic (v. 4), and with God's enabling, Jerusalem is delivered by "the clans/tents of Judah" (vv. 5–9). The "house of David" works jointly with the "ruler" or "inhabitants" of Jerusalem (v. 7; yōšēb could mean either). The Davidic house appears several times in the context of action by different clans and tribes, but it is God (rather than a messianic figure) who gives the victory (vv. 2–9).[36] As well, the "house of David" is among those who mourn for the one "whom they have pierced" (v. 10; root dāqar), with the people themselves somehow responsible for his death. The shepherd approved by God ("my shepherd") who is slain by the sword in 13:7 would seem to be the same person as the one pierced in 12:10,[37] and the figure of 13:7 may also be equated with the "good shepherd" of 11:4–14. In Zechariah's time, there is ambiguity as to who the shepherd will be, but he appears to be a Davidic royal figure (over whom his house will mourn). This material about the slaying of the shepherd is picked up in the New Testament and applied to Jesus both by the Fourth Evangelist (John 19:37; cf. Zech. 12:10) and the Synoptic writers (Matt. 26:31; Mark 14:27; cf. Zech. 13:7),[38] though without elaboration, presumably because they

34. Matthew combines what is said in Zechariah with material from Jer. 32.

35. Paul L. Redditt, "The Two Shepherds in Zechariah 11:4–17," CBQ 55 (1993): 676–86.

36. Anthony Petterson notes that v. 9 is a summary of vv. 2–8, with God the one who destroys the threatening nations. Anthony Petterson, Haggai, Zechariah and Malachi, ApOTC 25 (Nottingham: Apollos, 2015), 261.

37. For such piercing with the sword, see Judg. 9:54; 1 Sam. 31:4; 1 Chron. 10:4; these are references provided by Mark J. Boda, The Book of Zechariah, NICOT (Grand Rapids: Eerdmans, 2016), 715.

38. See Stephen L. Cook, "The Metamorphosis of a Shepherd: The Tradition History of Zechariah 11:17 + 13:7–9," CBQ 55 (1993): 463–66.

thought the key points were obvious—namely, the piercing/striking of the shepherd was in accord with the plan of God, and it resulted in the scattering of the flock, which will not be finally remedied until the dawning of God's kingdom.

How, then, are we to integrate the prophecy, especially in regard to what is said by Zechariah about the human and divine kingship? At the end of the book, the focus is YHWH as the universal king (14:9, 16),[39] but the "muted messianism" of the first half of the canonical book (the figure of the Sprout) is neither forgotten nor denied,[40] but rather sublimated into the figure of the suffering shepherd-king, who has a significant role in the purposes of God.

The Eschatology of Malachi

The prophecy of Malachi is to be read as an integral part of a larger canonical structure—namely, the Book of the Twelve—and Malachi comes straight after Zech. 14, in which the nations recognize God as King. The connections between Malachi and the preceding prophetic booklets of the Twelve (esp. Haggai and Zechariah) have been explored.[41] The links include the "messenger" (mal'āk) theme; the similar oracle titles in Zech. 9:1, 12:1, and Mal. 1:1; and the question-answer schema in Hag. 2:11–14, in Zechariah's night visions, and throughout Malachi.[42] The prophecy of Haggai ends with the anticipation of God's rule over the nations of the world (2:20–23). The call to "return" to YHWH and the contingent promise that YHWH will "return" to Jerusalem found in Zech. 1:3 is picked up in Mal. 3:7.[43] In Zech. 14:16–19, the nations share in the worship of God in a restored Jerusalem. Though Malachi does not mention a pilgrimage of the nations to Zion, international recognition of YHWH's rule is an important theme in Malachi's picture of the future, and several texts in Malachi (1:5, 11, 14; 3:12) describe that future

39. Paul L. Redditt, "Israel's Shepherds: Hope and Pessimism in Zechariah 9–14," *CBQ* 51 (1989): 641.

40. Eric M. Meyers, "Messianism in First and Second Zechariah and the 'End' of Biblical Prophecy," in *"Go to the Land I Will Show You": Studies in Honour of Dwight W. Young*, ed. Joseph E. Coleson and Victor H. Matthews (Winona Lake, IN: Eisenbrauns, 1996), 135.

41. E.g., Louis Stulman and Hyun Chul Paul Kim, *You Are My People: An Introduction to Prophetic Literature* (Nashville: Abingdon, 2010), 240–45. They do not, however, mention the theme of God's end-time rule over the nations.

42. E.g., Mark J. Boda, "Messengers of Hope in Haggai–Malachi," *JSOT* 32 (2007): 113–31; Ronald W. Pierce, "Literary Connectors and a Haggai/Zechariah/Malachi Corpus," *JETS* 27 (1984): 277–89; Ronald W. Pierce, "A Thematic Development of the Haggai/Zechariah/Malachi Corpus," *JETS* 27 (1984): 401–11.

43. Stulman and Kim, *You Are My People*, 243.

prospect and should be translated using the future tense (e.g., 1:11: "In every place incense *will be offered* to my name").[44] Malachi cites future international cultic recognition of YHWH in order to highlight current Judean cultic failure to properly honor God (1:6–10, 12–14a).

The only passage in Malachi where some readers have found reference to messianic agency in God's plans for his people and the world is in the opening verses of chapter 3 of that prophecy.[45] Malachi 3:1–5 reads:

> [1]Behold, I send my messenger, and he will prepare the way before me. And the Lord whom you seek will suddenly come to his temple; and the messenger of the covenant in whom you delight, behold, he is coming, says the LORD of hosts. [2]But who can endure the day of his coming, and who can stand when he appears? For he is like a refiner's fire and like fullers' soap. [3]He will sit as a refiner and purifier of silver, and he will purify the sons of Levi and refine them like gold and silver, and they will bring offerings in righteousness to the LORD. [4]Then the offering of Judah and Jerusalem will be pleasing to the LORD as in the days of old and as in former years.
>
> [5]Then I will draw near to you for judgment. I will be a swift witness against the sorcerers, against the adulterers, against those who swear falsely, against those who oppress the hired worker in his wages, the widow and the fatherless, against those who thrust aside the sojourner, and do not fear me, says the LORD of hosts.

Verse 1 answers the skeptical question of the people in 2:17b ("Where is the God of justice [*mišpāṭ*]?"), and the wrongs of the present age will be put right by God's coming (cf. v. 5a: "Then I will draw near to you for judgment [*mišpāṭ*]"). The coming of "the Lord" to the temple will, however, be preceded by the arrival of "[his] messenger" (3:1a), and this "Lord" is YHWH rather than a messianic figure.[46] God is the presumed speaker in 3:1a and 3:5, and verses 1b–4 speak of God in the third person, as is often the case when a prophet speaks as God's mouthpiece. The "messenger" in verse 1b ("even [*waw*] the messenger of the covenant," ESV alt.) is equated with "the Lord" (*hā'ādôn*), for similar relative clauses are applied to both figures ("whom you seek . . . in whom you delight") and both are said to be "coming" (using the same Hebrew verb). This prophecy is based on what is said about the angel of the LORD

44. For detailed argument, see Gregory Goswell, "The Eschatology of Malachi after Zechariah 14," *JBL* 132 (2013): 625–38.

45. We also recognize that Mal. 4:5, with its reference to God sending Elijah, may have messianic connotations, but the text has a prophetic, rather than royal, figure in view, so this falls outside the scope of our study.

46. As helpfully explained by Andrew S. Malone, "Is the Messiah Announced in Malachi 3:1?," *TynBul* 57 (2006): 215–28.

in Exod. 23:20 ("Behold, I send a messenger before you to guard your way," authors' trans.), another passage in which the roles of Yhwh and his messenger merge (vv. 21–22). The "messenger of the covenant" remains the subject of the following verse (Mal. 3:2), where divine action is clearly in view—the frightful prospect of God coming as "refiner and purifier" (v. 3). There are, then, two messengers in Mal. 3:1, the first prophetic and the second divine.[47]

Therefore, Mal. 3:1–5 describes what God will do when he comes to purify "the sons of Levi" and to judge wrongdoers. The passage prophesies of the time when "the offering of Judah and Jerusalem will be pleasing [root *'āreb*] to the Lord" (v. 4). This prospect reverses the earlier evaluation of Judean sacrifices as unacceptable to God (cf. 1:8b: "Present that to your governor; will he be pleased [root *rāṣâ*] with you or show you favor?," ESV alt.).[48] Malachi 3:4 is a "refinement text"[49] and idealizes the past ("as in the days of old and as in former years"); however, the idyllic past does not have a Davidic frame of reference (cf. Isa. 1:26).[50] In the prophecy of Malachi, the ideal past has already been alluded to (Mal. 2:4–7), so that the earlier period referred to in 3:4 is presumably the same ideal Levitical past in the Mosaic era. This is the case whether the background to the "covenant with Levi" alluded to in Mal. 2:4–7 is found in the Blessing of Levi in Deut. 33:8–11, the reward promised to Phinehas in Num. 25:11–13, or a combination of both pentateuchal passages.[51] Therefore, nothing suggests any messianic agency in the forecast reformation of the Jerusalemite cult; rather, Malachi announces that God himself will intervene to judge and refine.[52]

Postlude: Canonical Reflections

The Use of Zechariah 9:9 in the Gospels

A discussion of the use of Zech. 9:9 in the accounts of Jesus's entry into Jerusalem found in Matt. 21 and John 12 is required, for many think that the

---

47. Beth Glazier-McDonald, "*Mal'ak habberit*: The Messenger of the Covenant in Mal 3:1," *HAR* 11 (1987): 93–104.

48. As noted by Karl William Weyde, *Prophecy and Teaching: Prophetic Authority, Form Problems, and the Use of Traditions in the Book of Malachi*, BZAW 288 (Berlin: de Gruyter, 2000), 300–301, the roots are used in parallel in Jer. 6:20.

49. Weyde, *Prophecy and Teaching*, 302.

50. See Gregory Goswell, "Isaiah 1:26: A Neglected Text on Kingship," *TynBul* 62 (2011): 233–46.

51. For a discussion of the alternatives, see Julia M. O'Brien, *Priest and Levite in Malachi*, SBLDS 121 (Atlanta: Scholars Press, 1990), 104–6.

52. Rikk E. Watts, "Mark," in *CNTUOT*, 119: "The key point is that Mal. 3 makes no mention of a messianic figure."

Evangelists interpreted this key Old Testament verse in a different way from what is suggested above. In John 12, Jesus is hailed as "the King of Israel" by the crowd at his entry into Jerusalem (v. 13). In the severely shortened version of Zech. 9:9 provided in John 12:15, the Fourth Evangelist only includes the elements that reflect the two main features of his own presentation: Jesus's entrance into the city and his seated posture on the animal (cf. Matt. 21:5).[53]

John 12:14–15 reads:

[14]And Jesus found a young donkey and sat on it, just as it is written,

> [15]"Fear not, daughter of Zion;
> behold, your king is coming,
>   sitting on a donkey's colt!"

Even in the Synoptic Gospels, the words that the disciples were instructed to speak when procuring the animal(s), "*The Lord* needs them" (Matt. 21:3; cf. Mark 11:3; Luke 19:31), can be understood as hinting to the Christian reader that the animal requisitioned is to be used as a mount for God.[54] Unlike the other Gospels, the Fourth Gospel has no Davidic reference in the pericope where Jesus enters Jerusalem. In John 12:13, Jesus is designated "the King of Israel" rather than "the Son of David" (as in Matt. 21:9), and there is no mention of "the kingdom of our father David" (as in Mark 11:10). The Fourth Evangelist does not allude to Davidic kingship in the scene of the entrance of Jesus into Jerusalem.[55]

In the case of Matt. 21, it is not always noticed that more than one type of Christology is on display in the scene of Jesus's entry. In fact, there are three, and no one brand of Christology (e.g., Messiah) is to be used to deny the presence of the other two. The statement "The Lord needs them" (21:3) can be understood as pointing to the highest Christology of all (Jesus as divine Lord in human flesh), and this is immediately followed by the claim that Zech. 9:9 has been fulfilled.

53. Maarten J. J. Menken, *Old Testament Quotations in the Fourth Gospel: Studies in Textual Form*, CBET 15 (Kampen: Kok Pharos, 1996), 79–81.

54. As correctly noted by C. Kavin Rowe, who focuses on the Lukan form of the text; see *Early Narrative Christology: The Lord in the Gospel of Luke* (Grand Rapids: Baker Academic, 2006), 162.

55. For this paragraph, we acknowledge our dependence on Dae Woo Seo, "An Interpretation of the Key Johannine Christological Titles in John 1:19–51 on the Basis of Their Wider Use in the Narrative of the Gospel and in Dialogue with Their Old Testament Background" (master's diss., Australian College of Theology, 2012), chap. 8.

Matthew 21:1–5 reads:

¹Now when they drew near to Jerusalem and came to Bethphage, to the Mount of Olives, then Jesus sent two disciples, ²saying to them, "Go into the village in front of you, and immediately you will find a donkey tied, and a colt with her. Untie them and bring them to me. ³If anyone says anything to you, you shall say, 'The Lord needs them,' and he will send them at once." ⁴This took place to fulfill what was spoken by the prophet, saying,

> ⁵"Say to the daughter of Zion,
> 'Behold, your king is coming to you,
>   humble, and mounted on a donkey,
>   and on a colt, the foal of a beast of burden.'"

Several verses later, the acclamation of the crowds ("Hosanna to the Son of David!") testifies to their (partial at best) recognition of Jesus as Messiah (v. 9), but this is not connected by Matthew to the Zecharian verse quoted above, but to wording drawn from Ps. 118:25–26. Later still, on his entry into the city, the crowds acknowledge Jesus as a "prophet" (Matt. 21:11), and this understanding is supported by the cleansing of the temple viewed as a prophetic act (given that the evangelist quotes Jer. 7:11). In other words, the one event provides Matthew with the opportunity to present the person of Jesus from three vantage points (God, Messiah, prophet), and each view is supported by a different Old Testament citation. We only need to reiterate the key point that Matthew's use of Zech. 9:9 is linked to the revelation of and testimony to Jesus's divinity.

The Use of Malachi 3 in the Gospels

Confirmation that Davidic messianism is not on show in Mal. 3 is the fact that the New Testament identifies the messenger of Mal. 3:1a as John the Baptist (Matt. 11:10; Mark 1:2; Luke 7:27), and according to the evangelists, "the Lord" of Malachi 3:1b is Jesus, who is God in the flesh, with the divine identity of the one for whom John prepares made clear by the citation of Isa. 40 (cf. Mark 1:3 citing Isa. 40:3: "Prepare the way of the Lord").[56] John is preparing people for the coming of God.

Mark 1:2–3 reads:

²As it is written in Isaiah the prophet,

> "Behold, I send my messenger before your face,
>   who will prepare your way,

---

56. See Craig L. Blomberg, "Elijah, Election, and the Use of Malachi in the New Testament," *Criswell Theological Review* 2 (1987): 104.

³the voice of one crying in the wilderness:
  'Prepare the way of the Lord,
  make his paths straight.'"

Of course, John was also preparing for the coming of the Messiah (e.g., John 3:28: "I am not the Christ, but I have been sent *before him*"); however, Mal. 3:1 is not used in connection with this way of viewing John's role, and the wording of John 3:28, for example, is not close enough to that of Mal. 3:1 ("before your face") to prove that it is citing or alluding to this Old Testament verse.[57]

In summary, the widespread theme of YHWH's coming in the prophecy of Zechariah supports the interpretation of Zech. 9:9 as a description of the entrance of YHWH into Jerusalem. The figure seated on an ass is a metaphorical description of the coronation and enthronement of YHWH in the eschaton. In the Gospels of Matthew and John, Zech. 9:9 is used by the evangelists to proclaim the highest Christology of all, depicting Jesus as God entering Jerusalem. Messianism is also on show in Zechariah, both in the form of the Sprout, who is the future temple-builder and ruler over a peaceful domain, and in the figure of the rejected and dying shepherd-king (who is equated with Jesus in the passion narratives). On the other hand, the proclamation of Malachi does not feature a messianic figure in its vision of God's renovation of the Jerusalemite cult and the universal worship of YHWH among the nations.

---

57. *Pace* Petterson, *Behold Your King*, 368. He depends on Andreas J. Köstenberger ("John," in *CNTUOT*, 437), who only sees this as a possibility.

13

The Portrait of David in the Psalter

The Psalms are a part of the Old Testament much loved and comparatively well known by Christians. On that basis, given the general lack of interest in and neglect of the Old Testament, even by many pastors in their preaching, it has been remarked (not wholly in jest) that the Psalter must be part of the New Testament. Indeed, there are pocket-sized New Testaments published that include the book of Psalms in the back. The Old Testament was "the Bible of Jesus," and it is plain, if we count up the allusions to and quotations of the Psalms made by Jesus, that this was his favorite book. This chapter may help to explain why. Does a messianic hope find expression in the Psalter? In this chapter we examine the final form of the Hebrew Psalter as outlined by Gerald H. Wilson, whose sequential reading of the canonical Psalter—an approach that makes the position of individual psalms and/or groups of psalms significant for interpretation—caused him to discount the typical messianic reading, but that is not at all to say that the Psalter does not throw light on the person and work of Jesus.

The usual mode of discussion in contemporary Psalms scholarship is that the Psalter is either messianic or non-messianic. The premise is that if a book of the Bible is not entirely centered on a royal Messiah as the be-all and end-all of hope, it is non-messianic (e.g., Michael Snearly's published dissertation,

An earlier version of material in this chapter was published as Gregory Goswell, "The Non-Messianic Psalter of Gerald H. Wilson," *VT* 66 (2016): 524–41. Used by permission.

and the work of many others who respond to Wilson).[1] Instead, following the lead of Wilson, we construe the hope expressed in the Psalter as taking the form of a nuanced messianism wherein a future "David" depends upon and serves YHWH, the Divine King. In this way, messianic hope is not discarded but oriented in such a way that YHWH's kingship is given prominence.

The Editing of the Hebrew Psalter

The seminal work of Gerald Wilson shows that certain royal psalms are given prominent placement in the five-book structuring of the Psalter,[2] with Pss. 2, 41, 72, and 89 strategically placed at the "seams" of books 1, 2, and 3.[3] According to Wilson, the intervening psalms are to be read in light of this royal frame, which promotes Davidic kingship and the covenant that undergirds it. The postscript "The prayers of David, son of Jesse, are ended," at 72:20, helps identify books 1 and 2 as an earlier collection, introduced and concluded by royal psalms (Pss. 2; 72), with the bulk of the psalms being Davidic. The collection is capped by Ps. 72, bearing the title "For Solomon" (ESV alt.). The mention of David and Solomon, together with indications of God's commitment to his covenant promises to David, makes Pss. 2–72 a celebration of YHWH's faithfulness to the covenant, a covenant that found its fullest expression during the united monarchy.

Psalm 2

According to Wilson, an examination of Pss. 2, 41, 72, and 89 reveals a progression in thought about Israelite kingship and the Davidic covenant. Psalm 2 introduces and alludes to the Davidic covenant (vv. 7–9)—for example, the language of sonship in verse 7 (cf. 2 Sam. 7:14: "I will be to him a father, and he shall be to me a son"), though the word "covenant" (*bərît*) is not used (neither is it in 2 Sam. 7).[4] The king is depicted as world ruler (Ps. 2:2).

1. Michael K. Snearly, *The Return of the King: Messianic Expectation in Book V of the Psalter*, LHBOTS 624 (London: Bloomsbury T&T Clark, 2016).

2. Gerald H. Wilson, *The Editing of the Hebrew Psalter*, SBLDS 76 (Chico, CA: Scholars Press, 1985); Gerald H. Wilson, "Evidence of Editorial Divisions in the Hebrew Psalter," *VT* 24 (1984): 337–52; Gerald H. Wilson, "The Use of Royal Psalms at the 'Seams' of the Hebrew Psalter," *JSOT* 35 (1986): 85–94. Wilson's work has produced a sea change in Psalms scholarship.

3. Though Ps. 41 is not usually classified as a royal psalm, Wilson argues that it belongs to this category.

4. Cf. Gregory Goswell, "What Makes the Arrangement of God with David in 2 Samuel 7 a Covenant?," *ResQ* 60 (2018): 87–97.

Psalm 2:1–9 reads:

> ¹Why do the nations rage
>   and the peoples plot in vain?
> ²The kings of the earth set themselves,
>   and the rulers take counsel together,
>   against the LORD and against his Anointed, saying,
> ³"Let us burst their bonds apart
>   and cast away their cords from us."
> ⁴He who sits in the heavens laughs;
>   the Lord holds them in derision.
> ⁵Then he will speak to them in his wrath,
>   and terrify them in his fury, saying,
> ⁶"As for me, I have set my King
>   on Zion, my holy hill."
>
> ⁷I will tell of the decree:
> The LORD said to me, "You are my Son;
>   today I have begotten you.
> ⁸Ask of me, and I will make the nations your heritage,
>   and the ends of the earth your possession.
> ⁹You shall break them with a rod of iron
>   and dash them in pieces like a potter's vessel."

This is not just courtly hyperbole but indicates world dominance by an ideal Davidic ruler yet to come. Norman Whybray is right to find full-blown messianism in Ps. 2,[5] but this need not give the whole Psalter a messianic cast. This is where the Psalter begins, but it may end in quite a different place theologically. God's promise to thwart the plotting of the rebellious "kings of the earth" (vv. 1–6) is echoed in Ps. 41, the psalm that closes book 1, where David expresses his assurance of God's protection from his enemies (vv. 1, 2, 11–12). Psalm 2 provides the context for the early psalms, which are for the most part laments (e.g., Pss. 3–7). David typically laments his troubles and difficulties, most often caused by enemies, and the fulsome depiction of his suffering in Ps. 22 represents a high point in this theme.

Psalm 45

Psalm 45 alludes to the promise made to David that his dynasty would endure forever (vv. 6–7; cf. 2 Sam. 7:11b–16), and it does so with the king

---

5. Norman Whybray, *Reading the Psalms as a Book*, JSOTSup 222 (Sheffield: Sheffield Academic, 1996).

ostensibly addressed in verse 6a as "God" (*'ĕlōhîm*; we take the word as vocative). Psalm 45:6–7 reads:

> ⁶Your throne, O God, is forever and ever.
>   The scepter of your kingdom is a scepter of uprightness;
> ⁷you have loved righteousness and hated wickedness.
>   Therefore God, your God, has anointed you
>   with the oil of gladness beyond your companions.

The Greek Bible (LXX) does not significantly change the text of verse 6a ("O God" [*ho theos*]), and the translation of the Aramaic targum is paraphrastic but confirms a vocative address ("Your glorious throne, O Lord, endures for ever and ever"), though the distinction drawn in verse 7 ("God, your God") rules out ascribing actual divinity to the Davidic king, as do subsequent verses about the king's consort and their progeny (vv. 9–17). This exalted mode of address may be due to the king's role as the nation's chief law officer, delegated by God to exercise God's prerogative to judge, which is the explanation of the use of the word "gods" in application to *judges* in Ps. 82:6 ("You are gods"; cf. Jesus's use of this Old Testament verse in John 10:34–35).⁶ This judicial interpretation is supported by mention in Ps. 45 of "throne" and "uprightness" (*mîšōr*), as well as the "[loving] righteousness . . . [hating] wickedness" contrast.⁷ It is Jesus's supreme position as judge (a role not given to any angel) that justifies the citation of this psalm in application to Jesus by the writer of Hebrews (1:8–9), for Jesus fulfills what is said of the Davidic figure of Ps. 45 as well as being the God whose concern for justice explains why the figure is given this important legal role.

Psalm 72

Psalm 72, with its repeated petition on behalf of the "royal son" (v. 1), may represent the prayer of aged David (cf. 71:9, 18) for his son Solomon in view of the latter's ascension to the throne (understanding the psalm title *lišlōmōh* = "For Solomon"). The hope is expressed of a continuation of the blessings of the Davidic covenant in the experience of his descendants.

---

6. This is the view of the medieval rabbi Rashi. For other possible instances, see the KJV and NIV translations of Exod. 21:6 and 22:8 (22:7 MT). The alternate interpretation is that these verses about going *to* God refer to going to the sanctuary for judgment (cf. 1 Sam. 10:3), where the appointed judges reside; see Brevard S. Childs, *Exodus*, OTL (London: SCM, 1974), 469, 475.

7. Cf. Geoffrey W. Grogan, *Psalms*, THOTC (Grand Rapids: Eerdmans, 2008), 99.

Psalms 89 and 90

At the conclusion of book 3 and start of book 4, a less hopeful psalm regarding Davidic kingship (Ps. 89) gives way to a focus on the enduring kingship of God (Ps. 90). Psalm 89 makes explicit mention of the Davidic covenant (vv. 3–4, 20–21, 28), but the covenant is now viewed as established in the dim past ("of old"; vv. 19–20, 49). Psalm 89:49 reads:

> Lord, where is your steadfast love of old,
>   which by your faithfulness you swore to David?

Psalm 90:1–2 reads:

A Prayer of Moses, the man of God.

> [1]Lord, you have been our dwelling place
>   in all generations.
> [2]Before the mountains were brought forth,
>   or ever you had formed the earth and the world,
>   from everlasting to everlasting you are God.

The covenant is broken and failed (89:38–44), and the hope of its renewal is expressed (vv. 50–51). Book 3 ends at this climactic point. Wilson goes on to argue that, starting from Ps. 90, books 4 and 5 move away from this royal framework and that the final form of the Psalter encourages its readers to shift their focus "away from hope in human, Davidic kingship back to the premonarchic period with its (supposed) direct reliance on God's protection and the individual access guaranteed by the Law."[8] As noted by Wilson,[9] the Hebrew term for "king" (*melek*) is used of the kings of Israel and Judah in books 1–3 (2:6; 21:1, 7; 45:11; 89:18), but in books 4–5 this is lacking, showing a diminution of emphasis on the rulership of the Davidide normally associated with the word "king."[10]

An overwhelming focus on divine kingship in the later part of the Psalter (e.g., Pss. 93–99) appears to leave behind any messianic hope in the form of

8. Wilson, "Use of Royal Psalms," 92; Gerald H. Wilson, "King, Messiah, and the Reign of God: Revisiting the Royal Psalms and the Shape of the Psalter," in *The Book of Psalms: Composition and Reception*, ed. Peter W. Flint and Patrick D. Miller Jr., VTSup 99 (Leiden: Brill, 2005), 392; Gerald H. Wilson, "The Structure of the Psalter," in *Interpreting the Psalms: Issues and Approaches*, ed. Philip S. Johnston and David G. Firth (Leicester, UK: Apollos, 2005), 235.

9. Gerald H. Wilson, *Psalms*, NIVAC (Grand Rapids: Zondervan, 2002), 1:115–17; cf. Gerald H. Wilson, "Psalms and Psalter: Paradigm for Biblical Theology," in *Biblical Theology: Retrospect and Prospect*, ed. Scott Hafemann (Leicester: Apollos, 2002), 107.

10. The only possible exception is Ps. 144:10. A similar phenomenon is to be observed in the book of Isaiah, comparing chaps. 1–39 with chaps. 40–66.

revived Davidic rule (e.g., Ps. 97:1: "The LORD reigns, let the earth rejoice"). Gerald Wilson views these "The LORD reigns" (YHWH *mālāk*) psalms as "the theological 'heart' of the expanded final Psalter."[11] He sees book 4, with so many psalms without titles (thirteen out of seventeen), as "the editorial centre" of the final form of the Psalter, responding to the demise of the Davidic covenant as reflected in Ps. 89. Its message is that YHWH was Israel's King in the past (notably the Mosaic period) and that this is the shape of the future. "How long?" of 90:13 picks up the same question in 89:46. YHWH is Israel's refuge "in all generations" (90:1), in contrast to transient human monarchy, which shares the frailty of humanity generally (vv. 2–6, 9–10). In book 4, YHWH's kingship, not David's, is steadily reiterated, with the climactic statement found in 103:19 before the hallelujah psalms, 104–6, that close this book ("YHWH has established his throne in the heavens, / and his kingdom rules over all," ESV alt.).

Book 4, like book 3, ends with a plea: not a plea for YHWH to live up to his covenant obligations to the house of David, but the plea for restoration from exile (Ps. 106:47a: "Gather us from among the nations"). The concern is now the fate of the nation, not that of Davidic kingship. Book 5 shows that this plea will be answered, Ps. 107 giving examples of how God rescued his people when they cried to him, just as David cried to YHWH and was answered (Pss. 108–10). Wilson argues that there is a shift in theological perspective away from what prevailed in books 1–3. For Wilson, the Psalter is a historical retrospect (books 1–3) followed by an exhortation directing Israel's future hope to theocracy (rule by God) and depicting a reduced (though vital) role for the Davidic king (books 4–5).

Gerald Wilson on Book 5

A little more detail on Wilson's reading of book 5 is needed, for Pss. 110 and 132 are Davidic psalms that many see as having a messianic outlook. These two psalms are regularly viewed by scholars as a serious impediment to the acceptance of Wilson's thesis. Book 5 has three main components: Davidic psalms (108–10; 138–45) and the Songs of Ascents (120–34), each capped by hallelujah psalms (111–17; 135; 146–50). Psalm 107 answers the plea of Ps. 106, showing that the distress of the exile has been overcome (107:1–3). In this postexilic context, David becomes the model of piety for this new stage of salvation history. Two groups of Davidic psalms (108–10; 138–45) are placed

---

11. Wilson, "Use of Royal Psalms," 92.

near the beginning and end of the book. David reemerges at this late stage of
the Psalter as the "wise man" (107:43), who relies on the kindness of Yhwh,
and David at once takes up this theme in 108:4 ("For your kindness is great
above the heavens," ESV alt.).

Psalm 145 is the climax of the Psalter (according to Wilson) and is spoken
by David. Here David the king extols the superior kingship of Yhwh, who is
addressed as "my God and king" (145:1). Psalms 146–50 depend on 145:21
(the last verse of the psalm), wherein David says that he will "speak the praise
of Yhwh," and so Ps. 146 is (presumably) spoken by David, who contrasts
the mortality and weakness of human rulers (vv. 3–4) with the dependabil-
ity of God's help (v. 5). Yhwh fulfills the judicial and social responsibilities
of the former Israelite kings (vv. 6–9), and it is his eternal reign centered at
Zion that is proclaimed (v. 10). Yhwh the eternal King alone is worthy of
trust.[12] Wilson's reading of the Psalter is an impressive achievement, but he
is not without his critics.[13] In Wilson's sequential reading of the Psalter, is it
a problem that Pss. 110 and 132 come toward the end of the Psalter (book 5),
when any Davidic hope has supposedly been disposed of?

Psalm 110

Psalm 110 is one of a group of three psalms ascribed to David (108–10)
and can, in fact, be viewed as the linchpin of the first seven psalms in book 5:
Pss. 107–9 contain pleas for deliverance that are answered in Ps. 110, and Pss.
111–13 then praise God for the deliverance provided.[14] It needs to be noted
that the pleas for saving help (107:6, 13, 19, 28; 108:6, 12; 109:26) and the
subsequent praises (111:2, 9; 112:7; 113:7) cover a range of distressing situations that God has acted to reverse. As well, Pss. 111 and 112 are acrostics,
with a strong wisdom flavor, and especially obvious are the wisdom motto
about fearing God in 111:10 (cf. Prov. 1:7; 9:10) and the contrast of the righteous and the wicked in Ps. 112 (cf. Ps. 1). Such a setting suggests that Ps.
110 provides assurance of a more general nature that God is willing to rescue
his people. The partnering of several key royal psalms with a neighboring
wisdom psalm (Pss. 1/2; 72/73; 89/90; 118/119) suggests to Jamie A. Grant
that in the final form of the Psalter, these royal psalms now serve a didactic

12. Gerald H. Wilson, "Shaping the Psalter: A Consideration of Editorial Linkage in the
Book of Psalms," in *The Shape and Shaping of the Psalter*, ed. J. Clinton McCann, JSOTSup
159 (Sheffield: Sheffield Academic, 1993), 72–82.

13. E.g., David C. Mitchell, *The Message of the Psalter: An Eschatological Programme in
the Book of Psalms*, JSOTSup 252 (Sheffield: Sheffield Academic, 1997); David C. Mitchell,
"Lord, Remember David: G. H. Wilson and the Message of the Psalter," *VT* 56 (2006): 526–48.

14. Barry C. Davis, "Is Psalm 110 a Messianic Psalm?," *BSac* 157 (2000): 168.

purpose.[15] To this list of psalm pairs may be added Pss. 110/111. As well, the divine victory over the nations in 110:5–7 results in God "giving [his people] the inheritance of the nations" (111:6).

Psalm 110 reads:

A Psalm of David.

[1]The LORD says to my Lord:
　"Sit at my right hand,
until I make your enemies your footstool."

[2]The LORD sends forth from Zion
　your mighty scepter.
　Rule in the midst of your enemies!
[3]Your people will offer themselves freely
　on the day of your power,
　in holy garments;
from the womb of the morning,
　the dew of your youth will be yours.
[4]The LORD has sworn
　and will not change his mind,
"You are a priest forever
　after the order of Melchizedek."

[5]The Lord is at your right hand;
　he will shatter kings on the day of his wrath.
[6]He will execute judgment among the nations,
　filling them with corpses;
he will shatter chiefs
　over the wide earth.
[7]He will drink from the brook by the way;
　therefore he will lift up his head.

In Ps. 110, God promises to be at the right hand as ally and support (v. 5a: "The Lord is at your right hand"), with God referring to himself in the third person, which is not unusual in divine speech (either inside or outside the Psalter). The right side is the position of the advocate, and in the verse that immediately precedes Ps. 110 and provides its context (109:31), David vows to testify publicly that "[YHWH] stands at the right hand of *the needy*." This term is part of the "poor and needy" theme in the Psalter (cf. 12:5; 40:17; 70:5; 109:16). Therefore, the context provided by 109:31 implies

15. Jamie A. Grant, *The King as Exemplar: The Function of Deuteronomy's Kingship Law in the Shaping of the Book of Psalms*, AcBib 17 (Atlanta: Society of Biblical Literature, 2004).

that Yhwh's promises of support to the figure in Ps. 110 are democratized and illustrative of his willingness and ability to help his people when they are in need.[16] We do not, however, agree with a corporate interpretation of the individual of 110:1; rather, the individual acts as the representative of God's people, for in verse 3 the reference to "your people" distinguishes between the two.

It must also be noted that Ps. 110 is strongly theocratic in its orientation, with Yhwh the one who actively fights on behalf of the figure whom David addresses in the psalm (vv. 5–7).[17] The (Divine) "Lord" (*'ădōnāy*) is in view in verse 5a, the masoretic vocalization making this a divine title, and this is supported by many medieval Hebrew manuscripts that read Yhwh. As well, reference to "wrath" favors a divine subject in verse 5b (e.g., Ps. 2:5, 12; Isa. 63:6; Lam. 2:1), so verses 5–6 refer to Yhwh.[18] At first sight, 110:7 appears to revert to the human figure ("He will drink from the brook by the way; / therefore he will lift up his head"). Any such swapping of subject, however, is awkward, for "he" in verse 7 ought logically to refer to Yhwh, the subject of verses 5–6. The hero of the battle quenches his thirst and holds up his head in triumph (cf. Ps. 27:6). Both actions are a natural sequel to engagement in battle. If God can be depicted as fighting, he can also be portrayed as doing what other warriors do after the battle.

When all this is considered, we see that the human figure in Ps. 110 is a largely passive figure, as would be expected following the plea by David the psalmist in 109:26–27 for Yhwh's intervention and saving help. The figure of Ps. 110 is granted an exalted position; however, his position at God's right hand is a place of great honor rather than of personal power (cf. 1 Kings 2:19; Pss. 45:9; 80:17).[19] Certainly, this is the case in 1 Kings 2:19, where Solomon seats his mother, Bathsheba, on his right. Honor rather than power is indicated, as confirmed by what follows: "*until* I make your enemies your footstool."

16. For David speaking as one of the "poor," see Howard N. Wallace, "King and Community: Joining with David in Prayer," in *Psalms and Prayer: Papers Read at the Joint Meeting of the Society of Old Testament Study and Het Oudtestamentische Werkgezelschap in Nederland en België, Apeldoorn August 2006*, ed. Bob Becking and Eric Peels, OTS 55 (Leiden: Brill, 2007), 276.

17. As noted by Markus Saur, *Die Königspsalmen: Studien zur Entstehung und Theologie*, BZAW 340 (Berlin: de Gruyter, 2004), 218: the king is "usually relegated to a role of total passivity" (authors' trans.). Mitchell is mistaken in seeing a reference in these verses to "the messianic war" (*Message of the Psalter*, 262), and there is no textual support for his view that the figures of Yhwh and the king are conflated. Along the same lines, Snearly refers to the human figure as a "warrior-king" (*Return of the King*, 122).

18. T. Booij, "Psalm CX: 'Rule in the Midst of Your Foes,'" *VT* 41 (1991): 403–4.

19. Howard N. Wallace, *Psalms*, Readings: A New Biblical Commentary (Sheffield: Sheffield Phoenix, 2009), 171.

Psalm 132

Psalm 132 is also considered a problem for Wilson's thesis,[20] but again context is significant for interpretation. The psalm is immediately preceded by a call by David (note the word *ləd̄awid* [of David] in the title of Ps. 131) for Israel to "hope in the LORD from this time forth and forevermore" (131:3), picking up an earlier call in 130:7 ("O Israel, hope in the LORD"). What is more, the Songs of Ascents (Pss. 120–34) repeatedly reflect an ethic of reliance on YHWH's help alone (e.g., 121:2; 123:2; 124:8).[21] This setting does not encourage the reader to look for or find a strong messianic hope in Ps. 132. Wilson does not say that David is absent from books 4–5, but he does argue that the final two books of the Psalter provide a nuanced portrait of David that is best described as non-messianic.

Psalm 132:13–18 reads:

> [13]For the LORD has chosen Zion;
>   he has desired it for his dwelling place:
> [14]"This is my resting place forever;
>   here I will dwell, for I have desired it.
> [15]I will abundantly bless her provisions;
>   I will satisfy her poor with bread.
> [16]Her priests I will clothe with salvation,
>   and her saints will shout for joy.
> [17]There I will make a horn to sprout for David;
>   I have prepared a lamp for my anointed.
> [18]His enemies I will clothe with shame,
>   but on him his crown will shine."

Though Ps. 132 does speak of God's dynastic promise to David, God reiterates what he will do ("I will . . ."; vv. 14–18), stressing what God pledges to do on behalf of Zion/Jerusalem. The subsequent psalms (133–34) carry on the Zion focus, and the Songs of Ascents promote an ideal of Israel unified around Zion (122:3–4; 133:1–3; 134:3), much like the Chronicler, who desires all the tribes to be united in worship at Jerusalem.[22] Scholars argue

20. B. W. Anderson calls it "the 'Achilles' heel' of Wilson's hypothesis"; see B. W. Anderson with Steven Bishop, *Out of the Depths: The Psalms Speak for Us Today*, 3rd ed. (Louisville: Westminster John Knox, 2000), 209.

21. H. Viviers, "The Coherence of the *maʿǎlôt* Psalms (Pss. 120–134)," *ZAW* 106 (1994): 277.

22. As noted by Philip E. Satterthwaite, "Zion in the Songs of Ascent," in *Zion, City of Our God*, ed. Richard S. Hess and Gordon J. Wenham (Grand Rapids: Eerdmans, 1999), 127–28.

over whether Ps. 132 is primarily a royal or a Zion psalm,[23] but if context is at all determinative, situated as it is among the Songs of Ascents, the answer must be the latter. This psalm is structured around oaths, David's oath (vv. 3–5) and two oaths by Yhwh himself: God will support David's dynasty (vv. 11–12), and God will bless his people from Zion (vv. 14–18). The last oath is given the greater emphasis because of its bulk and final positioning, and it places what God promises to do for David in verses 17–18 under the larger heading of his purposes for Zion.[24] The conjunction "for" (v. 13a) is also to be noted,[25] for the causal relation indicated implies that God's promises to David (vv. 11–12) were given *for the sake of Zion*, the city that God elected as his dwelling, making Davidic arrangements subservient to God's favor toward Zion.

The psalm consists of two stanzas, each with ten lines; the first stanza contains a petition (Ps. 132:1–10), and the second the divine response (vv. 11–18).[26] The psalm refers to David by name four times (vv. 1, 10, 11, 17), with these four references forming *inclusios* around the two stanzas. Verses 1 and 10 provide a prayer-frame around verses 2–9, which show what is meant by David's efforts (v. 1)—namely, his sworn vow to find a permanent dwelling place for the ark (vv. 2–5) and the record of its fulfillment (vv. 6–9). Psalm 132 is a poetic version of what is recorded in narrative in 2 Sam. 6. The ark is the intended reference of "his footstool" (v. 7; cf. 1 Chron. 28:2), and, as in 2 Sam. 6, and so presumably here, the bringing up of the ark to David's new capital (Jerusalem) is godly David's acknowledgment of Yhwh's kingship over the nation. In other words, the strenuous efforts of David (v. 1) are aimed at glorifying Yhwh as king rather than promoting his own rule.

The animal "horn" (*qeren*) is a symbol of strength in the Old Testament (e.g., 1 Sam. 2:10; 2 Sam. 22:3) and can be used in relation to God's support of the Davidic king, as the preceding references show. In Ps. 132:17 this "horn" may represent God's provision of a future Davidide, but it is neither said nor implied that the future Davidide(s) will exercise the kind of high authority that was a feature in the monarchic period. The future "David" of books 4–5 is neither a conquering hero nor the world ruler; rather, the model set by David in verses 1–10 is of one whose chief concern is to properly honor the Divine King, whose rule over Israel is symbolized by the ark. A certain type

23. E.g., E. S. Gerstenberger calls it both a "Zion Psalm" and a "Messianic Hymn." E. S. Gerstenberger, *Psalms, Part 2, and Lamentations*, FOTL 15 (Grand Rapids: Eerdmans, 2001), 363.

24. Also Saur, *Die Königspsalmen*, 246–48.

25. Terence E. Fretheim, "Psalm 132: A Form-Critical Study," *JBL* 86 (1967): 298.

26. For the bipartite division of the psalm after v. 10, see Gianni Barbiero, "Psalm 132: A Prayer of 'Solomon,'" *CBQ* 75 (2013): 239–58.

of Davidism is in view, one in which David is a model of devotion to what the temple and Zion symbolize (God's palace and capital)—that is, this "David" embodies the implied ethic of loyal citizenship in God's kingdom, wherein the praise and worship of God takes pride of place. David is called the "lamp [*nēr*] of Israel" in 2 Sam. 21:17, so that this figure of speech in Ps. 132:17 may symbolize the continuity of the Davidic house (cf. 1 Kings 11:36; 15:4; 2 Kings 8:19), but this does not mandate a particular style of kingship, and it is consistent with an eschatological reversion to the circumscribed paradigm of human rulership found in Deut. 17—namely, the king as a model Israelite.

The theory of Gerald Wilson continues to attract attention and critical scrutiny, and we have sought to defend Wilson's sequential reading of the Hebrew Psalter, which gives it a distinctly non-messianic cast. Wilson is right to detect a major shift of theme at the juncture of books 3 and 4, with the Psalter moving away from hopes centering on the Davidic royal house toward an exclusive reliance on YHWH as king. We have argued that the presence of psalms normally classified as "royal" in book 5—namely, Pss. 110 and 132— does not undermine his thesis when the psalms are read in context. The Psalter in its final form is highly eschatological, for it looks forward to the fulfillment of the hope of the prophets in the coming reign of God, which Christians see as fulfilled in Jesus, who is God in the flesh; however, it would be a mistake to simply *equate* eschatology with messianism. The answer to the cry of the exiles in 137:4 ("How shall we sing the LORD's song in a foreign land?") is modeled by David in the minicollection of Davidic psalms that follow (Pss. 138–45).[27] Similarly, in 145:21 ("My mouth will speak the praise of the LORD") David "announces and leads the praise of YHWH that takes place in the last five psalms of the Psalter."[28] This portrait of David as worship leader is not at all far from the vision of Ezek. 40–48, which features a united Israel whose communal life focuses on the temple and whose leader, the "prince," is patron and sponsor of the cult and the chief lay participant in worship.

Postlude: Canonical Reflections

We view the expression *lədāwid* in the title of Ps. 110 as a *lamed auctoris* (i.e., as meaning "by David")—that is, it ascribes authorship of the psalm

27. As noted, for example, by Harm Van Grol, "David and His Chasidim: Place and Function of Psalms 138–145," in *The Composition of the Book of Psalms*, ed. Erich Zenger, BETL 238 (Leuven: Peeters, 2010), 309–37.

28. Nancy L. deClaissé-Walford, *Reading from the Beginning: The Shaping of the Hebrew Psalter* (Macon, GA: Mercer University Press, 1997), 99.

to David, identifying him as a prophet who delivers the LORD's message and using a prophetic idiom for introducing an oracle: "the utterance [nəʾum] of YHWH" (authors' trans.).[29] In this oracle, David speaks of an exalted figure ("my Lord") who is invited to sit at God's right hand. The wording about sitting at God's right hand (110:1) is echoed many times in the New Testament (e.g., Mark 14:62; Acts 2:34–35). In Mark 12:35–37 and parallel texts, Ps. 110:1 forms the substance of a riddle asked by Jesus, and the use of this verse by Jesus cannot in any straightforward sense be classified as "messianic."

Mark 12:35–37 reads:

[35]And as Jesus taught in the temple, he said, "How can the scribes say that the Christ is the son of David? [36]David himself, in the Holy Spirit, declared,

> 'The Lord said to my Lord,
> "Sit at my right hand,
>   until I put your enemies under your feet."'

[37]David himself calls him Lord. So how is he his son?" And the great throng heard him gladly.

In Mark 12, the conundrum propounded by Jesus implies, by way of rhetorical question, that the exalted figure designated "my Lord," with whom Jesus appears to identify himself, is *not* "the son of David," for it is a cultural given that fathers do not view their sons (descendants) as their superiors.[30] The riddle stumps his debating partners, and it has puzzled Christian interpreters ever since, who commonly resort to the explanation that Jesus is hinting that he is something more than the biological descendent of David, thereby stretching the category of "Messiah" to encompass his divine person as the Son of God,[31] but this is not the way to solve the dominical riddle. The matter is picked up in 14:61–62, where Jesus conflates Ps. 110:1 and Dan. 7:13,[32] and this supports the idea that the "Lord" of Ps. 110:1, like the "one like a son of man" in Dan. 7, is a passive human figure who receives a position of great honor and authority.

29. For David as a prophet, see Margaret Daly-Denton, "David the Psalmist, Inspired Prophet: Jewish Antecedents of a New Testament *Datum*," *ABR* 52 (2004): 32–47.

30. George Aichele, *The Control of Biblical Meaning: Canon as Semiotic Mechanism* (Harrisburg, PA: Trinity Press International, 2001), 178, 182–85.

31. E.g., Craig A. Evans, "Praise and Prophecy in the Psalter and the New Testament," in *The Book of Psalms: Composition and Reception*, ed. Peter W. Flint and Patrick D. Miller Jr., VTSup 99 (Leiden: Brill, 2005), 564.

32. For the association of Ps. 110 and Dan. 7 in Jewish tradition, see William G. Braude, *The Midrash on Psalms* (New Haven: Yale University Press, 1958), 40–41.

Mark 14:61–62 reads:

> [61]But he remained silent and made no answer. Again the high priest asked him, "Are you the Christ, the Son of the Blessed?" [62]And Jesus said, "I am, and you will see the Son of Man seated at the right hand of Power, and coming with the clouds of heaven."

Note the actual wording of 14:62: "You will see *the Son of Man* seated at the right hand of Power."[33] The figure of "one like a son of man" in Dan. 7 is not messianic, given the absence of any overt Davidic linkage in that chapter and the lack of interest in the figure of David in the book of Daniel generally.[34] Read in the context of the preceding psalms, the picture of the exaltation of an apocalyptic human figure in Ps. 110 gives encouragement to God's needy people that YHWH will likewise act on their behalf and exalt them from their lowly position. Again, the comparison with Dan. 7 is illuminating, for in verse 27 the people (= the saints) are given "the kingdom and the dominion" that the one like a son of man was given in verse 14. Though the exact connection is not explained, it is perhaps safest to say that the saints *share* the rule of the one like a son of man, and the aim of the vision of Dan. 7 seems to be to encourage the suffering people of God. In summary, we understand Ps. 110:1 (and the New Testament interpretation of this verse) to point to an apocalyptic figure with whom Jesus identified himself.

Bruce Waltke argues that the Christian reader must not limit the number of messianic psalms to the approximately fifteen psalms cited in the New Testament with respect to the Lord Jesus.[35] According to Waltke, the whole Psalter has Jesus Christ in view, for the human subject of most of the psalms is the king. Waltke accepts the work of J. H. Eaton, who followed up the work of Hermann Gunkel and Sigmund Mowinckel, such that all psalms relate to the king, who in the cult represents his people.[36] Since the final editing of the Psalter was in the postexilic context, with no Davidide sitting on the throne, Waltke views the Psalter in its final shape as prophetic and inveighs against any "democratization" of the Psalms. However, the placement of

33. Bruce K. Waltke states that "David's lord is Daniel's Son of Man" but provides no argument; see "Psalm 110: An Exegetical and Canonical Approach," in *Resurrection and Eschatology: Theology in Service of the Church; Essays in Honor of Richard B. Gaffin Jr.*, ed. Lane G. Tipton and Jeffrey C. Waddington (Phillipsburg: P&R, 2008), 85.

34. See chap. 14 in the present volume.

35. Bruce K. Waltke, "A Canonical Process Approach to the Psalms," in *Tradition and Testament: Essays in Honor of Charles Lee Feinberg*, ed. J. S. Feinberg and P. D. Feinberg (Chicago: Moody, 1981), 3–18.

36. J. H. Eaton, *Kingship and the Psalms*, SBT 2/32 (London: SPCK, 1976).

Ps. 1 as an introduction, the repeated pairing of royal and wisdom psalms (1/2; 72/73; 89/90; 110/111; 118/119), and the addition of books 4–5 require such a democratizing interpretation, and we suggest that Waltke's construal is only based on books 1–3. The Psalter reflects the experience of exile and dispersion after the failure of the Davidic house, leading to a recasting of the role of future "David." Jesus as God in the flesh, in his humanity, fulfills the model presented by David of the one who depends on God's help,[37] but he is also the Divine King celebrated throughout the Psalter.[38]

Not content to have the teaching about Christ in the Psalter limited to the traditional "messianic psalms," Richard Belcher Jr. also argues that *all* the Psalms are related in some way to Jesus Christ, anticipating and throwing light upon his person and work.[39] Belcher seeks to supply reasons for his "Christological approach" to the Psalms, which builds upon the earlier work of Waltke. He tries to interpret all the psalms as the prayers of Jesus—that is, he gives theological priority to Jesus as the active praying subject of all the psalms. Belcher goes so far as to say the Psalms are only *secondarily* our prayers. This approach, however, turns things on their head, for Belcher cannot say that the Psalms are *first of all* Jesus's prayers and then say that Jesus prays community laments "as a member of the covenant community." This implies that the psalms are our prayers and that Jesus prays them because he identifies with us in our distresses (famine, defeat in war, etc.). So too, when Belcher comes to Ps. 51, the great penitential prayer, he says that Christ prays this as our representative and priest. Christ is confessor of our sins (he has none of his own) and does so on our behalf. Again, it makes no sense to say that a prayer of confession like Ps. 51 is only *secondarily* ours. It is plain that something is not quite right with Belcher's methodology.

It is proper for the Christian to find Jesus in the Psalter. Indeed, his presence is more pervasive in the Psalter than often realized, for everything said of God in the book of Psalms directly applies to Jesus as God the Son. Our study has sought to show that Jesus is to be identified with the Divine King who helps his people in their distress, the apocalyptic human figure exalted by God in Ps. 110:1, and the promised "David" who models humble dependence on God.

---

37. See W. Dennis Tucker Jr., *Constructing and Deconstructing Power in Psalms 107–150*, AIL 19 (Atlanta: Society of Biblical Literature, 2014), 174–85.

38. E.g., the use made of Ps. 102:25–27 by the author of Hebrews (1:10–12).

39. Richard Belcher Jr., *The Messiah and the Psalms: Preaching Christ from all the Psalms* (Fearn, Scotland: Mentor, 2006).

14

Where Is David in the Book of Daniel?

Many believers have a kind of love-hate relationship with the book of Daniel. From Sunday school days they have delighted in the adventures of Daniel and his three friends in the first half of the book (Dan. 1–6); on the other hand, like scared children, many Christians do their best to avoid thinking about what they view as the weird and baffling symbols in the visions (Dan. 7–12). Indeed, the distinctive character of the two halves of the book (tales/visions) is probably what led to it being put in quite different positions in the Hebrew and Greek canons. In the latter (which became the Bible of the early church), due to the visionary character of chapters 7–12, Daniel is regarded as a prophet, and his book follows Ezekiel, as the last of the great prophets. In the Hebrew Bible, the book of Daniel comes after Esther and before Ezra-Nehemiah—that is, between other books that describe Jewish heroes in foreign courts. However, to properly understand the book of Daniel, we must consider both halves.

The futurist eschatology on display in the visions of Daniel, but not limited to the visions (e.g., the royal dream of Dan. 2), is a striking feature of the canonical book. In this chapter, the book of Daniel is surveyed with the aim of clarifying whether its eschatology is messianic or not, with "messianism"

An earlier version of material in this chapter was published as Gregory Goswell, "Where Is David in the Book of Daniel?," *ResQ* 56 (2014): 209–21. Used by permission.

defined as the expectation of the arrival of a future king in the line of David. To that end, we will look at the two references to an "anointed" that in Christian exegesis has often been viewed as a messianic figure (9:25, 26),[1] though it should be noted at the outset that the New Testament itself does not identify Jesus with either anointed figure as such.

Possible Davidic Connections in Daniel 1

The importance of the opening chapter is underlined if it is viewed as an introduction to the book, for this would make Dan. 1 the key to any evaluation of the book. It tells the story of the refusal by the four Jewish youths to eat the king's food. We argue that they take this stand due to the inordinate obligations inherent in partaking of the king's food.[2] In Dan. 1, the king's "rich food" (RSV; *pat-bag*) is mentioned repeatedly (1:5, 8, 13, 15, 16; cf. 11:26). The last reference provides a clue to the significance of the food ("Even those who eat his rich food shall be his undoing," RSV). Such rebellion against the king of the South in 11:26 is unexpected and wrong because the rebels eat from the king's table and this action is a symbol of political covenant and subservience (cf. 1 Sam. 20:26–34; 2 Sam. 9:9–13; 19:27–29).[3] To eat the king's food is tantamount to a pledge of loyalty. In line with this, it is the king-connection of the food that is stressed in Dan. 1—a connection mentioned twice: "a daily portion of the rich food *which the king ate*, and of the wine *which he drank*" (v. 5 RSV). By assigning such a diet, Nebuchadnezzar imposes binding political allegiance on his subjects.[4] However, "Daniel resolved that he would not defile himself with the king's rich food" (v. 8 RSV). Nothing in the narrative says or implies that they refuse to bind themselves irrevocably to Nebuchadnezzar because of their loyalty to the incumbent Davidic king, Jehoiakim; rather, it is their loyalty to God's kingship that causes them to act the way they do.

1. See Louis E. Knowles, "The Interpretation of the Seventy Weeks of Daniel in the Early Fathers," *WTJ* 7 (1944): 136–60; William Adler, "The Apocalyptic Survey of History Adapted by Christians: Daniel's Prophecy of 70 Weeks," in *The Jewish Apocalyptic Heritage in Early Christianity*, ed. James C. VanderKam and William Adler, Compendia Rerum Iudaicarum ad Novum Testamentum 3.4 (Minneapolis: Fortress, 1996), 201–38.

2. Cf. Daniel L. Smith-Christopher, "Hebrew Satyagraha: The Politics of Biblical Fasting in the Post-Exilic Period (Sixth to Second Century B.C.E.)," *Food and Foodways* 5 (1993): 285.

3. See Jan Jaynes Granowski, "Jehoiachin at the King's Table: A Reading of the Ending of the Second Book of Kings," in *Reading between Texts: Intertextuality and the Hebrew Bible*, ed. Danna Nolan Fewell (Philadelphia: Westminster John Knox, 1992), 183–84.

4. Cf. Danna Nolan Fewell, *Circle of Sovereignty: A Story of Stories in Daniel 1–6*, JSOTSup 20 (Sheffield: Sheffield Academic, 1988), 39–40; W. Sibley Towner, *Daniel*, IBC (Atlanta: John Knox, 1984), 24–26.

With regard to their line of descent, Daniel and his compatriots are first of all said to be "sons of Israel" (banê-yiśrā'ēl [i.e., Israelites]; Dan. 1:3), though this must be a theological use of the term (= members of the covenant people), for a little later the four youths are identified as "sons of Judah" (banê yəhûdâ [i.e., Judahites]; 1:6; cf. 2:25; 5:13; 6:13 [6:14 MT]). The designation "Israelites" is more closely qualified by what follows: "namely [waw], from the seed of kingship and from the nobles" (1:3, authors' trans.).[5] The first phrase is also found in 2 Kings 25:25 and identifies a member of the royal family; the second phrase refers to the nobility more generally (cf. Esther 1:3; 6:9); but it is uncertain to which group the four youths belonged. In Dan. 1, the only apparent narratival purpose in specifying their royal or noble lineage is that it provides them with the good breeding that made them suitable for service at court.[6]

The qualifications of the youths to be selected for training in Dan. 1:4 include the requirement that they be "handsome" (RSV; ṭôbê mar'eh). Though this can be viewed as a royal trait (e.g., David [1 Sam. 16:12]; cf. 1 Sam. 9:2; 10:23; 2 Sam. 14:25; 1 Kings 1:6; Ps. 45:2 [45:3 MT]), it does not need to be, for it can also be understood as a mark of divine favor more generally and have no connection to kingly rule (cf. the infant Moses in Exod. 2:2). On the other hand, being "handsome" is a prerequisite for court service (e.g., David in 1 Sam. 16:18; NIV: "fine looking" ['îš ṭō'ar]), and that is more likely the reason for the mention of this trait in Dan. 1, given the various parallels between the "court contest" stories of Dan. 1, 2, 4, and 5 and the story of Joseph, including Joseph's good looks (Gen. 39:6), his ability to interpret dreams, and his rise to the highest level in the service of a foreign king.

The most that can be said, therefore, is that Daniel and his friends may be of royal descent; however, the action and outcome of Dan. 1 do not depend on this tantalizing possibility, for the continuation of the Davidic house appears to be a nonissue in a chapter whose dominating interest is depicting the four heroes choosing loyalty to God (the King) over loyalty to Nebuchadnezzar.

The Eschatology of Daniel 2

In the prayer of Daniel in which he praises God for his revelation of the content and interpretation of the king's dream, the description of God as he who "removes kings and sets up kings" (2:21) is particularly significant,

---

5. Viewing the conjunction as an explicative waw.
6. Shane Kirkpatrick, Competing for Honor: A Social-Scientific Reading of Daniel 1–6, BIntS 74 (Leiden: Brill, 2005), 48–49.

though it is perhaps only on a second reading of the chapter that the reader perceives it to contain a hint of the content of the yet-to-be-narrated dream that depicts a succession of human kingdoms that will be judged and replaced by the eternal kingdom of God.

The "mountain" of the vision is a symbol for God's future universal rule centered on Zion (Dan. 2:34–35, 44–45), given the use of this image elsewhere in the Old Testament (e.g., Isa. 2:2–4: "the mountain of the house of the LORD").[7] Within the book of Daniel itself, references in 9:16 ("your city Jerusalem, your holy mountain," ESV alt.), 9:20 ("the holy mountain of my God," ESV alt.), and 11:45 ("the glorious holy mountain") confirm the postulated identification. In line with wider biblical usage, the "stone" that was cut from a mountain and, in turn, became a mountain represents the same thing (2:35, 45; cf. Isa. 28:16; Zech. 12:3; 4 Ezra 13:36). In the New Testament, the christological application of the "stone" imagery (e.g., Mark 12:10; Matt. 21:42, 43; Luke 20:17–18; 1 Pet. 2:4–8) draws on various Old Testament texts (Ps. 118:22; Isa. 8:14–15; 28:16).[8] A link to Dan. 2 need not be denied, for the second part of Luke 20:18 ("When it falls on anyone, it will crush him") appears to allude to the destructive stone of Dan. 2,[9] and the giving of the kingdom to "a people" in Matt. 21:43 is probably an allusion to Dan. 2:44 ("Nor shall the kingdom be left to another people").[10] The New Testament writers connect Zion theology with Jesus as the one through whom God's kingdom will come, but that does not need to be viewed as asserting that they saw the "stone" of Dan. 2 as simply a messianic cipher (stone = Messiah). As well, the statement that the stone that struck the image "was cut out by no human hand" would seem to allow no place for messianic agency in the destruction of the preceding kingdoms (2:34; cf. 2:45; 8:25).[11] In confirmation of this, it

---

7. Cf. C. L. Seow, "The Rule of God in the Book of Daniel," in *David and Zion: Biblical Studies in Honor of J. J. M. Roberts*, ed. Bernard F. Batto and Kathryn L. Roberts (Winona Lake, IN: Eisenbrauns, 2004), 225; see the extensive discussion provided by G. K. Beale, *The Temple and the Church's Mission: A Biblical Theology of the Dwelling Place of God*, NSBT 17 (Leicester, UK: Apollos, 2004), 145–53.

8. For Jewish use of the "stone" tradition, see John Hall Elliott, *The Elect and the Holy: An Exegetical Examination of 1 Peter 2:4–10 and the Phrase* Basileion Hierateuma, NovTSup 12 (Leiden: Brill, 1966), 26–28.

9. Elliott, *Elect and the Holy*, 29; Joseph A. Fitzmyer, *The Gospel according to Luke (X–XXIV): Introduction, Translation, and Notes*, AB 28A (Garden City, NY: Doubleday, 1985), 1286; Charles A. Kimball III, "Jesus' Exposition of Scripture in Luke 20:9–19: An Inquiry in Light of Jewish Hermeneutics," *BBR* 3 (1993): 77–92.

10. Klyne Snodgrass, *The Parable of the Wicked Tenants: An Inquiry into Parable Interpretation*, WUNT 27 (Tübingen: Mohr Siebeck, 1983), 67–70.

11. Cf. 4 Ezra 13:1–7 (ca. 100 CE), which develops the imagery of Dan. 2 in new directions and has the man who rises from the sea cut out a great mountain (*sculpsit montem magnum*); see Michael Stone, "The Concept of the Messiah in IV Ezra," in *Religions in Antiquity: Essays*

is explicitly stated that the enduring kingdom is set up by God himself (2:44: "The God of heaven will set up a kingdom that shall never be destroyed").

Daniel's theology of God as he who "removes kings and sets up kings" (2:21) is on show in the demotion and rehabilitation of Nebuchadnezzar (chap. 4) and the removal of Belshazzar (chap. 5). According to Robert D. Rowe, Nebuchadnezzar is measured against Davidic standards when he is warned by Daniel: "Break off your sins by practicing righteousness, and your iniquities by showing mercy to the oppressed" (4:27 [4:24 MT]; cf. Ps. 72:2, 4, 12);[12] however, this warning is better read against the background of the widespread expectation that ANE kings would uphold social justice.[13]

Is the Figure of One like a Son of Man Messianic?

The vision of Dan. 7 bears an obvious relation to the king's dream of chapter 2, but the four metals of the statue (= four kings/kingdoms) become four destructive beasts. Chapter 7 is divided into two parts: the vision (vv. 1–14) and the explanation of the vision (vv. 15–28). The vision of verses 1–14 is further subdivided into three sections based on the prefatory statement: "I saw in the night visions" (vv. 2, 7, 13). The first section describes the first three beasts arising out of the sea (vv. 2–6); the second section depicts the fourth beast and the judgment of the beasts (vv. 7–12; the fourth beast is slain, the other three are spared for a time); and the final section presents the son of man figure (vv. 13–14).[14]

It is important to note that "one like a son of man" (kəbar 'ĕnāš) is a description rather than title (Dan. 7:13). In such Aramaic (and Hebrew) expressions "son" can indicate having characteristics of what follows, so "a son of man" describes the figure as human in appearance in contrast to the preceding beasts, which at best parody human characteristics (e.g., in v. 4 it is said of the first

in Memory of Erwin Ramsdell Goodenough, ed. Jacob Neusner, Studies in the History of Religions (Supplements to Numen) 14 (Leiden: Brill, 1968), 303–10; G. K. Beale, The Use of Daniel in Jewish Apocalyptic Literature and in the Revelation of St. John (Lanham, MD: University Press of America, 1984), 130–35.

12. Robert D. Rowe, "Is Daniel's 'Son of Man' Messianic?," in Christ the Lord: Studies in Christology Presented to Donald Guthrie, ed. Harold H. Rowdon (Leicester, UK: Inter-Varsity, 1982), 83.

13. Moshe Weinfeld, Social Justice in Ancient Israel and in the Ancient Near East (Jerusalem: Magnes Press, 1995), 45–56. Cf. John J. Collins, The Scepter and the Star: Messianism in Light of the Dead Sea Scrolls, 2nd ed. (Grand Rapids: Eerdmans, 2010), 44: "The Gentile rulers [of Daniel 2–6] are not contrasted with a Davidic ideal."

14. For this division of the chapter, see Ziony Zevit, "The Structure and Individual Elements of Daniel 7," ZAW 80 (1968): 385–96.

beast, "[It] was . . . made to stand on two feet *like a man*, and the mind *of a man* was given to it"). The partial humanization of the beasts prepares for the figure in verse 13, who looks fully human. The authority abused by the bestial kingdoms and taken away from them by God (v. 12: "Their dominion was taken away") is given to this human figure as the proper seat of authority (v. 14a: "To him was given dominion"). The human figure is, therefore, their opposite and replacement. His humanity is not noted for the purpose of identifying him as the Messiah;[15] rather, the context suggests that "son of man" signals that he will exercise authority in a way that reflects the divine ordering of creation, wherein the animal kingdom is under human (Adamic) rule.[16] Note the earlier application of Adamic imagery to Nebuchadnezzar as world ruler in 2:38 (cf. Jer. 27:6; 28:14). The Davidic kings may have been understood to resemble Adam, but the inverse is not necessarily the case—namely, that every Adamic figure portends Davidic rule—for on that basis, we would have to view Nebuchadnezzar as a Davidic type, which is not at all a likely scenario. To say that the Adamic figure in Dan. 7:13–14 is messianic (in the absence of explicit Davidic motifs in Dan. 7) is to propound a species of panmessianism.

Some argue that the "one like the son of man" is a conquering figure and therefore messianic in nature. Although the fourth beast "was killed" (*qǝṭîlat*) and the passive verbal form implies that it was slain by God (Dan. 7:11), G. R. Beasley-Murray suggests that this was done by the one like the son of man, who then received the dominion as his reward. Beasley-Murray makes this deduction based on comparison with ANE myth (the cloud rider who slays the dragon).[17] The destruction of the fourth beast (v. 11) and the stripping of authority from the other three (v. 12) is a logical precondition for the giving of dominion to the one like a son of man (vv. 13–14). The ANE mythological root of the imagery does not need to be denied, but neither should it be pressed too far, for nothing in the Danielic text indicates that the son of man figure took an active part in the downfall of the beasts in section 2 of the vision (vv. 7–12), since any mention of him is confined to the description of his presentation before God in section 3 (vv. 13–14).

---

15. *Pace* Rowe, who seeks to forge a link with the role of the Davidic king as Primal Man (*Urmensch*) in the Jerusalem cult ("Is Daniel's 'Son of Man' Messianic?," 72–82); cf. Aage Bentzen, *King and Messiah*, ed. G. W. Anderson, 2nd ed. (Oxford: Basil Blackwell, 1970), 74–78; André Lacocque, *Daniel in His Time* (Columbia: University of South Carolina Press, 1988), 143–61.

16. André Lacocque, "Allusions to Creation in Daniel 7," in *The Book of Daniel: Composition and Reception*, ed. John J. Collins and Peter W. Flint, VTSup 83.1 (Leiden: Brill, 2001), 125–26 (esp. 126: "Kingship is here exercised by the human *qua* son of Adam, not *qua* son of David").

17. G. R. Beasley-Murray, "The Interpretation of Daniel 7," *CBQ* 45 (1983): 47–48. For the mythological background, see John J. Collins, *Daniel: A Commentary on the Book of Daniel*, Hermeneia (Minneapolis: Fortress, 1993), 286–94.

As well, the elaboration of the vision speaks in terms of a decisive *divine* intervention that brings the horn's war with the saints to an end (7:22: "until the Ancient of Days came, and judgment was given . . ."). In each case, the beast/horn is not slain in combat (à la Canaanite myth) but dealt with in a judicial assembly over which God presides as judge. The one like a son of man is, then, no messianic conqueror after the model of David (cf. the listing of David's victories in 2 Sam. 8).[18] Though John J. Collins thinks there are elements in the vision of Dan. 7 that lend themselves to a messianic interpretation,[19] he decides that "the one like a son of man" is a transcendent figure (whom he equates with Michael) rather than an earthly king in the line of David.[20]

The one like a son of man may be thought of as angel-like, given the comparable descriptions of the heavenly visitants in Dan. 8–12 (e.g., 8:15: "one having the appearance of a man [*geber*]"; cf. 9:21; 10:5–6, 16, 18; 12:6). Ziony Zevit wishes to equate the human figure of Dan. 7 with Gabriel (see 8:15; 9:21),[21] but many other scholars, like Collins, identify the figure with Michael.[22] Given repeated mention of the human appearance of the angelic figures, the Danielic context does suggest that the figure of 7:13 may be thought of as angel-like because the angelic beings are regularly described as having human form, but the text itself avoids explicitly identifying the figure as either Gabriel or Michael. As well, in the book of Daniel, angelic figures are divine agents sent either to deliver God's people[23] or to reveal God's plans to them.[24] On the other hand, the one like a son of man in Dan. 7 is not said to play either

---

18. Daniel 7 was later interpreted messianically in some streams of Jewish tradition, as 1 Enoch 48:10 and 52:4 show, where the term "anointed" is applied to the Son of Man (cf. 62:2: "The spirit of righteousness has been poured out upon him"), but that does not mean that this understanding should be read back into the text of Dan. 7. Translations of 1 Enoch are taken from James H. Charlesworth (ed.), *The Old Testament Pseudepigrapha*, vol. 1, AYBRL (New Haven: Yale University Press, 1983).

19. He is thinking of the giving of "dominion and glory and kingdom" and the Baal/El imagery rooted in ancient Canaanite mythology.

20. Collins, *Daniel*, 310.

21. Ziony Zevit, "The Exegetical Implications of Daniel VII 1, IX 21," *VT* 28 (1978): 488–92; cf. Jarl E. Fossum, *The Name of God and the Angel of the Lord: Samaritan and Jewish Concepts of Intermediation and the Origin of Gnosticism*, WUNT 36 (Tübingen: Mohr Siebeck, 1985), 279n61.

22. E.g., Benedikt Otzen, "Michael and Gabriel: Angelological Problems in the Book of Daniel," in *The Scriptures and the Scrolls: Studies in Honour of A. S. van der Woude on the Occasion of His 65th Birthday*, ed. F. Garcia Martinez, A. Hilhorst, and C. J. Labuschagne, VTSup 49 (Leiden: Brill, 1992), 114–24.

23. E.g., the angelic deliverer in the furnace (3:25) and in the lions' den (6:22 [6:23 MT]) and the militant figure of Michael (10:13, 21; 12:1). See Aleksander R. Michalak, *Angels as Warriors in Late Second Temple Jewish Literature*, WUNT 2/330 (Tübingen: Mohr Siebeck, 2012), 101–7.

24. Gabriel is primarily an *angelus interpres* (interpreting angel), yet note 10:13, 20, 21 (if these verses do refer to him). Cf. Michalak, *Angels as Warriors*, 124–25.

role (deliverer or revealer) and so is not to be classified as an angelic figure; rather, he is a passive human figure who receives authority from God.

The Prayer and Revelation of Daniel 9

In the prayer of Daniel that occupies the first half of chapter 9, he confesses the nation's failings and prays for the restoration of the desolate sanctuary (vv. 3–19). He acknowledges, "We [the nation] have not listened to your servants the prophets, who spoke in your name to our kings, our princes, and our fathers, and to all the people of the land" (v. 6). The result is that shame belongs "to our kings, to our princes, and to our fathers" (v. 8) and calamity has come "against us and against our *rulers* who *ruled* us" (v. 12; root *šāpaṭ* [2x]), with the word "rulers" used to sum up the various official classes listed in verses 6 and 8. In these listings of officials, no particular focus is placed on the earlier (Davidic) kings, and this is confirmed by verse 16, which speaks in general terms of the failings of the contemporary and previous generations ("For our sins, and for the iniquities of our fathers [= ancestors], Jerusalem and your people have become a byword"; cf. Neh. 9:2). If the earlier Davidic kings are not singled out as chiefly to blame for the nation's predicament, it is unlikely (though not impossible) that the divine response to Daniel's prayer will take the form of a promise of a future Davidide (= Messiah) who will set things right.

The difficulty of interpreting Dan. 9:24–27 is universally acknowledged, and that is why we have delayed considering this passage until this point, believing as we do that a survey of the rest of the book is a necessary preliminary to any attempt to understand the revelation brought by Gabriel. The meaning and import of almost every word and phrase of these four verses is disputed by scholars. To contain the discussion within workable limits, we will keep to our brief—namely, that of determining whether a messianic theology is to be found in these verses. The sanctuary is clearly the focus of the angelic communication, especially when it is noted at what time Gabriel arrives to speak with Daniel (v. 21: "at the time of the evening sacrifice").[25] It is specifically stated that the prediction concerns "your people and your holy city" (v. 24), and the city is holy because it is the site of God's sanctuary. Daniel 9:24–27 reads:

[24]Seventy weeks are decreed about your people and your holy city, to finish the transgression, to put an end to sin, and to atone for iniquity, to bring in

25. Jacques Doukhan, *Le soupir de la terre: Étude prophétique du livre de Daniel* (Dammarie-les-Lys Cedex: Editions Vie et Santé, 1993), 199.

everlasting righteousness, to seal both vision and prophet, and to anoint a most holy place. [25]Know therefore and understand that from the going out of the word to restore and build Jerusalem to the coming of an anointed one, a prince, there shall be seven weeks. Then for sixty-two weeks it shall be built again with squares and moat, but in a troubled time. [26]And after the sixty-two weeks, an anointed one shall be cut off and shall have nothing. And the people of the prince who is to come shall destroy the city and the sanctuary. Its end shall come with a flood, and to the end there shall be war. Desolations are decreed. [27]And he shall make a strong covenant with many for one week, and for half of the week he shall put an end to sacrifice and offering. And on the wing of abominations shall come one who makes desolate, until the decreed end is poured out on the desolator.

As is commonly noted by commentators, the six actions of 9:24 provide a panoramic overview of the period described in verses 25–27. The two references to "an anointed one" (vv. 25, 26 [māšîaḥ]) pick up the earlier mention of the *anointing* (root māšaḥ) of "a most holy [people? place?]," which is the climactic highpoint of the series of actions in verse 24.[26] Either interpretation (people or place) is possible, given the mention of "your people and your holy city" in the same verse, but most likely, the reference is to "a most holy *place*" (qōdeš qodāšîm), the temple. On this understanding, the action in verse 24 reverses the predicted treading down of "the holy place" in 8:13 and 8:14 (both verses using qōdeš, which picks up the earlier mention of the "sanctuary" [miqdāš] in v. 11). It is foretold that the sanctuary will be reconsecrated after its defiling, so that the angelic communication is a restatement of the prophetic vision of chapter 8 (notably v. 14). Yet another destruction of the city and the "sanctuary" (qōdeš) is forecast in 9:26 ("desolations [šōmēmôt] are decreed"), together with the cessation of sacrifice and offering through the action of a "desolator" (v. 27; šōmēm). Chapter 9, therefore, shares with chapter 8 a focus on the disruption of the temple cult (cf. the "transgression that makes desolate [šōmēm]" in 8:13), though finally the interest in the temple is not as a physical structure[27] but as a symbol and expression of God's reign.

Given that the center of interest in Dan. 9:24–27 is the temple, if verses 25 and 26 are viewed as referring to an anointed *individual*, or, more probably, to two such individuals appearing after successive periods of seven weeks and sixty-two weeks ("to the coming of an anointed one, a prince, . . . an anointed one shall be cut off"), this still leaves royal and sacerdotal options—namely,

26. Tim Meadowcroft, "Exploring the Dismal Swamp: The Identity of the Anointed One in Daniel 9:24–27," *JBL* 120 (2001): 429, 436.

27. As rightly stressed by Ron Haydon, *"Seventy Sevens Are Decreed": A Canonical Approach to Daniel 9:24–27*, JTISup 15 (Winona Lake, IN: Eisenbrauns, 2016), 87–93.

whether the "anointed one" is a king or priest. The choice of one or two figures depends on the acceptance or otherwise of the masoretic punctuation of verse 25, which places a break between "seven weeks" and "sixty-two weeks."[28] The break does not need to be viewed as a reaction against a messianic interpretation promoted by Christians or the Bar Kokhba movement.[29] In the earliest known commentary on Daniel, Hippolytus of Rome (died 235 CE) divided the seventy weeks into three stages (7 + 62 + 1).[30]

In Dan. 9:25, there is ambiguity in the designations "anointed one" (māšîaḥ) and "prince" (nāgîd),[31] for incumbents in both royal and priestly offices can be referred to under these terms.[32] As well, both offices (each in its own way) are connected to the proper functioning of the temple (cf. the roles of kings and priests in the history of the temple as an institution recounted by the Chronicler).[33] The prevailing historicist reading (e.g., J. A. Montgomery, John J. Collins) identifies the "anointed one" in verse 25 and in verse 26 with priestly figures known from history, two postexilic high priests: Joshua son of Jehozadak and Onias III, whose murder is recorded in 2 Macc. 4:33–38 (ca. 171 BCE). The weakness of this approach is that it takes the Danielic sabbatical-heptadic periodization of history literally, turning these highly allusive verses into a mundane timetable of historical events (seventy weeks/sevens = 490 years).[34] Due to the prominence of the priesthood and absence of kings during this late period of Israelite history,[35] it is almost inevitable that those who approach the material in this way identify the anointed figures as priests.

28. For a defense of the MT, see Thomas E. McComiskey, "The Seventy 'Weeks' of Daniel against the Background of Ancient Near Eastern Literature," *WTJ* 47 (1985): 18–45.

29. *Pace* Roger T. Beckwith, *Calendar and Chronology, Jewish and Christian: Biblical, Intertestamental and Patristic Studies*, AGJU 33 (Leiden: Brill, 1996), chap. 8.

30. Katharina Bracht, "*Logos parainetikos*: Der Danielkommentar des Hippolyt," in *Die Geschichte der Daniel-Auslegung in Judentum, Christentum und Islam: Studie zur Kommentierung des Danielbuches in Literatur und Kunst*, ed. Katharina Bracht and David S. du Toit, BZAW 371 (Berlin: de Gruyter, 2007), 87–88.

31. Joyce G. Baldwin, *Daniel: An Introduction and Commentary*, TOTC (Leicester, UK: Inter-Varsity, 1978), 170.

32. E.g., Lev. 4:3, 5, 16; 6:22 (6:15 MT); Num. 35:25; 1 Sam. 9:16; 2 Sam. 2:4, 10; 1 Chron. 9:11; Neh. 11:11; Jer. 20:1; Dan. 11:22.

33. See William M. Schniedewind, "King and Priest in the Book of Chronicles and the Duality of Qumran Messianism," *JJS* 45 (1994): 71–78. According to Schniedewind, Chronicles "evaluates the history of Israel in terms of bicephalic leadership administered by the temple and the palace. . . . In its idealized vision, an anointed king (the Davidides) and an anointed priest (the Aaronites) provided dual leadership" (72); cf. 1 Chron. 29:22: "They *anointed* him [Solomon] as prince for the Lord, and Zadok as priest."

34. This is a criticism made by Meadowcroft ("Exploring the Dismal Swamp," 433, 447) and Haydon ("*Seventy Sevens Are Decreed*," 67–85).

35. See Deborah W. Rooke, *Zadok's Heirs: The Role and Development of the High Priesthood in Ancient Israel*, Oxford Theological Monographs (Oxford: Oxford University Press,

It is only at this point in the book of Daniel that there is the possibility of reference to a messianic figure. Even so, it is not said what *function* the anointed figures perform (assuming there are two). What is said about them merely reflects the time and situation in which they are present. In Dan. 9:25, the appearance of the first "anointed one" (king or priest) coincides with the rebuilding of the city (and sanctuary, presumably), though the anointed figure is not said to be its builder or to offer sacrifice. The second "anointed one" is cut off (*yikkārēt*) at the time of the destruction of the city and sanctuary (v. 26), and nothing more is said about him, unless he is to be equated with "the prince" whose "people" (= army [a recognized meaning of *'am*]) destroy the city and the sanctuary, but the identification of the two is unlikely. Neither reference, therefore, gives any information that would assist in determining whether the predicted figures are kings or priests.

Postlude: Canonical Reflections

It seems that John Collins is right in stating that "there is no clear reference in Daniel to the restoration of the Davidic line."[36] The introductory chapter of Daniel shows the clash of a pagan king and the Divine King, who each require the total loyalty of their Jewish subjects. Loyalty to the house of David, however, is not said to play a part in Daniel's resolution to resist the claims of Nebuchadnezzar. In Dan. 2, Daniel interprets one of Nebuchadnezzar's dreams. This dream tells of a series of future kingdoms but does not mention a Davidic kingdom. Nor is the dream against a Davidic ideal that the kings of chapters 4–5 are measured and found wanting. The human (nonangelic) figure granted supreme authority in Dan. 7 is also non-messianic, given the absence of any demonstrable David connection. Finally, it does not seem possible to determine with any certainty whether the anointed figures alluded to in 9:25 and 9:26 are royal or priestly. These negative conclusions do not, however, call into question the validity of the later ecclesial use of Dan. 7, with Jesus recorded as identifying himself with *both* the divine Judge who gives universal authority and the human figure who receives it.

Though Dan. 7 is non-messianic, it feeds into the high Christology of the New Testament. For example, the vision of "one like a son of man" in Rev. 1:13–16 (identified as the risen Jesus, given v. 18) shows the combined influence of Dan. 7:9 and 7:13 and the description of the angelic figures in Dan. 8–10.

2000). Despite the cultic importance of the high priest, Rooke's conclusion is that the office itself did not bestow civil authority on the one who occupied it.

36. Collins, *Scepter and the Star*, 45.

The vision amalgamates the separate descriptions of the one like a son of man, the one that was ancient of days, and the angelic figures.[37] Most notable is the use of elements of the portrait of the one that was ancient of days in John's vision (e.g., his hair like white wool [Rev. 1:14; cf. Dan. 7:9]). A similar merging of the son of man figure and the enthroned figure of Dan. 7:9 is the explanation behind Matt. 25:31 (cf. 19:28), where it is said that "[the son of man] will sit on his glorious throne" as world judge. The origin of the *judging* function of the Son of Man in Matt. 25 lies in the merging of the human figure of Dan. 7:13 and the divine Judge of 7:9, for the one like a son of man in Dan. 7 is not said to be a judge. A precedent is found in the elaboration of the Danielic tradition in the Similitudes (Parables) of 1 Enoch (esp. 62:5: "the Son of Man sitting on the throne of his glory"; 69:29: "that the Son of Man has appeared and has seated himself on the throne of his glory").[38]

The enthronement of the son of man in 1 Enoch and Matthew is not derived from the use of "thrones" (plural) in Dan. 7:9. This need not refer to a judgment bench (cf. Ps. 122:5; Matt. 19:28; Rev. 20:4),[39] and in Dan. 7 it is best understood as a plural of amplification (= God's enormous throne).[40] Certainly, no one is said to be seated in Dan. 7 except for the one that was ancient of days. The myriads of 7:10 are all pictured as standing, and the one like a son of man is not invited to sit down.

The merging of the two figures of Dan. 7 is the best explanation of the enthronement of the son of man in both Matthew and 1 Enoch. This is preferable to positing the influence of Ps. 110:1 on 1 Enoch texts,[41] nor should an explanation of the dominical sayings in Matt. 19:28 and 25:31 seek recourse

37. E.g., Christopher Rowland, "The Vision of the Risen Christ in Rev. i. 13ff.: The Debt of an Early Christology to an Aspect of Jewish Angelology," *JTS* 31 (1980): 1–11; Thomas Hieke, "The Reception of Daniel 7 in the Revelation of John," in *Revelation and the Politics of Apocalyptic Interpretation*, ed. Richard B. Hays and Stefan Alkier (Waco: Baylor University Press, 2012), 56–57; Peter R. Carrell, *Jesus and the Angels: Angelology and the Christology of the Apocalypse of John*, SNTSMS 95 (Cambridge: Cambridge University Press, 1997), 148–74.

38. Leslie Walck argues that the Matthean redaction draws on Enoch (not on Dan. 7 directly); see "The Parables of Enoch and the Synoptic Gospels," in *Parables of Enoch: A Paradigm Shift*, ed. James H. Charlesworth and Darrell L. Bock, T&T Clark Jewish and Christian Texts Series 11 (London: Bloomsbury T&T Clark, 2013), 254–58.

39. *Pace* Barnabas Lindars, *Jesus Son of Man: A Fresh Examination of the Son of Man Sayings in the Gospels in the Light of Recent Research* (London: SPCK, 1983), 126.

40. See J. C. L. Gibson, *Davidson's Introductory Hebrew Grammar: Syntax*, 4th ed. (Edinburgh: T&T Clark, 1994), §21 Rem.3; *GKC* §123d–f; Doukhan, *Le soupir de la terre*, 163–64; Richard Bauckham, *Jesus and the God of Israel: God Crucified and Other Studies on the New Testament's Christology of Divine Identity* (Grand Rapids: Eerdmans, 2008), 161–62.

41. *Pace*, e.g., David M. Hay, *Glory at the Right Hand: Psalm 110 in Early Christianity*, SBLMS 18 (Nashville: Abingdon, 1973), 26–27; Donald Juel, *Messianic Exegesis: Christological Interpretation of the Old Testament in Early Christianity* (Philadelphia: Fortress, 1988), 137–38.

to Ps. 110, for these texts do not use the phrase "the right hand (of God)," which is a telltale sign of its influence. Furthermore, as noted by Richard Bauckham, it is not a second throne but the *one* divine throne on which the Son of Man takes his seat in 1 Enoch, so that this feature would seem to rule out the influence of Ps. 110:1.[42] As well, the key motif of judging in Matt. 25 and 1 Enoch (e.g., 61:8–9; 69:27) cannot be derived from Ps. 110, wherein the overthrow of enemies is by means of warfare (vv. 5–7), not by judicial procedure as in Dan. 7. Bauckham's own explanation is that the author of the Similitudes of Enoch noted that the terms in which sovereignty is described in Dan. 7:14 are the same as used of God's sovereignty (4:3, 34; 6:26 [3:33; 4:31; 6:27 MT]) and so portrayed the son of man as seated on God's throne.[43] This theory is correct as far as it goes, but it does not go far enough, for none of the earlier Danielic texts contain the motif of sitting on a throne. The crucial point is that the noted similarity of terms gave permission for later readers to *merge* the two figures in the throne scene of Dan. 7, and it is this merger that explains the enthronement of the one like a son of man and his role as world judge. We argue, therefore, Jesus's self-referential use of the expression "son of man" is a shorthand way of referring to the scene of 7:13–14 in toto wherein Jesus identifies himself with *both* figures: the enthroned divine Judge who gives authority and the human figure who receives it.

42. Bauckham, *Jesus and the God of Israel*, 162, 169–70; cf. Charles A. Gieschen, *Angelomorphic Christology: Antecedents and Early Evidence*, AGJU 42 (Leiden: Brill, 1998), 84–88.

43. Richard Bauckham, "The Throne of God and the Worship of Jesus," in *The Jewish Roots of Christological Monotheism: Papers from the St. Andrews Conference on the Historical Origins of the Worship of Jesus*, ed. Carey C. Newman, James R. Davila, and Gladys S. Lewis, JSJSup 63 (Leiden: Brill, 1999), 58.

15

Kingship and the Temple in 1–2 Chronicles

When I (Andrew) was an undergraduate taking a class on the Pentateuch and the historical books, we jumped from 2 Kings to Ezra. So, I asked the professor why we were skipping over Chronicles. He answered, "We've already covered its contents in Samuel and Kings, so we won't spend our time there." Although I did not have the courage to ask, I wondered why Chronicles is in the Bible if it simply presents stories from Samuel and Kings. It was not until later that I began to recognize the importance of Chronicles and to ponder why the book occurs at the conclusion of the Hebrew Bible. First and 2 Chronicles do more than regurgitate contents found elsewhere; the Chronicler draws upon known stories, reworks them, and incorporates stories of his own to craft a unique message for postexilic Israel. In fact, by comparing Chronicles with parallel passages in Samuel and Kings,[1] we can more readily grasp its theology.[2]

1. A useful resource for comparing Chronicles with parallels is John C. Endres, William R. Millar, and John Barclay Burns, eds., *Chronicles and Its Synoptic Parallels in Samuel, Kings, and Related Biblical Texts* (Collegeville, MN: Liturgical Press, 1998).

2. Rodney Duke cautions against an author expecting an audience to detect minute adjustments in language between the source texts and 1–2 Chronicles. It is more likely that the book should be read "in a loose, synoptic sense" in coordination with the other traditions. Rodney Duke, "A Rhetorical Approach to Appreciating the Books of Chronicles," in *The Chronicler as Author: Studies in Text and Texture*, ed. M. Patrick Graham and Steven L. McKenzie, JSOTSup 263 (Sheffield: Sheffield Academic, 1999), 109.

Although Chronicles holds out hope for an era when a Davidic king will reign in Jerusalem, the central intention of the book lies elsewhere. The Chronicler's primary objective is to help the postexilic community recognize that their identity can be meaningfully lived out by centering on God's royal presence in the temple under the leadership of the Levites and priests, even without a Davidic king on the throne. The emphasis, then, is on fortifying the identity of a kingless, postexilic community as the people of the Divine King, YHWH, under temple leadership.[3] Messianic expectations are secondary to this, so this chapter will begin by considering the primary objective of 1–2 Chronicles before offering a few modest claims about royal messianic hopes in the book.

A Kingless Community with YHWH as King

Chronicles divides into two major sections: genealogies (1 Chron. 1–9) and narratives (1 Chron. 10–2 Chron. 36). Both sections present story lines that culminate with postexilic Israel focusing on the temple. As we will see below, the respective frameworks of the genealogies and narratives help postexilic Israel clarify that they can faithfully live as God's people without a Davidic king.

Israel's Story according to the Genealogies

First Chronicles opens by tracing Israel's history through genealogies. These begin by swiftly moving from Adam through to Abraham and Jacob (chap. 1) before camping out for three chapters on Judah and David (2:1–4:23). If the Chronicler had finished the genealogies in chapter 4, the impression might be that the Davidic king is at the center of God's plans for Israel amid all nations.[4]

The second half of the genealogies clarifies that Israel's identity involves much more than Judah and David. First, all of Israel, not just Judah, is important to Israel's story. This is apparent when 1 Chron. 5:1–2 says that Judah did not receive Reuben's forfeited birthright; instead, it went to the sons of Joseph: Ephraim and Manasseh. Even though Judah was strong and had a chief, this was not due to birthright (5:2). By clarifying this point, the Chronicler displays

3. Jonathan E. Dyck captures this sentiment well: "The Chronicler adapted the history of the First Temple to this purpose by showing how the temple in Jerusalem was, from the beginning, the theocratic capital of all Israel. Identity and legitimacy are thereby secured in terms of the origins of [the] theocratic 'kingdom of Yahweh.'" Jonathan E. Dyck, *The Theocratic Ideology of the Chronicler*, BIntS 33 (Leiden: Brill, 1998), 227–28.

4. On the significance of other nations within 1 Chron. 1–9, see Gary N. Knoppers, "Shem, Ham and Japheth: The Universal and the Particular in the Genealogy of Nations," in *The Chronicler as Theologian: Essays in Honor of Ralph W. Klein*, ed. M. Patrick Graham, Steven L. McKenzie, and Gary N. Knoppers, JSOTSup 371 (London: T&T Clark, 2003), 13–31.

that a "Judah-David-centric" view of Israel's history misses the significance of the other tribes of Israel in God's plans, even if Judah's prowess results in it being the first tribe listed in the genealogy. For this reason, over the following chapters, there are genealogies for Simeon, Reuben, Gad, the two half tribes of Manasseh, Levi, Issachar, Benjamin (including Saul), Naphtali, Ephraim, and Asher (4:24–8:40). "All Israel" is equally a part of God's plan. Second, amid this emphasis on "all Israel," the Chronicler highlights the importance of the Levites. As the Chronicler lists the genealogies of the tribes, the Levites occur at the center of the list of the tribes.[5] What is more, the length of Levi's genealogy (eighty-one verses!) is gargantuan in comparison with the other tribes' genealogies (chap. 6). Thus, the genealogies teach that the significance of David and Judah must be seen in light of God's concern for all Israel and the important place of the priests and Levites within Israel. For a postexilic community that would aim to incorporate tribes from the Northern and Southern Kingdoms, this focus on all Israel is vital for community reconstruction.

In chapter 9, the emphases on "all Israel" and the Levites find expression as the postexilic era comes into view. "The first to dwell again in their possessions in their cities were Israel, the priests, the Levites, and the temple servants. And some of the people of Judah, Benjamin, Ephraim, and Manasseh lived in Jerusalem" (1 Chron. 9:2–3).[6] Three observations are important here. First, "all Israel" is apparent in the mention that "Israel" possessed their cities and that various tribes had representatives dwelling in Jerusalem, likely reflecting the account in Neh. 11 of Jerusalem's settlement with a tenth of the general population.[7] Second, the mention of "the priests, the Levites, and the temple servants" in 1 Chron. 9:2 develops across verses 10–34 through lists of priests, Levites, and temple workers. Third, although there is no mention of a Davidic king among the postexilic returnees, the capital city established by David and the temple that was built by his son remain important. The contributions of David's lineage to God's story with Israel endure in the postexilic era, even without a Davidic king.

Thus, the genealogies in chapters 1–9 tell an important story that begins with Adam (1:1), continues through Abraham, Jacob, Judah, David, and all

5. Sara Japhet, *I and II Chronicles*, OTL (Louisville: Westminster John Knox, 1993), 8; William Johnstone, *1 Chronicles 1–2 Chronicles 9: Israel's Place among the Nations*, vol. 1 of *1 and 2 Chronicles*, JSOTSup 253 (Sheffield: Sheffield Academic, 1997), 12, 36–40, 82.

6. The ESV's translation adds an "again" that is not in the Hebrew text. The Hebrew is ambiguous as to whether verses 2–3 recount those who originally dwelt in Jerusalem and the land during the time of David or whether this refers to the postexilic era. Due to the mention of exile in verse 1 and similarities with Neh. 11, Klein is correct that 9:2–34 is a postexilic list. See Ralph W. Klein, *1 Chronicles*, Hermeneia (Minneapolis: Fortress, 2006), 263–67.

7. For an extensive listing of connections between Neh. 11 and 1 Chron. 9, see Japhet, *I and II Chronicles*, 206–19.

of Israel, and extends into the postexilic era. This is a story where "all Israel" is, at its core, a people who orient around the temple in Jerusalem through the mediating service of the priests and Levites. Therefore, 1 Chron. 1–9 is an appropriate start to the book that concludes the Hebrew Bible.

Israel's Story in the Narratives

The narratives that make up the rest of Chronicles retell Israel's story from David's appointment after Saul's fall to Cyrus's decree for the exiles to return to rebuild the temple (1 Chron. 10–2 Chron. 36). By comparing the Chronicler's accounts with those in Samuel and Kings, two prominent emphases come to the fore: temple/priesthood and all of Israel.

TEMPLE AND PRIESTHOOD

Although the temple is important in Samuel and Kings, its significance reaches new heights in 1 Chron. 10–2 Chron. 36. This focus on the temple is apparent in several ways. First, the arc of these narratives begins with David and Solomon establishing the temple and concludes with a Persian king, Cyrus, commissioning exiles to return to Jerusalem to rebuild the temple. This arc differs from 1–2 Kings, in which no mention is made of Cyrus and his commission to rebuild the temple. As will become more apparent below, this framing arc reveals that the primary objective of the Davidic king continues during an era without a Davidic king; the postexilic community can continue to prioritize God's presence in the temple, even under the direction of a Persian king.[8]

Second, the David-Solomon narrative (1 Chron. 10–2 Chron. 9) primarily focuses on the king's role in establishing the temple.[9] The Chronicler does not recount the obstacles David (1 Sam. 16–2 Sam. 4) and Solomon (1 Kings 1–2) overcame en route to becoming king over all Israel. The Chronicler also has little interest in the major sins of David and Solomon—there is no mention of Bathsheba, Uriah, and the ensuing strife within David's kingdom (2 Sam. 11–20), nor do we read about Solomon's harem, idolatrous ways, and ensuing condemnation (1 Kings 11).[10] What is most important for the Chronicler is how David and Solomon prioritize the temple and priesthood. Whereas 2 Sam. 6 narrates the transfer of the ark to Jerusalem in twenty verses, the

8. Ehud Ben Zvi, "When the Foreign Monarch Speaks," in *The Chronicler as Author: Studies in Text and Texture*, ed. M. Patrick Graham and Steven L. McKenzie, JSOTSup 263 (Sheffield: Sheffield Academic, 1999), 222–23.

9. On the close connection between David and Solomon in Chronicles, see Roddy L. Braun, "Solomonic Apologetic in Chronicles," *JBL* 92 (1973): 503–16. See also Roddy L. Braun, *1 Chronicles*, WBC 14 (Dallas: Word, 1986), xxxii–xxxv.

10. For more on these omissions, see under the heading "The Ideal" below.

Chronicler's account stretches across seventy-two verses in 1 Chron. 15–16, with further details added about David's appointment of priests and Levites to specific tasks regarding the ark and leading the community in musical celebration. This focus on God's presence and on priestly leadership continues with respect to the temple. Although 2 Sam. 7 notes David's interest in building a temple for God, 1 Chron. 22–29 extensively recounts how David gathered resources for the temple, assigned duties to the priests and Levites for service at the temple, and issued instructions to Solomon about building the temple. Solomon carries out this important task of building and dedicating the temple (2 Chron. 2–7), and, "according to the ruling of David his father" (8:14), appoints priests and Levites to their assigned tasks in the temple. It is apparent, then, that the central feature of David and Solomon's kingship is the prioritization of the temple and establishment of temple leadership.

Third, the temple and priesthood remain priorities for Davidic kings in 2 Chron. 10–36. On numerous occasions, materials not found in Kings occur in 2 Chron. 10–36 to highlight a king's commitment to the temple and priesthood. For instance, the reigns of King Rehoboam (11:13–15) and King Abijah (13:8–12) become safe havens for faithful priests who fled Jeroboam's wicked ways in the North. Asa leads the community in covenant renewal and sacrifice (15:1–15), and Jehoshaphat puts priests and Levites into place as judges to handle disputes in light of Torah, with Amariah the chief priest in charge (19:8–11). These instances are in addition to the stories already noted in Kings about Joash, Hezekiah, and Josiah instituting temple reform. The Chronicler speaks further than 1–2 Kings of Hezekiah restoring the temple, celebrating Passover, and providing for the priests and Levites (chaps. 29–31) and of Josiah mobilizing the Levites to lead a Passover celebration (35:1–19).[11] There is little doubt, then, that the Chronicler wants to double down on Davidic kings as upholders of the temple and priesthood.

Fourth, as the narratives unfold, religious and political crises become occasions for highlighting the importance of the priesthood in upholding David's priorities. For instance, when Athaliah seizes the throne, the chief priest, Jehoiada, ensures both Davidic lineage and David's priorities by preserving Joash (a.k.a. Jehoash). Several details that only occur in Chronicles give us clearer perspective on Jehoiada's actions. When Jehoiada gives the Levitical priests authority over the temple, the Chronicler clarifies that these Levitical priests were those "whom David had organized to be in charge of the house

11. On Hezekiah as a second David and Solomon in Chronicles, see Mark A. Throntveit, "The Relationship of Hezekiah to David and Solomon in the Books of Chronicles," in *The Chronicler as Theologian: Essays in Honor of Ralph W. Klein*, ed. M. Patrick Graham, Steven L. McKenzie, and Gary N. Knoppers, JSOTSup 371 (London: T&T Clark, 2003), 105–21.

of the LORD" and that Jehoiada's actions were "according to the order of David" (2 Chron. 23:18).[12] The priesthood could carry on David's priorities when kingship was in crisis. Later, King Joash apostatizes after Jehoiada's death (24:17), and he ignores the exhortations of Jehoiada's son, Zechariah, and kills him (vv. 20–22).[13] The priests also step in when Uzziah's pride leads him to transgress the boundaries of a priest, as he offers incense in the temple (26:16). The priest Azariah assembles eighty priests to confront Uzziah and usher the leprous king out of the temple (vv. 17–20). Thus, by further clarifying how Jehoiada's actions align with David's priorities and by adding stories where priests attempt to redirect kings, the Chronicler is placing a spotlight on a motif that is not as prominent in Kings. Although the best Davidic kings appoint and collaborate with the Levitical priests to promote temple purity (David, Solomon, Hezekiah, Josiah), priests strove to uphold this ideal at times when Davidic kingship was in a precarious state.

In summary, the narratives of David-Solomon (1 Chron. 10–2 Chron. 9) and the rest of the kings (2 Chron. 10–36) tell a story that kicks off with King David prioritizing the temple and its leadership. Two excerpts from David's prayers—both of which do not appear in 1–2 Samuel—capture the heart behind his program: "The LORD reigns" (1 Chron. 16:31) and "Yours is the kingdom, O LORD, and you are exalted as head above all" (29:11). Since YHWH is truly the king of heaven and earth, the primary role of the human king is to lead Israel and the nations in aligning with God as King. As Magne Sæbø puts it, "The kingship and kingdom of Yahweh—his theocracy—has included and is superior to the Davidic kingship and kingdom; in the end there is only one kingdom, that of Yahweh—and the Davidic king is its representative."[14] David's son, Solomon, and many subsequent kings continue David's prioritization of God's kingship in the temple and priestly leadership. As the narrative progresses, however, Davidic kings stray at times, and the task of continuing David's initiatives falls into the hands of the Levitical priests. The entire book closes with a pagan king taking over David's initiative of temple building and therefore commanding God's people to return. By doing so, this pagan king enables the postexilic community to recognize their place in Israel's narrative by carrying forth David's initiatives regarding the temple and its leadership into a new era in the land without a king.

12. Raymond Dillard, *2 Chronicles*, WBC 15 (Grand Rapids: Zondervan Academic, 2015), 184, notes, "Concern with Davidic praxis is a fitting accompaniment to the reinstitution of Davidic rule." The priest is taking initiative in reinstalling a Davidic king (Joash) and in reestablishing David's temple program.

13. On the contrast in aligning with the temple between the two parts of Joash's reign, see Japhet, *I and II Chronicles*, 848–50.

14. Magne Sæbø, "Messianism in Chronicles? Some Remarks to the Old Testament Background of the New Testament Christology," *HBT* 2 (1980): 101 (italics removed).

ALL ISRAEL

Although our discussion of temple and priesthood above captures the overarching emphasis of the book, the concept of "all Israel" is also important throughout the narratives to a far greater extent than in Samuel–Kings.[15] In the David-Solomon narrative, "all Israel" conquers Jerusalem with David (1 Chron. 11:4) and brings the ark to Jerusalem (11:5–6, 8; 15:3, 25). During Solomon's reign, he addresses "all Israel" (2 Chron. 1:2), and they join in bringing the ark into the temple (5:2–6 // 1 Kings 8:1–5). This focus continues throughout the rest of the narratives. Even after the North and the South divide, faithful priests and "those who had set their hearts to seek the LORD God of Israel came after them from all the tribes of Israel" (2 Chron. 11:14–16) to Jerusalem to worship. When King Asa repents after the prophecy of Azariah son of Oded, sojourners from Ephraim, Manasseh, and Simeon (15:9) join Judah and Benjamin in gathering in Jerusalem. Jehoshaphat's reforms involve those from Ephraim (19:4). Moreover, many from Israel participated in the Passover celebrations under Hezekiah (30:1–31:1, 21) and Josiah (35:2–18). Significantly, then, the Chronicler wants to make it clear that Jerusalem and the temple are of interest not only to David and the priests; all Israel also partook in Jerusalem's establishment, and the faithful from all Israel continually viewed it as their religious capital. The importance of this for the postexilic era cannot be overstated. Since exiles from tribes other than Judah returned, it was essential to recover the truth that all the tribes of Israel, not simply Judah, could continue orienting their lives around the temple in Jerusalem.

Thus, both the genealogies (1 Chron. 1–9) and the narratives (1 Chron. 10–2 Chron. 36) present a view of Israel's history that helps postexilic Israel cope with a kingless existence. Although they do not have a Davidic king, postexilic Israel lives out of a history where all Israel under the leadership of priests and Levites prioritizes the temple, the presence of the Divine King. In this way, a kingless community carries on the priorities of David.

Royal Messianic Hope in Chronicles?

Many scholars hold the view that Chronicles offers no hope for future kingship from the line of David.[16] Instead, the task and mission of David is de-

---

15. For an overview of "all Israel" across the book, see Braun, *1 Chronicles*, xxxv–xxxvii; H. G. M. Williamson, *1 and 2 Chronicles*, NCB (Grand Rapids: Eerdmans, 1982), 24–26.

16. For surveys of positions, see H. G. M. Williamson, "Eschatology in Chronicles," *TynBul* 28 (1977): 115–54; Braun, "Solomonic Apologetic in Chronicles," 503–7.

mocratized to the community of Israel under the leadership of the priests. If this is correct, the office of the Davidic king played an important role in God's plans for a season within Israel's history, but postexilic Israel should not expect the office to continue; instead, the ideals would continue within the community as a whole.

Although we express the *primary* focus of 1–2 Chronicles in a similar way—namely, postexilic Israel can meaningfully live their identity around the temple without a Davidic king—other aspects in Chronicles point forward to hopes that would include a Davidic king.

Hope in General

Although life in postexilic Israel could still be meaningful for Israel, this does not mean life was optimal.[17] On the one hand, the Chronicler addresses the following questions that Peter Ackroyd identifies as arising in this historical moment: "What must the community be if it is to be true to its ancestral faith and tradition when it finds itself quite evidently on a more permanent basis under the aegis of an imperial power? How can a subject people be the people of God?"[18] The people need a word so that they can carry out their historical calling, even if everything is not ideal. On the other hand, the community would likely be asking other questions too: "Will life under imperial power ever end? Will this temple that does not compare to the glory of Solomon's become even greater? How can our postexilic community, with so few returnees, be close to God's ideal? Will there ever be a Davidic king again?" The Chronicler also addresses these questions, as we will see.

Along with helping postexilic Israel to grasp their calling during a less-than-ideal time, the book offers a pathway toward fulfilling their hopes for more: seeking the LORD in humility.[19] One of the most well-known passages from Chronicles is 2 Chron. 7:14. It is a window into a major motif in the book. After Solomon dedicates the temple, the LORD states: "If my people who are called by my name humble [*kānaʿ*] themselves, and pray [*pālal*] and seek [*bāqaš*] my face and turn from their wicked ways, then I will hear from heaven and will forgive their sin and heal their land." The fulcrum between barrenness and blessing for Israel is God's willingness to respond to a people who seek him in humility. Since this verse does not occur in 1 Kings, its inclusion

17. For a helpful historical sketch of the time, see Peter Ackroyd, "The Age of the Chronicler," in *The Chronicler in His Age*, JSOTSup 101 (Sheffield: Sheffield Academic, 1991), 1–86.

18. Ackroyd, "Age of the Chronicler," 13.

19. See Williamson, "Eschatology in Chronicles," esp. 149–54, who also appeals to this motif as a basis for hope beyond the present of postexilic Yehud.

in Chronicles suggests its importance for the postexilic community; humility before the LORD will usher in an era of blessing.

A brief survey of the use of key terms from 2 Chron. 7:14 in the rest of the book displays the importance of seeking the LORD across the book.[20] When Rehoboam and the people "humble [kānaʿ]" themselves (12:6–7), God preserves Judah from an attack by Shishak of Egypt. When Israel threatens Judah during the time of Abijah, Judah relies on the LORD and experiences victory (13:18; cf. vv. 4–12).[21] During the time of King Asa, the entire community "sought [dāraš] the LORD" (14:7 [14:6 MT]), and the king models this by "calling" (ESV: "cried"; v. 11 [v. 10 MT]) on the LORD, with God responding by bringing victory and blessing to Judah (vv. 10–13). This leads to a season of rest during the time of Asa, as the community continued seeking (bāqaš) the LORD (15:15) by putting away other gods. During a time of threat from Moab and Ammon, King Jehoshaphat and Judah "assembled to seek" (bāqaš) the LORD (20:4), resulting again in deliverance. When Hezekiah invites the northern tribes to join in the Passover, some from Asher, Manasseh, and Zebulun humble themselves (kānaʿ) and come (30:11). Hezekiah later humbles himself (kānaʿ), along with the community, and this wards off the wrath of God (32:26). In one of the most surprising additions to Chronicles, Manasseh becomes an exemplar of humility, as he humbles himself (kānaʿ) amid exile in Babylon and prays (pālal) to God (33:12).[22] The LORD frees him from captivity, enabling Manasseh's return to Jerusalem. Due to Josiah's humility in response to the law of the LORD, God promises to delay the ruin awaiting Jerusalem until after his death (34:27–28).[23]

Several insights emerge from the survey above. In every case except for Manasseh, the entire community—not only the king—seeks the LORD in humility. This is a communal affair. Also, in nearly every case, seeking the LORD results in God delivering and blessing his people. What is more, every occasion mentioned above only occurs in the book of Chronicles and not in Kings. Why, then, does the Chronicler emphasize these patterns so much? The Chronicler wants the entire postexilic community to trust that if they

20. Williamson, 1 and 2 Chronicles, 225–26.

21. Although no terms from 2 Chron. 7:14 are present in 13:18, the concepts expressed through "cry out" (ṣ'q) and "reliance" (š'n) in 13:14 and 13:18 resonate with Solomon's prayer.

22. On the Chronicler's depiction of Manasseh as an exemplar for the postexilic community, see Philippe Abadie, "From the Impious Manasseh (2 Kings 21) to the Convert Manasseh (2 Chronicles 33): Theological Rewriting by the Chronicler," in The Chronicler as Theologian: Essays in Honor of Ralph W. Klein, ed. M. Patrick Graham, Steven L. McKenzie, and Gary N. Knoppers, JSOTSup 371 (London: T&T Clark, 2003), 89–104.

23. Negatively, Rehoboam (2 Chron. 12:14), Asa (16:12), Amon (33:23), and Zedekiah (36:12) are critiqued for not seeking the LORD in humility.

humbly seek God in his temple, a new era of blessing will come about when God responds to them. Although the blessings that the postexilic community hopes for will be numerous—deliverance from pestering nations, national sovereignty, flourishing agriculture, and so on—the question before us now is whether the Chronicler envisages a Davidic king among the future blessings awaiting a postexilic Israel that humbly seeks the LORD.

Davidic Hope

If 1–2 Chronicles invites postexilic Yehud to hope for more, while also affirming their identity and calling in a less-than-ideal situation, two lines of evidence support an enduring hope for Davidic kingship.[24]

THE IDEAL

First, the Chronicler's portrayal of Israel's best kings establishes an ideal of a partnership between Davidic kings and the temple priesthood. By sensing this ideal in reading Chronicles, a postexilic community with only temple leadership would yearn for a Davidic king to enter the equation. Chronicles presents David and Solomon far more positively than 2 Samuel and 1 Kings. Although David's sin in taking the census is mentioned (1 Chron. 21)—likely because this leads to the purchase of the temple mount—there is not a word about Bathsheba, Uriah, and the ensuing discord. As for Solomon, he is impeccable, with no mention of his idolatry that results in the division of the kingdom.[25] These positive portrayals of David and Solomon lead Raymond Dillard to state, "[The Chronicler] presents us not only the David and Solomon of history, but also the David and Solomon of his messianic expectation."[26] Their positive religious and moral behavior, however, does not exhaust the Chronicler's attempt to depict his ideal for a Davidic king. It is significant that David and Solomon were kings during a time when Israel was a unity;[27] united Israel is at its best with a Davidic king. Since the Chronicler wants to recover a sense of "unity" within Israel, the important place of the Davidic

---

24. See Braun, "Solomonic Apologetic in Chronicles," 503–7, and Williamson, "Eschatology in Chronicles," for an overview of positions that reject any messianic hopes in 1–2 Chronicles.

25. Braun, "Solomonic Apologetic in Chronicles," 506–7 (cf. 512), overstates Solomon's depiction: "The Chronicler presents Solomon even more consistently as one who, from first to last, was completely faithful to Yahweh." Twice the Chronicler mentions that Solomon imported horses from Egypt (2 Chron. 1:16; 9:28), an obvious violation of Deut. 17:16. See Andrew Hill, *1 & 2 Chronicles*, NIVAC (Grand Rapids: Zondervan, 2003), 382.

26. Dillard, *2 Chronicles*, 2.

27. On the support of "all Israel" being the ideal set within David-Solomon, see Braun, "Solomonic Apologetic in Chronicles," 508–15.

king in the time of the united monarchy likely yields hope for this happening
once again. Most importantly, since David and Solomon are representatives
of the Divine King,[28] their rule finds its central expression in their appointing priests and Levites to leadership and prioritizing the construction and
maintenance of the temple.

David and Solomon's establishment of these institutions does not bring
this ideal to completion. Instead, the David-Solomon ideal persists through
the office of subsequent kings. When temple leadership leads the way, without the partnership of the king, the benefits are limited and local. For instance, when the priest Jehoiada takes charge to oversee temple leadership and to direct king Joash, this leads to reform only in Judah (2 Chron.
23:16–21; 24:1–14). What is more, after Jehoiada dies, Joash goes astray
to the great detriment of Judah (24:17–25). When we compare this with
occasions where kings take the lead, the results are much different. The
account of Hezekiah begins with him assembling the priests and Levites,
consecrating the temple, and celebrating the Passover. Through the king's
leadership, some from the North join with the South to celebrate Passover,
and idols are destroyed across Judah, Benjamin, Ephraim, and Manasseh
(31:1). Similarly, Josiah takes the initiative in purging idols throughout the
South and North (34:6–7, 33) and responds to the priests' recovery of the
Torah by instituting nationwide reform. He even leads a Passover celebration
with priests, Levites, Judah, and those from Israel who came to Jerusalem
(35:1–19). Although temple leadership can have a positive impact in promoting reform, as one sees with Jehoiada, all Israel can be united in temple
worship when a Davidic king takes initiative in the partnership between
king, priests, and the community.[29]

Through the accounts of the best kings—David, Solomon, Hezekiah, and
Josiah—an ideal emerges where temple worship for "all Israel" is at its best
when there is a Davidic king in place who partners with the priests and Levites.
In the postexilic era, temple leadership is in place, but a piece is missing. The
narratives of David, Solomon, Hezekiah, and Josiah prompt hope within the
community for a renewal of Davidic kingship. Led by such a king, the temple
leadership and all of Israel will live in allegiance to God in his temple.[30]

---

28. Sæbø, "Messianism in Chronicles?," 101.

29. Sæbø comes close to capturing this ideal when he says: "What the Chronistic History,
then, is concentrated upon is *the history of the one kingdom: one people under one king*, namely
David and after him the Davidic kings, *gathered around one shrine*, the temple on Zion." Sæbø,
"Messianism in Chronicles?," 99.

30. For more on the Chronicler's coordination of divine supremacy and Davidic kingship, see
Matthew Lynch, *Monotheism and Institutions in the Book of Chronicles: Temple, Priesthood,
and Kingship in Post-Exilic Perspective*, FAT 64 (Tübingen: Mohr Siebeck, 2014), esp. 209–60.

The Promise

Along with the ideal projected by Chronicles, the promises to David contribute to the book's hopes in Davidic rule. The promises to David from 2 Sam. 7 are restated in 1 Chron. 17 with several new emphases. The overall gist remains the same: God turns the tables on David's desire to build God a house; God will instead build David a house. One of David's children will build a house for God, and God will establish his throne forever (vv. 10b–14). Several observations illuminate the significance of these promises in Chronicles. First, and related to the "ideal" above, the Chronicler adds the following to the end of the promise: "I will position him in my house and in my kingdom forever" (17:14, authors' trans.). The verb that we translated as "position him in" is the *hiphil* form of *ʿāmad* followed by the preposition *bə*. In 6:31 [6:16 MT], the same verb form occurs but with the preposition *ʿal*, to say that David "put [priests] in charge" of singing in the temple. Since the preposition chosen in 17:14 is "in" (*bə*) rather than "over" (*ʿal*), the message is not that David's offspring will have superiority over God's house and kingdom; God retains sovereignty over his own kingdom. This is an important reminder for the postexilic community that God's kingship is ultimate.[31] As is apparent in the David-Solomon narratives, the king's position "in God's house" will be in having a lead role in collaborating with the priests to promote allegiance to the Divine King in the temple throughout Israel.

Second, the obvious referent throughout 1 Chron. 17:10b–14 is Solomon. Solomon will fulfill much of what 17:10b–14 describes when he builds the temple. Does this mean God's promise to David is exhausted in Solomon? Hugh Williamson identifies three important passages in 2 Chronicles that make clear that God's promises to David's offspring extend beyond Solomon: 13:5–8; 21:7; 23:3.[32] King Abijah presumes a general knowledge that God pledges to be with Davidic kings after Solomon when he warns Ephraim: "Ought you not to know that the LORD God of Israel gave the kingship over Israel forever to David and his sons by a covenant of salt?" (13:5). He goes on to express the close connection with God's kingdom: "And now you think to withstand the kingdom of the LORD in the hand of the sons of David" (v. 8).[33] Additionally, when speaking of the wicked King Jehoram, the Chronicler says: "Yet the LORD was not willing to destroy the house of David, because of the covenant that he had made with David, and since he had promised to give a lamp to him and to his sons forever" (21:7). Finally, after Athaliah attempts to

---

31. Williamson, *1 and 2 Chronicles*, 136.
32. Williamson, "Eschatology in Chronicles," 143–49.
33. Williamson, "Eschatology in Chronicles," 146–47.

seize the throne in Judah, the priest Jehoiada declares: "The king's son [Joash]! Let him reign, as the LORD spoke concerning the sons of David" (23:3). Thus, whether it is just after the division of the nation (Abijah), during the reign of a wicked king (Jehoram), or amid an attempted coup (Athaliah and Joash), the Chronicler reiterates God's faithfulness to the promises he made to David's dynasty. This leads Williamson to conclude, "Although the term 'messianic' is perhaps too strong, it must be concluded that the Chronicler still cherished the hope that one day the Davidic dynasty would be re-established over Israel."[34]

Thus, the Chronicler invites the community to seek the LORD in humility in the hope that God will bring about an even greater era of blessing for Israel. Since Chronicles depicts Israel at its best under Davidic kings who prioritize God's temple in partnership with the priests, this ideal would almost certainly have invited hope for a new era of Davidic kingship. With promises that God would have an important place for David's offspring in God's house and kingdom forever, the postexilic community would wonder when God's faithfulness to this promise would again be evident.

Conclusion

So, does Chronicles promote the hope that God's kingdom will one day have a Davidic king ruling over it? It has been argued that Chronicles clearly invites the postexilic community to hope for an era of renewal beyond what they were experiencing at the time. Why else would there be such an emphasis on how seeking the LORD in humility would usher in a time of blessing? The ensuing question, then, is this: Would the Chronicler expect there to be a Davidic king reigning during a future era of blessing? Although priests are fundamental to Israel's well-being, the best eras in the Chronicler's history are when Davidic kings take the lead in partnering with temple leadership to guide "all Israel" to align with God in his temple. Additionally, the Chronicler displays God's faithfulness to the promises made to David that a descendant of Solomon would be upon the throne "forever." As Sæbø observes, "The strong concentration upon the promises to the Davidic dynasty *in a period without a Davidic king* is in itself a significant expression of a living longing for the fulfillment of these promises, even in their theocratically stamped form."[35]

Although Chronicles does promote hope in the renewal of the Davidic dynasty, the overarching purpose of the book is to help postexilic Israel recognize that faithfulness to their identity does not require a Davidic king. Under the

34. Williamson, *1 and 2 Chronicles*, 134.
35. Sæbø, "Messianism in Chronicles?," 101.

leadership of the temple, "all Israel" can carry out their calling to focus on the presence of the Divine King in the temple. In doing so, they carry out the initiatives of David and Solomon, even if they are lacking a king. Without a Davidic king, however, the postexilic community would read of the idyllic times under Israel's best kings and remember God's promises to David, yearning for an era of greater renewal when God's throne would once again have someone from the line of David upon it. This tension between faithfulness in the moment and yearning for more is an apt conclusion to the Hebrew Bible.

Postlude: Canonical Reflections

There are several resonances between Chronicles and the New Testament's witness. First, the church finds itself in a time between the times like the audience of Chronicles. The postexilic audience needed to recover a sense of identity, whereby they could continue their mission as the people of God during a time that was less than ideal. Sure, they had come back to the land, had a new temple, and were under the leadership of priests, yet they awaited so much more. As they awaited a new era of restoration, which would include a renewal of Davidic kingship, the community could faithfully seek the LORD in his temple under priestly leadership. The church finds itself further along the line of fulfillment, yet also living amid a longing for more. The church now is a kingdom of priests (1 Pet. 2:8–10) that acknowledges Jesus as the Davidic king, yet the church still awaits an era of great blessing that includes a greater realization of the rule of the Davidic king when Christ comes again. In this way, Chronicles bears witness to a God who wishes for the people of God to embrace the validity of their calling amid the less than ideal, while seeking God earnestly as they await the new era of blessing to come.

Second, just as the David-Solomon narrative provides an ideal that finds its best expressions in Hezekiah and Josiah, so this ideal finds an even greater fulfillment in Jesus Christ. In Jesus, we have a Davidic king (Matt. 1:1) who takes on the role of priest (Heb. 4:14–16), becomes the new temple (John 1:14; 2:19–22), and provides a way for people from all nations—not merely Judah and Israel—to have access to the throne of grace (Heb. 4:16) in the heavenly Jerusalem (12:22).

16

Looking Forward
to the New Testament

Many a church member after listening to a sermon on the Old Testament has echoed the request of those who approached Philip in John 12: "Sir, we wish to see Jesus" (v. 21). For Christians this is where the rubber meets the road: How does the Old Testament throw light on Jesus? In line with the subject of this book, the question could be rephrased in this way: How does the messianic hope found in the Old Testament help us to understand the early Christian proclamation of Jesus as the Christ? It is a common pattern in churches of all persuasions that preaching is more often based on New Testament texts than Old Testament texts. This, however, is not a crime, for a Christian reading of the Old Testament views it as pointing to the one who would fulfill its hopes. Indeed, Jesus himself instructed his followers to read the Old Testament in this way (e.g., Luke 24:27, 44; John 5:39). For this reason, in the preceding chapters, after examining an Old Testament book for what it teaches on the subject of messianism, we have included a postlude, titled "Canonical Reflections," in which we *began* to connect what was found in that particular book with what is on show in the New Testament. In this chapter we carry this process further by looking at what the authors of the New Testament say about Jesus, for they announce that the "Christ" has come.

However, we wrote a book that concentrates on what the Old Testament says of the expectations of a coming human king (our definition of "messianism"), for we believe that too often Christian authors writing on this subject

224

rush to the New Testament after only a hurried survey of Old Testament texts. The theme of the Messiah is both wider and narrower than is often thought. There is, for example, *by implication*, a messianic theology in Samuel and Kings. We also discovered that a number of texts routinely labeled "messianic" (e.g., Ps. 110:1; Dan. 7:13; Zech. 9:9) are nothing of the sort, though they do point to Jesus, but in a different way. What is the purpose of such precision? Are distinctions like this a needless sophistication? We seek to demonstrate that careful thinking about Old Testament texts pays dividends when we turn to consider the New Testament.

Do readers *need* the assistance of the Old Testament to properly understand who Jesus is and what he did to save his people? We wrote this book because we believe they do. Which testament is the harder to understand? Most Christians would answer that question by saying that they struggle with the Old Testament more than with the New. However, this probably only reflects their greater *familiarity* with the contents of the New Testament, for, if the truth be told, the revelation of Jesus as the God-man in the New Testament is something far more difficult to grasp than anything revealed in the pages of the Old Testament. Only after spending extended time in the Old Testament are we ready to understand and appreciate the better things we have in Jesus Christ. For that reason, having sought to elucidate what the Old Testament says about the Messiah, we now turn to see if the New Testament fulfillment matches these expectations.

Our claim here is not that all the Old Testament's messianic expectations find fulfillment in the New Testament. To be sure, some of the Old Testament passages that promote messianic expectations are quoted or alluded to by the New Testament authors in their witness to Jesus, but New Testament usage does not exhaust the Old Testament's witness to messianic hopes. We prefer to affirm instead that all the Old Testament's messianic expectations have found and/or will find their fulfillment in Jesus. Our aim in this chapter is to survey the various ways the New Testament authors bore witness to Jesus as Christ, often via recourse to Old Testament texts.

Jesus as the Christ in the Gospel of Matthew

The messianic status of Jesus as the expected king in David's line is obviously important to the First Evangelist, given the superscription of his gospel: "The book of the genealogy of Jesus Christ, the son of David, the son of Abraham" (Matt. 1:1). This literary work is introduced as a "book" (*biblos*). The superscription, on analogy with Gen. 5:1 (LXX), may be intended to cover no more than the genealogy (Matt. 1:2–17), and the repetition (in reverse order) in 1:2–17 of the triad of names found in the opening line could be construed as evidence for limiting the intent of the superscription to this: Abraham (v. 2), David (v. 6), and Jesus, "who is called Christ" (v. 16).[1] W. D. Davies and Dale C. Allison Jr., however, opt for the view that 1:1 is the title for the entire gospel,[2] with the introductory use of "the book of the genealogy" (*biblos geneseōs*) intended to set the story of Jesus as a counterpart to another "book of origins," Genesis. If that is the intention, it signals that Matthew's book tells of the renewal of creation through the person and work of Jesus (cf. Matt. 19:28 with its use of *palingenesia* = "new world" [ESV] or "regeneration"), who, of course, can only bring about the renewal of all things because he is God in the flesh.

As we have seen, the book of Ruth fits within the trajectory of Davidic hope found in the Old Testament historical books (especially Samuel and Kings). It is highly appropriate, therefore, to find that the one reference to the name of Ruth in the New Testament is as an ancestor of Jesus Christ in the genealogy in the opening chapter of Matthew's Gospel (1:5). The genealogy indicates that "the birth of Jesus Christ" (v. 18) represents a revival in the fortunes of the house of David after the low point of the exile (v. 11). This is confirmed by the Evangelist's use of the prophecy of Jesus's Bethlehemite origins found in Mic. 5:2 and the "clash of kings" motif (Herod versus Jesus) in the next chapter (Matt. 2:2, 4, 6). Jesus is the ruler who will shepherd God's people as Micah predicted. Soon after, Matthew quotes what is said in Isaiah about the dawning of light in the ministry of Jesus in Galilee: "The people who walked in darkness / have seen a great light" (Isa. 9:2; cf. Matt. 4:12–16). In the following chapter of Isaiah, "the light of Israel" (10:17) is an appellation for God, so that the "great light" mentioned in Isa. 9 is presumably a metaphor for the saving action of God, and the evangelist uses this Isaianic text to assert his high Christology of Jesus as God the Savior.

The picture that emerged from our earlier study of the prophecy of Mic. 5, similar to what was found in Isa. 9, 11, and 16,[3] is that these prophecies are fulfilled by Jesus on *two levels*. Jesus is the promised Davidide, whose rule ensures that God's people receive justice and care, and he is also the Divine King who overthrows evil and establishes the kingdom of God on earth.[4]

1. As noted by Davies in W. D. Davies and Dale C. Allison Jr., *The Gospel according to Saint Matthew*, ICC (Edinburgh: T&T Clark, 1988), 1:149.

2. They give their reasons in *Gospel according to Saint Matthew*, 1:150–54.

3. See chaps. 6 and 11 in the present volume.

4. This distribution of tasks is noted by Joel Willitts after his survey of prophetic texts— namely, God brings about the restoration and the Davidic ruler maintains the new order; see

In Matthew's Gospel, Jesus's miracles (chaps. 8–9) are labeled "the deeds of the Christ" (11:2), presumably reflecting the perspective of imprisoned John, but Jesus's own summary of his activities in 11:5 clearly reflects Isa. 35:5–6, which depicts the end-time renewal to be brought about by the action of God himself.

As we have seen from our study of the Old Testament, coordinating a theology of divine and human kingship leads to a more nuanced interpretation of what kind of Messiah is in view in the various books, and the same applies to what the New Testament says about Jesus, where his divine identity is on show more often than sometimes thought. In the case of Matthew, Jesus is depicted as the Divine Shepherd-King who seeks, saves, and refines his flock (10:6; 14:14; 15:24, 32; 25:31–46), and he is also the human shepherd-king who is killed, resulting in the scattering of the flock (26:31; cf. Zech. 13:7), but whose vindication will lead to the regathering of God's flock. What are *separate* strands of hope in the Old Testament—the Messiah is coming and God is coming—are dramatically brought together in the New Testament in one person, the Lord Jesus Christ. This is the leading example of how the teaching of the New Testament both confirms and adjusts the messianic expectations of the Old Testament.

Jesus as the Christ in the Gospel of Mark

The convictions of the evangelist Mark are on show in the opening verse of his action-packed account of the life of Jesus: "The beginning of the gospel of Jesus Christ" (1:1).[5] This immediately reveals that the work of Jesus in his capacity as Messiah will play an important part in Mark's presentation. The Second Gospel has the same major turning point as Matthew, where Peter confesses, "You are the Christ" (8:29; cf. Matt. 16:16), with this being the second use of the title in the gospel (Mark 1:1). But Jesus forbids his disciples to say anything of this to others (8:30), and he himself switches terminology ("the son of man") when going on to speak of what the future holds for him (v. 31). Why must his messianic credentials not be broadcast? Is it because they are likely to be misconstrued before the cross and resurrection? The repetition of the demand for secrecy, linked to the same postresurrection time frame (9:9),

Joel Willitts, *Matthew's Messianic Shepherd-King: In Search for the "Lost Sheep of the House of Israel,"* BZNW 147 (Berlin: de Gruyter, 2007), 67.

5. The words that follow in the RSV ("the Son of God") may not be original; see Peter M. Head, "A Text-Critical Study of Mark 1:1: 'The Beginning of the Gospel of Jesus Christ,'" *NTS* 37 (1991): 621–29. Its addition to this text may be due to the climactic declaration by the centurion in Mark 15:39 of the dying Jesus as "the son of God."

supports that explanation. Or do messianic claims have awkward political and military overtones in Roman-occupied Palestine? The charge brought against Jesus at his trial (15:2, 9, 12), the mocking salutation of the soldiers (v. 18), the title on the cross ("The King of the Jews"; v. 26), and the derision of the religious leaders at the foot of the cross (v. 32) offer support for that way of construing Jesus's motivation and suggest that he died as a messianic pretender. All this demonstrates the use of dramatic irony by Mark, for only by suffering and dying will Jesus fulfill his messianic destiny and role.

Whatever the true explanation of the dominical command for silence, the instruction was not understood by Mark as a denial by Jesus of his messianic status (cf. 9:41).[6] Mark's use of imagery drawn from Ps. 22 in the passion narrative (e.g., the casting of lots, Jesus surrounded by enemies, the mocking of his trust in God),[7] together with the quoted prophecy of Zechariah about the slaying of the (royal) shepherd (Mark 14:27; cf. Matt. 26:31; John 19:37), demonstrates that suffering is not foreign to the evangelists' views of the messiahship of Jesus.[8] In the Old Testament, this aspect of the messianic role is muted, but it does exist (as Ps. 22 and Zechariah show) and does not need to be *manufactured* by trying to turn the Isaianic Servant of the LORD (a suffering *prophetic* figure) into a royal messianic personage.[9] The prominence given to the suffering of Jesus as the Christ is another example of how the cruciform theology of the New Testament both confirms and adjusts the messianic expectations of the Old Testament.

The cleansing of the temple recorded in all four Gospels (e.g., Mark 11:15–19) can be viewed as a messianic action, for in one strand of Old Testament messianic expectation, the future David figure is depicted as having a key role in association with a new temple as its builder or as the patron of the

6. M. de Jonge, "The Earliest Christian Use of *Christos*: Some Suggestions," *NTS* 32 (1986): 321–43; Martin Hengel, "Jesus, the Messiah of Israel: The Debate about the 'Messianic Mission' of Jesus," in *Crisis in Christology: Essays in Quest of Resolution*, ed. William R. Farmer (Livonia, MI: Dove, 1995), 217–40.

7. The connections are mainly, but not exclusively, with the lament section of this psalm. See John H. Reumann, "Psalm 22 at the Cross: Lament and Thanksgiving for Jesus Christ," *Int* 28 (1974): 39–58, who focuses on its use in Mark's Gospel.

8. This feature is more explicitly linked to the messianic identity of Jesus in Luke-Acts.

9. *Pace*, e.g., Michael R. Stead, "Suffering Servant, Suffering David, and Stricken Shepherd," in *Christ Died for Our Sins: Essays on the Atonement*, ed. Michael R. Stead (Canberra: Barton, 2013), 63–66. Stead views the Isaianic suffering servant as a development of the suffering David of the Psalms, but it would be more accurate to say that the fourth Servant Song picks up the motif of the righteous sufferer from the Old Testament lament tradition, exemplified in the Psalter and in Jeremiah's confessions, but it has no essential connection to David (e.g., the image of the lamb led to the slaughter in Isa. 53:7 is found in Ps. 44:22 [44:23 MT]; Jer. 11:19; 12:3); cf. Lothar Ruppert, *Jesus als der leidende Gerechte? Der Weg Jesu im Lichte eines alt- und zwischentestamentlichen Motivs*, SBS 59 (Stuttgart: Katholisches Bibelwerk, 1972), 19–20.

cult (e.g., the type of "David" found in Psalms book 5; the "prince" of Ezek. 40–48; the "Sprout" in Zech. 6:12–13), though in other Old Testament texts it is predicted that God himself will cleanse and restore the temple (e.g., Amos 9:11; Hag. 2:7–9; Mal. 3:1–4). We do not need to set one type of prediction against the other; rather, the point is that Jesus as the God-man fulfills both.

Jesus as the Christ in Luke-Acts and Non-Pauline Epistles

The Lukan infancy story contains six explicit references to David (Luke 1:27, 32, 69; 2:4 [2x], 11). The connection to David is reinforced by the Song of Mary (echoing that of Hannah in 1 Sam. 2:1–10), the stress on the Bethlehemite location of Jesus's birth, and the motif of shepherds who pasture flocks near Bethlehem as David once did.[10] Later, as Jesus travels toward Jerusalem, his identity as the "Son of David" is announced by a blind man (Luke 18:38, 39), whose healing leads to *God* being glorified (v. 43), such that the kind and powerful actions of Jesus on display in his ministry are being interpreted on more than one level in this gospel as well.

Jesus is depicted as the shepherd-king who comes to seek and to save the lost in Luke 19:10,[11] a verse that appears to sum up the message of salvation in Luke's Gospel as a whole,[12] but understanding what is said here depends on Ezek. 34:16, 22 ("I [YHWH] will seek the lost. . . . I will rescue [save] my flock"). Jesus is not claiming to be the Davidic shepherd who tends the flock (as per most scholars) but the Divine Shepherd who saves. Likewise, Jesus uses the parable of the lost sheep (Luke 15:3–7) to rebuke the failed shepherd-leaders of his day (= the Pharisees and scribes of v. 2) who did not care for the flock and also to depict God as the shepherd who seeks and finds lost sheep, such that Jesus is saying that he acts in the capacity of God, the Savior of his people (2:11; cf. 1:47 ["God my Savior"]).[13] Sarah Harris acknowledges that in both Ezek. 34 and Luke 15 the focus is on God pictured as a shepherd; however, she goes on to claim that in Ezek. 34 "his [God's] hands and feet in the task of shepherding are his servant David,"[14] and therefore she wishes to see Jesus

---

10. For this paragraph we acknowledge our dependence on Sarah Harris, *The Davidic Shepherd King in the Lukan Narrative*, LNTS 558 (London: Bloomsbury T&T Clark, 2016), 37.

11. According to Yuzuru Miura, *David in Luke-Acts: His Portrayal in the Light of Early Judaism*, WUNT 2/232 (Tübingen: Mohr Siebeck, 2007), 225.

12. I. Howard Marshall, *Luke: Historian and Theologian* (Exeter, UK: Paternoster, 1970), 116.

13. Cf. Nina Henrichs-Tarasenkova, *Luke's Christology of Divine Identity*, LNTS 542 (London: Bloomsbury T&T Clark, 2016), 159–63.

14. Harris, *Davidic Shepherd King*, 104.

as the *Davidic* shepherd. But this is not the way to read the prophet Ezekiel—the Davidic "prince" is not a savior figure in Ezekiel—nor at this point in the Gospel should the Christology be limited to that of Jesus as a Davidic figure.

The accusation that Jesus claimed to be "Christ, a king" (*christon basilea*) is submitted to Pilate by the Sanhedrin (Luke 23:2), and in Luke's version of the interrogation of Jesus by the high priest as to whether he is the Christ, the answer of Jesus is evasive but does not need to be read as a denial (22:67–68; cf. Mark 14:61–62; Matt. 26:63–64). His subsequent admission under questioning that he is "the Son of God" (Luke 22:70) brings the two titles into relation with each other but without precisely equating them.[15] The use of the language of sonship in certain Davidic passages in the Old Testament about the dynastic promise (esp. 2 Sam. 7:14: "I will be to him a father, and he shall be to me a son"; Ps. 2:7: "You are my son") is probably due to the fact that the role of a covenant is to give permanency to a relationship with the aim of securing lasting benefits; hence, covenants in the ANE and in the Bible can use the father-son relation as a metaphor (e.g., God's commitment to Israel in Exod. 4:22).[16] However, in noncovenantal contexts in the Old Testament, the (present or promised) king in David's line is not referred to as God's son.

The author of Acts places a summary of early Christian proclamation in the mouth of Peter, who tells the people of Jerusalem that Jesus is "both Lord and Christ" (2:36). This summary is preceded by the apostle's argument linking Jesus to David, making Jesus the fulfillment of God's oath to David that "he would set one of his descendants on his throne" (2:30; cf. 2 Sam. 7).[17] According to Peter, the resurrection and ascension lead to the vindication of Jesus as the messianic king (= Christ),[18] and also to his enthronement at God's right hand as the apocalyptic figure designated as David's "Lord" in Ps. 110:1 (quoted in Acts 2:34). This is the best *contextual* reading of the claim that Jesus is "both Lord and Christ,"[19] with the two titles differentiated in the way indicated.

---

15. A valid point made by Joseph A. Fitzmyer, *The One Who Is to Come* (Grand Rapids: Eerdmans, 2007), 138, disagreeing with Brendan Byrne, "Jesus as Messiah in the Gospel of Luke: Discerning a Pattern of Correction," *CBQ* 65 (2003): 85, 91.

16. According to F. M. Cross, the effect of a covenant is to forge fictive kinship relations between those who are not blood relatives; see "Kinship and Covenant in Ancient Israel," in *From Epic to Canon: History and Literature in Ancient Israel* (Baltimore: Johns Hopkins University Press, 1998), 7.

17. As pointed out by Fitzmyer, *One Who Is to Come*, 137.

18. Mark L. Strauss, *The Davidic Messiah in Luke-Acts: The Promise and Its Fulfillment in Lukan Christology*, JSNTSup 110 (Sheffield: Sheffield Academic, 1995), 141.

19. Strauss also sees "Lord" in v. 36 as drawn in the first instance from the quotation of Ps. 110:1, but he thinks it is a messianic reference. Strauss, *Davidic Messiah in Luke-Acts*, 143.

In Acts, Jesus as the "Christ" features, often to the exclusion of other christological titles, in summaries of early preaching (5:42; 8:5; 9:22; 17:3; 18:5, 28), such that this is a key term for Lukan Christology. From where does the author of Luke-Acts draw the idea of a *suffering* Messiah? The following examples show that this was for Luke a settled way of speaking: Luke 24:26, 46; Acts 3:18; 17:3; 26:23; and this Lukan phraseology is not without parallel elsewhere (cf. 1 Cor. 15:3; 1 Pet. 1:11). As noted by Mark L. Strauss, it is only after the resurrection, starting from Luke 24:26, that the motif of suffering is joined to the title "Christ" and is said to fulfill Old Testament expectations ("Was it not necessary that the Christ should suffer these things?"),[20] but Luke fails to explain what Old Testament passages he has in mind. For example, he does not record the cry of dereliction that quotes from Ps. 22:1 (cf. Mark 15:34; Matt. 27:46). Presumably, he too is drawing on the image of the righteous sufferer in the Psalter and possibly Zechariah.

As an addendum to Acts, a brief discussion of the epistles of James, Peter, Jude, and Hebrews is in order. In all Greek textual witnesses, Acts prefaces the Catholic Letters, and these are treated as a fixed and coherent canonical unit (*Praxapostolos*).[21] This settled pattern of conjoining Acts and the Catholic Epistles (almost always in that order) suggests that these letters are to be viewed "through the lens of Acts."[22] There are two references to Jesus as the "Lord Jesus Christ" in the Letter of James (1:1; 2:1), but the Christology of James is mostly implicit and oriented to eschatology—notably, "the coming of the Lord," at which time suffering believers will receive from God "the crown of life" (1:12; 5:7–8). This is best viewed as referring to the return of Jesus, but given that both God and Jesus are called "Lord" in this letter (for God as "Lord," see, e.g., 3:9; 4:15; 5:4),[23] there is ambiguity—no doubt deliberate on the part of James—as to whether the Lord Jesus is said to be coming as God or as the Messiah. First Peter is focused on the common experience of believers suffering for their faith. Peter assures his readers that just as Christ suffered and was glorified (1 Pet. 1:11, 21), so also believers will be rewarded (2:21; 4:13, 19; 5:4, 10) "at the revelation of Jesus Christ" (1:13). The day of vindication for believers is both "the day of the Lord" and "the day of God" (2 Pet. 3:10, 12), and both expressions allude to the coming of "our Lord and Savior Jesus Christ" (3:18; cf. Jude 25).

20. Strauss, *Davidic Messiah in Luke-Acts*, 257.
21. David C. Parker, *An Introduction to the New Testament Manuscripts and Their Texts* (Cambridge: Cambridge University Press, 2008), 283–86.
22. David R. Nienhuis and Robert W. Wall, *Reading the Epistles of James, Peter, John, and Jude as Scripture* (Grand Rapids: Eerdmans, 2013), 53.
23. William R. Baker, "Christology in the Epistle of James," *EvQ* 74 (2002): 53–54.

In Hebrews, as elsewhere in the New Testament, it would be a mistake to limit our attention to uses of the term "Christ," and a messianic theology is present in this anonymous document.[24] The strongest thematic links between Hebrews and the Catholic Epistles are those between Hebrews and 1 Peter.[25] They congregate around the theme of suffering—the suffering of Christ (Heb. 2:14; 4:15; 1 Pet. 4:1) and that of the Christian community (Heb. 12:2–11; 1 Pet. 2:21–25; 3:13–22)—and indeed the two matters are closely and essentially linked. The first two chapters of Hebrews are united by the theme of the status of Jesus relative to the angels—Jesus is superior to the angels (1:5–14)—but at the incarnation he was "made lower than the angels" (2:5–18).[26] The focus in Hebrews is the high priesthood of Jesus (starting in 2:17), yet it is not the only theme, and the special attention given to Ps. 8 in Heb. 2 is a case in point. Hebrews 2:6–8 contains a lengthy quotation of Ps. 8:5–7 (LXX). In 1 Cor. 15:27 and Eph. 1:22, the generic "man" of Ps. 8:6 is transformed into a specific person—namely, Jesus, the one perfect representative of the human race. This move is justified by the psalm's presentation of humanity in royal (Davidic) terms as ruling over creation. Taking seriously the ordering of the psalms, we can see that the lament of Ps. 7 concludes with the vow of David, "I will sing praise to the name of the LORD, the Most High" (7:17 [7:18 MT]), and that Ps. 8 should be read as the fulfillment of the king's vow,[27] which means that its content is related to his royal status. On that basis, the writer to the Hebrews is right to view Ps. 8 as alluding to the messianic role, prefigured by the first man, then by David, but finally fulfilled by Jesus (Heb. 2:9).[28] That role involved suffering on behalf of his "brothers" (2:11); however, the fuller explication of the atoning significance of his death is explored by means of the theme of the high priesthood of Jesus.

24. Cynthia Long Westfall is right to attend to an assortment of motifs such as the enthronement of Jesus, his victory over enemies, and his link to the temple, all of which potentially relate to the kingly status and role of Jesus; see Cynthia Long Westfall, "Messianic Themes of Temple, Enthronement, and Victory in Hebrews and the General Epistles," in *The Messiah of the Old and New Testaments*, ed. Stanley E. Porter (Grand Rapids: Eerdmans, 2007), 210–29.

25. L. D. Hurst, *The Epistle to the Hebrews: Its Background of Thought*, SNTSMS 65 (Cambridge: Cambridge University Press, 1990), 125–30.

26. Cf. David A. deSilva, *Perseverance in Gratitude: A Socio-Rhetorical Commentary on the Epistle to the Hebrews* (Grand Rapids: Eerdmans, 2000), 72.

27. See Patrick D. Miller, "The Beginning of the Psalter," in *The Shape and Shaping of the Psalter*, ed. J. Clinton McCann, JSOTSup 159 (Sheffield: Sheffield Academic, 1993), 89–90.

28. Cf. Brevard S. Childs, "Psalm 8 in the Context of the Christian Canon," *Int* 23 (1969): 20–31; Brevard S. Childs, *Biblical Theology in Crisis* (Philadelphia: Westminster, 1970), 151–63.

Jesus as the Christ in the Writings of John

Among the plethora of christological titles found in the first chapter of John's Gospel is the announcement by Andrew, "We have found the Messiah [*ton Messian*]" (1:41), which title the author immediately explains to his Greek-speaking readers as meaning "the Christ" (*christos*). Andrew responds correctly to Jesus, but the full meaning of the messiahship of Jesus is beyond his understanding and will only be grasped by reading what is recorded in this Gospel.[29] Unlike in the Synoptic Gospels, in the Fourth Gospel Jesus's messianic status is openly proclaimed at the beginning of his public ministry.[30] What exactly is the relation of that proclamation to what Nathaniel says shortly afterward by way of acclamation to Jesus, "You are the Son of God! You are the king of Israel" (v. 49)? Are these merely two other ways of saying that Jesus is the Messiah? More likely, in a Johannine context the term *Son* is to be understood in relation to the unique Father-Son relationship, and the title "the king of Israel" identifies Jesus as the Divine King (see below). Again, it is not necessary to think that Nathaniel understood the full purport of what he said, but the writer uses his confession to depict "the ideal Johannine belief-response."[31]

With so many christological titles in John's repertoire, is "Christ" an important one in his eyes? It is by no means insignificant, for the word *christos* is found nineteen times in the Fourth Gospel. The Samaritan woman tells Jesus that she believes in the coming of the Messiah (*Messias*; 4:25), and Jesus identifies himself with this figure of hope ("I who speak to you am he," v. 26).[32] The evangelist describes the witness of various prominent figures to Jesus in terms of the title "Messiah/Christ," especially Andrew (1:41), the Samaritan woman (4:29), and Martha of Bethany (11:27), though it is not clear that they fully understand Jesus's true identity. Notably, the strategic placement of the title near the beginning (1:41) and end of the Gospel (20:31) suggests a Johannine focus on Jesus's messianic identity and role.[33]

29. For what follows in this section, we acknowledge our substantial dependence on Dae Woo Seo, "An Interpretation of the Key Johannine Christological Titles in John 1:19–51 on the Basis of Their Wider Use in the Narrative of the Gospel and in Dialogue with Their Old Testament Background" (master's diss., Australian College of Theology, 2012), chap. 8.

30. Stephen S. Smalley, *John: Evangelist and Interpreter* (Exeter, UK: Paternoster, 1978), 217.

31. Cornelius Bennema, *Encountering Jesus: Character Studies in the Gospel of John* (Milton Keynes, UK: Paternoster, 2009), 67.

32. No doubt her words reflect her own expectation of a Messiah in accordance with Samaritan traditions (*Taheb*); see John P. Meier, "The Historical Jesus and the Historical Samaritans: What Can Be Said?," *Bib* 81 (2000): 202–32.

33. See Mavis M. Leung, *The Kingship-Cross Interplay in the Gospel of John: Jesus' Death as Corroboration of His Royal Messiahship* (Eugene, OR: Wipf & Stock, 2011), 48.

There is debate among the Jews as to whether Jesus is the Christ (John 7:25–31, 41–42; 9:22; 10:24; 12:34). That Jesus was known to come from Nazareth was seen as a problem by some (7:27, 41–42);[34] on the other hand, the miracles that Jesus performed confirmed his messianic status in the eyes of others (v. 31). The popular expectation that the Messiah will reign forever (12:34) could be supported by Isa. 9:7 (9:6 MT) or Ezek. 37:25, such that the prospect of Jesus dying was a stumbling block in accepting his messianic identity. The claims of Jesus include messiahship but also go beyond it, for the figure of the "good shepherd" who regathers the people of God in John 10 draws on Ezek. 34 and depicts the active *divine* role played by Jesus in rescuing and regathering God's scattered people. Likewise, in John 10:24–25, when Jesus responds to the Jewish leadership ("the Jews") who demanded that he tell them plainly whether he is the Christ, he does not reject the title but prefers to reveal his identity by referring to his unique relationship with the Father, speaking of his oneness with the Father (v. 30) and his identification as "the Son of God" (v. 36). This discussion moves well beyond the concept of Messiah asked about by the Jews, and Jesus's status as the Son of God in John is not to be reduced to his messianic identity and role.

Some scholars, like Mark Appold, argue in regard to John 1:49 and 12:13 that "the original connotation of the King of Israel title was determined by a distinctly Davidic messianology,"[35] but something more is involved. The motif of kingship is extensively featured throughout the Johannine passion narrative (chaps. 18–19), and it is mainly expressed using the titles "the King" and "the King of the Jews," whereas the title "the Christ" is completely absent from the trial narrative.[36] In fact, the title "King" is the only one used of Jesus, except for one (ironic) use of the title "the Son of God" by the Jews (19:7).[37] This suggests that the issue of Jesus's kingship forms the "main focus of the trial."[38] As John Painter notes, "'King of Israel' is the Palestinian

34. On this issue, see Richard Bauckham, "Messianism according to the Gospel of John," in *Challenging Perspectives on the Gospel of John*, ed. John Lierman, WUNT 2/219 (Tübingen: Mohr Siebeck, 2006), 60–63.

35. Mark L. Appold, *The Oneness Motif in the Fourth Gospel: Motif Analysis and Exegetical Probe into the Theology of John*, WUNT 2/1 (Tübingen: Mohr Siebeck, 1976), 76.

36. Reimund Bieringer, "'My Kingship Is Not of This World' (John 18:36): The Kingship of Jesus and Politics," in *The Myriad Christ: Plurality and the Quest for Unity in Contemporary Christology*, ed. Terrence Merrigan and Jacques Haers (Leuven: Leuven University Press, 2000), 159–75.

37. Bieringer, "'My Kingship Is Not of This World' (John 18:36)," 160.

38. Matthew L. Skinner, *The Trial Narrative: Conflict, Power, and Identity in the New Testament* (Louisville: Westminster John Knox, 2010), 95.

Jewish form of which 'king of the Jews' is the Gentile and dispersion Jewish variant."[39] The evangelist does not aim to distinguish the two titles. When Pilate calls Jesus "your [the Jews'] King," the chief priests reject his designation of Jesus by saying, "We have no king but Caesar" (v. 15). According to David Rensberger, "[This] is a renunciation of Israel's profession to have no king but God. . . . With this cry, 'the Jews' reject the kingship not only of Jesus but of God as well."[40] In other words, the rejection of Jesus as king is equivalent to the rejection of God as King. Likewise, in John's version of the entry of Jesus into Jerusalem, he reports that the people give Jesus the title "the King of Israel," which was normally reserved for God (12:13); thus the evangelist equates Jesus with the God of the Old Testament. Although the theme of Jesus's kingship in John can have messianic overtones (e.g., 6:15), his kingship revealed under the titles "the King of Israel" and "the King of the Jews" is connected to his divine identity rather than simply his messianic identity.

In the book of Revelation God is repeatedly described as the one "who is seated on [or "sits on"] the throne" (e.g., Rev. 4:9; 5:13), and God and the Lamb (= Jesus) are paired and jointly praised for the work of salvation (5:13; 7:10). The connection of the two is so close that John can even speak of "the Lamb in the midst of the throne" (7:17) and of "the throne of God and of the Lamb" (22:1, 3).[41] Likewise, in 3:21, the risen Jesus says that he has conquered and sat with his Father on his throne. According to Darrell Hannah, the placement of these statements in chapters 3 and 22 is highly significant, for it means that the visions of John are framed by declarations that Jesus sits on the very throne of God.[42] In the context of this high Christology, using what is a complementary image for Jesus and his place in the unfolding of God's purposes, John says that the seals of the scroll are opened by "the Lion of the tribe of Judah, the Root of David" (5:5). These titles are drawn from and adapt Gen. 49:9 and Isa. 11:1, 10. The lamb imagery is pervasive in the book of Revelation, whereas the lion of the tribe of Judah does not appear elsewhere. This does not mean that messianic theology is unimportant to John but indicates that Jesus conquered and will reign because of his sacrificial

---

39. John Painter, "Christ and the Church in John 1:45–51," in *L'Évangile de Jean: Sources, rédaction, théologie*, ed. Marinus de Jonge, BETL 44 (Leuven: Leuven University Press, 1977), 360.

40. David Rensberger, "The Politics of John: The Trial of Jesus in the Fourth Gospel," *JBL* 103 (1984): 406.

41. It is probable that the Lamb also occupies the throne of God in Rev. 5:6; see Laszlo Gallusz, *The Throne Motif in the Book of Revelation*, LNTS 487 (London: Bloomsbury T&T Clark, 2014), 153–58.

42. See Darrell D. Hannah, "The Throne of His Glory: The Divine Throne and Heavenly Mediators in Revelation and the Similitudes of Enoch," *ZNW* 94 (2003): 69.

work on the cross.[43] The conquering and triumphant lamb in the book of Revelation (e.g., 6:16; 14:10; 17:14) can be linked to the soteriology of John's Gospel in which the cross is "the place of eschatological triumph," where sin, death, and the devil are defeated (John 12:31; 16:11; 19:30).[44]

In the Letters of John, belief in the messiahship of Jesus is deemed essential (1 John 2:22; 5:1), and those who deny this are labeled "antichrists" (2:18, 22; 4:3; cf. 2 John 7). First John insists on the reality of the physical resurrection of Jesus, the author claiming to have seen and handled the risen Christ (1:1; cf. John 20:24–29), presumably in response to heretical claims to the contrary.[45] The bold joint insistence of Peter and John on the truth of the resurrection of Jesus (Acts 4:20: "We cannot but speak of what we have seen and heard") is echoed in the opening of 1 John (1:1: "which we have heard, which we have seen with our eyes"). On this basis, whatever the particular thematic emphases of the individual works, the Johannine writings give a unified witness to the truthfulness of the claim that the Christ, the Son of God, is Jesus (cf. the authorial statements of purpose in John 20:31 and 1 John 5:13).[46]

Jesus as the Christ in the Pauline Letters

An example of Paul's use of *christos* in application to Jesus is Rom. 9:5, where it is clearly not a proper name (Matthew Novenson calls it an honorific).[47] The preceding verse and this one together supply a list of Jewish privileges, Paul picking up where he left off in 3:2 ("To begin with, the Jews are entrusted with the oracles of God"). He speaks of the physical descent of Jesus ("From their race, according to the flesh [*kata sarka*], is the Christ," 9:5), recalling what he said in the opening verses of the letter—namely, that Jesus "was descended from David according to the flesh [*kata sarka*]" (1:3). It is not possible, therefore, to agree with the claim of Nils Dahl that "in no case in Paul can *Christos*

43. As rightly pointed out by Gallusz (*Throne Motif*, 153).

44. Dorothy A. Lee, "Paschal Imagery in the Gospel of John: A Narrative and Symbolic Reading," *Pacifica* 24 (2011): 18.

45. Matthew D. Jensen, *Affirming the Resurrection of the Incarnate Christ: A Reading of 1 John*, SNTSMS 153 (Cambridge: Cambridge University Press, 2012), 60–65.

46. For the Johannine writings addressed to a Jewish Christian audience, dealing with the situation where previous members of the community were denying that the Christ is Jesus, see Matthew D. Jensen, "John Is No Exception: Identifying the Subject of *eimi* and Its Implications," *JBL* 135 (2016): 341–53.

47. His argument is provided in Matthew V. Novenson, *Christ among the Messiahs: Christ Language in Paul and Messiah Language in Ancient Judaism* (Oxford: Oxford University Press, 2012), 64–97.

be translated 'Messiah.'"[48] As well, those occasions in Paul's writings when he inverts the order of the names, referring to "Christ Jesus" (e.g., Rom. 6:3, 11; 8:1, 39; Gal. 2:4; 1 Thess. 2:14), show that "Christ" is not being used as a proper name, for such inversions are impossible for two proper names (e.g., Julius Caesar, Simon bar Jonah),[49] with the result that "Christ Jesus" must be a combination of a personal name (Jesus) with an honorific (Christ).[50]

Just as in the Old Testament there are messianic passages that do not use the term "anointed one" (māšîaḥ; e.g., Jer. 23:5–6), so, too, in the letters of Paul, the presence or absence of the word christos does not by itself determine whether or not Paul is discussing the messianic status and role of Jesus; rather, it is the overall content and argument of a text that is determinative. For example, the first and last paragraphs of the Letter to the Romans contain a collation of messianic themes—namely, Paul's gospel ministry, summed up as "the preaching of Jesus Christ" (16:25), fulfills Old Testament prophecy (1:2; 16:26) and aims to bring about "the obedience of faith" among all the nations (1:5; 16:26; cf. 15:18).[51] These two passages frame the letter and set the argument of the letter in the context of God's revealed purpose that Jesus as the Messiah will rule the nations.[52]

It was Paul's encounter with the risen Christ on the Damascus Road that caused a revolution in his thinking, resulting in his conversion and commissioning as the apostle to the gentiles. On that road Paul came to believe that the crucified Jesus was not a messianic pretender (1 Cor. 1:23; 2 Cor. 5:16) but the Messiah (Gal. 1:16; 2:20). This suggests that Jesus's royal messianic status is fundamental to Paul's teaching and ministry. In fact, the theological presupposition behind Paul's gentile mission is "the future hegemony of the Davidic messiah over the Gentile nations,"[53] as is made clear by Paul's citation of Isa. 11:10 (LXX) in Rom. 15:12, which depicts the subjection of foreign nations to "the root of Jesse." It is significant that in verses near the beginning and end of the body of the Letter to the Romans Paul connects the

---

48. Nils A. Dahl, "The Messiahship of Jesus in Paul," in *Jesus the Christ: The Historical Origins of Christological Doctrine*, ed. Donald H. Juel (Minneapolis: Fortress, 1991), 17n11. For Novenson's critique of Dahl, see *Christ among the Messiahs*, 98–115.

49. Novenson, *Christ among the Messiahs*, 101.

50. Novenson, *Christ among the Messiahs*, 134.

51. This is an ambiguous phrase that signifies both the obedience that springs from faith and the obedience (= proper response to God) that consists of faith; see Don Garlington, *Faith, Obedience, and Perseverance: Aspects of Paul's Letter to the Romans*, WUNT 2/79 (Tübingen: Mohr Siebeck, 1994), 13–31.

52. Cf. Matthew V. Novenson, "The Jewish Messiahs, the Pauline Christ, and the Gentile Question," *JBL* 128 (2009): 357–73.

53. Novenson, "Jewish Messiahs," 366.

messiahship of Jesus to his own mission to the gentiles; indeed, as pointed out by Christopher Whitsett, "Isaiah 11:10 is the note on which Paul concludes the entire argumentative body of Romans."[54] Citing Isaiah, Paul says of Christ, "He . . . arises to rule the Gentiles" (Rom. 15:12). The resurrection of Jesus shows that he has been elevated to the throne of David (1:4), and now through the gospel mission led by Paul, Jesus is extending his rightful messianic rule over the gentiles.

Conclusion

In this book we have stressed the importance of coordinating the themes of divine and human kingship, for in the person of Jesus we see both the coming of God and the coming of the promised human king (= Messiah). Knowing that Jesus is both the Messiah and the Divine King, we see Jesus more often in the Old Testament than we did before, for everything said of God can be applied to Jesus. Likewise, in the New Testament, studying these themes in tandem pays dividends, for Jesus does what God alone can do (e.g., he is the Divine Shepherd who rescues his people), and his humanity is essential for the carrying out of his messianic office (he is the dying shepherd-king predicted by Zechariah).

Every use of "Christ" in the New Testament writings is not necessarily an indicator that a messianic theology is on show, for the messiahship of Jesus was a fundamental article of faith in early Christian communities, so that the honorific "Christ" could easily substitute for the personal name Jesus when making statements about his person and work. This means that the reader should not assume that every use of "Christ" means that what is said about Christ is something inherent to the term. On the other hand, it is not mandatory that a New Testament author use the word *christos* when discussing the messiahship of Jesus.

When we find in the New Testament a collation of christological titles—notably, Christ and Son of God (John 11:27; cf. Matt. 16:16; 2 Cor. 1:19; 1 John 4:15) and Christ and Lord (e.g., Luke 2:11; Rom. 5:1; 1 Pet. 3:15)—this is best understood as predicating the one person Jesus with alternate (and finally compatible) titles denoting roles and status without asserting that these different categories with Old Testament roots can simply be collapsed into one—that is, that Christ equals Son of God or that Christ equals Lord.

---

54. Christopher G. Whitsett, "Son of God, Seed of David: Paul's Messianic Exegesis in Rom. 1:3–4," *JBL* 119 (2000): 671.

Conclusion

After our journey through most of the books in the Old Testament, it is time to ask: How do the pieces fit together? In answering this question, it is important to allow the Old Testament itself to shape and perhaps modify our expectations. Some expect the royal messianic expectations in the Old Testament to be like a constellation—if we connect the dots, a clear outline of the Messiah will emerge. The "constellation" approach does not work. God chose to speak in diverse ways and from diverse angles, such that there are varying emphases in various periods in the history of revelation. Under God's providence and inspiration, no individual passage exhausts Old Testament messianic expectations; there is not a network of texts that neatly outlines the likeness of the Messiah; and there is not an evolutionary process by which the latest messianic expression rules them all. Instead of the metaphor of a constellation, an *abstract mosaic* is a more suitable metaphor for viewing the whole. A mosaic is a work of art consisting of many pieces of tile; it is considered "abstract" when it presents its subject through a profusion of effects rather than a linear portrayal. Imagine a gigantic mosaic with the Divine King as its central image and variations of a motif emerging across the landscape of the work. The motif manifesting itself across the backdrop of the mosaic is the royal messianic expectation, complementing the central image of the Divine King. Below, we will use *abstract mosaic* as a metaphor to gain perspective on the profusion of messianic hopes we have seen across the Old Testament.

Modes of Expressing Messianic Hope

There are numerous modes of expression within mosaic art. For one, the choice of tile type (stone, glass, painted, imprinted, etc.) greatly influences a mosaic, and it is not uncommon to mix tile types or other media in the creation of an abstract mosaic. Similarly, there is not simply one mode in the Old Testament for expressing messianic expectations. Naturally, *explicit promises* receive a great deal of attention in most studies on messianic expectations. In the Pentateuch, there are promises that kings will come from Abraham's line (Gen. 17:16), that "the scepter shall not depart from Judah" (49:10), and that "a scepter shall rise out of Israel" (Num. 24:17). In the Former Prophets, Hannah prophesies that the LORD will "exalt the horn of his anointed" (1 Sam. 2:10), and God promises through Nathan that David's "throne shall be established forever" (2 Sam. 7:16). Nathan's promises are reiterated throughout 1–2 Kings. In the Latter Prophets (Isaiah–Malachi), promises of a new era of kingship find expression in Isaiah (9:6–7; 11:1–5; 16:5; cf. 32:1), Jeremiah (3:15; 17:25; 23:1–4, 5–6; 30:9, 21; 33:14–26), Ezekiel (34:23–24; 37:24; 44:1–4; 46:1–3, 8–10, 12), Hosea (1:11; 3:5), possibly Amos (9:11), Micah (5:2–4 [5:1–3 MT]), and Zechariah (3:8; 6:12–13). The Psalter, too, contains psalms that express promises regarding God's commitment to Davidic kingship (Pss. 2:6–8; 72; 132). These explicit promises of hope total less than one hundred verses, so as you imagine our mosaic, keep in mind that these tiles—as brightly as they shine—are only one of the modes God uses to convey messianic expectations.

Another mode for giving rise to messianic expectation is *narrative*. Generally speaking, the Pentateuch includes within its redemptive story line the expectation that kingship will play some role as God fulfills his promises to Israel to bless the entire world. Not all narratives operate in the same manner. In the book of Judges, for instance, the refrain "In those days there was no king in Israel" (17:6; cf. 18:1; 19:1; 21:25) figures into the greater narrative of the book, which presents human kingship as an alternative to judgeship; perhaps a human king will be able to lead the nation to live under God's kingship. In Samuel and Kings, especially in David's early reign and narratives about Solomon and Josiah, the narratives create a paradigmatic ideal of kingship that projects beyond the lives of these kings. These ideals in Samuel and Kings find their background in the law of Deut. 17:14–20, yet another mode of expression. In Chronicles, comparisons with synoptic passages from Samuel and Kings reveal how its narratives uphold the ideal of Davidic kingship as a hope that endures in the postexilic era. The book of Ruth culminates with a genealogy, inviting a rereading of the book in light of God's providence in preserving the house of David. Our mosaic, then, should include swaths of narrative that give rise to messianic expectations.

In addition to the various types of tile, a mosaic can contain a range of *vantage points*. Certain images may appear near or distant, jagged or smooth, prominent or peripheral, depending upon the vantage point in the mosaic. In our mosaic of messianic expectations, multiple vantage points emerge in view of the historical situation within the text. The book of Hosea's northern and preexilic provenance uniquely shapes how we view its expression of hope for a time when both houses will be under the reign of a Davidide (3:5). Isaiah and Micah express their expectations from within Judah during a time of Assyrian threat. They envisage a restoration of Davidic kingship after the threat of Assyria has been quelled (Isa. 10:32–11:5; Mic. 5:1–5). Naturally, Jeremiah's up-close depiction of Jerusalem's fall to Babylon and Zedekiah's removal inform the way he focuses on how God can justly put the line of David to death and how there is hope that God will resuscitate David's dynasty. Throughout most of these prophets, messianic hopes often contrast with the corrupt rulers at the time, as we saw in the play on Zedekiah's name in Jer. 23:6. The book of Kings makes a case to an exilic or early postexilic audience regarding how God can justly reject the line of David, while simultaneously setting forth an ideal for what kingship should look like should God's favor continue through exile. Chronicles has yet another vantage point, as it was written later in the postexilic era. The Chronicler's concern is to help Israel recognize that their identity as a nation centered around the temple does not depend on having a Davidic king, while the book also maintains hope for the restoration of Davidic kingship. Under God's inspiration, the Old Testament expresses messianic expectations in a way that would resonate with and be suitable for a wide range of original audiences and situations. The mosaic, then, will capture the circumstances that gave rise to such visions of messianic renewal.

Finally, a motif can recur throughout a mosaic yet express itself in a range of *forms*. The same is apparent regarding motifs of messianic expectation in the Old Testament. Kingship finds expression through the images of the lion and scepter in Gen. 49:9–10 and through the star and scepter in Num. 24:17. In 2 Sam. 7, "house" and "shepherd" are the prominent metaphors that capture Nathan's promise to David. Isaiah 11:1, 10; Jer. 23:6; 33:17–18; and Zech. 3:8; 6:12 draw upon horticultural imagery to speak of a new era of Davidic kingship: the Sprout. Jeremiah (3:15; 23:1–5) and Ezekiel (34:23–24; 37:24) utilize the image of a shepherd to envisage the renewal of Davidic kingship. So, our mosaic should have a great deal of variation in the forms it uses to capture the recurring motif of messianic expectation in the Old Testament.

Although the initial instinct of some might be to wish for one mode of expressing messianic hopes, there is a remarkable richness to this profusion of modes. Through promises, law, genealogy, and narratives, from northern and southern, preexilic, exilic, and postexilic vantage points, and through metaphorical lenses such as the lion, shepherd, and sprout, messianic expectations become far more colorful and impactful than what one mode of expression could attain.

Characteristics of the Messianic Hope

Not only is there a wide range of *modes* of expression in an abstract mosaic, but a motif can repeat itself with similar and differing *characteristics* pertaining to the subject matter. For instance, imagine a motif of "human flourishing" across a mosaic. The motif might manifest itself as people eating fruit, children at play, people of different races embracing, and jails emptying. Variations in the motif enable the conveying of a range of characteristics of human flourishing: joy, satisfaction, peace, reconciliation, freedom, and more. Similarly, royal messianic expectations include a range of characteristics, with some characteristics more prominent than others.

The most prominent characteristic, especially in the narratives, is that *the messiah promotes the centrality of the Divine King and his temple.* In the books of Samuel and Kings, David, Solomon, and Josiah-like kings led Israel to celebrate the rule of God by bringing the ark to Jerusalem, constructing the temple, and instituting reform to eradicate idols and centralize the exclusive worship of the LORD in the temple. Not only did these kings build the temple, but they were exemplars in living in exclusive allegiance to God, as Deut. 17:14–20 states and as the end of Judges hopes for (17:6; 18:1; 19:1; 21:25). Chronicles directs even greater attention to the temple, as it recounts how Davidic kings established temple leadership to guide the community in worship. The Latter Prophets also share an emphasis on the Davidic king being temple centric. In Ezek. 40–48, the "prince" will primarily promote the worship of the LORD (44:1–4; 46:1–3, 8–10, 12). Also, in Isa. 16:4–5 and Amos 9:11, a renewal of Davidic kingship coordinates with the restoration of the "tent of David," the temple of God. Zechariah's "Sprout" will build the temple of the LORD (Zech. 6:12–13). Indeed, even in book 5 of the Psalter, the ideal Davidide leads Israel to praise the Divine King in the temple (132:1–10; 145:21).

The second-most-recurring characteristic of the ideal king is his role in *ensuring justice in society.* Within the Old Testament narratives, the quality of the king doing "justice and righteousness" occurs, although it is not all that prominent. In the book of Samuel, Israel requests a king who will "judge" them (1 Sam. 8:5) because Samuel's sons perverted "justice" (v. 3). The narrator describes David's rule by saying: "David ruled over all of Israel, and David was doing justice and righteousness for all of his people" (2 Sam. 8:15, authors' trans.). In the book of Kings, divine wisdom enables Solomon to execute justice and righteousness for Israel (1 Kings 3:28; 10:9), but this characteristic is of little importance in the construction of the royal ideal in the rest of Kings and Chronicles. Within the Latter Prophets, establishing justice is a chief characteristic of Davidic kingship. In Isaiah, the king's throne will be established "with justice and with righteousness" (9:7 [9:6 MT]); God's Spirit will endow the king with wisdom, so that "with righteousness he shall judge" (11:2–5); the king will seek justice as he judges and hastens righteousness (16:5). In Jeremiah, shepherds who align with God's heart will shepherd with the wisdom and knowledge that promote justice and righteousness (3:15 [cf. 9:23–24]; 23:1–4); the king will be a "righteous sprout" who reigns with wisdom, doing what is just and right (23:5; 33:15). In Ezekiel, God will shepherd his people through a Davidic shepherd to ensure they receive justice (34:16, 23). Micah (5:1 [4:14 MT]) depicts Judah's king as a judge. In Psalms, amid a prayer for a Davidic descendant whose rule will span from sea to sea, the lead request is that God will endow him with God's justice and righteousness to ensure the fair treatment of the afflicted (72:1–2).

In contrast to the dominance of the characteristics above, it is significant to observe that there are only a few instances where it is explicit that Israel's king will be victorious in battle. Although there may be others, Num. 24:17, 2 Sam. 8, and Ps. 2:9 are among the most definitive texts that envisage the ideal king bringing about military victory. More regularly in the prophets, it is God who brings about military victory, and hope as it relates to the Davidic king pertains to his rule in the aftermath of this salvation to establish justice within a kingdom established by God.

There are of course other characteristics of the Messiah that can only be listed here: emerging from decimation (Isa. 11:1; Jer. 23:5–6; 33:15–16); aligning with God's heart (1 Sam. 13:14; 16:7; Jer. 3:15); ruling with a scepter (Gen. 49:10; Num. 24:17; Ps. 2:9); extending blessing to the nations (Ps. 72:17; Isa. 11:10); being equipped by the Spirit of God (1 Sam. 16; Isa. 11:2–3); suffering (Ps. 22; Zech. 12:10); and more.

Thus, various characteristics appear in the portrayal of Davidic kingship. All these characteristics coordinate around the Divine King, who is the central image in the mosaic. The Davidic king lives in allegiance to God and aims to unite the people around the rule of God. The Davidic king receives wisdom from God to establish justice in God's kingdom. The Davidic king lives in obedience to the instruction of the great Suzerain. The Davidic king finds his rebirth in the creative power of God, which brings life out of what appears to be dead. In fact, the Old Testament is so theocentric in its outlook that the king even bears names that point to the very God who is at work through the agency of the king (Isa. 9:6–7 [9:5–6 MT]; Jer. 23:6).

Messianic Hope Then and Now

In this book, our primary question has been, What hopes does the Old Testament set forth pertaining to a future royal agent who will carry out God's kingdom purposes? We have answered this question primarily from the perspective of ancient Israel, *looking forward*. The ideals that the Old Testament teaches are not realized within the Old Testament, and, in fact, many of these ideals were expressed for audiences that did not see a Davidic king upon the throne during their lifetimes (exile, postexile). In this way, the Old Testament looks forward to a time when these royal messianic expectations will be realized. As we look from the Old Testament forward to Jesus, we wonder how these promises relate to God's revelation in Jesus Christ, the professed Messiah of the Christian faith. Discontinuities are readily apparent—the Old Testament typically looks for a renewal of a dynasty, not simply one individual; for a king who will bring about justice and righteousness in a geopolitical setting of Israel; for a king who will organize temple leadership.

It is at this point of observing discontinuities that a return to the metaphor of the abstract mosaic can prove helpful. Mosaics are meant to look different depending on lighting, time of day, and vantage point of the viewer. Similarly, *looking back* at these expressions of expectation through the light of Christ uncovers additional dimensions of meaning beyond what could be seen by only looking forward. As we have argued throughout, Christ's divinity creates a remarkable fusion between the Old Testament's witness to the Divine King and to his Davidic king. Additionally, Jesus certainly exudes the characteristics the Old Testament hopes for in its king: zeal for God's house and a concern for justice and righteousness. There is, then, accord between the Old Testament's messianic hopes and the coming of Jesus, even if a surplus of expectation remains.

Humility, though, demands that we acknowledge several limits as we conclude this volume. First, we have limited our scope to *royal* messianic expectations. In doing so, we have on occasion bumped up against *prophetic* and *priestly* expectations, such as Isaiah's suffering servant and anointed messenger, Zechariah's high priest, or Malachi's coming messenger. It would be a mistake to believe that only *royal* messianic expectations are important for understanding Jesus; in fact, these realms of expectation merge together throughout the New Testament. Second, humility calls for us to recognize our limits in knowing and explaining exactly how the Old Testament's *royal* messianic expectations meet their match in Jesus. Although we can have confidence that Jesus is King, we do not know precisely how God will fulfill the surplus of expectation remaining from the Old Testament throughout the church age and at Christ's second coming. Will Jesus fulfill his office as king in Israel when he comes again? Were the geopolitical promises types for a nonpolitical reign of the Davidic king in the church? Will King Jesus's implementation of justice against crimes within the church look different from his justice toward unbelievers? Many, many questions remain, yet the Old Testament's mosaic of royal messianic expectations invites us to see the Divine King at work establishing justice and orienting his people around his presence in Christ's first coming, through Christ's body today, and in anticipation of Christ's second coming. This mosaic is abstract, and, although its profusion of effects makes its sense graspable, it remains for the Master Artist to make clear over the course of history how the mosaic will be most fully expressed and realized when the Kingdom of God reaches its culmination.

Bibliography

Abadie, Philippe. "From the Impious Manasseh (2 Kings 21) to the Convert Manasseh (2 Chronicles 33): Theological Rewriting by the Chronicler." Pages 89–104 in *The Chronicler as Theologian: Essays in Honor of Ralph W. Klein*. Edited by M. Patrick Graham, Steven L. McKenzie, and Gary N. Knoppers. JSOTSup 371. London: T&T Clark, 2003.

Abernethy, Andrew T. *The Book of Isaiah and God's Kingdom: A Thematic-Theological Approach*. NSBT 40. Downers Grove, IL: IVP Academic, 2016.

———. "Theological Patterning in Jeremiah: A Vital Word through an Ancient Book." *BBR* 24 (2014): 149–61.

Ackroyd, Peter. "The Age of the Chronicler." Pages 1–86 in *The Chronicler in His Age*. JSOTSup 101. Sheffield: Sheffield Academic, 1991.

Adler, William. "The Apocalyptic Survey of History Adapted by Christians: Daniel's Prophecy of 70 Weeks." Pages 201–38 in *The Jewish Apocalyptic Heritage in Early Christianity*. Edited by James C. VanderKam and William Adler. Compendia Rerum Iudaicarum ad Novum Testamentum 3.4. Minneapolis: Fortress, 1996.

Agamben, Giorgio. *The Time That Remains: A Commentary on the Letter to the Romans*. Translated by Patricia Dailey. Stanford, CA: Stanford University Press, 2005.

Aichele, George. *The Control of Biblical Meaning: Canon as Semiotic Mechanism*. Harrisburg, PA: Trinity Press International, 2001.

Alexander, T. Desmond. "Further Observations on the Term 'Seed' in Genesis." *TynBul* 48 (1997): 363–67.

———. "Genealogies, Seed and the Compositional Unity of Genesis." *TynBul* 44 (1993): 255–70.

———. "Messianic Ideology in the Book of Genesis." Pages 19–39 in *The Lord's Anointed: Interpretation of Old Testament Messianic Texts*. Edited by P. E. Satterthwaite, Richard S. Hess, and Gordon J. Wenham. Carlisle, UK: Paternoster, 1995.

————. "The Regal Dimension of the תולדות־יעקב." Pages 196–212 in *Reading the Law: Studies in Honour of Gordon J. Wenham*. Edited by J. G. McConville and Karl Möller. LHBOTS 461. New York: Continuum, 2007.

————. "Royal Expectations in Genesis to Kings: Their Importance for Biblical Theology." *TynBul* 49 (1998): 191–212.

Allen, Leslie C. *The Books of Joel, Obadiah, Jonah and Micah*. NICOT. Grand Rapids: Eerdmans, 1976.

————. *Ezekiel 20–48*. WBC 29. Waco: Word, 1990.

————. *Jeremiah*. OTL. Louisville: Westminster John Knox, 2008.

Amit, Yairah. *The Book of Judges: The Art of Editing*. Translated by Jonathan Chipman. BIntS 38. Leiden: Brill, 1999.

————. *Hidden Polemics in Biblical Narrative*. Translated by Jonathan Chipman. BIntS 25. Leiden: Brill, 2000.

Andersen, Francis I. "Yahweh, the Kind and Sensitive God." Pages 41–88 in *God Who Is Rich in Mercy: Essays Presented to Dr. D. B. Knox*. Edited by Peter T. O'Brien and David G. Peterson. Homebush West, NSW: Lancer Books, 1986.

Andersen, Francis I., and David Noel Freedman. *Amos: A New Translation with Introduction and Commentary*. AB 24A. New York: Doubleday, 1989.

————. *Hosea: A New Translation with Introduction and Commentary*. AB 24. Garden City, NY: Doubleday, 1980.

————. *Micah: A New Translation with Introduction and Commentary*. AB 24E. New York: Doubleday, 2000.

Anderson, A. A. *2 Samuel*. WBC 11. Dallas: Word, 1989.

Anderson, B. W., with Steven Bishop. *Out of the Depths: The Psalms Speak for Us Today*. 3rd ed. Louisville: Westminster John Knox, 2000.

Angel, Hayyim. "The Eternal Davidic Covenant in II Samuel Chapter 7 and Its Later Manifestations in the Bible." *Jewish Biblical Quarterly* 44 (2016): 83–90.

Appold, Mark L. *The Oneness Motif in the Fourth Gospel: Motif Analysis and Exegetical Probe into the Theology of John*. WUNT 2/1. Tübingen: Mohr Siebeck, 1976.

Arnold, Bill T. *1 & 2 Samuel*. NIVAC. Grand Rapids: Zondervan, 2003.

Auld, A. Graeme. *I & II Samuel*. Rev. ed. OTL. Louisville: Westminster John Knox, 2011.

Baker, William R. "Christology in the Epistle of James." *EQ* 74 (2002): 47–58.

Baldwin, Joyce G. *Daniel: An Introduction and Commentary*. TOTC. Leicester, UK: Inter-Varsity, 1978.

————. *Haggai, Zechariah, Malachi: An Introduction and Commentary*. TOTC. Leicester, UK: Inter-Varsity, 1988.

————. "*Ṣemaḥ* as a Technical Term in the Prophets." *VT* 14 (1964): 93–97.

Barbiero, Gianni. "Psalm 132: A Prayer of 'Solomon.'" *CBQ* 75 (2013): 239–58.

Bar-Efrat, Shimon. "Some Observations on the Analysis of Structure in Biblical Narrative." *VT* 30 (1980): 154–73.

Barr, Colin. "The Failure of Newman's Catholic University of Ireland." *Archivum hibernicum* 55 (2001): 126–39.

Barré, Michael L. "The Meaning of *l' 'šybnw* in Amos 1:3–2:6." *JBL* 105 (1986): 611–31.

Bartlett, J. R. "The Use of the Word *rō'š* as a Title in the Old Testament." *VT* 19 (1969): 1–10.

Bauckham, Richard. "James and the Jerusalem Church." Pages 415–80 in *The Book of Acts in Its Palestinian Setting*. Edited by Richard Bauckham. Grand Rapids: Eerdmans, 1995.

———. *Jesus and the God of Israel: God Crucified, and Other Studies on the New Testament's Christology of Divine Identity*. Grand Rapids: Eerdmans, 2008.

———. "Messianism according to the Gospel of John." Pages 34–68 in *Challenging Perspectives on the Gospel of John*. Edited by John Lierman. WUNT 2/219. Tübingen: Mohr Siebeck, 2006.

———. "The Throne of God and the Worship of Jesus." Pages 43–69 in *The Jewish Roots of Christological Monotheism: Papers from the St. Andrews Conference on the Historical Origins of the Worship of Jesus*. Edited by Carey C. Newman, James R. Davila, and Gladys S. Lewis. JSJSup 63. Leiden: Brill, 1999.

Baumann, Gerlinde. *Love and Violence: Marriage as Metaphor for the Relationship between YHWH and Israel in the Prophetic Books*. Collegeville, MN: Liturgical Press, 2003.

Beale, G. K. *The Temple and the Church's Mission: A Biblical Theology of the Dwelling Place of God*. NSBT 17. Leicester, UK: Apollos, 2004.

———. *The Use of Daniel in Jewish Apocalyptic Literature and in the Revelation of St. John*. Lanham, MD: University Press of America, 1984.

Beasley-Murray, G. R. "The Interpretation of Daniel 7." *CBQ* 45 (1983): 44–58.

Beattie, D. R. G. *Jewish Exegesis of the Book of Ruth*. JSOTSup 2. Sheffield: JSOT Press, 1977.

———. *The Targum of Ruth*. Aramaic Targums 19. Edinburgh: T&T Clark, 1994.

Becker, Joachim. *Messianic Expectation in the Old Testament*. Translated by David E. Green. Philadelphia: Fortress, 1980.

Beckwith, Roger T. *Calendar and Chronology, Jewish and Christian: Biblical, Intertestamental and Patristic Studies*. AGJU 33. Leiden: Brill, 1996.

———. *The Old Testament Canon of the New Testament Church and Its Background in Early Judaism*. Grand Rapids: Eerdmans, 1985.

Beekman, John, John Callow, and Michael Kopesec. *The Semantic Structure of Written Communication*. 5th ed. Dallas: SIL, 1981.

Begg, Christopher. "Zedekiah and the Servant." *ETL* 62 (1986): 393–98.

Belcher, Richard, Jr. *The Messiah and the Psalms: Preaching Christ from all the Psalms*. Fearn, Scotland: Mentor, 2006.

Bennema, Cornelius. *Encountering Jesus: Character Studies in the Gospel of John*. Milton Keynes, UK: Paternoster, 2009.

Bentzen, Aage. *King and Messiah*. Edited by G. W. Anderson. 2nd ed. Oxford: Basil Blackwell, 1970.

Ben Zvi, Ehud. *Hosea*. FOTL 21A/1. Grand Rapids: Eerdmans, 2005.

———. *Micah*. FOTL 21B. Grand Rapids: Eerdmans, 2000.

———. "When the Foreign Monarch Speaks." Pages 209–28 in *The Chronicler as Author: Studies in Text and Texture*. Edited by M. Patrick Graham and Steven L. McKenzie. JSOTSup 263. Sheffield: Sheffield Academic, 1999.

Berger, Yitzhak. "Ruth and Inner-Biblical Allusion: The Case of 1 Samuel 25." *JBL* 128 (2009): 253–72.

Berlin, Adele. "Hannah and Her Prayers." *Scriptura* 87 (2004): 227–32.

———. *Poetics and Interpretation of Biblical Narrative*. BLS 9. Sheffield: Almond, 1983.

Bertman, Stephen. "Symmetrical Design in the Book of Ruth." *JBL* 84 (1965): 165–68.

Beuken, Willem A. M. *Isaiah, Part II, Volume 2: Isaiah Chapters 28–39*. HCOT. Leuven: Peeters, 2000.

———. "'Lebanon with Its Majesty Shall Fall. A Sprout Shall Come Forth from the Stump of Jesse' (Isa. 10:34–11:1): Interfacing the Story of Assyria and the Image of Israel's Future in Isaiah 10–11." Pages 17–33 in *The New Things: Eschatology in Old Testament Prophecy; Fss. for Henk Leene*. Edited by J. W. Dyk, P. J. Midden, K. Spronk, and G. J. Venema. Maastricht: Uitgeverij Shaker, 2002.

Beyse, Karl-Martin. *Serubbabel und die Königserwartungen der Propheten Haggai und Sacharja: Eine historische und traditionsgeschichtliche Untersuchung*. AzTh 1.48. Stuttgart: Calver, 1972.

Bieringer, Reimund. "'My Kingship Is Not of This World' (John 18:36): The Kingship of Jesus and Politics." Pages 159–75 in *The Myriad Christ: Plurality and the Quest for Unity in Contemporary Christology*. Edited by Terrence Merrigan and Jacques Haers. Leuven: Leuven University Press, 2000.

Biggs, Charles R. "The Role of the *Nasi* in the Programme for Restoration in Ezekiel 40–48." *Colloquium* 16 (1983): 46–57.

Birch, Bruce C. *Let Justice Roll Down: The Old Testament, Ethics, and Christian Life*. Louisville: Westminster John Knox, 1991.

Blenkinsopp, Joseph. *Isaiah 1–39: A New Translation with Commentary*. AB 19. New York: Doubleday, 2000.

Block, Daniel I. *The Book of Ezekiel: Chapters 25–48*. NICOT. Grand Rapids: Eerdmans, 1998.

———. "Bringing Back David: Ezekiel's Messianic Hope." Pages 167–88 in *The Lord's Anointed: Interpretation of Old Testament Messianic Texts*. Edited by P. E. Satterthwaite, Richard S. Hess, and Gordon J. Wenham. Carlisle, UK: Paternoster, 1995.

———. *Judges, Ruth*. NAC 6. Nashville: Broadman & Holman, 1999.

Blomberg, Craig L. "Elijah, Election, and the Use of Malachi in the New Testament." *Criswell Theological Review* 2 (1987): 99–117.

———. "Interpreting Old Testament Prophetic Literature in Matthew: Double Fulfillment." *TJ* 23 (2002): 17–33.

Boda, Mark J. *The Book of Zechariah*. NICOT. Grand Rapids: Eerdmans, 2016.

———. "Messengers of Hope in Haggai–Malachi." *JSOT* 32 (2007): 113–31.

Booij, T. "Psalm CX: 'Rule in the Midst of Your Foes.'" *VT* 41 (1991): 396–407.

Bracht, Katharina. "*Logos parainetikos*: Der Danielkommentar des Hippolyt." Pages 79–97 in *Die Geschichte der Daniel-Auslegung in Judentum, Christentum und Islam: Studie zur Kommentierung des Danielbuches in Literatur und Kunst*. Edited by Katharina Bracht and David S. du Toit. BZAW 371. Berlin: de Gruyter, 2007.

Braude, William G. *The Midrash on Psalms*. New Haven: Yale University Press, 1958.

Braun, Roddy L. *1 Chronicles*. WBC 14. Dallas: Word, 1986.

———. "Solomonic Apologetic in Chronicles." *JBL* 92 (1973): 503–16.

Brettler, Marc Zvi. *God Is King: Understanding an Israelite Metaphor*. JSOTSup 76. Sheffield: Sheffield Academic, 1989.

Briggs, Charles Augustus, and Emilie Grace Briggs. *The Book of Psalms*. 2 vols. ICC. Edinburgh: T&T Clark, 1906.

Bruce, F. F. *The Epistle to the Galatians: A Commentary on the Greek Text*. NIGTC. Grand Rapids: Eerdmans, 1982.

Brueggemann, Walter. *A Commentary on Jeremiah: Exile and Homecoming*. Grand Rapids: Eerdmans, 1998.

———. *1 & 2 Kings*. SHBC 8. Macon, GA: Smyth & Helwys, 2000.

———. "I Samuel 1: A Sense of a Beginning." *ZAW* 102 (1990): 33–48.

———. *Solomon: Israel's Ironic Icon of Human Achievement*. Studies on Personalities of the Old Testament. Columbia: University of South Carolina Press, 2005.

Bryant, David J. "Micah 4:14–5:14: An Exegesis." *ResQ* 21 (1978): 210–30.

Bush, Frederic William. *Esther*. WBC 9. Dallas: Word, 1996.

———. "Ruth 4:17: A Semantic Wordplay." Pages 3–14 in *"Go to the Land I Will Show You": Studies in Honor of Dwight W. Young*. Edited by Joseph E. Coleson and Victor H. Matthews. Winona Lake, IN: Eisenbrauns, 1996.

Byrne, Brendan. "Jesus as Messiah in the Gospel of Luke: Discerning a Pattern of Correction." *CBQ* 65 (2003): 80–95.

Campbell, Edward F., Jr. *Ruth: A New Translation with Introduction, Notes and Commentary*. AB 7. Garden City, NY: Doubleday, 1975.

Caquot, André. "Le Messianisme d'Ézéchiel." *Semitica* 14 (1964): 5–23.

———. "Osée et la Royauté." *RHPR* 41 (1961): 123–46.

Carrell, Peter R. *Jesus and the Angels: Angelology and the Christology of the Apocalypse of John*. SNTSMS 95. Cambridge: Cambridge University Press, 1997.

Carroll, Robert P. *From Chaos to Covenant: Prophecy in the Book of Jeremiah*. New York: Crossroad, 1981.

Carroll R., M. Daniel. "God and His People in the Nations' History: A Contextualised Reading of Amos 1–2." *TynBul* 47 (1996): 39–70.

Cassuto, Umberto. *A Commentary on the Book of Genesis, Part II: From Noah to Abraham*. Jerusalem: Magnes Press, 1964.

Chapman, Stephen B. *1 Samuel as Christian Scripture: A Theological Commentary*. Grand Rapids: Eerdmans, 2016.

Charlesworth, James H., ed. *The Old Testament Pseudepigrapha*. Vol. 1. AYBRL. New Haven: Yale University Press, 1983.

Childs, Brevard S. *Biblical Theology in Crisis*. Philadelphia: Westminster, 1970.

———. *Exodus*. OTL. London: SCM, 1974.

———. "Psalm 8 in the Context of the Christian Canon." *Int* 23 (1969): 20–31.

Christensen, Duane L. *Nahum: A New Translation with Introduction and Commentary*. AB 24F. New Haven: Yale University Press, 2009.

Chrysostom, John. *Homilies on Hannah, David and Saul*. Translated by Robert Charles Hill. Vol. 1 of *Old Testament Homilies*. Brookline, MA: Holy Cross Orthodox, 2003.

Clements, Ronald E. "The Immanuel Prophecy of Isa. 7:10–17 and Its Messianic Interpretation." Pages 225–40 in *Die Hebräische Bibel und ihre zweifache Nachgeschichte: Festschrift für Rolf Rendtorff zum 65. Geburtstag*. Edited by Christian Macholz and Ekkehard Stegemann. Neukirchen-Vluyn: Neukirchener Verlag, 1990.

Cogan, Mordechai. *I Kings*. AB 10. New Haven: Yale University Press, 2001.

Cogan, Mordechai, and Hayim Tadmor. *II Kings*. AB 11. Garden City, NY: Doubleday, 1988.

Cohen, Mordechai. "*Ḥesed*: Divine or Human? The Syntactic Ambiguity of Ruth 2:20." Pages 11–38 in *Hazon Nahum: Studies in Jewish Law, Thought, and History Presented to Dr. Norman Lamm on the Occasion of His Seventieth Birthday*. Edited by Yaakov Elman and Jeffrey S. Gurock. Hoboken, NJ: Ktav, 1997.

Cole, R. Dennis. *Numbers*. NAC 3B. Nashville: Broadman & Holman, 2000.

Collins, C. John. *Genesis 1–4: A Linguistic, Literary, and Theological Commentary*. Phillipsburg, NJ: P&R, 2006.

———. "A Syntactical Note (Genesis 3:15): Is the Woman's Seed Singular or Plural?" *TynBul* 48 (1997): 139–48.

Collins, John J. *Daniel: A Commentary on the Book of Daniel*. Hermeneia. Minneapolis: Fortress, 1993.

———. *The Scepter and the Star: Messianism in Light of the Dead Sea Scrolls*. 2nd ed. Grand Rapids: Eerdmans, 2010.

Collins, Terence. "The Literary Contexts of Zechariah 9:9." Pages 29–40 in *The Book of Zechariah and Its Influence*. Edited by Christopher Tuckett. Aldershot, UK: Ashgate, 2003.

———. *The Mantle of Elijah: The Redaction Criticism of the Prophetical Books*. Biblical Seminar 20. Sheffield: JSOT Press, 1993.

Cook, Joan E. *Hannah's Desire, God's Design: Early Interpretations of the Story of Hannah*. JSOTSup 282. Sheffield: Sheffield Academic, 1999.

Cook, Stephen L. "The Metamorphosis of a Shepherd: The Tradition History of Zechariah 11:17 + 13:7–9." *CBQ* 55 (1993): 453–66.

Coote, Robert B. *Amos among the Prophets: Composition and Theology*. Philadelphia: Fortress, 1981.

Craigie, Peter C., Page H. Kelley, and Joel F. Drinkard Jr. *Jeremiah 1–25*. WBC 26. Dallas: Word, 1991.

Crane, Ashley S. *Israel's Restoration: A Textual-Comparative Exploration of Ezekiel 36–39*. VTSup 122. Leiden: Brill, 2008.

Creach, Jerome F. D. *Yahweh as Refuge and the Editing of the Hebrew Psalter*. JSOTSup 217. Sheffield: Sheffield Academic, 1996.

Cross, F. M. "Kinship and Covenant in Ancient Israel." Pages 3–21 in *From Epic to Canon: History and Literature in Ancient Israel*. Baltimore: Johns Hopkins University Press, 1998.

———. "The Priestly Tabernacle in the Light of Recent Research." Pages 169–80 in *Temples and High Places in Biblical Times*. Edited by A. Biran. Jerusalem: Keter, 1981.

Dahl, Nils A. "The Messiahship of Jesus in Paul." Pages 15–25 in *Jesus the Christ: The Historical Origins of Christological Doctrine*. Edited by Donald H. Juel. Minneapolis: Fortress, 1991.

Daly-Denton, Margaret. "David the Psalmist, Inspired Prophet: Jewish Antecedents of a New Testament *Datum*." *ABR* 52 (2004): 32–47.

Daniels, Dwight R. *Hosea and Salvation History: The Early Traditions of Israel in the Prophecy of Hosea*. BZAW 191. Berlin: de Gruyter, 1990.

Davies, G. Henton. "Amos—The Prophet of Re-Union." *ExpTim* 92 (1981): 196–200.

Davies, G. I. *Hosea*. NCB. Grand Rapids: Eerdmans, 1992.

Davies, W. D., and Dale C. Allison Jr. *The Gospel according to Saint Matthew*. Vol. 1. ICC. Edinburgh: T&T Clark, 1988.

Davis, Barry C. "Is Psalm 110 a Messianic Psalm?" *BSac* 157 (2000): 160–73.

Dearman, J. Andrew. *The Book of Hosea*. NICOT. Grand Rapids: Eerdmans, 2010.

deClaissé-Walford, Nancy L. *Reading from the Beginning: The Shaping of the Hebrew Psalter*. Macon, GA: Mercer University Press, 1997.

de Jonge, M. "The Earliest Christian Use of *Christos*: Some Suggestions." *NTS* 32 (1986): 321–43.

Dekker, John T., and Anthony H. Dekker. "Centrality in the Book of Ruth." *VT* 68 (2018): 41–50.

deSilva, David A. *Perseverance in Gratitude: A Socio-Rhetorical Commentary on the Epistle to the Hebrews*. Grand Rapids: Eerdmans, 2000.

Dillard, Raymond. *2 Chronicles*. WBC 15. Grand Rapids: Zondervan Academic, 2015.

Donaldson, Laura E. "The Sign of Orpah: Reading Ruth through Native Eyes." Pages 130–44 in *Ruth and Esther: A Feminist Companion to the Bible*. Edited by Athalya Brenner. 2nd series. Sheffield: Sheffield Academic, 1999.

Doukhan, Jacques. *Le soupir de la terre: Étude prophétique du livre de Daniel*. Dammarie-les-Lys Cedex: Editions Vie et Santé, 1993.

Driver, S. R. *Notes on the Hebrew Text and the Topography of the Books of Samuel*. Oxford: Clarendon, 1913.

Duguid, Iain M. *Ezekiel and the Leaders of Israel*. VTSup 56. Leiden: Brill, 1994.

Duke, Rodney. "A Rhetorical Approach to Appreciating the Books of Chronicles." Pages 100–135 in *The Chronicler as Author: Studies in Text and Texture*. Edited by M. Patrick Graham and Steven L. McKenzie. JSOTSup 263. Sheffield: Sheffield Academic, 1999.

Dumbrell, William J. "The Content and Significance of the Books of Samuel: Their Place and Purpose within the Former Prophets." *JETS* 33 (1990): 49–62.

———. *The Faith of Israel: A Theological Survey of the Old Testament*. 2nd ed. Leicester, UK: Apollos, 2002.

———. "'In Those Days There Was No King in Israel; Every Man Did What Was Right in His Own Eyes': The Purpose of the Book of Judges Reconsidered." *JSOT* 25 (1983): 23–33.

Dyck, Jonathan E. *The Theocratic Ideology of the Chronicler*. BIntS 33. Leiden: Brill, 1998.

Eaton, J. H. *Kingship and the Psalms*. SBT 2/32. London: SPCK, 1976.

Elledge, Roderick. *Use of the Third Person for Self-Reference by Jesus and Yahweh: A Study of Illeism in the Bible and Ancient Near Eastern Texts and Its Implications for Christology*. LNTS 575. London: Bloomsbury T&T Clark, 2017.

Elliott, John Hall. *The Elect and the Holy: An Exegetical Examination of 1 Peter 2:4–10 and the Phrase* Basileion Hierateuma. NovTSup 12. Leiden: Brill, 1966.

Ellis, E. Earle. "The Old Testament Canon in the Early Church." Pages 653–90 in *Mikra: Text, Translation, Reading and Interpretation of the Hebrew Bible in Ancient Judaism and Early Christianity*. Edited by Martin Jan Mulder. Peabody, MA: Hendrickson, 2004.

Emmerson, Grace I. *Hosea: An Israelite Prophet in Judean Perspective.* JSOTSup 28. Sheffield: Sheffield Academic, 1987.

Endres, John C., William R. Millar, and John Barclay Burns, eds. *Chronicles and Its Synoptic Parallels in Samuel, Kings, and Related Biblical Texts.* Collegeville, MN: Liturgical Press, 1998.

Eskenazi, Tamara Cohn, and Tikva Frymer-Kensky. *Ruth.* JPS Bible Commentary. Philadelphia: JPS, 2001.

Eslinger, Lyle M. *House of God or House of David: The Rhetoric of 2 Samuel 7.* JSOTSup 164. Sheffield: Sheffield Academic, 1994.

———. *Kingship of God in Crisis: A Close Reading of 1 Samuel 1–12.* BLS 10. Sheffield: Almond, 1985.

———. "Viewpoints and Point of View in 1 Samuel 8–12." *JSOT* 26 (1983): 61–76.

Evans, Craig A. "Praise and Prophecy in the Psalter and the New Testament." Pages 551–79 in *The Book of Psalms: Composition and Reception.* Edited by Peter W. Flint and Patrick D. Miller Jr. VTSup 99. Leiden: Brill, 2005.

Fay, Ron C. "The Narrative Function of the Temple in Luke-Acts." *TJ* 27 (2006): 255–70.

Feeley-Harnik, Gillian. "Naomi and Ruth: Building Up the House of David." Pages 163–84 in *Text and Tradition: The Hebrew Bible and Folklore.* Edited by Susan Niditch. Atlanta: Scholars Press, 1990.

Fewell, Danna Nolan. *Circle of Sovereignty: A Story of Stories in Daniel 1–6.* JSOTSup 20. Sheffield: Sheffield Academic, 1988.

Firth, David G. *1 & 2 Samuel.* ApOTC 8. London: Apollos, 2009.

Fitzmyer, Joseph A. *The Gospel according to Luke (X–XXIV): Introduction, Translation, and Notes.* AB 28A. Garden City, NY: Doubleday, 1985.

———. *The One Who Is to Come.* Grand Rapids: Eerdmans, 2007.

Floyd, Michael H. *Minor Prophets, Part 2.* FOTL 22. Grand Rapids: Eerdmans, 2000.

Fossum, Jarl E. *The Name of God and the Angel of the Lord: Samaritan and Jewish Concepts of Intermediation and the Origin of Gnosticism.* WUNT 36. Tübingen: Mohr Siebeck, 1985.

France, R. T. *The Gospel of Matthew.* NICNT. Grand Rapids: Eerdmans, 2007.

Freedman, David Noel. "But Did King David Invent Musical Instruments?" *Bible Review* 1 (1985): 49–51.

Fretheim, Terence E. "Psalm 132: A Form-Critical Study." *JBL* 86 (1967): 289–300.

Gale, Warren Austin. "Ruth upon the Threshing Floor and the Sin of Gibeah: A Biblical-Theological Study." *WTJ* 51 (1989): 369–75.

Gallusz, Laszlo. *The Throne Motif in the Book of Revelation.* LNTS 487. London: Bloomsbury T&T Clark, 2014.

Garlington, Don. *Faith, Obedience, and Perseverance: Aspects of Paul's Letter to the Romans.* WUNT 2/79. Tübingen: Mohr Siebeck, 1994.

Garsiel, Moshe. *Biblical Names: A Literary Study of Midrashic Derivations and Puns.* Revised edition. Ramat Gan: Bar-Ilan University Press, 1991.

Geiger, Abraham. *Urschrift und Übersetzungen der Bibel in ihrer Abhängigkeit von der innern Entwickelung des Judenthums.* Breslau: Julius Hainauer, 1857.

Gelston, Anthony. "Kingship in the Book of Hosea." Pages 71–85 in *Language and Meaning: Studies in Hebrew Language and Biblical Exegesis; Papers Read at the Joint British-Dutch Old Testament Conference held at London, 1973.* Edited by A. S. van der Woude. OTS 19. Leiden: Brill, 1974.

———. *The Twelve Minor Prophets.* Vol. 13 of *BHQ.*

Gerstenberger, E. S. *Psalms, Part 2, and Lamentations.* FOTL 15. Grand Rapids: Eerdmans, 2001.

Gibson, J. C. L. *Davidson's Introductory Hebrew Grammar: Syntax.* 4th ed. Edinburgh: T&T Clark, 1994.

Gieschen, Charles A. *Angelomorphic Christology: Antecedents and Early Evidence.* AGJU 42. Leiden: Brill, 1998.

Gillingham, Susan E. "The Messiah in the Psalms: A Question of Reception History and the Psalter." Pages 209–37 in *King and Messiah in Israel and the Ancient Near East: Proceedings of the Oxford Old Testament Seminar.* Edited by John Day. JSOTSup 270. Sheffield: Sheffield Academic, 1998.

Ginsburg, C. D. *Introduction to the Massoretico-Critical Edition of the Hebrew Bible.* New York: Ktav, 1966. First published in 1897 by Trinitarian Bible Society (London).

Gisin, Walter. *Hosea: Ein literarisches Netzwerk beweist seine Authentizität.* BBB 139. Berlin: Philo, 2002.

Glazier-McDonald, Beth. "*Mal'ak habberit*: The Messenger of the Covenant in Mal 3:1." *HAR* 11 (1987): 93–104.

Glenny, W. Edward. *Finding Meaning in the Text: Translation Technique and Theology in the Septuagint of Amos.* VTSup 126. Leiden: Brill, 2009.

Glück, J. J. "Nagid-Shepherd." *VT* 13 (1963): 144–50.

Glueck, Nelson. *Ḥesed in the Bible.* Translated by Alfred Gottschalk. Cincinnati: Hebrew Union College Press, 1967.

Golding, William. *Lord of the Flies.* New York: Riverhead, 1954.

Goldingay, John. "The Compound Name in Isaiah 9:5(6)." *CBQ* 61 (1999): 239–44.

———. *Isaiah.* NIBC. Peabody, MA: Hendrickson, 2001.

Gordon, Robert P. *I & II Samuel: A Commentary.* Library of Biblical Interpretation. Grand Rapids: Zondervan, 1999.

Görg, M. "*yāšab.*" *TDOT* 6:420–38.

Gosse, Bernard. "La nouvelle alliance et les promesses d'avenir se référant à David dans les libres de Jérémie, Ezéchiel, et Isaie." *VT* 41 (1991): 419–28.

———. "Le salut et le messie en 1 Sam. 2,1–10, et Yahvé juge, à l'œuvre sur la terre et dans l'histoire, dans la tradition des cantiques et du Psautier." *BN* 111 (2002): 18–22.

Goswell, Gregory. "The Absence of a Davidic Hope in Ezra-Nehemiah." *TJ* 33 (2012): 19–31.

———. "The Attitude to the Persians in Ezra—Nehemiah." *TJ* 32 (2011): 191–203.

———. "The Book of Ruth and the House of David." *EQ* 86 (2014): 116–29.

———. "David in the Prophecy of Amos." *VT* 61 (2011): 243–57.

———. "'David Their King': Kingship in the Prophecy of Hosea." *JSOT* 42 (2017): 213–31.

———. "Davidic Rule in the Prophecy of Micah." *JSOT* 44 (2019): 153–65.

———. "The Eschatology of Malachi after Zechariah 14." *JBL* 132 (2013): 625–38.

———. "Farewell to Davidic Kingship: The Meaning and Significance of Isaiah 39." *ResQ* 61 (2019): 87–106.

———. "The Fate and Future of Zerubbabel in the Prophecy of Haggai." *Bib* 91 (2010): 77–90.

———. "Isaiah 1:26: A Neglected Text on Kingship." *TynBul* 62 (2011): 233–46.

———. "Isaiah 16: A Forgotten Chapter in the History of Messianism." *SJOT* 28 (2014): 91–103.

———. "Is Ruth Also among the Wise?" Pages 115–33 in *Exploring Old Testament Wisdom: Literature and Themes*. Edited by David G. Firth and Lindsay Wilson. London: Apollos, 2016.

———. "Joshua and Kingship." *BBR* 23 (2013): 29–42.

———. "King and Cultus: The Image of David in the Book of Kings." *JESOT* 5 (2016–17): 167–86.

———. "Messianic Expectation in Isaiah 11." *WTJ* 79 (2017): 123–35.

———. "The Non-Messianic Psalter of Gerald H. Wilson." *VT* 66 (2016): 524–41.

———. "The Prince Forecast by Ezekiel and Its Relation to Other Old Testament Messianic Portraits." *BN* 178 (2018): 53–73.

———. "Royal Names: Naming and Wordplay in Isaiah 7." *WTJ* 75 (2013): 97–105.

———. "The Shape of Kingship in Deut. 17: A Messianic Pentateuch?" *TJ* 38 (2017): 169–81.

———. "The Shape of Messianism in Isaiah 9." *WTJ* 77 (2015): 101–10.

———. "A Theocratic Reading of Zechariah 9:9." *BBR* 26 (2016): 7–19.

———. "What Makes the Arrangement of God with David in 2 Samuel 7 a Covenant?" *ResQ* 60 (2018): 87–97.

———. "Where Is David in the Book of Daniel?" *ResQ* 56 (2014): 209–21.

Gow, Murray D. *The Book of Ruth: Its Structure, Theme and Purpose*. Leicester, UK: Apollos, 1992.

Granowski, Jan Jaynes. "Jehoiachin at the King's Table: A Reading of the Ending of the Second Book of Kings." Pages 173–88 in *Reading between Texts: Intertextuality and the Hebrew Bible*. Edited by Danna Nolan Fewell. Philadelphia: Westminster John Knox, 1992.

Grant, Jamie A. *The King as Exemplar: The Function of Deuteronomy's Kingship Law in the Shaping of the Book of Psalms*. AcBib 17. Atlanta: Society of Biblical Literature, 2004.

Gray, John. *I and II Kings: A Commentary*. 2nd ed. OTL. Philadelphia: Westminster John Knox, 1964.

Grogan, Geoffrey W. *Psalms*. THOTC. Grand Rapids: Eerdmans, 2008.

Gross, H. "*māšal* II." *TDOT* 9:68–71.

Gross, Walter. "Israel's Hope for the Renewal of the State." *JNSL* 14 (1988): 101–33.

Groves, Joseph W. *Actualization and Interpretation in the Old Testament*. SBLDS 86. Atlanta: Scholars Press, 1987.

Guthrie, George H. "Hebrews." Pages 919–95 in *CNTUOT*.

Hagstrom, David Gerald. *The Coherence of the Book of Micah: A Literary Analysis*. SBLDS 89. Atlanta: Scholars Press, 1988.

Hals, Ronald M. *The Theology of the Book of Ruth*. FBBS 23. Philadelphia: Fortress, 1969.

Hamilton, James. "'The Virgin Will Conceive': Typological Fulfillment in Matthew 1:18–23." Pages 228–47 in *Built upon the Rock: Studies in the Gospel of Matthew*. Edited by Daniel Gurtner and John Nolland. Grand Rapids: Eerdmans, 2008.

Hamilton, Victor P. *The Book of Genesis: Chapters 18–50*. NICOT. Grand Rapids: Eerdmans, 1995.

Hannah, Darrell D. "The Throne of His Glory: The Divine Throne and Heavenly Mediators in Revelation and the Similitudes of Enoch." *ZNW* 94 (2003): 68–96.

Hanson, Paul D. *The Dawn of Apocalyptic: The Historical and Sociological Roots of Jewish Apocalyptic Eschatology*. Rev. ed. Philadelphia: Fortress, 1979.

Harris, Sarah. *The Davidic Shepherd King in the Lukan Narrative*. LNTS 558. London: Bloomsbury T&T Clark, 2016.

Hauser, Alan Jon. "Genesis 2–3: The Theme of Intimacy and Alienation." Pages 383–98 in *I Studied Inscriptions from before the Flood: Ancient Near Eastern, Literary, and Linguistic Approaches to Genesis 1–11*. Edited by Richard S. Hess and David Toshio Tsumura. Winona Lake, IN: Eisenbrauns, 1994.

Hay, David M. *Glory at the Right Hand: Psalm 110 in Early Christianity*. SBLMS 18. Nashville: Abingdon, 1973.

Haydon, Ron. *"Seventy Sevens Are Decreed": A Canonical Approach to Daniel 9:24–27*. JTISup 15. Winona Lake, IN: Eisenbrauns, 2016.

Hayward, Robert, trans. *The Targum of Jeremiah*. ArBib 12. Collegeville, MN: Liturgical Press, 1987.

Head, Peter M. "A Text-Critical Study of Mark 1:1: 'The Beginning of the Gospel of Jesus Christ.'" *NTS* 37 (1991): 621–29.

Heil, John Paul. "Ezekiel 34 and the Narrative Strategy of the Shepherd and Sheep Metaphor in Matthew." *CBQ* 55 (1993): 698–708.

Hengel, Martin. "Jesus, the Messiah of Israel: The Debate about the 'Messianic Mission' of Jesus." Pages 217–40 in *Crisis in Christology: Essays in Quest of Resolution*. Edited by William R. Farmer. Livonia, MI: Dove, 1995.

Henrichs-Tarasenkova, Nina. *Luke's Christology of Divine Identity*. LNTS 542. London: Bloomsbury T&T Clark, 2016.

Heskett, Randall. *Messianism within the Scriptural Scrolls of Isaiah*. LHBOTS 456. London: T&T Clark, 2007.

Hieke, Thomas. "The Reception of Daniel 7 in the Revelation of John." Pages 47–67 in *Revelation and the Politics of Apocalyptic Interpretation*. Edited by Richard B. Hays and Stefan Alkier. Waco: Baylor University Press, 2012.

Hill, Andrew. *1 & 2 Chronicles*. NIVAC. Grand Rapids: Zondervan, 2003.

Holladay, William L. *Isaiah: Scroll of a Prophetic Heritage*. Grand Rapids: Eerdmans, 1978.

———. *Jeremiah 1: A Commentary on the Book of the Prophet Jeremiah, Chapters 1–25*. Hermeneia. Philadelphia: Fortress, 1986.

House, Paul R. *The Unity of the Twelve*. JSOTSup 97. Sheffield: Almond, 1990.

Hubbard, Robert L., Jr. *The Book of Ruth*. NICOT. Grand Rapids: Eerdmans, 1988.

Hurst, L. D. *The Epistle to the Hebrews: Its Background of Thought*. SNTSMS 65. Cambridge: Cambridge University Press, 1990.

Irwin, Brian P. "Not Just Any King: Abimelech, the Northern Monarchy, and the Final Form of Judges." *JBL* 131 (2012): 443–54.

Jacobs, Mignon R. *The Conceptual Coherence of the Book of Micah*. JSOTSup 322. Sheffield: Sheffield Academic, 2001.

Japhet, Sara. *I and II Chronicles*. OTL. Louisville: Westminster John Knox, 1993.

Jensen, Matthew D. *Affirming the Resurrection of the Incarnate Christ: A Reading of 1 John*. SNTSMS 153. Cambridge: Cambridge University Press, 2012.

———. "John Is No Exception: Identifying the Subject of *eimi* and Its Implications." *JBL* 135 (2016): 341–53.

Jenson, Philip Peter. *Obadiah, Jonah, Micah: A Theological Commentary*. LHBOTS 496. New York: T&T Clark International, 2008.

Jeremias, Jörg. *Hosea und Amos: Studien zu den Anfängen des Dodekapropheton*. FAT 13. Tübingen: Mohr Siebeck, 1996.

———. *Das Königtum Gottes in den Psalmen: Israels Begegnung mit dem kanaanäischen Mythos in den Jahwe-König-Psalmen*. FRLANT 141. Göttingen: Vandenhoeck & Ruprecht, 1987.

———. *Kultprophetie und Gerichtsverkündigung in der späten Königszeit Israels.* WMANT 35. Neukirchen-Vluyn: Neukirchener Verlag, 1970.

Johnstone, William. *1 Chronicles 1–2 Chronicles 9: Israel's Place among the Nations.* Vol. 1 of *1 and 2 Chronicles.* JSOTSup 253. Sheffield: Sheffield Academic, 1997.

Joseph, Alison L. *Portrait of the Kings: The Davidic Prototype in Deuteronomistic Poetics.* Minneapolis: Fortress, 2015.

Joüon, Paul, and T. Muraoka. *A Grammar of Biblical Hebrew.* Rev. English ed. SubBi 27. Rome: Pontifical Biblical Institute, 2006.

Joyce, Paul M. "King and Messiah in Ezekiel." Pages 323–37 in *King and Messiah in Israel and the Ancient Near East: Proceedings of the Oxford Old Testament Seminar.* Edited by John Day. JSOTSup 270. Sheffield: Sheffield Academic, 1998.

Juel, Donald. *Messianic Exegesis: Christological Interpretation of the Old Testament in Early Christianity.* Philadelphia: Fortress, 1988.

Kaiser, Walter C., Jr. *The Messiah in the Old Testament.* Studies in Old Testament Biblical Theology. Grand Rapids: Zondervan, 1995.

Kasari, Petri. *Nathan's Promise in 2 Samuel 7 and Related Texts.* Publications of the Finnish Exegetical Society 97. Helsinki: Finnish Exegetical Society, University of Helsinki, 2009.

Keil, C. F. *The Minor Prophets.* Translated by J. Martin. Vol. 10 of *Commentary on the Old Testament.* 1869. Reprint, Grand Rapids: Eerdmans, 1980.

Kelle, Brad E. *Hosea 2: Metaphor and Rhetoric in Historical Perspective.* AcBib 20. Atlanta: Society of Biblical Literature, 2005.

Kennedy, James. "Yahweh's Strongman? The Characterization of Hezekiah in the Book of Isaiah." *PRSt* 31 (2004): 383–97.

Kessler, Martin. "The Scaffolding of the Book of Jeremiah." Pages 57–66 in *Reading the Book of Jeremiah: A Search for Coherence.* Edited by Martin Kessler. Winona Lake, IN: Eisenbrauns, 2004.

Kimball, Charles A., III. "Jesus' Exposition of Scripture in Luke 20:9–19: An Inquiry in Light of Jewish Hermeneutics." *BBR* 3 (1993): 77–92.

Kirkpatrick, Shane. *Competing for Honor: A Social-Scientific Reading of Daniel 1–6.* BIntS 74. Leiden: Brill, 2005.

Klein, Ralph W. *1 Chronicles.* Hermeneia. Minneapolis: Fortress, 2006.

Knierim, Rolf P. "Messianic Concept in the First Book of Samuel." Pages 20–51 in *Jesus and the Historian: Written in Honor of Ernest Cadman Colwell.* Edited by F. Thomas Trotter. Philadelphia: Westminster, 1968.

Knoppers, Gary N. "Shem, Ham and Japheth: The Universal and the Particular in the Genealogy of Nations." Pages 13–31 in *The Chronicler as Theologian: Essays in Honor of Ralph W. Klein.* Edited by M. Patrick Graham, Steven L. McKenzie, and Gary N. Knoppers. JSOTSup 371. London: T&T Clark, 2003.

Knowles, Louis E. "The Interpretation of the Seventy Weeks of Daniel in the Early Fathers." *WTJ* 7 (1944): 136–60.

Koch, Klaus. "*'ōhel*." *TDOT* 1:118–30.

Koester, Craig R. *The Dwelling of God: The Tabernacle in the Old Testament, Intertestamental Jewish Literature, and the New Testament*. CBQMS 22. Washington, DC: Catholic Biblical Association of America, 1989.

Konkel, Michael. *Architektonik des Heiligen: Studien zur zweiten Tempelvision Ezechiels (Ez 40–48)*. BBB 129. Berlin: Philo, 2001.

Korpel, Margo C. A. *The Structure of the Book of Ruth*. Pericope 2. Assen: Van Gorcum, 2001.

Köstenberger, Andreas J. "John." Pages 415–512 in *CNTUOT*.

Köstenberger, Andreas J., and Peter T. O'Brien. *Salvation to the Ends of the Earth: A Biblical Theology of Mission*. Downers Grove, IL: IVP Academic, 2001.

Laato, Antti. *Who Is Immanuel? The Rise and the Foundering of Isaiah's Messianic Expectations*. Åbo: Åbo Academy Press, 1988.

Lacocque, André. "Allusions to Creation in Daniel 7." Pages 114–31 in *The Book of Daniel: Composition and Reception*. Edited by John J. Collins and Peter W. Flint. VTSup 83.1. Leiden: Brill, 2001.

———. *Daniel in His Time*. Columbia: University of South Carolina Press, 1988.

———. *Ruth: A Continental Commentary*. Translated by K. C. Hanson. CC. Minneapolis: Fortress, 2004.

LaMarche, Paul. *Zacharie IX—XIV: Structure littéraire et messianisme*. Paris: Gabalda, 1961.

Laniak, Timothy. *Shepherds after My Own Heart: Pastoral Traditions and Leadership in the Bible*. NSBT 15. Downers Grove, IL: IVP Academic, 2006.

Lau, Peter H. W. *Identity and Ethics in the Book of Ruth: A Social Identity Approach*. BZAW 416. Berlin: de Gruyter, 2011.

Lau, Peter H. W., and Gregory Goswell. *Unceasing Kindness: A Biblical Theology of Ruth*. NSBT 41. London: Apollos, 2016.

Laubscher, Frans du T. "The King's Humbleness in Zechariah 9:9: A Paradox?" *JNSL* 18 (1992): 125–34.

Leclerc, Thomas L. *Yahweh Is Exalted in Justice: Solidarity and Conflict in Isaiah*. Minneapolis: Fortress, 2001.

Lee, Dorothy A. "Paschal Imagery in the Gospel of John: A Narrative and Symbolic Reading." *Pacifica* 24 (2011): 13–28.

Leske, Adrian M. "Context and Meaning of Zechariah 9:9." *CBQ* 62 (2000): 663–78.

Leung, Mavis M. *The Kingship-Cross Interplay in the Gospel of John: Jesus' Death as Corroboration of His Royal Messiahship*. Eugene, OR: Wipf & Stock, 2011.

Levenson, Jon D. "The Last Four Verses in Kings." *JBL* 103 (1984): 353–61.

————. *Theology of the Program of Restoration of Ezekiel 40–48*. HSM 10. Missoula, MT: Scholars Press, 1976.

Levine, Baruch A. *Numbers 21–36*. AB 4B. New York: Doubleday, 2000.

Levinson, Bernard M. "The Reconceptualization of Kingship in Deuteronomy and the Deuteronomistic History's Transformation of Torah." *VT* 51 (2001): 511–34.

Lindars, Barnabas. *Jesus Son of Man: A Fresh Examination of the Son of Man Sayings in the Gospels in the Light of Recent Research*. London: SPCK, 1983.

Linville, James R. *Amos and the Cosmic Imagination*. SOTSMS. Aldershot, UK: Ashgate, 2008.

————. "Visions and Voices: Amos 7–9." *Bib* 80 (1999): 22–42.

————. "What Does 'It' Mean? Interpretation at the Point of No Return in Amos 1–2." *BibInt* 8 (2000): 400–424.

Long, Burke O. *1 Kings*. FOTL 9. Grand Rapids: Eerdmans, 1984.

Longman, Tremper, III. *Jeremiah, Lamentations*. NIBC. Peabody, MA: Hendrickson, 2008.

————. *Song of Songs*. NICOT. Grand Rapids: Eerdmans, 2001.

Lovell, Nathan. "The Shape of Hope in the Book of Kings: The Resolution of Davidic Blessing and Mosaic Curse." *JESOT* 3 (2014): 3–27.

Luker, Lamontte M. "Beyond Form Criticism: The Relation of Doom and Hope in Micah 2–6." *HAR* 11 (1987): 285–301.

Lynch, Matthew. *Monotheism and Institutions in the Book of Chronicles: Temple, Priesthood, and Kingship in Post-Exilic Perspective*. FAT 64. Tübingen: Mohr Siebeck, 2014.

Machinist, Peter. "Hosea and the Ambiguity of Kingship in Ancient Israel." Pages 153–81 in *Constituting the Community: Studies on the Polity of Ancient Israel in Honor of S. Dean McBride Jr.* Edited by John T. Strong and Steven S. Tuell. Winona Lake, IN: Eisenbrauns, 2005.

Macintosh, A. A. *Hosea*. ICC. Edinburgh: T&T Clark, 1997.

Malone, Andrew S. "Is the Messiah Announced in Malachi 3:1?" *TynBul* 57 (2006): 215–28.

Marlow, Hilary. "The Spirit of Yahweh in Isaiah 11:1–9." Pages 220–32 in *Presence, Power and Promise: The Role of the Spirit of God in the Old Testament*. Edited by David Firth and Paul Wegner. Downers Grove, IL: IVP Academic, 2011.

Marshall, I. Howard. *Luke: Historian and Theologian*. Exeter, UK: Paternoster, 1970.

Martens, Elmer A. *Jeremiah*. Scottdale, PA: Herald, 1986.

Mathews, Danny. *Royal Motifs in the Pentateuchal Portrayal of Moses*. LHBOTS 571. New York: T&T Clark International, 2012.

Mathews, Kenneth A. *Genesis 1–11:26*. NAC 1A. Nashville: Broadman & Holman, 1996.

Matthews, Victor H. *Judges and Ruth*. New Cambridge Bible Commentary. Cambridge: Cambridge University Press, 2004.

Mays, James L. *Micah: A Commentary*. OTL. London: SCM, 1976.

McCarter, P. Kyle, Jr. *I Samuel: A New Translation with Introduction, Notes and Commentary*. AB 8. Garden City, NY: Doubleday, 1980.

———. *II Samuel: A New Translation with Introduction, Notes and Commentary*. AB 9. Garden City, NY: Doubleday, 1984.

McComiskey, Thomas E. "The Seventy 'Weeks' of Daniel against the Background of Ancient Near Eastern Literature." *WTJ* 47 (1985): 18–45.

McConville, J. G. *Deuteronomy*. ApOTC. Downers Grove, IL: InterVarsity, 2002.

———. *Judgment and Promise: An Interpretation of the Book of Jeremiah*. Leicester, UK: Apollos, 1993.

———. "King and Messiah in Deuteronomy and the Deuteronomistic History." Pages 271–95 in *King and Messiah in Israel and the Ancient Near East: Proceedings of the Oxford Old Testament Seminar*. Edited by John Day. JSOTSup 270. Sheffield: Sheffield Academic, 1998.

———. "Law and Monarchy in the Old Testament." Pages 69–88 in *A Royal Priesthood? The Use of the Bible Ethically and Politically: A Dialogue with Oliver O'Donovan*. Edited by Craig Bartholomew, Jonathan Chaplin, Robert Song, and Al Wolters. Scripture & Hermeneutics Series 3. Carlisle, UK: Paternoster, 2002.

McKane, William. *Jeremiah*. Vol. 1. ICC. Edinburgh: T&T Clark, 1986.

Meadowcroft, Tim. "Exploring the Dismal Swamp: The Identity of the Anointed One in Daniel 9:24–27." *JBL* 120 (2001): 429–49.

Meek, Theophile J., trans. "The Code of Hammurabi." In *Ancient Near Eastern Texts relating to the Old Testament*. Edited by James B. Pritchard. 3rd ed. Princeton: Princeton University Press, 1969.

Meier, John P. "The Historical Jesus and the Historical Samaritans: What Can Be Said?" *Bib* 81 (2000): 202–32.

Menken, Maarten J. J. *Old Testament Quotations in the Fourth Gospel: Studies in Textual Form*. CBET 15. Kampen: Kok Pharos, 1996.

Meyers, Carol L., and Eric M. Meyers. *Zechariah 9–14*. AB 25C. New York: Doubleday, 1993.

Meyers, Eric M. "Messianism in First and Second Zechariah and the 'End' of Biblical Prophecy." Pages 127–42 in *"Go to the Land I Will Show You": Studies in Honour of Dwight W. Young*. Edited by Joseph E. Coleson and Victor H. Matthews. Winona Lake, IN: Eisenbrauns, 1996.

Michalak, Aleksander R. *Angels as Warriors in Late Second Temple Jewish Literature*. WUNT 2/330. Tübingen: Mohr Siebeck, 2012.

Milgrom, Jacob. *Numbers*. JPS Torah Commentary. Philadelphia: Jewish Publication Society, 1989.

Miller, Patrick D. "The Beginning of the Psalter." Pages 83–92 in *The Shape and Shaping of the Psalter*. Edited by J. Clinton McCann. JSOTSup 159. Sheffield: Sheffield Academic, 1993.

Mitchell, David C. "Lord, Remember David: G. H. Wilson and the Message of the Psalter." *VT* 56 (2006): 526–48.

———. *The Message of the Psalter: An Eschatological Programme in the Book of Psalms*. JSOTSup 252. Sheffield: Sheffield Academic, 1997.

Miura, Yuzuru. *David in Luke-Acts: His Portrayal in the Light of Early Judaism*. WUNT 2/232. Tübingen: Mohr Siebeck, 2007.

Moberly, R. W. L. "Whose Justice? Which Righteousness? The Interpretation of Isaiah v 16." *VT* 51 (2001): 55–68.

Montgomery, James A. *The Book of Kings*. Edited by Henry Snyder Gehman. ICC. Edinburgh: T&T Clark, 1950.

Moo, Douglas J. *Galatians*. BECNT. Grand Rapids: Baker Academic, 2013.

Moore, Michael S. "To King or Not to King: A Canonical-Historical Approach to Ruth." *BBR* 11 (2001): 27–41.

Motyer, J. Alec. *The Prophecy of Isaiah: An Introduction and Commentary*. Downers Grove, IL: InterVarsity, 1993.

Mowinckel, Sigmund. *He That Cometh: The Messiah Concept in the Old Testament and Later Judaism*. Translated by G. W. Anderson. Grand Rapids: Eerdmans, 2005.

Nägele, Sabine. *Laubhütte Davids und Wolkensohn: Eine auslegungsgeschichtliche Studie zu Amos 9,11 in der jüdischen und christlichen Exegese*. AGJU 24. Leiden: Brill, 1995.

Neusner, Jacob, William Scott Green, and Ernest S. Frerichs, eds. *Judaisms and Their Messiahs at the Turn of the Christian Era*. Cambridge: Cambridge University Press, 1987.

Newman, John Henry. *The Idea of a University*. Edited by Frank M. Turner. New Haven: Yale University Press, 1996.

Nielson, Kirsten. *Ruth: A Commentary*. Translated by Edward Broadbridge. OTL. Louisville: Westminster John Knox, 1997.

Nienhuis, David R., and Robert W. Wall. *Reading the Epistles of James, Peter, John, and Jude as Scripture*. Grand Rapids: Eerdmans, 2013.

Nihan, Christophe. "The *nāśîʾ* and the Future of Royalty in Ezekiel." Pages 229–46 in *History, Memory, Hebrew Scriptures: A Festschrift for Ehud Ben Zvi*. Edited by Ian Douglas Wilson and Diana V. Edelman. Winona Lake, IN: Eisenbrauns, 2015.

Noble, Paul R. "Israel among the Nations." *HBT* 15 (1993): 56–62.

———. "'I Will Not Bring "It" Back' (Amos 1:3): A Deliberately Ambiguous Oracle?" *ExpTim* 106 (1994–95): 105–9.

Nogalski, James D. "Joel as 'Literary Anchor' for the Book of the Twelve." Pages 91–109 in *Reading and Hearing the Book of the Twelve*. Edited by James D.

Nogalski and Marvin A. Sweeney. SBL Symposium Series 15. Atlanta: Society of Biblical Literature, 2000.

———. *Literary Precursors to the Book of the Twelve*. BZAW 217. Berlin: de Gruyter, 1993.

———. "Recurring Themes in the Book of the Twelve: Creating Points of Contact for a Theological Reading." *Int* 61 (2007): 125–36.

Novakovic, Lidija. *Raised from the Dead according to Scripture: The Role of Israel's Scripture in the Early Christian Interpretations of Jesus' Resurrection*. Jewish and Christian Texts in Contexts and Related Studies 12. London: Bloomsbury T&T Clark, 2012.

Novenson, Matthew V. *Christ among the Messiahs: Christ Language in Paul and Messiah Language in Ancient Judaism*. Oxford: Oxford University Press, 2012.

———. "The Jewish Messiahs, the Pauline Christ, and the Gentile Question." *JBL* 128 (2009): 357–73.

Nowack, W. *Die kleinen Propheten*. Göttingen Handkommentar zum Alten Testament. Göttingen: Vandenhoeck & Ruprecht, 1903.

O'Brien, Julia M. *Priest and Levite in Malachi*. SBLDS 121. Atlanta: Scholars Press, 1990.

Oegema, Gerbern S. *The Anointed and His People: Messianic Expectations from the Maccabees to Bar Kochba*. JSPSup 27. Sheffield: Sheffield Academic, 1998.

Ortlund, Dane. "Is Jeremiah 33:14–26 a 'Centre' to the Bible? A Test Case in Intercanonical Hermeneutics." *EQ* 84 (2012): 119–38.

Osborne, William R. *Trees and Kings: A Comparative Analysis of Tree Imagery in Israel's Prophetic Tradition and the Ancient Near East*. BBRSup 18. University Park, PA: Eisenbrauns, 2018.

Oswalt, John. *The Book of Isaiah: Chapters 1–39*. NICOT. Grand Rapids: Eerdmans, 1986.

Otzen, Benedikt. "Michael and Gabriel: Angelological Problems in the Book of Daniel." Pages 114–24 in *The Scriptures and the Scrolls: Studies in Honour of A. S. van der Woude on the Occasion of His 65th Birthday*. Edited by F. Garcia Martinez, A. Hilhorst, and C. J. Labuschagne. VTSup 49. Leiden: Brill, 1992.

Painter, John. "Christ and the Church in John 1:45–51." Pages 359–62 in *L'Évangile de Jean: Sources, rédaction, théologie*. Edited by Marinus de Jonge. BETL 44. Leuven: Leuven University Press, 1977.

Parker, David C. *An Introduction to the New Testament Manuscripts and Their Texts*. Cambridge: Cambridge University Press, 2008.

Paul, Shalom M. *Amos*. Hermeneia. Minneapolis: Fortress, 1991.

Petersen, David L. *Zechariah 9–14 and Malachi*. OTL. Louisville: Westminster John Knox, 1995.

Peterson, Brian Neil. *The Authors of the Deuteronomistic History: Locating a Tradition in Ancient Israel.* Minneapolis: Fortress, 2014.

Petterson, Anthony R. *Behold Your King: The Hope for the House of David in the Book of Zechariah.* LHBOTS 513. New York: T&T Clark International, 2009.

———. "The Eschatology of Zechariah's Night Visions." Pages 119–34 in *"I Lifted My Eyes and Saw": Reading Dream and Vision Reports in the Hebrew Bible.* Edited by Elizabeth R. Hayes and Lena-Sofia Tiemeyer. LHBOTS 584. London: Bloomsbury T&T Clark, 2014.

———. *Haggai, Zechariah and Malachi*, ApOTC 25. Nottingham: Apollos, 2015.

———. "A New Form-Critical Approach to Zechariah's Crowning of the High Priest Joshua and the Identity of 'Shoot' (Zechariah 6:9–15)." Pages 285–304 in *The Book of the Twelve and the New Form Criticism.* Edited by Mark J. Boda, Michael H. Floyd, and Colin M. Toffelmire. SBL Ancient Near East Monographs 10. Atlanta: SBL Press, 2015.

———. "The Shape of the Davidic Hope across the Book of the Twelve." *JSOT* 35 (2010): 225–46.

Pierce, Ronald W. "Literary Connectors and a Haggai/Zechariah/Malachi Corpus." *JETS* 27 (1984): 277–89.

———. "A Thematic Development of the Haggai/Zechariah/Malachi Corpus." *JETS* 27 (1984): 401–11.

Polley, Max E. *Amos and the Davidic Empire: A Socio-Historical Approach.* New York: Oxford University Press, 1989.

Polzin, Robert. *Samuel and the Deuteronomist: A Literary Study of the Deuteronomic History, Part Two: 1 Samuel.* Bloomington: Indiana University Press, 1993.

Pomykala, Kenneth E. *The Davidic Dynasty Tradition in Early Judaism: Its History and Significance for Messianism.* SBLEJL 7. Atlanta: Scholars Press, 1995.

———. "Jerusalem as the Fallen Booth of David in Amos 9:11." Pages 275–93 in *Biblical Studies in Honor of Simon John De Vries.* Vol. 1 of *God's Word for Our World.* Edited by J. Harold Ellens, Deborah L. Ellens, Rolf P. Knierim, and Isaac Kalimi. JSOTSup 388. London: T&T Clark International, 2004.

Porten, Bezalel. "The Scroll of Ruth: A Rhetorical Study." *Gratz College Annual of Jewish Studies* 7 (1978): 23–49.

Porter, Stanley E., ed. *The Messiah in the Old and New Testaments.* Grand Rapids: Eerdmans, 2007.

Provan, Iain. "The Messiah in the Books of Kings." Pages 67–85 in *The Lord's Anointed: Interpretation of Old Testament Messianic Texts.* Edited by P. E. Satterthwaite, Richard S. Hess, and Gordon J. Wenham. Carlisle, UK: Paternoster, 1995.

Radine, Jason. *The Book of Amos in Emergent Judah.* FAT 2.45. Tübingen: Mohr Siebeck, 2010.

Redditt, Paul L. "Israel's Shepherds: Hope and Pessimism in Zechariah 9–14." *CBQ* 51 (1989): 631–42.

———. "The Production and Reading of the Book of the Twelve." Pages 394–419 in *SBL 1997 Seminar Papers*. Atlanta: Scholars Press, 1997.

———. "The Two Shepherds in Zechariah 11:4–17." *CBQ* 55 (1993): 676–86.

Reimer, David J. "Redeeming Politics in Jeremiah." Pages 121–36 in *Prophecy in the Book of Jeremiah*. Edited by Hans M. Barstad and Reinhard G. Kratz. BZAW 388. Berlin: de Gruyter, 2009.

Renaud, B. *La Formation du Livre de Michée: Tradition et Actualisation.* Études Bibliques. Paris: J. Gabalda, 1977.

Rendtorff, Rolf. "How to Read the Book of the Twelve as a Theological Unity." Pages 75–86 in *Reading and Hearing the Book of the Twelve*. Edited by James D. Nogalski and Marvin A. Sweeney. SBL Symposium Series 15. Atlanta: Society of Biblical Literature, 2000.

Rensberger, David. "The Politics of John: The Trial of Jesus in the Fourth Gospel." *JBL* 103 (1984): 395–411.

Renz, Thomas. *The Rhetorical Function of the Book of Ezekiel.* VTSup 76. Leiden: Brill, 1999.

Reumann, John H. "Psalm 22 at the Cross: Lament and Thanksgiving for Jesus Christ." *Int* 28 (1974): 39–58.

Ringgren, Helmer. "Behold Your King Comes." *VT* 24 (1974): 207–11.

Roberts, J. J. M. "The Davidic Origin of the Zion Tradition." *JBL* 92 (1973): 329–44.

———. "Whose Child Is This? Reflections on the Speaking Voice in Isaiah 9:5." *HTR* 90 (1997): 115–29.

Rofé, Alexander. "David Their King (Whom God Will Raise): Hosea 3:5 and the Onset of Messianic Expectation in the Prophetic Books." Pages 130–35 in *Leshon Limmudim: Essays on the Language and Literature of the Hebrew Bible in Honour of A. A. Macintosh*. Edited by David A. Baer and Robert P. Gordon. LHBOTS 593. London: Bloomsbury T&T Clark, 2013.

Rooke, Deborah W. *Zadok's Heirs: The Role and Development of the High Priesthood in Ancient Israel.* Oxford Theological Monographs. Oxford: Oxford University Press, 2000.

Rose, Wolter H. "Zechariah and the Ambiguity of Kingship in Postexilic Israel." Pages 219–31 in *Let Us Go Up to Zion: Essays in Honour of H. G. M. Williamson on the Occasion of His Sixty-Fifth Birthday*. Edited by Iain Provan and Mark J. Boda. VTSup 153. Leiden: Brill, 2012.

———. *Zemah and Zerubbabel: Messianic Expectations in the Early Postexilic Period.* JSOTSup 304. Sheffield: Sheffield Academic, 2000.

Rowe, C. Kavin. *Early Narrative Christology: The Lord in the Gospel of Luke.* Grand Rapids: Baker Academic, 2006.

Rowe, Robert D. "Is Daniel's 'Son of Man' Messianic?" Pages 71–96 in *Christ the Lord: Studies in Christology Presented to Donald Guthrie*. Edited by Harold H. Rowdon. Leicester, UK: Inter-Varsity, 1982.

Rowland, Christopher. "The Vision of the Risen Christ in Rev. i 13ff.: The Debt of an Early Christology to an Aspect of Jewish Angelology." *JTS* 31 (1980): 1–11.

Rudnig-Zelt, Susanne. "Vom Propheten und seiner Frau, einem Ephod und einem Teraphim—Anmerkungen zu Hos 3:1–4:5." *VT* 60 (2010): 373–99.

Ruppert, Lothar. *Jesus als der leidende Gerechte? Der Weg Jesu im Lichte eines alt- und zwischentestamentlichen Motivs*. SBS 59. Stuttgart: Katholisches Bibelwerk, 1972.

Sæbø, Magne. "Messianism in Chronicles? Some Remarks to the Old Testament Background of the New Testament Christology." *HBT* 2 (1980): 85–109.

Sailhamer, John H. *Introduction to Old Testament Theology: A Canonical Approach*. Grand Rapids: Zondervan, 1995.

———. *The Meaning of the Pentateuch: Revelation, Composition and Interpretation*. Downers Grove, IL: IVP Academic, 2009.

Sakenfeld, Katharine Doob. *Faithfulness in Action: Loyalty in Biblical Perspective*. OBT. Philadelphia: Fortress, 1985.

———. *The Meaning of Ḥesed in the Hebrew Bible: A New Inquiry*. HSM 17. Missoula, MT: Scholars Press, 1978.

———. *Ruth*. IBC. Louisville: John Knox, 1999.

Sasson, Jack M. *Ruth: A New Translation with a Philological Commentary and a Formalist-Folkloric Interpretation*. Baltimore: Johns Hopkins University Press, 1979.

Satterthwaite, Philip E. "David in the Books of Samuel: A Messianic Expectation?" Pages 41–65 in *The Lord's Anointed: Interpretation of Old Testament Messianic Texts*. Edited by P. E. Satterthwaite, Richard S. Hess, and Gordon J. Wenham. Carlisle, UK: Paternoster, 1995.

———. "'No King in Israel': Narrative Criticism and Judges 17–21." *TynBul* 44 (1993): 75–88.

———. "Zion in the Songs of Ascent." Pages 105–28 in *Zion, City of Our God*. Edited by Richard S. Hess and Gordon J. Wenham. Grand Rapids: Eerdmans, 1999.

Satterthwaite, Philip E., Richard S. Hess, and Gordon J. Wenham, eds. *The Lord's Anointed: Interpretation of Old Testament Messianic Texts*. Carlisle, UK: Paternoster, 1995.

Saur, Markus. *Die Königspsalmen: Studien zur Entstehung und Theologie*. BZAW 340. Berlin: de Gruyter, 2004.

Schart, Aaron. *Die Entstehung des Zwölfprophetenbuchs: Neubearbeitungen von Amos im Rahmen schriftübergreifender Redaktionsprozesse*. BZAW 260. Berlin: de Gruyter, 1998.

Schibler, Daniel. "Messianism and Messianic Prophecy in Isaiah 1–12 and 28–33." Pages 87–104 in *The Lord's Anointed: Interpretation of Old Testament Messianic Texts*. Edited by P. E. Satterthwaite, Richard S. Hess, and Gordon J. Wenham. Grand Rapids: Baker, 1995.

Schniedewind, William M. "King and Priest in the Book of Chronicles and the Duality of Qumran Messianism." *JJS* 45 (1994): 71–78.

Schreiner, Thomas R. *Galatians*. ZECNT. Grand Rapids: Zondervan, 2010.

Seitz, Christopher. *The Goodly Fellowship of the Prophets: The Achievement of Association in Canon Formation*. Grand Rapids: Baker Academic, 2009.

———. *Isaiah 1–39*. IBC. Louisville: Westminster John Knox, 1993.

———. *Zion's Final Destiny: The Development of the Book of Isaiah; A Reassessment of Isaiah 36–39*. Minneapolis: Fortress, 1991.

Seo, Dae Woo. "An Interpretation of the Key Johannine Christological Titles in John 1:19–51 on the Basis of Their Wider Use in the Narrative of the Gospel and in Dialogue with Their Old Testament Background." Master's diss., Australian College of Theology, 2012.

Seow, C. L. "The Rule of God in the Book of Daniel." Pages 219–46 in *David and Zion: Biblical Studies in Honor of J. J. M. Roberts*. Edited by Bernard F. Batto and Kathryn L. Roberts. Winona Lake, IN: Eisenbrauns, 2004.

Seybold, Klaus. *Das davidische Königtum im Zeugnis der Propheten*. FRLANT 107. Göttingen: Vandenhoeck & Ruprecht, 1972.

Shaw, Charles S. *The Speeches of Micah: A Rhetorical-Historical Analysis*. JSOTSup 145. Sheffield: Sheffield Academic, 1993.

Skinner, Matthew L. *The Trial Narrative: Conflict, Power, and Identity in the New Testament*. Louisville: Westminster John Knox, 2010.

Smalley, Stephen S. *John: Evangelist and Interpreter*. Exeter, UK: Paternoster, 1978.

Smith, Gary V. *Amos*. Mentor. Fearn, Scotland: Christian Focus, 1998.

———. "The Concept of God/the Gods as King in the Ancient Near East and the Bible." *TJ* 3 (1982): 20–38.

———. *Isaiah 1–39*. NAC 15A. Nashville: B&H, 2007.

———. *Isaiah 40–66*. NAC 15B. Nashville: B&H, 2009.

Smith, J. M. Povis. *Micah, Zephaniah and Nahum*. ICC. Edinburgh: T&T Clark, 1911.

Smith, Ralph L. *Micah–Malachi*. WBC 32. Waco: Word, 1984.

———. *Micah–Malachi*. Word Biblical Themes. Dallas: Word, 1990.

Smith-Christopher, Daniel L. "Hebrew Satyagraha: The Politics of Biblical Fasting in the Post-Exilic Period (Sixth to Second Century B.C.E.)." *Food and Foodways* 5 (1993): 269–92.

———. *Micah: A Commentary*. OTL. Louisville: Westminster John Knox, 2015.

Snearly, Michael K. *The Return of the King: Messianic Expectation in Book V of the Psalter.* LHBOTS 624. London: Bloomsbury T&T Clark, 2016.

Snodgrass, Klyne. *The Parable of the Wicked Tenants: An Inquiry into Parable Interpretation.* WUNT 27. Tübingen: Mohr Siebeck, 1983.

Speiser, E. A. "Background and Function of the Biblical *Nasi'*." Pages 113–22 in *Oriental and Biblical Studies: Collected Writings of E. A. Speiser.* Edited by J. J. Finkelstein and Moshe Greenberg. Philadelphia: University of Pennsylvania Press, 1967.

Stead, Michael R. "Suffering Servant, Suffering David, and Stricken Shepherd." Pages 59–79 in *Christ Died for Our Sins: Essays on the Atonement.* Edited by Michael R. Stead. Canberra: Barton, 2013.

Steinmann, Andrew E. "The Oracle of Amos's Oracles against the Nations: 1:3–2:16." *JBL* 111 (1992): 683–89.

Steussy, Marti J. *David: Biblical Portraits of Power.* Columbia: University of South Carolina Press, 1999.

Stevenson, Kalinda Rose. *The Vision of Transformation: The Territorial Rhetoric of Ezekiel 40–48.* SBLDS 154. Atlanta: Scholars Press, 1996.

Stone, Michael. "The Concept of the Messiah in IV Ezra." Pages 295–312 in *Religions in Antiquity: Essays in Memory of Erwin Ramsdell Goodenough.* Edited by Jacob Neusner. Studies in the History of Religions (Supplements to *Numen*) 14. Leiden: Brill, 1968.

Story, Cullen I. K. "Amos—Prophet of Praise." *VT* 30 (1980): 67–80.

Strauß, Hans. *Messianisch ohne Messias: Zur Überlieferungsgeschichte und Interpretation der sogenannten messianischen Texte im Alten Testament.* Europäische Hochschulschriften XXIII/232. Frankfurt am Main: Peter Lang, 1984.

Strauss, Mark L. *The Davidic Messiah in Luke-Acts: The Promise and Its Fulfillment in Lukan Christology.* JSNTSup 110. Sheffield: Sheffield Academic, 1995.

Stuart, Douglas K. *Hosea–Jonah.* WBC 31. Waco: Word, 1987.

Stulman, Louis. *Jeremiah.* AOTC. Nashville: Abingdon, 2005.

———. "The Prose Sermons as Hermeneutical Guide to Jeremiah 1–25: The Deconstruction of Judah's Symbolic Word." Pages 34–63 in *Troubling Jeremiah.* Edited by A. R. Diamond and K. M. O'Connor. JSOTSup 260. Sheffield: Sheffield Academic, 1999.

Stulman, Louis, and Hyun Chul Paul Kim. *You Are My People: An Introduction to Prophetic Literature.* Nashville: Abingdon, 2010.

Swaim, Gerald G. "Hosea the Statesman." Pages 177–83 in *Biblical and Near Eastern Studies: Essays in Honor of William Sanford LaSor.* Edited by Gary A. Tuttle. Grand Rapids: Eerdmans, 1978.

Sweeney, Marvin A. *I & II Kings.* OTL. Louisville: Westminster John Knox, 2007.

———. *Hosea, Joel, Amos, Obadiah, Jonah.* Vol. 1 of *The Twelve Prophets.* Berit Olam. Collegeville, MN: Liturgical Press, 2000.

———. "Jeremiah's Reflection on the Isaian Royal Promise: Jeremiah 23:1–8 in Context." Pages 308–21 in *Uprooting and Planting: Essays on Jeremiah for Leslie Allen.* Edited by John Goldingay. LHBOTS 459. New York: T&T Clark, 2007.

Swete, H. B. *An Introduction to the Old Testament in Greek, with an Appendix Containing the Letter of Aristeas.* Edited by H. St. J. Thackeray. Cambridge: Cambridge University Press, 1902. Revised by R. R. Ottley. New York: Ktav, 1968.

Thompson, J. A. *The Book of Jeremiah.* NICOT. Grand Rapids: Eerdmans, 1980.

Thompson, M. E. W. "Amos—A Prophet of Hope?" *ExpTim* 104 (1992): 71–76.

Throntveit, Mark A. "The Relationship of Hezekiah to David and Solomon in the Books of Chronicles." Pages 105–21 in *The Chronicler as Theologian: Essays in Honor of Ralph W. Klein.* Edited by M. Patrick Graham, Steven L. McKenzie, and Gary N. Knoppers. JSOTSup 371. London: T&T Clark, 2003.

Tollington, Janet E. *Tradition and Innovation in Haggai and Zechariah 1–8.* JSOTSup 150. Sheffield: JSOT Press, 1993.

Towner, W. Sibley. *Daniel.* IBC. Atlanta: John Knox, 1984.

Trotter, James M. *Reading Hosea in Achaemenid Yehud.* JSOTSup 328. London: Sheffield Academic, 2001.

Tsumura, David Toshio. *The First Book of Samuel.* NICOT. Grand Rapids: Eerdmans, 2007.

Tucker, W. Dennis, Jr. *Constructing and Deconstructing Power in Psalms 107–150.* AIL 19. Atlanta: Society of Biblical Literature, 2014.

Tuell, Steven Shawn. *The Law of the Temple in Ezekiel 40–48.* HSM 49. Atlanta: Scholars Press, 1992.

Vancil, Jack W. "Sheep, Shepherd." *ABD* 5:1187–90.

VanderKam, James, and Peter Flint. *The Meaning of the Dead Sea Scrolls: Their Significance for Understanding the Bible, Judaism, Jesus and Christianity.* San Francisco: Harper, 2002.

van der Kooij, Arie. "The Septuagint of Zechariah as Witness to an Early Interpretation of the Book." Pages 53–64 in *The Book of Zechariah and Its Influence.* Edited by Christopher Tuckett. Aldershot, UK: Ashgate, 2003.

Van Grol, Harm. "David and His Chasidim: Place and Function of Psalms 138–145." Pages 309–37 in *The Composition of the Book of Psalms.* Edited by Erich Zenger. BETL 238. Leuven: Peeters, 2010.

Van Leeuwen, Raymond C. "Scribal Wisdom and Theodicy in the Book of the Twelve." Pages 31–49 in *In Search of Wisdom: Essays in Memory of John G. Gammie.* Edited by L. G. Perdue, B. Scott, and W. Wiseman. Louisville: Westminster John Knox, 1993.

van Wolde, Ellen. *Ruth and Naomi.* London: SCM, 1997.

Viviers, H. "The Coherence of the *ma'ᵃlôt* Psalms (Pss. 120–134)." *ZAW* 106 (1994): 275–89.

Vogt, Peter T. *Deuteronomic Theology and the Significance of Torah: A Reappraisal.* Winona Lake, IN: Eisenbrauns, 2006.

von Rad, Gerhard. *Old Testament Theology.* Vol 1. Translated by D. M. G. Stalker. Peabody, MA: Hendrickson, 2005.

———. "The Royal Ritual in Judah." Pages 222–31 in *The Problem of the Hexateuch, and Other Essays.* Translated by E. W. Trueman Dicken. Edinburgh: Oliver & Boyd, 1966.

Walck, Leslie. "The Parables of Enoch and the Synoptic Gospels." Pages 231–68 in *Parables of Enoch: A Paradigm Shift.* Edited by James H. Charlesworth and Darrell L. Bock. T&T Clark Jewish and Christian Texts Series 11. London: Bloomsbury T&T Clark, 2013.

Wallace, Howard N. "King and Community: Joining with David in Prayer." Pages 267–77 in *Psalms and Prayer: Papers Read at the Joint Meeting of the Society of Old Testament Study and Het Oudtestamentische Werkgezelschap in Nederland en België, Apeldoorn August 2006.* Edited by Bob Becking and Eric Peels. OTS 55. Leiden: Brill, 2007.

———. *Psalms.* Readings: A New Biblical Commentary. Sheffield: Sheffield Phoenix, 2009.

Waltke, Bruce K. "A Canonical Process Approach to the Psalms." Pages 3–18 in *Tradition and Testament: Essays in Honor of Charles Lee Feinberg.* Edited by J. S. Feinberg and P. D. Feinberg. Chicago: Moody, 1981.

———. *A Commentary on Micah.* Grand Rapids: Eerdmans, 2007.

———. "Psalm 110: An Exegetical and Canonical Approach." Pages 60–85 in *Resurrection and Eschatology: Theology in Service of the Church; Essays in Honor of Richard B. Gaffin Jr.* Edited by Lane G. Tipton and Jeffrey C. Waddington. Phillipsburg: P&R, 2008.

Walton, John H. *Genesis.* NIVAC. Grand Rapids: Zondervan, 2001.

———. *Genesis 1 as Ancient Cosmology.* Winona Lake, IN: Eisenbrauns, 2011.

———. "Isa. 7:14: What's in a Name?" *JETS* 30 (1987): 289–306.

Ward, James M. "The Message of the Prophet Hosea." *Int* 23 (1969): 387–407.

Watts, James W. "The Legal Characterization of God in the Pentateuch." *HUCA* 67 (1996): 1–14.

Watts, Rikk E. "Immanuel: Virgin Birth Proof Text or Programmatic Warning of Things to Come (Isa. 7:14 in Matt 1:23)?" Pages 92–113 in *From Prophecy to Testament: The Function of the Old Testament in the New.* Edited by Craig Evans. Peabody, MA: Hendrickson, 2004.

———. "Mark." Pages 111–249 in *CNTUOT.*

Way, Kenneth C. "Donkey Domain: Zechariah 9:9 and Lexical Semantics." *JBL* 129 (2010): 105–14.

Webb, Barry G. *The Book of Judges.* NICOT. Grand Rapids: Eerdmans, 2012.

———. *The Book of the Judges: An Integrated Reading.* JSOTSup 46. Sheffield: JSOT Press, 1987.

Wegner, Paul. *An Examination of Kingship and Messianic Expectation in Isaiah 1–35.* Lewiston, NY: Mellen, 1992.

———. "A Re-examination of Isaiah IX 1–6." *VT* 42 (1992): 109–12.

Weinfeld, Moshe. *Social Justice in Ancient Israel and in the Ancient Near East.* Jerusalem: Magnes Press, 1995.

Wenham, Gordon J. "*Bĕtûlāh*, 'A Girl of Marriageable Age.'" *VT* 22 (1972): 326–47.

———. *Genesis 1–15.* WBC 1A. Nashville: Nelson, 1987.

Westermann, Claus. *Genesis 37–50.* Translated by John J. Scullion. CC. Minneapolis: Fortress, 2002.

Westfall, Cynthia Long. "Messianic Themes of Temple, Enthronement, and Victory in Hebrews and the General Epistles." Pages 210–29 in *The Messiah of the Old and New Testaments.* Edited by Stanley E. Porter. Grand Rapids: Eerdmans, 2007.

Weyde, Karl William. *Prophecy and Teaching: Prophetic Authority, Form Problems, and the Use of Traditions in the Book of Malachi.* BZAW 288. Berlin: de Gruyter, 2000.

Whitelam, Keith W. *The Just King: Monarchical Judicial Authority in Ancient Israel.* JSOTSup 12. Sheffield: JSOT Press, 1979.

Whitsett, Christopher G. "Son of God, Seed of David: Paul's Messianic Exegesis in Rom 1:3–4." *JBL* 119 (2000): 661–81.

Whybray, Norman. *Reading the Psalms as a Book.* JSOTSup 222. Sheffield: Sheffield Academic, 1996.

Widmer, Michael. *Moses, God and the Dynamics of Intercessory Prayer.* FAT 2.8. Tübingen: Mohr Siebeck, 2004.

Wilde, Oscar, *Nothing . . . except My Genius.* Compiled by Alastair Rolfe. London: Penguin, 1997.

Williamson, H. G. M. *A Critical and Exegetical Commentary on Isaiah 1–5.* ICC. London: T&T Clark, 2006.

———. "Eschatology in Chronicles." *TynBul* 28 (1977): 115–54.

———. *1 and 2 Chronicles.* NCB. Grand Rapids: Eerdmans, 1982.

———. *Variations on a Theme: King, Messiah and Servant in the Book of Isaiah.* Didsbury Lectures 1997. Carlisle, UK: Paternoster, 1998.

Williamson, Paul R. *Sealed with an Oath: Covenant in God's Unfolding Purpose.* NSBT 23. Downers Grove, IL: IVP Academic, 2007.

Willis, John T. "The Authenticity and Meaning of Micah 5:9–14." *ZAW* 81 (1969): 353–68.

———. "Micah 4:14–5:5, a Unit." *VT* 18 (1968): 529–47.

Willitts, Joel. *Matthew's Messianic Shepherd-King: In Search for the "Lost Sheep of the House of Israel."* BZNW 147. Berlin: de Gruyter, 2007.

Wilson, Gerald H. *The Editing of the Hebrew Psalter.* SBLDS 76. Chico, CA: Scholars Press, 1985.

———. "Evidence of Editorial Divisions in the Hebrew Psalter." *VT* 24 (1984): 337–52.

———. "King, Messiah, and the Reign of God: Revisiting the Royal Psalms and the Shape of the Psalter." Pages 391–406 in *The Book of Psalms: Composition and Reception.* Edited by Peter W. Flint and Patrick D. Miller Jr. VTSup 99. Leiden: Brill, 2005.

———. *Psalms.* Vol. 1. NIVAC. Grand Rapids: Zondervan, 2002.

———. "Psalms and Psalter: Paradigm for Biblical Theology." Pages 100–110 in *Biblical Theology: Retrospect and Prospect.* Edited by Scott Hafemann. Leicester, UK: Apollos, 2002.

———. "Shaping the Psalter: A Consideration of Editorial Linkage in the Book of Psalms." Pages 72–82 in *The Shape and Shaping of the Psalter.* Edited by J. Clinton McCann. JSOTSup 159. Sheffield: Sheffield Academic, 1993.

———. "The Structure of the Psalter." Pages 229–46 in *Interpreting the Psalms: Issues and Approaches.* Edited by Philip S. Johnston and David G. Firth. Leicester, UK: Apollos, 2005.

——— "The Use of Royal Psalms at the 'Seams' of the Hebrew Psalter." *JSOT* 35 (1986): 85–94.

Wilson, Lindsay. *Joseph, Wise and Otherwise: The Intersection of Wisdom and Covenant in Genesis 37–50.* Paternoster Biblical Monographs. Carlisle, UK: Paternoster, 2004.

Wolfenson, L. B. "Implications of the Place of the Book of Ruth in Editions, Manuscripts, and Canon of the Old Testament." *HUCA* 1 (1924): 151–78.

Wolff, Hans W. *Hosea: A Commentary on the Book of the Prophet Hosea.* Translated by Gary Stansell. Hermeneia. Philadelphia: Fortress, 1974.

———. *Joel and Amos.* Translated by Waldemar Janzen, S. Dean McBride Jr., and Charles A. Muenchow. Hermeneia. Philadelphia: Fortress, 1977.

———. *Micah: A Commentary.* Translated by Gary Stansell. CC. Minneapolis: Augsburg, 1990.

Wong, Gregory T. K. *Compositional Strategy of the Book of Judges: An Inductive, Rhetorical Study.* VTSup 111. Leiden: Brill, 2006.

Wood, Joyce Rilett. *Amos in Song and Book Culture.* JSOTSup 337. London: Sheffield Academic, 2002.

Wray Beal, Lissa M. *1 & 2 Kings*. ApOTC 9. Nottingham: Apollos, 2014.

Wright, Christopher J. H. *The Mission of God: Unlocking the Bible's Grand Narrative*. Downers Grove, IL: IVP Academic, 2006.

Wright, N. T. *The Climax of the Covenant: Christ and the Law in Pauline Theology*. Edinburgh: T&T Clark, 1991.

———. *Paul and the Faithfulness of God*. Christian Origins and the Question of God 4. Minneapolis: Fortress, 2013.

Yarbro Collins, Adela, and John J. Collins. *King and Messiah as Son of God: Divine, Human, and Angelic Messianic Figures in Biblical and Related Literature*. Grand Rapids: Eerdmans, 2008.

Yee, Gale A. *Composition and Tradition in the Book of Hosea: A Redaction Critical Investigation*. SBLDS 102. Atlanta: Scholars Press, 1987.

Younger, K. Lawson. *Judges and Ruth*. NIVAC. Grand Rapids: Zondervan, 2002.

Zakovitch, Yair. *Das Buch Rut: Ein jüdischer Kommentar; Mit einem Geleitwort von Erich Zenger*. SBS 177. Stuttgart: Katholisches Bibelwerk, 1999.

Zapff, Burkard M. *Redaktionsgeschichtliche Studien zum Michabuch im Kontext des Dodekapropheton*. BZAW 256. Berlin: de Gruyter, 1997.

Zevit, Ziony. "The Exegetical Implications of Daniel VII 1, IX 21." *VT* 28 (1978): 488–92.

———. "The Structure and Individual Elements of Daniel 7." *ZAW* 80 (1968): 385–96.

Zimmerli, Walther. *Ezekiel 1: A Commentary on the Book of the Prophet Ezekiel, Chapters 1–24*. Translated by Ronald E. Clements. Hermeneia. Philadelphia: Fortress, 1979.

———. *Ezekiel 2: A Commentary on the Book of the Prophet Ezekiel, Chapters 25–48*. Translated by James D. Martin. Hermeneia. Philadelphia: Fortress, 1983.

———. "Planungen für den Wiederaufbau nach der Katastrophe von 587." *VT* 18 (1968): 229–55.

Scripture and Ancient Writings Index

276

Name Index

Subject Index